Teachings on Usury in Judaism, Christianity and Islam

Y0-BNP-366

TEACHINGS ON USURY IN JUDAISM, CHRISTIANITY AND ISLAM

Susan L. Buckley

Texts and Studies in Religion
Volume 85

The Edwin Mellen Press
Lewiston•Queenston•Lampeter

WITHDRAWN

HIEBERT LIBRARY
FRESNO PACIFIC UNIV.-M. B. SEMINARY
FRESNO, CA 93702

Library of Congress Cataloging-in-Publication Data

Buckley, Susan L. (Susan Louise)
  Teachings on usury in Judaism, Christianity and Islam / Susan L. Buckley.
    p. cm. -- (Texts and studies in religion ; v. 85)
  Includes bibliographical references and index.
  ISBN 0-7734-7656-3
  1. Usury. 2. Usury--Biblical teaching. 3. Usury--Religious aspects--Judaism. 4.
Usury--Religious aspects--Christianity. 5. Usury--Religious aspects--Islam. I.Title. II.
Series.

HB551 .B83 2000
291.5'644--dc21   00-055434

This is volume 85 in the continuing series
Texts and Studies in Religion
Volume 85 ISBN 0-7734-7656-3
TSR Series ISBN 0-88946-976-8

A CIP catalog record for this book is available from the British Library.

Copyright © 2000 Susan L. Buckley

All rights reserved. For information contact

The Edwin Mellen Press
Box 450
Lewiston, New York
USA 14092-0450

The Edwin Mellen Press
Box 67
Queenston, Ontario
CANADA L0S 1L0

The Edwin Mellen Press, Ltd.
Lampeter, Ceredigion, Wales
UNITED KINGDOM SA48 8LT

Printed in the United States of America

In Memory of Jim

Contents

Foreword

This is a ground breaking study of one of the most important questions facing the world today, namely that of achieving social and economic justice for the majority of the world's population. It is ground breaking because, so far as I know, it is the first sustained and systematic attempt to look at the international banking system - responsible for many of the world's woes – from the point of view of the three great monotheistic faiths, Judaism, Christianity and Islam, all of which have had things to say about interest and profit, but only one of which, Islam, has so far attempted to put into practice and to work out a viable, practical banking system which seeks to give substance to what that religion has to say about social and economic justice. There are today many Muslims living in the English speaking world and pressure from them is having the consequence that the English speaking world is at last beginning to take Muslim concerns about the existing, and essentially Western banking system, at local, national and international levels, seriously. Dr. Buckley puts these concerns, and the growing contemporary awareness on the part of many Jews and Christians that there are, indeed, fundamental ethical issues at stake in the way banking is practiced in the Western world into context by looking both at what the Hebrew Bible, the Christian Scriptures, and the Qur'an have to say about these matters, and at how what they say has been understood in the past and how it is being understood in the present. This, in an area long neglected, is a necessary beginning, but Dr. Buckley's book is no ivory tower, academic, historical study, but a book which makes some very timely, and some very practical suggestions which those in a position to influence international economic policies, and particularly those who claim to adhere to one or other of the three faiths with which she deals, might well ponder with profit. it should also be required reading for all those in universities and colleges in the Western World who teach and study Christian (or Jewish or Islamic) Ethics, for Dr. Buckley's study of that side of banking, known more familiarly as her title indicates, as 'moneylending' is at bottom a study of nothing less than the ethical dimension of the three faiths to which she refers and which, alone of the world's religions, have concerned themselves, in theory if not always in practice, with social and economic justice in this world, a world which, so these faiths believe, has been created by God as the arena in which the salvation or otherwise of humanity is to be played out.

James Thrower
Professor of the History of Religions
The University of Aberdeen
21.9.99

Preface

Traditionally, it is alleged that Rome was founded in 753 BCE on the site of the lowest bridgeable point of the River Tiber. The early Romans built a temple to Jupitor on the Capitol, one of Rome's famous seven hills and the temple became a secure place for storing money – in whatever form it presented at that time. In 390 BCE when the Gauls supposedly overran most of Rome the cackling of the temple geese on the Capitol averted a surprise attack and defeat. In gratitude the Romans erected a shrine to Moneta, the goddess of warning, or advice, and it is from 'Moneta' that we derive our name for money.[1]

Perhaps, today, as with cigarettes, money should come with a Government health warning – too much money can seriously damage your health – nothing exceeds like excess! Equally, and more soberingly, too little money throughout the world not only seriously damages innocent peoples' lives but also leads to mayhem, massacres, malnutrition and mortalities.

This book is intended to challenge the morality of money in the sense of its absolute unequal distribution throughout our McLuhan defined 'global village'. It questions our concept of money, and our concept of those who have it and those who do not. It examines the religious teaching on moneylending within Judaism, Christianity and Islam which has raised fierce debate down the centuries, and in some cases still does, with regard to the moral usage of money. In particular, I address the question of 'usury' (defined at its simplest as charging exorbitant interest on a loan)

---

[1] See Glyn Davies, A History of Money, (University of Wales Press, 1994/paperback edition with postscripts 1996) p.87.

within these three monotheistic traditions because I believe and posit that their respective traditions produced differing concepts of 'economic man' however that is defined; and it raises serious considerations today about how money is addressed not so much in terms of wealth redistribution, but in terms, for the very poor, of wealth creation. How can we help the poor and poorest to have access to finance and financial institutions to improve their lot in life? How do we address issues of Third World debt? Can Islamic Banking practice, Credit Unions, Co-operative Movements, Local Exchange Trading Systems provide 'via medias' – a 'Third Way' in this respect? What are, not just our rights, but our responsibilities to humanity, the planet, human resources – and God – as we plough into the next millenium?

This book is an interdisciplinary study which engages with theology, religious studies, economics, and sociology with regard to the historical development of and key principles behind Jewish, Christian and Islamic attitudes, and teachings, toward the subjects of moneylending, debt, usury and related topics. In essence, it deals in the subject of religious ethics, specifically the ethics of moneylending, textually based, as they have been understood and developed in each of these traditions. As you will discover, I posit differing models of 'economic man' with regard to the issue of moneylending within these traditions and look for a model of 'seconomic man' – within the prevailing economic ethos of modern secular society (although that does not necessarily mean a non-religious society). I discuss important contemporary issues and offer significant pointers toward establishing a more just, interest-free economic system at both the micro and macro levels based on an evaluation of the historical development of the teachings on 'usury' within these three monotheistic faiths.

The words of Tensin Gyatso, the fourteenth Dalai Lama are an inspiration:

"Therefore, if in the midst of your enjoyment of the world you have a moment, try to help in however small a way, those who are downtrodden and those who, for whatever reason, cannot or do not help themselves. Try not to turn away from those whose appearance is disturbing, from the ragged and unwell. Try never to think of them as inferior to yourself. If you can , try not even to think of yoursellf as better than the humblest beggar. You will look the same in your grave."[2]

Susan Louise Buckley,
Houston, Texas,
February 2000

---

[2]Tensin Gyatso, *Ancient Wisdom, Modern World – Ethics for a New Millenium*, (Little, Brown & Co.London) 1999 p.245.

Acknowledgments

I am extremely indebted to Dr. Malise Ruthven and Rev. Dr. Ian Bradley who were my supervisors at Aberdeen University when this book started out as research material for a Ph.D. within the Department of Divinity. Their invaluable advice and knowledgeable insights helped to shape this book. I enjoyed their encouragement and friendship and am deeply grateful for the time and effort they exercised on my behalf. It is a debt which cannot fully be expressed simply by my thanks and this acknowledgement.

I would also like to extend my gratitude to staff of the Department of Divinity with Religious Studies who, during various stages of my research, provided me with very useful information: Professor Alan Main, Professor James Thrower, Professor William Johnstone, Professor David Fergusson, Dr. William Storrar, and Dr. Iain Torrance.

Many people informed my research and I acknowledge my appreciation to them in my endnotes. I am particularly grateful to Dr. Michael Schluter at the Jubilee Centre in Cambridge and to Dr. Richard Higginson at Ridley Hall Theological College, Cambridge. Various people whom I met during a 'Finance against Poverty' conference at Reading University in March, 1995, also furnished me with very interesting material. These include: Amanda Rowlatt from CDI; Lucy Charrington and Nicholas Colloff from Opportunity Trust; Dr. Mohammad El-Karaki from the University of Jordan, Amman; and Dr. Howard Jones from Reading University. I should also like to thank Jackie Burns and Bill Mearns from the social strategy unit in Aberdeen, for the time they spent in discussing the burgeoning Credit

Union movement in the Grampian region with me and for the handbook which was willingly supplied. Rev. Dr. Henry Awoniyi from Aberdeen University, was also kind enough to loan me a report on the Church and the external debt in Nigeria.

I am also grateful for the many conversations and discussions I shared with other post-graduate students during the three years of my research, and in particular, my greatest thanks go to my dear friend Gillian McCulloch for the gift of her faithful friendship.

So many people have been of enormous help both directly and indirectly, not least my silent, but at the same time, paradoxically, eloquent travelling companions confined between the covers of the many books I have experienced. I would like to acknowledge a debt to them and to their ideas and stimulating thoughts.

I am also extremely grateful to Ms. Sylvia A. Macey for the excellent preparation and formatting of my manuscript for The Mellen Press.

Not least, of course, I would like to express my sincerest thanks to my loving husband, Bruce, for his constant encouraging support, and to my dear children, Robin and Keira for all their kindness and patience and intelligent observations.

Sadly, Professor James Thrower, Head of the Centre for the Study of Religions and also my Ph.D examiner, friend and colleague, died in November, shortly after he had written this preface for my book. I should like to dedicate it to him in memory of his wit and wisdom, always kind, and always courteous.

※

Introduction

Religion can provide a moral framework within which people orientate themselves ethically. A relationship with God, with other people, and with the earth and its resources is a response to this. Religion has always, therefore, had to address economic issues because an attitude toward wealth and poverty reflects, from a religious viewpoint, an attitude toward God, other people, and the resources available for distribution. This book, therefore, traces the historical development and theological interpretation of the three great monotheistic religions, Judaism, Christianity and Islam, in their respective scriptures, with regard to their teaching on the concept of usury, and asks what relevance it has in the modern, or postmodern, world.

As we enter the twenty-first century, it is difficult to imagine the intensity of the intellectual debate on usury which raged especially in the sixteenth and seventeenth centuries, when it was regarded as a vice which corrupted cities and Church alike. Usury today, however, is not the dead issue that might be imagined. Since the 1960's the implementation of risk-sharing, interest-free Islamic banking systems, not only in the Islamic world but also in other areas, has raised the profile of the usury issue again. The concept of interest-free or low cost credit systems in co-operative banking, credit unions, and local exchange trading schemes have also gained attention; and it is a consideration in terms of Third World debt, highlighted especially by the Jubilee 2000 campaign, and based on scripture from the Hebrew Bible in terms of the cancellation of debts. In order to address the problem perceptively, an understanding of its development from early Judaic times, and its interpretation by the Christian church, up to the present day must be attempted, followed by an examination of the way in which the issue is now being interpreted in terms of Islamic banking and the concept of interest-free economies. Indeed, it is the model of Islamic banking which may provide a twenty-first century paradigm for interpreting the concept of interest-free lending today.

Chapter One, therefore, examines the Judaic teaching found in the Torah with particular reference to the significance of the Deuteronomic teaching, in which the Jews were permitted to lend at usury to the foreigner, but enjoined to extend non-usurious loans to one another. In order to understand this, it is important to appreciate the nature of the covenantal relationship between God and his 'chosen people'; the necessity of this teaching as the Israelites were about to enter their 'promised land'; and the economic difficulties that that would entail. It is this *theological* significance which is of paramount importance. This book obviously cannot ignore the economic issues which are raised by this teaching, but it is a theological exposition, and its conclusions are drawn with a practical theological application as its *modus operandi*. In this chapter, therefore, I propose that the spirit of capitalism was embryonic from the very start of Jewish money-changing in the Temple which took place in order that sacrifices could be purchased for use in Temple rites. This economic activity developed into moneylending as capital was accumulated, and this atavistic characteristic was as much a reason for the Jews becoming the money-lenders of Europe in both the Christian and the Islamic world, as the fact that persecution debarred them from holding land and high positions. It was also easier to flee in times of persecution with liquid assets which were amassed as trade routes opened up to the east and south. The Jewish commitment to its own community also played a vital role in its economic development as the Judaic religious teaching fostered an attitude of *chesed* towards its needy members of the community, which was more than an act of charity, but one of 'loving kindness' associated with the idea of righteousness. This was to be expressed in non-usurious loans to one another; it was a system which developed in diasporan communities, and one which still operates within Judaism today. The concept of *tzedekah*, which one might define as 'charitable justice', will also be discussed in conclusion.

Chapter Two focuses on the struggle of the Christian Church in interpreting the texts found in the Hebrew Bible with regard to usury, and in particular the difficulties experienced with the Deuteronomic teaching on lending at usury to the 'foreigner', and the rather vague interpretation of Luke 6:35 in the New Testament, where it is reported that Jesus said, 'Lend, hoping for nothing again.' The historical development of the theological arguments which proceeded from this is traced through the Church's rulings with regard to this issue, firstly by the early Church Fathers and Church Councils, and then the Scholastics of the Medieval period. The rulings of Calvin are discussed with regard to the controversy in the Reformation era, and the various responses and teachings of the Church to the present day.

The term 'usury' itself is not easy to define, and its interpretation evolved throughout the centuries. In Judaic terms, any interest charged on a loan, be it two or two hundred per-cent, was considered usurious. Gradually the term usury came to mean the voluntary taking of payment on a loan – as a 'use' charge, whereas interest was conceded as compensation for the loss of gain. It can be argued that the Christian Church moved in order to accommodate the changing economic developments of the day, but one thing it never condoned was injustice to the poor. In the twentieth century, there are Christians who believe that the Church should be reconsidering its Biblical teaching with regard to the question of 'usury', and an interest-free economy is advocated in order to help eradicate injustice to the poor.

Can the model of interest-free Islamic Banking, at present in a fairly embryonic stage, provide a new paradigm for the future?

Chapter Three, therefore, focuses on the Islamic teaching on usury, which is defined in the Qur'an as *riba*. I consider the development of this teaching in the *hadith* traditions and literature, and the way in which it was discussed in the schools of law. This is brought up to date with a consideration of Islamic banking with regard to risk, and profit-and-loss-sharing partnerships (PLS). Both Iran and Pakistan have theoretically abolished interest since the early 1980's, operating instead an Islamic economic system according to the teachings of the *Shari'ah*. It is also possible for Islamic Banking to exist in other non-Islamic countries with a Muslim population, or for ordinary commercial banks to operate with an 'Islamic window'. The City of London is experimenting in this way.

The place where interest-free finance has the most potential for successful operation is amongst the poor not only in low income countries but also in first world countries; failing that, there are other methods of instigating low cost finance such as those found within the co-operative movement, credit unions, or local exchange trading systems. These schemes may all be considered at an individual level, but equally important is the collective aspect, and nowhere is that more obvious than in the area of Third World debt. This concern is considered in terms of its cancellation especially with regard to a 'Jubilee' ethic, with its roots in the Judaic tradition, and the eradication of grinding poverty. These are only the first steps, however, because it has to be remembered that 'credit is also debt'.

This book, therefore, aims to examine the teaching on 'usury' within these three great religious traditions and to ask whether a new theological interpretation today can help to alleviate the plight of the poor. Is an interest-free banking system a workable solution towards helping to eradicate poverty and introduce fairer systems to control and redistribute wealth, as well as to create it? Is the Islamic banking system a twenty-first century paradigm which could be utilised by other communities, religious or secular (acknowledging, of course, an obvious point that I shall discuss, that 'Islamic Banking' is naturally and inevitably *per se* a 'product' of Islam defined by its teaching and set within its own cultural, religious, economic, social and political milieu), in order to help the poor and poorest people in societies? Did the religious teaching with regard to usury within these three monotheistic traditions produce different models of a Judaic, Christian, and Islamic 'economic man' because of it? And, in a proposed interest-free, pluralist, stake-holder society – based on the concept of non-usurious lending – can 'seconomic man' be found, i.e. secular economic man, in whom believer and non-believer alike are combined in a spirit of toleration, in order to work together toward a fairer distribution of wealth, the eradication of poverty throughout this 'global village', and in an attempt to find justice in wealth creation for the poor and poorest?

Chapter One

Toward a Judaic Understanding of Usury

The Torah: Pentateuchal Exegesis

In order to understand the Judaic interpretation of the concept of 'usury' – which differs from our present-day understanding of the term – we need to start with the Hebrew Bible and especially the books of Exodus, Leviticus and Deuteronomy. The most important element here is the covenantal relationship clearly demonstrated between God and his 'chosen people.' It was the Deuteronomic redactor's contribution to remould Exodus from law-code to covenant-code, and although this code follows similar Near Eastern treaty patterns, there are significant differences within the Hebrew Bible material which make Israel's position so distinctive. These are an uncompromising monotheism, a community spirit, and a remarkable concern for the underprivileged. The important aspect of community and brotherhood in this respect will also be examined. One of the more perplexing questions, which is often glossed over in terms of interpreting the Hebrew Bible's proscription on usurious lending, is the fact that in Deuteronomy 23:20, God 'allows' the Israelites to extract usury from the foreigner, but not from each other. The complexity of this situation will be addressed.

The term 'usury' in modern language denotes a rate of interest greater than that which the law or public opinion permits, usually interpreted as exorbitant interest:

1

> "But the Biblical law, in all dealings among Israelites, forbids all 'increase' of the debt by reason of lapse of time or forbearance, be the rate of interest high or low, while it does not impose any limit in dealings between Israelites and Gentiles. Hence in discussing Jewish law the words 'interest' and 'usury' may be used indiscriminately."[1]

It is important from the beginning to understand that the word 'usury' in Judaic terms meant something other than its modern day interpretation. It meant not only the charge of excessive or exorbitant interest but of *any* interest at all. The same issue will be addressed in Islamic terms where usury is understood by the term *riba*, and which, again, has a different interpretation to the modern day understanding of the term 'usury,' in addition to a different understanding of its usage in the Hebrew Bible.

The following passages from the Torah contain the important Mosaic injunctions with regard to usury. Other biblical references are dealt with in this book: usually they exist as prophetic tirades against those who ignore its teaching, or to remind God's people of his blessings toward those who do not act as usurers toward their brother. It is very significant that the teaching with regard to usury is cited in the Pentateuchal books of Exodus, Leviticus, and Deuteronomy, as this constitutes the religious law by which the Jews ordered the moral life of their society, and is representative of God's covenant between himself and his 'chosen people.'

> "If thou lend money to any of my people that is poor by thee, thou shalt not be to him as an usurer, neither shalt thou lay upon him usury." Exodus 22:25 (AV)

> "And if thy brother be waxen poor, and fallen in decay with thee; ... Take thou no usury of him, or increase: but fear thy God; that thy

---

[1] *The Jewish Encyclopedia*, Vol. xii, (Funk and Wagnells Co., New York and London, 1905), p.388.

brother may live with thee. Thou shalt not give him thy money upon usury, nor lend him thy victuals for increase." Leviticus 25:35-37 (AV)

"Thou shalt not lend upon usury to thy brother; usury of money, usury of victuals, usury of anything that is lent upon usury: Unto a stranger thou mayest lend upon usury; but unto thy brother thou shalt not lend upon usury: that the Lord thy God may bless thee in all that thou settest thine hand to in the land whither thou goest to possess it." Deuteronomy 23:19-20 (AV)

I have quoted the Authorised Version here, the King James Version of 1611, because it uses the word 'usury' in its translation. However, it is interesting to compare the relevant terminology in a recent translation, the New Revised Standard Version (Collins, London, 1989) where the word credit or interest is used synonymously with usury. Later on in medieval practice, the concept of 'interest' became acceptable, whereas the concept of 'usury' was still unacceptable. But this, I believe, is a question of semantics, because at whatever stage of the historic development on the teaching of usury, both concepts imply a payment above the principal, whether one recognises it as a just compensation for time or lost revenue, or unjust profit on a loan:

"If you lend money to my people, to the poor among you, you shall not deal with them as a creditor, you shall not exact interest from them." Exodus 22:25 (NRSV)

"If any of your kin fall into difficulty and become dependent on you, (you shall support them; they shall live with you as though resident aliens.) Do not take interest in advance or otherwise make a profit from them, but fear your God: let them live with you. You shall not lend them your money at interest taken in advance, or provide them food at a profit." Leviticus 25:35-37 (NRSV)

"You shall not charge interest on loans to another Israelite, interest on money, interest on provisions, interest on anything that is lent. On loans to a foreigner you may charge interest, so that the Lord your God may bless you in all your undertakings in the land that you are about to enter and possess." Deuteronomy 23:19-20 (NRSV)

These verses also stress the importance of the concept of 'brotherhood/kinship' and the relational responsibilities, whether economic or social, that the small group engenders with regard to its sense of community. G.E.Mendenhall states that "beyond the truly primitive band of food gatherers, kinship is rarely functional in the formation or preservation of large social units."[2] In one sense this is true. It is probably easier to have a sense of 'community' in small kinship groups where the sense of 'brotherhood'[3] is more keenly felt, than in larger, less homogeneous, social groupings, although Christian and Islamic interpretations of the notion of 'brotherhood' are extended to incorporate a more universalistic concept. In terms of the Israelites, however, in a paper entitled, 'The Social Unit: Family, Clan, Tribe, and Nation,' M. Burrows emphasises the importance of their concept of brotherhood:

"The basic social unit of the Hebrews was the patriarchal family, which included not only a man with his wives and unmarried children but also his married sons and their wives and children, and also the

---

[2] G.E.Mendenhall, *The Tenth Generation: The Origins of the Biblical Tradition*, (The John Hopkins University Press, Baltimore and London, 1973), p.174.

[3] In the preface to the NRSV, Bruce Metzger remarks that many people in the churches during the last half-century since the publication of the RSV have become sensitive to the danger of linguistic sexism arising from the inherent bias of the English language towards the masculine gender, which in the Bible has often restricted or obscured the meaning of the original text. I am also sensitive to this issue. I use the term 'brotherhood' because I believe that it gives a greater indication of the very patriarchal nature of society during this period, which paradoxically, could be obscured by 'inclusive' language. *New Revised Standard Version Bible*, (Collins, London, 1973), preface.

slaves with their wives and children. Membership in the family
therefore did not necessarily mean actual blood relationship. In fact,
by drinking blood together or by mingling their own blood, as well
as by other forms of covenant, men became brothers."[4]

The definition of 'brother,' 'family,' 'kin,' 'clan,' 'tribe,' 'community,'
'nation,' etc., is, therefore, during this period, a complex issue, and it is too easy to
superimpose twentieth, or twenty-first, century interpretations on to early cultures.
The concepts of 'brotherhood' and 'community' are essential, therefore, but
differently expressed, features within Judaism, Christianity, and Islam. It would
appear that the concept of 'brotherhood' within the Judaic understanding relates
specifically to small Jewish, and after the destruction of the Temple, diasporan
communities; in Islamic terms 'brotherhood' is seen, theoretically, as a concept
which embraces all Islamic communities wherever they might be in one great Islamic
ummah; in Christian terms, 'brotherhood' is to embrace all humankind in a
universalistic acceptance of inter-relationship. Differences in the religious teaching
on usurious lending within these three traditions, have resulted, I believe, in differing
interpretations of these concepts of 'brotherhood.' It is important to note that these
are idealized definitions, and homogeneity is a difficult concept to define in terms of
community. Is an homogeneous community defined in terms of social status, ethnic
or racial characteristics, political affiliation, religious belief, employment, some other
factor, or a combination of factors? Arnold Toynbee has some interesting comments
to make on this issue which I shall address in my conclusion. If it exists at all,
however, in anything other than an idealized form, it is easier to exist in very small
social groupings associated with the concept of 'brotherhood,' rather than larger ones

---

[4]M. Burrows, *"The Social Institutions of Israel."* in *Peake's commentary on the Bible*, (NT ed.
M.Black; OT ed. H.H.Rowley, Van Rostrand Reinhold (UK) Co. Ltd., 1962), p.134.

which because of their size, necessarily incorporate the concept and image of 'foreigner.'[5] (Although, of course, the concept can be used in a totally universalistic sense in such definitions as 'the brotherhood of man.')

Before defining the Hebraic terms used in connection with the teaching on usury, it is important to try and set these biblical sources, or redactions, in their historical and social context – their *'Sitz im Leben'* as defined by the form-critic, Hermann Gunkel, who thought it possible, in principle, to reconstruct the social situation which generated an individual tradition.[6] In Exodus the text is taken from the part of Exodus known as 'The Book of the Covenant'; in Leviticus it is found in the second part of the book known as the 'Holiness Code'; and the Deuteronomic text is an expansion, or rather, a redaction, of this law/covenant code.

In the southern kingdom of Judah certain traditions were collected together in the ninth century BCE to produce the sacred Judean history, or the 'Jahwistic' tradition, designated 'J' – according to the Wellhausen 'New Documentary Hypothesis' which was formulated in the 1870's, maintaining that the Hexateuch (Joshua/Judges was also included) comprised of four main literary documents: 'J'; 'E'; 'P'; and 'D.'[7] Somewhat later, in the Kingdom of Israel, the same traditions were brought together in the writings of a sacred history of the North ('E') even though the roots of the material are to be found long before Moses, in the ancient

---

[5]R.J.Rushdoony interprets this concept of 'foreigner' as 'unbeliever.' See Rousas John Rushdoony, *Politics of Guilt and Pity*, (The Craig Press, New Jersey, 1970), p.249.

[6]See Joseph Blenkinsopp, *The Pentateuch*, (SCM Press Ltd., 1992), p.126. This method of investigation was further developed by such scholars as Albrecht Alt, Gerhard van Rad, and Martin Noth, who by means of impressive hypotheses aimed to explain the origin of the traditions in the social activity, and especially the cultic activity, of the Israelite tribes in the pre-state period, and to show how these traditions eventually coalesced into continuous narrative form.

[7]J.Wellhausen, *Prolegomena to the History of Israel*, [New York, 1957 (1883)].

Near Eastern society of the third and second millennium BCE.[8] The Mosaic law is more concerned with a person's moral duty toward God and neighbour than the correct procedure for cultic celebration. The 'Book of the Covenant' (Exodus 20:22-23:33) is Elohistic and derived from pre-existing written sources. It is interesting to note that this law-code, containing the prohibition on usurious lending, is embedded within the framework of the covenantal ceremony in Exodus 19:1-24:11. Similarly, Leviticus 25, which also contains demands with regard to the concept of usury, as well as the sabbath of the land and the jubilee teaching, demonstrates the development of the incorporation of the ancient obligations of the cultus, as legal corpus, into that of covenantal code between God and his people as 'revealed' to Moses at Sinai, and is found embedded among material which in other respects was concerned with canons of holiness within the so-called 'Holiness Code' (Lev. 17-26).

At the time when Deuteronomy, which came from the north, was being edited, and everything was centred on the *covenant* and election on the part of God, the Jerusalem priests, wanted to codify the customs practiced in the Temple, all centred on the *cult*, to remind people that God is holy and utterly different. Leviticus itself is a collection of enactments intended to constitute the legal basis for the organised civil and religious life of the 'chosen people.' Unlike Deuteronomy, which is a popular exposition of the more esoteric priestly writings and is related more specifically to the idea of covenant obligations and election, Leviticus, according to R.K.Harrison, is composed of technical cultic material that was the prerogative of the priesthood, and the place it occupies in the pentateuchal corpus exhibits the clear intention of the compiler to continue the narrative of the experience at Sinai and to relate the legislation to the role of Israel as witness to the power of God in human

---

[8]Etienne Charpentier, *How to Read the Old Testament*, (Translated by John Bowden, SCM Press Ltd., London, 1988; first published Les Editions du Cerf, Paris, 1981), p.50.

affairs.[9]   If this is taken further with regard to the Book of Deuteronomy, whose compilation is dated seventh century BCE, William Johnstone states that by comparing the 'Book of the Covenant' in Exodus with the code in Deuteronomy, 12:1-26:15: "a process of assimilation of law-code to covenant-code was indeed taking place in the presentation of the Pentateuch."[10]

It must be noted that even today, as John Drane points out, some scholars are still arguing about the dates of the so-called source documents, and their conclusions vary widely with even the 'J' source being variously dated in periods as far apart as the ninth century and the post-exilic age. Y.Kaufmann postulated the existence of a monotheistic world-view among the Hebrews from a very early stage,[11]completely rejecting J.Wellhausen's theory of a faith which evolved from primitive beginnings through to the ethical monotheism of the major prophets.[12] It would appear that they did indeed have a strong 'Yahwistic' identity and a strong awareness of a covenantal relationship from a very early stage in their nomadic wanderings. Others have suggested that there is no such thing as an E source, while others argue that the four-source theory is inadequate, and that the Pentateuch contains many more sources; or, contradictorily they reject the hypothesis in toto (e.g. U.Cassuto and M.H.Segal.). Some have further claimed to be able to trace J, E and P not only in the Pentateuch, but also in Joshua, Judges, Samuel and even Kings. Much of this debate has been engendered by the fact that the so-called sources are not actually consistent in their

---

[9]R.K.Harrison, *Introduction to the Old Testament*, (W.B.Eerdmans, Michigan, 1969), p.589/590.

[10]William Johnstone, *Exodus*, (Sheffield Academic Press, 1990), p.58.

[11]Y.Kaufman, *History of the Religion of Israel*, (Vol. IV, Union of American Hebrew Congregations, New York, 1970), p.xiv.

[12]R.K.Harrison, *op. cit.*, p.75.

use of the different names for God, even though, it may be wryly noted, this was supposed to be their characteristic feature. Although there is controversy about the identitification of these source documents and their datings, they are still significant and the results of previous investigation should not be ignored, as Joseph Blenkinsopp points out:

> "It is true that the documentary hypothesis has increasingly been shown to be flawed, and will survive, if at all, only in a greatly modified form, but that does not mean that we should ignore the results of the last two centuries of investigation."[13]

What is more important is to see how these texts in the Torah concerning usury reflect the stage of the Israelite people with regard to their social and economic position, and also how this is affected by the theological development of their relationship with God in terms of a *covenant* code as opposed to simply a cultic or law code. The law-code is being transformed into covenant-code and this is clearly demonstrated in Exodus. Exodus 22:25-27, the specific text with regard to the teaching on usury, shows vestiges of the *mishpat*, an ordinance which means both 'custom' and 'precedent.' It is the variety of law identified by Albrecht Alt as 'casuistic (i.e. case) law,' as opposed to the *hoq* – statute; *mitswah* – commandment; and *dabar* – word, types of law, which Alt combined under the term 'apodeictic (i.e. unconditional) law.'[14] The *mishpat* material is normally formulated objectively in the third person, (e.g. if he/they . . .), and the *dabar/mitswah* as direct second person address, (e.g. you do/do not . . .). In this case the, '*if you* lend money,' of Exodus

---

[13] Joseph Blenkinsopp, *op. cit.*, p.28.

[14] Albrecht Alt, *Essays on Old Testament History and Religion*, (Tr. R.A.Wilson, Blackwell, Oxford,1966). See essay *'The Origins of Israelite Law,'* p.88ff. on casuistic law; p.103ff. on apodeictic law.

22:25 is a combinaton of both the 'if . . .' *mishpat* formulation, and the second person, 'you,' *dabar/mitswah* address. According to William Johnstone, the 'statute and ordinance' material, the *hoq umishpat*, of Exodus 21:1-22:20, originally a law-code, is now being incorporated secondarily into a covenant-code in the *dabar/mitswah* – word/commandment – formulation, held as it is within a *dabar/mitswah* formulation of Exodus 20:22-26 and 22:21-23:19; the Exodus 22:25 text showing, as has been noted, a trace of *mishpat,* which may provide valuable evidence for this proposition:

> "Thus material which appears in Exodus in the third person *mishpat* formulation of the law-code is reformulated in Deuteronomy in the second person *dabar/mitswah* of the covenant code . . . Exod.22:21-27 thus represents an intermediate stage of development in the reformulation of law-code as covenant-code, between the pure *mishpat* form and its full-scale assimilation to the *dabar/mitswah* form in Deut.12:1-26:15. The basic character of the 'Book of the Covenant' as a law-code remains essentially unchanged: it has been transformed into a covenant-code by the addition of the outer framework (which includes Exod.22:25-27) . . . By contrast, Deuteronomy represents a full-scale transformation of law-code to covenant-code."[15]

It would not be surprising, concludes Johnstone, if the material in Exodus proved itself to be of an earlier date than Deuteronomy. This would reflect the thinking that the laws recorded in Exodus, Leviticus, and Numbers are brought together in Deuteronomy as a covenant-code between God and his 'chosen people,' and applied specifically to the settled life of Canaan which was about to begin. It is the transformation of a cultic law-code which has now become symbolic of God's covenant with his people. His 'chosen people' know that he will look after them, as

---

[15]W. Johnstone, *op.cit.*, p.58.

a distinct community, and bless them as they settle into the land which he has given them. As Paul Johnson maintains:

> "The Jews were thus burdened with a religious law which forbade them to lend at interest among themselves, but permitted it towards strangers. The provision seems designed to protect and keep together a poor community whose chief aim was collective survival. Lending therefore became philanthropy – but you were not obliged to be charitable towards those you did not know or care for. Interest was thus synonymous with hostility."[16]

What we find in Deuteronomy is essentially a re-giving of the laws of the covenant made with Israel on Mount Horeb/Sinai. These are formulated as a speech of Moses – a farewell admonition to Israel on the eve of their entry into the promised land after wandering for forty years in the wilderness because of Israel's disobedience to God. The title, Deuteronomy, which comes from the Greek translation, implies a second law-giving, but, as noted above, the book contains a restatement and reaffirmation of the Sinai covenant. It was, after all, the Deuteronomic redactor's contribution to remould Exodus from law-code to covenant-code, and it follows a similar Near Eastern treaty pattern.[17]

From this premise we can assume that the Hebrew Bible material shows a distinct affinity with a long and widespread legal tradition in the ancient Near East; for example, according to C.H.W.Johns, a contemporary, or at least very early, copy from Nippur, of the Babylonian 'Code of Hammurabi,' states that if a man borrow grain or money from a merchant and has not sufficient grain or money to repay him, he must give the merchant whatever he has in his power to replace the debt that he

---

[16]Paul Johnson, *A History of the Jews*, (Orion Books Ltd., London, 1987), p.173 ff.

[17]R.E.Clements, *Deuteronomy*, (JSOT Press, Sheffield, 1989), p.7.

owes in the presence of the city elders, and the merchant may not decline to accept it.[18] It was from the Babylonians who were accustomed to charge interest at the rate of twenty per cent per annum that the post-exilic Jews learned much in the way of legal terms and forms: "Nearly if not quite all of their contract tablets show this rate of increase. The first allusion in the Babylonian Talmud to a rate of interest (*BB* 60a) is to one of twenty per cent."[19]

The Deuteronomistic pronouncements display clear similarities with ancient Near Eastern law-codes, with regard to language, covenant, and form[20] illustrating the fact that Israel was of eastern Mediterranean culture. However, there were also significant differences within the Old Testament material which made Israel's position distinctive – as already mentioned, an uncompromising monotheism relating everything to their one God, Yahweh – as maintained by A.C.Welch;[21] a community spirit which was based on the covenant relationship shared by all Israel with God; and a remarkable concern for the underprivileged – slaves, women, orphans, and strangers. Even within the outer framework section of the 'Book of the Covenant' in Exodus 22:21-23:19, the first and third parts (Ex.22:21-27 and Ex.23:1-9) which concern a variety of interpersonal relationships are linked together by the prohibition "you shall not oppress a stranger" – Ex. 22:21 and Ex.23:9. Despite this, however,

---

[18]*Encyclopaedia of Religion and Ethics*, ed. James Hastings, Vol. xii, (T. & T. Clark, Edinburgh, 1921), p.556.

[19]*The Jewish Encyclopedia*, *op. cit.*, p. 388.

[20]The Near Eastern law codes consisted of a six-part structure: a preamble introducing the author of the treaty; an historical prologue; stipulations explaining the mutual responsibilities of the partners; a document clause; and the sanction of curses and blessings. Gordon Wenham, "Covenants and Near Eastern Treaties," in *Handbook to the Bible*, (Lion Publishing plc, Herts., 1973.) p.198/199.

[21]A.C.Welch, *The Code of Deuteronomy*, (James Clarke & Co. Ltd., London,1924), see Chapter II, p. 24ff.

the Deuteronomic teaching on the subject of usury allowed for the taking of interest from the 'stranger.'

More than any other part of the Torah, Deuteronomy stresses Israel's obligation to love God; nothing is said, however, unlike in the New Testament, about man's obligation to love the 'alien,'[22] although the love of God does imply justice and sympathy for one's fellow men. This disregard for the stranger was entertained, therefore, and sanctioned by God, as the Hebrews were about to enter their 'Promised Land.' They were mindful of their own kinship values and brotherly love as well as their special relationship and covenant with God as his 'chosen people,' and fearful of the threat of the foreigner they were about to encounter. It has to be remembered that Deuteronomy was edited by the D-redactor reacting to the conditions of the time, and in the context of exile. It would appear that this was to show God's judgment on a pagan people. It was also a reminder of the special relationship between God and his chosen people, as the Near Eastern concept of covenant turned from the interhuman, horizontal plane, to the vertical relationship between Yahweh and Israel. This is a very clear example of how the law-code was reformulated into covenant-code in this respect because of the very special nature and relationship of God and his people, so that the teaching on usury moved from the concept expressed in Leviticus and Exodus of not exploiting the poor within their own community, to the Deuteronomic teaching which allowed for 'exploitation' of the stranger, and upon which 'horns of dilemma' the Christian Church wrestled for many centuries. According to R.Brinker, for example, the guiding principle of Deuteronomy was not that of the centralisation of worship in Jerusalem, as maintained by the critical

---

[22]Jay Williams, *Understanding the Old Testament*, (Barron's Educational Series Inc., New York, 1972), p.137.

school, but the protection of the people from the threat of Canaanite idolatry.[23] Similarly, Welch maintained that only the law in Deuteronomy 12:1-7 unquestionably demands the centralisation of the cult. The rest he states must have been intended to form a guide for the actual life of the community.[24] From the above discussion, and the reasons given, therefore, it could be assumed that this was why the Deuteronomic exception with regard to the prohibition on usury was made. The NRSV makes it very plain in its rendering: "On loans to a foreigner you may charge interest, *so that* the Lord your God may bless you in all your undertakings in the land that you are about to enter and possess" (italics mine). If this 'commandment' was followed it would, as Johnson maintains, protect and keep together a poor community whose chief aim was collective survival. In this case the emphasis would be on the charge not to exact payment for loans to one's brother, rather than emphasising the principle that payment may be exacted from a 'foreigner.' Any small community which might find itself surrounded and threatened by an 'alien' force must develop survival strategies, especially with regard to its economic situation. This is what the Deuteronomic teaching is about.

Whatever difficulties there are in determining the dating of the source material, it can be assumed that Deuteronomy was formed through a complex process that stretched from at least the eighth century to the sixth century, from the time of the divided monarchy to the exile. According to Patrick Miller[25] its affinities with other material that originated in the Northern Kingdom such as Hosea and the Elohist stratum of the Pentateuch suggests that possibly some of the traditions and materials

---

[23]R.Brinker, *The Influence of Sanctuaries in Early Israel*, (1946).

[24]A.C.Welch, *op. cit.*, p.195.

[25]Patrick D.Miller, *Deuteronomy: Interpretation*, (John Knox Press, Louisville, 1990), p.3.

originated there (See Moshe Weinfeld).[26] If that is so, they may have come into Judah in the eighth century, coinciding with the book's first stages in the eighth and seventh centuries. The many connections between Deuteronomy and the reform of Josiah depicted in 2Kings suggest that the time of Josiah and the events of his reign may have been the period when the book (i.e., chapters 4:44-26:68) most likely received its basic form.

What *is* important in trying to address the context in which the 'exemption clause' in Deuteronomy might have originated, is to recognise the relation of the Deuteronomic teaching to three significant periods in the history of Israel:

> "The words of this book, then, could speak to the people of God in sharply different circumstances: (1) when they had not yet received or enjoyed the abundant gifts and prosperity of the land but had known only the difficulties of life in the wilderness; (2) when they had lived long on the land, enjoying and becoming accustomed to all the benefits of land ownership; and, (3) when all the good gifts of God – the land, its abundance, and the temple – had been lost completely. Thus the book is, by necessity, engaged in a significant hermeneutical endeavour, speaking to new situations in light of the past, new situations that may be very different from previous ones."[27]

This answers the question, therefore, of why the Deuteronomic exemption, or exception, was permitted. As Israel prepared to enter the 'Promised Land,' this text, *theologically*, was a reminder of God's covenantal relationship and protection. The 'alien' could be exploited, possibly because they were pagan and idolatrous, but equally to provide the Israelites with a sense of their own corporate and covenantal

---

[26]Moshe Weinfeld, *Deuteronomy and the Deuteronomic School*, (Clarendon Press, Oxford, 1972). pp. 366-370.

[27]P.Miller, *op. cit.*, p.3.

relationship with God, who would bless them if they were obedient to his divine will. This text would equally apply in time of prosperity and despair – both of which followed.

Economically, however, according to Benjamin Nelson, this teaching resulted in a two-tier economic system: an internal, exclusive, clan ethic with the exclusion of seeking gain in respect of the 'brother,' and an external system with no ethical restriction on the pursuit of gain when applied to the 'other.'[28] This interpretation gains support from Gerhard van Rad who states that 'the prohibition against taking interest from a fellow countryman, actually known amongst other nations too, arose from the consciousness of a blood brotherhood which was still alive amongst early people.' However, he equally maintains that 'since Israel even as late as the time of Deuteronomy was almost exclusively a nation of peasants, it was really only foreigners who acted as traders and merchants.'[29] Meislin and Cohen amplify this position but argue that although private trading would be small, investment with foreign merchants would have taken place requiring the legality of interest, and this verse would have permitted these investment loans to the non-resident foreigner – *nokri*. Interest on loans to the poor, however, would remain usury-free and inclusive of the resident foreigner – *toshab/ger* (who often became converts to Judaism). A loan to a foreigner, therefore, is identified as a business loan, whilst a loan to a 'brother' is identified with a consumption loan. Within this argument, therefore, the distinction is between business and consumption and not brother and foreigner.[30]

---

[28]Benjamin Nelson, *The Idea of Usury*, (London: The University of Chicago Press, Ltd. 1949), p.xvi.

[29]Gerhard van Rad, *Deuteronomy, a Commentary* (London, 1964; 1976) p.148.

[30]B.J.Meislin/M.L.Cohen, *Backgrounds of the Biblical Law against Usury* (Comparative Studies in Society and History 6, 1963-64) pp. 264-265.

Barry Gordon, however, questions both analyses. Nelson's view, he contends, overemphasizes the tribal element in the religion of the Hebrews at the expense of the tradition's universalistic tendencies. Yahweh, he maintains, is not merely a tribal god. He is the one and only God, and the fate of all other peoples depends on him. 'An exclusively tribal understanding of social morality is not compatible with such conceptions.'[31] This I feel, in the light of my above argument rather undermines the concept of the covenantal relationship specifically developed in Deuteronomy. Equally, he maintains that a distinction between two general classes of loan – commercial and consumption – is putting too modern a construction on economic relationships in ancient societies. This is an important point as he states:

> "The predominant microeconomic institution in antiquity was the household, and this was not merely the modern organisation consisting of a group of consumers. At the same time it was 'the firm,' a group of producers. Hence, there was the most intimate relationship in institutional terms between production possibilities, consumption potential, and household capital. When a householder borrowed he was necessarily borrowing as consumer-producer. It is not surprising that it is difficult to discover unambiguous differentiation of business and consumption loans in the literature of antiquity. Certainly one finds lending to the poor distinguished from lending to others. However, 'poor loan' does not necessarily equate with 'consumer loan.'"[32]

This is an important consideration when we begin to think about loans on a micro-enterprise level to the poor even in this day and age, not only in the poor

---

[31]Barry Gordon, "Lending at Interest: Some Jewish, Greek, and Christian Approaches, 800BC-100AD" (*History of Political Economy*, 14:3, Duke University Press. 1982) pp. 407-412.

[32]*Ibid.* p.411.

village communities of the Third World countries but in areas in the First World where 'households' still need access to finance on a consumer-producer basis.

Gordon actually posits a rather innovative view in suggesting that perhaps the Deuteronomic support for taking from foreigners is best understood as an application to credit arrangements of the *Lex talionis:*

> "The latter prevailed as a general precept for the regulation of punishment for damages among the Babylonians and the Arabs of the desert. It is embodied in the Code of Hammurabi and the Sumerian laws, and it is repeated in Ex.21:23-25; Deut.19:21; and Lev.24:17-22. The Deuteronomic formulation reads: 'Life for life, eye for eye, tooth for tooth, hand for hand, foot for foot.' To this Leviticus adds (24:22): 'The sentence you pass shall be the same whether it be on native or on stranger.' The *Lex talionis* might be construed as relevant to loans, in that when Israelites borrow from foreigners whose civil legal codes permit interest taking (as did the Code of Hammurabi) the borrowers suffer 'damages' from the standpoint of Mosaic law. It would be equitable and just, then, that equivalent compensation for those damages is taken when Israelites assume the role of lender. Such reasoning is compatible with the exemption of the *ger* from interest payment, and its necessarily communal character finds support in the concept of 'corporate personality' which many modern scholars believe was predominant in early Jewish thought."[33]

It is an interesting hypothesis and if it is serving to emphasize the 'corporate personality' in early Jewish thought, it is not that far removed from the concept of tribal brotherhood. It is an obvious point, however, that as the Israelites could not forbid foreigners to lend to them money on interest, it would have been foolish to give the foreigner a cheaper loan which could then be lent on profit again to another Jew. But this did not prevent an operation of interest-free loans from existing within

---

[33] *Ibid.* p.413.

the corporate brotherhood of the Jewish community in accordance with this Deuteronomic injunction And the reason I have emphasisied this particular aspect is because I think that from a *theological* point of view it stressed the covenantal and protective element in the relationship between God and his 'chosen people.' At the same time it provided economic protection in an alien land. From the time of entering the land of Canaan its teaching was extended into diasporan communities which developed throughout the known world, especially after the destruction of the Second Temple in 70CE.

The Christian Church, therefore, was left to wrestle with the problem of how far this Deuteronomic teaching was to be adhered to in the light of economic development and Judaeo-Christian fortunes; and the question still remains as to how this teaching might be re-interpreted today.

Usury: Definition and Interpretation – *Neshekh; Marbit and Tarbit*

Although the Hebraic terms used in the Hebrew Bible do not throw much light on the *moral* and *religious* ideas connected with the concept of usury/interest, they must be noted in order to provide some understanding as to the way in which they came to be understood in Jewish economic life set within its own cultural milieu. The various interpretations of the Hebraic words which were translated as 'usury' will, therefore, be examined in this section. The significance of its teaching in various other texts throughout the Hebrew Bible will be considered, as well as the development of a specific '*Judaic* economic ethic' in the light of its teaching on usurious lending, especially with regard to the Deuteronomic 'exemption,' which resulted in, according to Nelson as I have already discussed, a two-tier economic system: an internal, exclusive, clan ethic with the exclusion of the quest for gain in respect of the 'brother,' and an external system where no ethical restriction in the pursuit of gain was to apply to the 'other.' It is, therefore, I argue, within the development of this *Judaic* clan ethic, as opposed to Weber's Calvinistic Protestant ethic aligned to 'calling,' that the embryonic spirit of modern capitalism is nurtured.

The Hebrew word for 'usury' is *neshekh* meaning literally 'a bite' from its painfulness to the debtor (Ex. 22:25; Deut. 23:19,20) but in the Levitical text, (Leviticus 25:36,37) 'increase' is the rendering of the Hebrew *marbit* or *tarbit* which denotes the gain on the creditor's side and which in later Hebrew becomes *ribbit.* This will be discussed later with regard to the Talmud, but it is worth noting here that the Talmudic prohibitions on interest are known as *avak ribbit,* i.e. the dust of interest, as distinguished from *ribbit kezuzah,* i.e. interest proper in an amount, or at a rate agreed upon between lender and borrower: see 'The Babylonian Talmud,' *Seder Nezikin II, Baba Mezia,* 61b and 67a.[34]

The prohibition on taking interest in Exodus and Leviticus seems to be confined to the poor in dire straits and not to extend to moneylending in the normal course of business, but the Deuteronomic prohibition clearly applies to all moneylenders, excluding only business dealings with foreigners. 'The Jewish Publication Society' renders *neshekh* as 'advance interest' and *marbit* or *tarbit* as 'accrued interest' – the one being deducted in advance, the other being added at the time of repayment.[35] This, however, was only one of many interpretations which was made of the terms *neshekh* and *tarbit* from the time of the Mishnah onward.

---

[34]*The Babylonian Talmud, "Seder Nezikin II, Baba Mezia,"* Translated into English under the Editorship of Rabbi Dr. I. Epstein, (The Soncino Press, London, 1935). Folios 1- 24b by Salis Daiches and Folios 25a to the end by H.Freedman. BM 61b, pp. 365-369; BM 67a, pp.391-393.

[35]*Encyclopaedia Judaica,* Volume 16, UR-Z, (Keter Publishing House, Jerusalem Ltd., 1972), p.27. And for further definition see *Baba Mezia, op. cit.,* pp. 361 ff.

The most authoritative view is that of Rava, a fourth century Babylonian amora. Almost every page of the Talmud reports discussions between Rava and his colleague Abbaye, based on their profound knowledge of the Oral Law and great analytical powers. With six exceptions the decision in each case is in accordance with the views of Rava who headed the academy at Mahoza. He stressed the importance of study and also emphasised ethical conduct. After the death of Abbaye, his Pumbedita school merged with the academy at Mahoza, and Rava, thus, became the undisputed talmudic authority in Babylonia.[36] Rava maintained that essentially there was no difference in meaning between these two terms, *neshekh* and *tarbit*, and the Torah used two synonyms to make the prohibiton of interest a two-fold one. However, the better explanation, etymologically, would be that *neshekh*, meaning bite, was the term used for the exaction of interest from the point of view of the debtor, and *marbit* or *tarbit*, meaning increase, was the term used for the recovery of interest by the creditor.[37]

As has been noted, the prohibition on interest is not a prohibiton on usury as it has now come to be understood, i.e. as excessive or exorbitant interest, but of *all*, even minimal, interest. There is no difference in Judaic law between various rates of interest, as all interest is prohibited, except, with the greatest of significance, in the Deuteronomic exemption of that 'unto a stranger, or foreigner.' Indeed, lending on usury or increase is classed by Ezekiel among the worst of sins (Ezekiel 18:13,17), and in Psalm 15:5 among the attributes of a righteous man is reckoned the fact that he does not lend on usury.

---

[36] *The Encyclopedia of the Jewish Religion*, ed. Dr. R.J. Zwi Werblowsky and Dr. Geoffrey Wigoder, (Phoenix House, London, 1967).

[37] *Encyclopaedia Judaica, op. cit.*, p.28

However, the prohibition on taking interest does not appear to have been generally observed in biblical times. The creditor far from giving free loans is often described as exacting and implacable (e.g. 1Samuel 22:2; 2Kings 4:1; Isaiah 50:1); and the prophet decries those who have taken 'interest' and 'increase' and forgotten God (Ezekiel 22:12). Nehemiah had to rebuke the noble and the rich for exacting interest, 'every one to his brother' (Neh. 5:7).[38] The exact nature of the reproach in this verse, though, has caused some controversy. Was it because of levying interest (RSV), or imposing burdens (cf. JB and GNB)? The normal word for 'interest' is not used here, and 'imposing burdens' does not follow the theme in verse 10 – 'I pray you let us leave off this usury.' According to Derek Kidner the terms in verses 7 and 10 mean, at their simplest, 'lending' (not 'exacting'), and 'a loan,' not interest; but the words implied a strict business relationship and Nehemiah's charge is therefore that the lenders were behaving like pawnbrokers, and harsh ones at that, instead of like brothers.[39]

From the Elephantine papyri, Aramaic documents written by a Jewish community who were living at roughly the time of Nehemiah and Ezra,[40] it appears that among the Jews in Egypt in the fifth century BCE it was a matter of course that interest would be charged on loans. Not only did they disregard the biblical injunctions as far as the taking of interest was concerned, but they made no attempt to justify it in legal terms in order to evade the prohibiton. In other words, however 'illegal' it may have been in terms of moral or religious law, because it did not

---

[38] *Ibid.* p.28.

[39] Derek Kidner, *Ezra and Nehemiah*, (Tyndale Old Testament Commentaries, Inter-Varsity Press, Leicester 1979), p.95.

[40] John Drane, *Introducing The Old Testament*, (Lion Publishing, Herts., 1987), p.185.

infringe on any state law, the biblical injunctions were not sufficient to stir the conscience into its strict adherence.

That is not to say, however, that there was no attempt to adhere to the biblical injunction on taking usury between fellow Jews. Although the biblical record has shown that the law was constantly evaded, the religious authorities did try to enforce the law strictly. They laid down that concealed interest was wrong – rent-free premises supplied by the borrowers; gifts; useful information – all these were termed 'the dust of interest' and banned. Talmudic rulings show amazing efforts over the years to block loopholes created by cunning usurers or desperate would-be borrowers.[41] The Mosaic law forbade the taking of interest between fellow Jews and required the interest-free loan as part of the economic system, apart from, that is, loans to a foreigner. I examine the development of Jewish usurious and non-usurious moneylending, the earliest form of banking, in terms of monetary currency as opposed to bartered goods, in order to see how it was made harmonious with this teaching, and how, in fact, it resulted in two differing economic policies, the one internal and associated with the 'brother'; and the other 'external' and associated with the 'other.'

In modern times this whole concept of usury, or interest on a loan, affects the treatment of bank credit, instalment buying, inflation, and exchange rates; and since Jews enjoyed a great measure of autonomy throughout the centuries, even after they lost political independence in their own homeland, they also enjoyed the sovereign right to tax members of their own communities. First and foremost, according to Meir Tamari, this was a method of financing the needs of the Jewish community, for defence, health facilities, free education and charity in its widest sense, not just, even

---

[41]P.Johnson, *op.cit.*, p.173.

in earliest biblical times, a method of collecting taxes to be paid to the non-Jewish authorities. Indeed, as will be discussed, Jewish and non-Jewish sources throughout the ages have agreed that charity and social welfare are hallmarks of Jewish life.

Although I have cited biblical evidence to show some general disregard for the prohibition of usury – prophetic tirades against 'sinful' behaviour – there did develop, over time, a specific Jewish economic system with regard to this teaching. Tamari maintains that for centuries Jews maintained in many countries of the 'Diaspora'[42] rabbinical courts of law which regulated and governed their economic activity preserving its special Jewish characteristics. The Hebrew Bible and the homiletical literature established an ethical and moral framework within which Jewish communities operated, introducing non-materialistic considerations, a unique social structure, and distinctive role models. Legal tradition dating back to the earliest days of Jewish national independence had already been codified in the early years of the Common Era. This tradition, written and oral, covered the economic aspects of life in addition to such areas as ritual observance, marriage and divorce. There is no reason to suppose that it simply represented an economic utopian model when the existence of Jewish life with regard to these other observances, based on these same codes, is universally accepted, for example, Rabbi Hanasi divided his Mishnah into six orders, or '*sedarim.*' The *Zera'im* dealt with the agricultural laws; the *Moed* dealt with the yearly cycle and the festivals; the *Nashim* dealt with marriage and divorce; the *Nezikin* dealt with the criminal, commercial, and civil codes of law – it is this *seder* which forms the legal basis for the treatment of

---

[42]As well as reading Keller, (*op. cit.*), on the Diaspora, for further information with regard to 'diasporan communities' and their effect on economic life, see Professor Arnold Toynbee's fascinating insight on the use of the diasporan Jewish people as a model for a special type of community, which I draw attention to in my conclusion. Arnold Toynbee, *A Study of History*, (Oxford University Press, 1972), p.65ff.

economic matters in Judaism, primarily in the tractates *Baba Kama, Baba Mezia,* and *Baba Bathra,* and the *Kodashim* dealt with the Temple service and sacrifices. Finally, the *Toharot* dealt with the laws of ritual purity.[43]

Throughout the ages, Jews turned to the rabbinical authorities for guidance and judgment in applying the law to problems arising out of all aspects of economic activity. The resulting response – rabbinical answers to questions on Jewish law and observance – provide a rich source of data and a wealth of detail on the actuality of Jewish economic life in various countries and at various periods of times. For a very long period, religious teaching was enshrined in the Talmud, and Jews through many centuries lived in it, for it, and through it. The responsa continue today, as the rabbinical authorities in Israel, England, and the United States continue to receive and answer such questions.

Legal decisions and legislation, however, are not in themselves sufficient to maintain the social and economic fabric of a society. That requires a value structure and moral code acceptable to the majority of that society. So, despite the centrality of rabbinical law to Judaism it is essential to pay attention to the ethical teachings that constituted the ideological framework of Jewish society, although, as I have already suggested in connection with the references in the Hebrew Bible to the disregard of anti-usury practice, where there was no legal implementation of the law to uphold it, a moral framework, however rigid in its ethic, will not deter those who wish to ignore it.

However, much of Jewish life until the middle of the nineteenth century was characterised by communal rule expressed in independent legislative and fiscal

---

[43]Meir Tamari, "With All Your Possessions," *Jewish Ethics and Economic Life,* (The Free Press, A Division of Macmillan Inc., New York, 1987), p.15.

authority and this shows that the moral tenets of Judaism and the decisions of the rabbinic courts were actually translated into every day practice. The autonomous Jewish communities must not be viewed as the voluntary religious or social entities with which we are familiar today, but, rather, the community, or *'kehilla'* – which is at once the political-legal structure of a local Jewish community and also the essence of that community – was comparable to the public sector of modern times, at the local, regional, or national level.[44] Community at this stage reflected a much larger homogeneous, group identity, and Jews maintained this sense of identity in terms of their racial and religious status. Today, in non-Jewish terms, it would be more comparable to equate this concept of community with 'the people,' and community itself would be defined as a concept within a much smaller grouping. It was within this Judaic framework, however, that the Jewish individual's economic aims, his methods of achieving them, and the degree of his social responsibilities were formed and nurtured, and were reflected in the application of rabbinical and communal legislation. In the modern world in which Jews live, in an open society exposed to non-Jewish cultural and social pressures – as that world in which the Christian and the Muslim also finds himself – this ethical value structure is perhaps even more important in defining a specific economic personality than it was in the closed, autonomous societies of previous generations, although in the Islamic world we shall find modern-day Islamic economic ethics being affected by a reversal to more closed, autonomous societies.

Thus, whilst economic activity is considered by Judaism a legitimate pursuit in the normal world – and legal and literary sources do show that there exists a Jewish economic wisdom – nevertheless, there exists a distinctly Jewish framework

---

[44] *Ibid.*, p.8.

within which this activity may take place. This framework seeks to sanctify man's everyday actions in this field, just as it introduces holiness into the domain of other basic needs, like food, shelter, sex, and social organisation. Attitudes and behaviour with respect to poverty, money, finance, trade, and welfare are determined by Jewish conceptions of man's partnership with God; man's duty and ability to sanctify and save himself through righteous acts; the recognition of the claims of others on one's property; and an overriding understanding of the demands of justice, mercy, and righteousness.[45] The result, reflected through centuries of Jewish life, is a specifically Jewish economic system, resulting, I believe, in what one might define as a distinctive 'Judaic Economic Man.'

At the heart of this system is the Deuteronomic teaching on the concept of usury which promoted the 'brother' at the expense of the 'other.' This is not an unnatural phenomenon in itself, most minority communities will adopt a policy of self-preservation when in a perceived threatening situation, but it would appear that in this case it was persistently adhered to throughout history, and what is, perhaps, more surprising, given religious sanctification. There exists a certain embryonic 'spirit of capitalism' in this Judaic economic ethic, even in these earliest biblical times, despite the fact that it was an agrarian economy, and, of course, depending on how one defines the concept of capitalism. In this respect it is encouraging to note that Benjamin Nelson wrote, with regard to Max Weber's later insights, that:

> "it was not until the end of his (Weber's) life that he detected the fruitfulness of taking the usury question as a point of departure for the history of the capitalist spirit."[46]

---

[45]*Ibid.*

[46]Benjamin Nelson, *The Idea of Usury*, (The University of Chicago Press, Ltd., London, 1949), p.74.

The biblical legal character of prohibition on usury rests on two grounds: firstly, that the prosperous ought to help the poor, if not by gifts then at least by free loans; and, secondly, that usury (or excessive interest) was seen to lie at the root of social ruin and was therefore to be completely banned. Both these considerations, however, would apply only *internally*. There could be no obligation to help foreigners nor was public policy concerned with their well-being; moneylending transactions with foreigners were motivated solely by the legitimate desire to make profits, while the internal economy was eminently agrarian and had, at that time, no money markets of any importance. From the charitable nature of the prohibiton on interest it follows that its violation was not regarded as a criminal offence but rather as a moral transgression, hence the prophetic tirades. On the other hand, while taking interest would not entail any punishment, granting free loans and refraining from taking interest would lead to God's rewards and blessings (Deut. 23:20). It was only in the prophesies of Ezekiel that usury came to be identified with the gravest of crimes – it is mentioned in the context of larceny, adultery, homicide, and other such 'abominations' which are worthy of death (Ez. 18:10-13). The threat of death for usury was later interpreted as the divine sanction against irrecoverable and illegitimate self-enrichment. 'He that augments his wealth by interest and increase' is listed among the 'evil men' (Proverbs 28:8); while as has been noted 'He who does not put out his money at interest' is among the upright and righteous (Ps. 15:5).[47]

From the very beginning, therefore, we can trace the development of a clan ethic; what ensued were two opposite attitudes toward the pursuit of gain which grew to exist in combination, and which might be classed as traditonal welfare socialism on the one hand, and free-enterprise exploitative capitalism on the other; because, on

---

[47]*Encyclopaedia Judaica, op. cit.* p.28.

the one hand, there developed internally an attachment to tradition and to the pietistic relations of fellow members of tribes, clan and house community with the *exclusion* of the quest for gain within the circle bound by religious ties; whilst, on the other hand, externally, there is absolutely unrestricted play of the gain spirit (i.e. profit) in economic relations where, according to Nelson,[48] no ethical restrictions applied to the foreigner who was, as we have seen from the Deuteronomic viewpoint, originally perceived as an 'alien' – an external factor, someone outside the internal 'brotherhood.'

It is an irony that over the centuries Jews, too, due firstly to the Diaspora and later to persecution, were almost everywhere themselves strangers in the sense that they became newcomers. As Werner Sombart maintains, Jews looked upon themselves as a 'peculiar' people; and as a 'peculiar' people the nations regarded them[49] in an age where the concept of world-citizenship was as yet non-existent. The development of this concept, however, does not insure it from coming under attack. Even in late twentieth century history it is being broken down yet again into its 'tribalistic' elements. As F.Fields, L.Halligan, and M.Owen remark:

> "As nation states disintegrate, tribalism is re-establishing itself in parts of Europe and what was the USSR. The search for territorial gain by well-armed gangs poses a threat to Europe's stability. A new dark age has already descended on lands surrounding much of Europe's borders. Europe has a vested interest in preventing tribalism dominating the politics of what were nation states on its borders."[50]

---

[48]Benjamin Nelson, *op. cit.*, p.xvi.

[49]W.Sombart, *The Jews and Modern Capitalism*, (tr. M.Epstein, Burt Franklin, New York, and London, 1913), p.177.

[50]See Frank Fields, Liam Halligan, and Matthew Owen, *Europe Isn't Working*, (The Institute of Community Studies, 1994).

Today this disintegration masquerades under the name of ethnicity, which is normally defined as relating to race or culture, but it also involves explicit overtones of religious discrimination. One has only to consider recent conflict in Bosnia and Kosovo, for example, to prove this point.

Furthermore, Nelson contends, it was as Weber suggested, upon the ruins of the tribalistic communalism of the Hebrew brotherhood, that modern capitalism arose.[51] I, however, argue, in terms of the development of a clan ethic, that it was not so much on the ruins of the tribalistic communalism of the Hebrew brotherhood upon which modern capitalism arose, but *because* of its formation in the first place, and the resultant attitude toward the 'other.' What may be arguable, however, is the *type* of capitalism which ensued. As Weber writes:

> "Jewish capitalism was speculative pariah-capitalism, while the Puritan was bourgeois organisation of labour."[52]

R.H.Tawney, however, in discussing Jean Calvin's treatment of capitalism, shows how he (Calvin) changed the plane on which the discussion was conducted.[53] This will be discussed later on in more detail but it is noted here that Calvin treated the ethics of moneylending not as a matter to be decided by an appeal to a special body of doctrine on the subject of usury, but, rather, with regard to specific cases within the social relations of a Christian community, which must be solved in the light of existing circumstances.

---

[51]Benjamin Nelson, *op. cit.*, p.xvii.

[52]Max Weber, *The Protestant Ethic and the Spirit of Capitalism*, (Unwin University Books, London, 1930), p.271.

[53]R.H.Tawney, *Religion and the Rise of Capitalism*, (Penguin Books, Middlesex, 1922), p.116.

The significant feature in his discussion of the subject is that, although he makes certain provisos which were subsequently ignored, he assumes credit to be a normal and inevitable incident in the life of society. He therefore dismisses the much quoted passages from the Hebrew Bible and the Church Fathers as irrelevant, designed for conditions which no longer exist, arguing that the payment of interest for capital is as valid as the payment of rent for land. He makes a fresh start and appeals from Christian tradition to commercial common sense in the hope that all extortion is to be avoided by Christians relying on behavioural 'norms' - natural justice and the golden rule: 'Love thy neighbour as thyself.' Capital and credit are indispensible; the financier is not a pariah, he maintains, but a useful member of society; and lending at interest, provided that the rate is reasonable and that loans are made freely to the poor, is not, per se, more extortionate than any other form of economic transactions within which human affairs are carried out. That acceptance of the realities of commercial practice as a starting-point was of momentous importance, especially for the Christian Church, and I shall return to it. However, in accepting the Protestant ethic as attributable to the spirit of capitalism is no more than to reinforce the *Judaic* notion that sanctification can be 'won' through righteous acts, a point made earlier, although in Protestant terms it is aligned to an understanding of 'calling.' For Calvin, the central paradox of religious ethics revolves around the concept that although good works are not a way of attaining salvation, they are indispensable as a proof that salvation has been attained.

I argue that capitalism did not arise like a phoenix from the ashes of the Protestant ethic, or, indeed, a Catholic one, but, rather from a Judaic one, based on the Deuteronomic understanding that one 'shalt' or 'may' (whether it is translated as a commandment or as an allowance, the Mishnah gave it '*mitswah*' status,[54] i.e. a commandment that the Jew is obliged to obey, or a good deed performed, which, as has been discussed, was developing through Leviticus and Exodus into the Deuteronomic *dabar/mitswah* formulation), 'unto a stranger lend upon usury, but unto thy brother thou shalt not lend upon usury, that the Lord thy God may bless thee.' This meant that the essence of profit making was incorporated into the Jewish economic way of life, which led to the rise of a two-tier system, or if not two-tier at least two parallel systems, one internal, and the other external in which the Judaic ethic nurtured the spirit of capitalism, be it defined as pariah, rather than its later Protestant manifestation which had more to do with, in Weberian terms, "the rational capitalistic organisation of (formally) free labour."[55]

In Judaic terms, as perceived in the Deuteronomic book of the Torah, the ethics of internal and external relations with regard to the concept of usury were categorically distinct. *Internally*, there existed the clan/tribal/brotherhood ethic, dependent ideally, on helping each other, especially the poor amongst them, with interest free loans; *externally*, there was no obligation to help foreigners, indeed moneylending transactions were motivated solely by a legitimate desire to make profit. However, once accountability, as I shall consider in Christian terms, (in so far as it is not Judaic), is established into the traditional 'brotherhood,' it displaces

---

[54]The Code of Maimonides states: "For it is written *Thou shalt not lend upon interest to thy brother* – to thy brother it is forbidden, but to the rest of the world it is permissible. Indeed, it is an affirmative comandment to lend money at interest to a heathen. For it is written *Unto the heathen thou shalt lend upon interest.* From the oral tradition it has been learned that this is to be construed as an affirmative commandment. This is the rule of the Law." *The Code of Maimonides (Mishneh Torah) Book Thirteen: The Book of Civil Laws*, (Yale Judaica Series, Vol.II, tr. from the Hebrew by J.J.Rabinowitz, Yale University Press, New York, 1949), Treatise Three: Creditor and Debtor, p.93.

[55]Max Weber, *op. cit.*, p.21.

the old Judaic religious/ethical relationship within the family community, for Christians that is, but, not necessarily Jews. As Sombart points out:

> "Jewish law, in fact, is as much a part of the religious system as are Jewish ethics. The Law is from God, and moral law and divine ordinances are inseparable in Judaism. Hence in reality there are no special ethics of Judaism. Jewish ethics are the underlying principles of the Jewish religion."[56]

This is where Calvin's teaching, as distinct from Martin Luther's, becomes so important, because it let Christians 'off the hook' in economic terms with regard to legitimising the profit motive. As Ronald Preston remarks:[57] "Luther was thoroughly mediaeval in the matter of usury, Calvin was more far-seeing." Various devices were sanctioned to get round the prohibiton of usury, and the discussions went on for another two hundred years or more, becoming increasingly ignored in practice, and finally expiring into a state of disuse. Today, as I shall examine further with regard to the Qur'anic teaching on this issue, it is a matter that is being given a great deal more consideration in terms of justice and equality for the poor.

Nonetheless, the whole history of this particular economic ethic was something which dominated the intellectual interest throughout the sixteenth and seventeenth centuries, and it is difficult to imagine the intensity of the debate today. The Christian Church maintained that the vice of usury implicated every part of Western society, corrupting cities and Church. The biggest problem was in defining, in the light of Christ's teaching, the whole concept of community in terms of *universal* brotherhood. For the Christian, according to Nelson's Weberian premise,

---

[56]W. Sombart, *op. cit.*, p.192.

[57]Ronald H. Preston, *Religion and the Ambiguities of Capitalism*, (SCM Press Ltd., London, 1991), p.36.

the "economic relations are no longer strictly communistic, there is an end of the naive piety and its repression of the economic impulse; . . . at the same time there is a tempering of the unrestricted quest of gain with the adoption of the economic principle into the internal economy."[58] The result is, ideally, a regulated life with the economic impulse functioning within bounds, both internally and externally. However, in accordance with the Torah, in Deuteronomic terms, the differences, economically, between the internal and external relationships continue to apply.

The Talmud: Usury – Rabbinical Interpretation

This section will consider how the teaching in the Hebrew Bible with respect to the concept of usury, was brought together from the oral tradition and formulated in the Talmud in the light of rabbinical interpretation.

The Jewish religion in all its stages was generally incorporated in a book, and these books may be looked upon as the sources of the Jewish religion. Besides the Bible, i.e. the 'Old Testament' until the destruction of the Second Temple in 70CE, which was read in Hebrew in Palestine and in Greek (Septuagint) in the Diaspora, there was the Talmud, more especially the Babylonian Talmud, which from the second to the sixth century of the Common Era, was the principle depository of Jewish religious teaching. In the Talmud usury is indicated either by the Biblical word *neshekh* or, as is more frequently the case, as I mentioned, by the term, *ribbit.* Although it is debated in the *Baba Mezia,*[59] it is acknowledged that both terms can denote money, food, or any article which a man gives on loan to his fellow man, on

---

[58]B.Nelson, *op. cit.*, p.xvi.

[59]See *Baba Mezia, op. cit.*, p. 361 – "You must draw no distinction between money and provisions, *neshekh* and *ribbit.*"

the condition that the latter repays something for the loan in addition to the original sum lent. The Talmud and the medieval Jewish codes – the twelfth century Code of Maimonides; the *Turim* Code of Jacob ben Asher (1248-1340); and the sixteenth century Code of Joseph Caro, the *Shulchan Arukh* – enumerate several kinds of 'increase.' These are 'fixed increase'; 'the mere dust of increase'; 'the semblance of increase'; and 'increase payable by some other means than money.'[60] They all refer on the internal level to dealings between Jew and Jew.

'Fixed increase' denotes the ordinary transaction where interest in money is paid directly on a loan, in violation of the express command of Scripture. This was frequently known as 'increase under the Mosaic law.' Secondly, 'Rabbinical increase,' also referred to as the 'mere dust of increase,' denotes interest paid in some indirect way – the amount of which was not stipulated nor mentioned at all when the loan was first transacted, but which was paid more or less gratuitously by the borrower or taken voluntarily by the lender with the consent of the borrower. Thus the Talmud says:

> "A man may not say to his neighbour, 'Lend me a kor of wheat and
> I will repay you at harvest time; lest it become dearer'"[61] (i.e. because
> the market-price of wheat might rise in the meantime and the lender
> would profit).

The third kind, the 'semblance of increase,' refers to interest paid out of sheer gratitude for a past loan or as the motive for inducing a future one: for example, after repayment of a loan a borrower might send a gift to the lender on the mere grounds that the lender's money had been in his (the borrower's) hands. This is forbidden.

---

[60] *Encyclopaedia of Religion and Ethics, op. cit.*, p.556.

[61] See *Baba Mezia, op. cit.*, 75a, p.432.

Or, if A has received a loan from B, he should not greet B in the street – out of gratitude – unless he had been in the habit of doing so before. The fourth form of increase – 'that payable by some other means than money' – is illustrated by the case of a Jew who after receiving a loan from a friend, honoured the latter by allowing him to perform some religious duty in connection with synagogue worship or home-ritual.

The Talmudic Rabbis laid a great amount of emphasis on all these sins of 'moral' usury – a loan from one Jew to another should be an act of kindness without the least expectation of profit. Kindness, in fact, was not simply an act of charity but rather the fulfillment of a *legal obligation*. Indeed, the duties and obligations imposed by Judaism on one's property go beyond the connotations of 'charity' and include acts of righteousness. The prime example of this is the commandment to make interest-free loans:

> "This exists as a separate positive commandment, distinct both from the injunction against taking interest as well as from the obligation to give charity. It is an act of righteousness, granted both to the rich man who is temporarily in financial straits and to the poor man trying to improve his economic situation."[62]

Exodus 22:25 is the basis for this positive precept of extending interest-free loans. Although the Hebrew word *'im'* is usually translated as, 'if' (the *mishpat* formulation already discussed), in this verse – 'if thou lend money to any of my people . . . thou shalt not be to him as an usurer, neither shalt thou lay upon him usury.' – the sages considered it to mean 'when.' This interpretation made giving interest-free loans a binding obligation rather than a voluntary act. This positive

---

[62]Meir Tamari, *op. cit.*, p.53.

commandment to lend money to a fellow Jew is one of the examples in Judaism of *chesed* – an act of loving kindness, considered to be an obligation to which the law prescribed no limits, since *chesed* was something rendered to people primarily when they were not entitled to it. Indeed, unlike charity, *tzedakah*, which is something one gives to the poor, *chesed* can be directed at rich and poor alike in times of need.[63]

Although it may appear that the interest-free loan commanded by the Torah might only seem relevant in a primitive agrarian economy, where most financial transactions would be between a neighbour and his fellow farmer, this was not the case. From the earliest days of Jewish society, the interest-free loan was relevant beyond the needs of an agrarian economy and was not simply limited to the simple act of making small temporary loans. What is amazing is that irrespective of the country in which Jews lived, the sophistication of its economy, or the particular economic conditions of the Jewish community, these free loans were an integral part of the Jewish economic world. Throughout history, and down to the present day, almost no Jewish community in an organised form has ever existed without the free-loan as a permanent part of its communal structure. The development of Jewish economic life in trade and commerce was no doubt assisted by the existence of its free-loan society in all of these countries. This enabled them to build up a strong internal economy, and then, externally, employing a usurious loan system, they nurtured the 'spirit of capitalism,' not in terms of gain as greed, but as Weber defines it, as gain in terms of profit, the basis of a capitalistic economy.

Meir Tamari suggests that perhaps one of the reasons for the difficulties which minority groups have had in establishing themselves financially today in, for instance, the United States, may be that no such tradition of the free-loan society

---

[63]See Tamari, *ibid.*, p.50 and p.248ff.

exists in their cultures.[64] There are exceptions, however, such as the Church of the Latter Day Saints who operate free loan schemes within their Mormon community.

Despite the centuries old Islamic ban on interest, and I shall be discussing the relevance of Islamic thought on this issue, it is only recently that rich Muslim countries have begun to develop the concept of interest-free loans. Until then, the objection to taking interest existed, but organised communal implementation of the interest-free loan did not. In Judaism, not only was the interest-free loan seen as a positive religious act, but separate and distinct from this also was the negative *mitswah* of not taking interest, that is to say, *ideally*, one positively gave and one also positively did not take.

The question to be addressed, therefore, is how defensible is it to assume the solidarity of the *mishpaha*, the clan, to the exclusion of the *nokri* – the foreigner (as distinguished from other Hebraic terms such as *ger* meaning the protected sojourner, or *toshab* meaning the resident stranger)[65] from the privileges and obligations of a fraternity, by enacting interest on a loan not to the 'brother,' but to the 'other,' and what have been, and what are, the consequences of that? The Deuteronomic teaching formed a cornerstone of the blood brotherhood morality of the Hebrew tribesmen; and it is upon the horns of the dilemma of this Deuteronomic double standard that the Christian Church has wrestled for almost the last two thousand years. In this chapter I am outlining the brotherhood morality, and economic privileges and prejudices, of a tribal society based on the religious injunctions of this teaching. In following chapters I shall consider the shift in focus with regard to the universal brotherhood of medieval Christianity, and propose that, based on this Deuteronomic teaching the

---

[64]*Ibid.*, p.171.

[65]Nelson, *op.cit.*, p.xix.

road to capitalism in the west was already paved by the Judaic implementation of it, and cemented with the good intentions of Christian universalism, based on the grapplings, and eventual reversal, of this Deuteronomic injunction.

This reversal in the anti-usury principle is also, interestingly, found in the mainstream of rabbinical thinking today as Rabbi Wasserman intimated to Tamari that lending money at interest is not only *not* intrinsically bad but is essential to the economy.[66] Extending interest bearing loans is actually beneficial to the borrower, who would be worse off if these loans were withheld. There is a corollary here with the issue of Third World debt when the loans made by rich oil-producing countries during 1975-82 proved very beneficial to them. There is also, however, a tremendous downside – repayments have proved to be crippling burdens for many countries struggling with the various problems of war, severe malnutrition, famine, disease, and recession which has hit, in different measure, both rich and poor countries. It is not just the debt, either, which in some cases has been fully repaid, but the interest repayments on the debt which is destroying the future economic growth of most Third World countries, and, because of world recession – the leap in interest rates in the developed countries and the fall in export commodity prices for the low income countries – the once economically bouyant countries have great difficulty in being able to ameliorate conditions in the Third World, even though, by comparison, they are still so much better off.[67]

This does raise some interesting considerations. Richard Higginson suggests, as too does the Jubilee Centre Research Paper on 'Families in Debt,'[68] that perhaps

---

[66]Tamari, *op.cit.*, p.182.

[67]I consider in greater detail the problem of debt in the Third World in my conclusion.

[68]"*Families in Debt,*" Jubilee Centre Research Paper, No.7, (Jubilee Centre Publications Ltd., Cambridge, 1988), p.7 ff.

what is needed is some mutually agreed solution which enshrines in a balanced way the principles of *justice*, i.e. the borrowing institution makes some attempt to discharge its obligations; *mercy*, so that a significant portion of the debt is actually written off; and, *hope*, working out new arrangements which hold more promise for the future.[69] The prophet Micah wrote similarly: 'And what does the Lord require of you but to do justice, and to love kindness, and to walk humbly with your God?' (Micah 6:8 RSV).

One might argue that the Jewish refraining from taking interest from one another is no different to similar regulations of many trade and other associations in which the members provide each other with special benefits. Such benefits are not available to outsiders, yet there is nothing to prevent others from establishing similar associations and providing the same help. However, in this context it must be acknowledged that for Jews not to charge interest to non-Jews, who themselves lent money at interest, would have been economically non-viable and doomed to failure.

One further argument remains. It must be remembered that Judaism does not see anything intrinsically wrong with lending money at interest. It is a perfectly normal and beneficial part of economic activity, like the supply of other forms of capital. The Torah does not view interest taking as akin to murder or theft, as in Ezekiel, or it would have forbidden it altogether, why then was it forbidden between Jews? I have been arguing for a clan/tribal/brotherhood perspective which as history unfolds places Jews economically, socially, and psychologically in a very unique, and, potentially dangerous, position; but there is also the other reason I noted. The Mosaic injunction against interest, between Jews, flows from a desire to place this

---

[69]Richard Higginson, *Called to Account*, (Eagle (IPS) Ltd., Surrey, 1993), p.111.

action within the framework of righteousness – *chesed* – of wholeness, of holiness, of purity. The rights and obligations, therefore, of both lender and borrower reflect, perhaps more than any other economic transaction, the ethical and moral value structure of Judaism.

There exists in this respect a perfect balance between the private wealth of the individual, his moral obligations, and his legal rights. On the one hand there is the religious obligation to lend fellow Jews money in the form of an interest-free loan, since the lender is in reality only a trustee or steward of his own wealth; and, on the other hand, the debtor, too, has religious obligations. The debtor is obligated to return the loan at the date agreed upon. This unconditional obligation to repay is an important concept in Judaism, which has implications not only in the sphere of credit but also for many aspects of modern economy. It has to be seen within the Jewish framework of mutual assistance but also communal responsibility – obligations as well as rights, a consideration often blurred in modern welfare economics.

There exists, therefore, an ethical and moral framework for economic activity which is intrinsic to Judaism. This framework created a special economy of its own, affective at two levels, that of the individual as both consumer and producer, and that of the community or state; and, equally, that which was operative internally toward the 'brother,' and that which operated externally toward the 'other.'

Today, the response to economic and social issues has become for Jews a matter of private and individual choice. Before we examine the factors involved there, especially with regard toward a Judaic understanding of the concept of usury, we must first turn our attention to an historical overview of the birth of 'Judaic economic man,' as I agree with Tamari, that there does indeed exist, as a result of the Jewish value system, a separate and distinct 'Jewish economic man' moulded by religious law and communal practice.[70] It is a mistake, I believe, to dissociate Jewish economic behaviour from the practices of Judaism and its ethical and moral codes, as though Jews have been living an economic existence divorced completely from their religious and cultural milieu.

This is especially important to comprehend because the somewhat disproportionate tendency of Jews, even in recent times, to follow the trade of moneylending is often set down as a piece of sheer atavism, although racial characteristics have a way of surviving long after the original causes which created them have disappeared. In this case I will later claim that this particular Jewish characteristic stemmed from the money-changing days in the Temple. The existence of racial characteristics is, of course, an important theory, and Sombart maintains that four elements are the corner-stones of Jewish character: intellectuality; teleology (everything must have a *tachlis* – a purpose or aim); energy; and mobility.[71] Two further qualities are also of special importance in economic life: extreme activity, and adaptability, both of which Jews manifest. These alone, however, do not account for their economic success based on moneylending. This success was able to come about partly from the external influences which almost forced Jews into moneylending, especially in those countries in Western Europe where legislation prevented Jews from owning land – although in Islamic countries and eastern Europe Jewish farming did exist, but also, and perhaps, more importantly, from the Judaic religious teaching which formed the economic ethical framework within which Jews operated i.e. Deuteronomy 23:20. Moneylending to a stranger, with payment of interest, was not only scripturally sanctioned but also permitted within the rabbinical

---

[70]Meir Tamari, *op. cit.*, p.1.

[71]W.Sombart, *op. cit.*, p.268.

tradition. The question I address, therefore, is how far 'Jewishness' is responsible for the economic success of Jews in terms of characteristics, as well as extraneous forces at work e.g., the Diaspora, persecution, debarrment from holding land or position, etc., and how far the Judaic teaching expressed in the Deuteronomic attitude toward 'brother' and 'other' influenced this success, and led, perhaps surprisingly, but eventually, to the development of the spirit of capitalism, however that might be defined.

After discussing the Jewish understanding of the concept of usury in terms of Hebrew Bible teaching and Rabbinic interpretation, therefore, it is important to consider in more detail the very complex issue of how and why Jews, worldwide, came to play such a major role in moneylending, banking and other forms of financing.

Debt and the Law of Jubilee

Because usurious loans necessarily entail borrowing and lending, the concept of debt will obviously be a consideration. In the Hebrew Bible debt is seen as the product of misfortune, and a generous attitude toward the debtor is encouraged. The biblical texts with regard to this will be examined, and also the work being done by a particular organisation in Cambridge called, 'The Jubilee Centre,' as it has used Old Testament teaching as a paradigm for twentieth century living with regard to debt; to 'kinship' institutions – related to both the home and the work-place; to the ownership of land or property; and to a pattern for 'relationism.'

The foundation of economic affairs was from the earliest Babylonian days the farming of sheep and cattle or of agricultural products for which there are cuneiform sources e.g. the Code of Hammurabi. The natural increase of flocks and herds and the abundance of crops in the fertile soil of Mesopotamia meant that a fortunate landowner would soon have owned more than he could possibly farm or protect, and the situation was full of possibilities for the oppression and exploitation of labour by capital. The rich or prosperous farmer would become master, or partial owner, of poorer brethren indebted to him, and debt and the servitude to which it led, despite regulations, were very common features of Babylonian society. Occasionally it may have been alleviated by a general amnesty from debt, or *seisachtheia,* proclaimed by many sovereigns apparently to inaugurate their new reign. This would be intended to secure popularity and encourage loyalty and thereby achieve power to maintain the sovereign's rule.[72] The ability thus to remit debts lay in the power which the king had over temple revenues. The temples were the chief holders of credit, and the kings were the stewards of this wealth for the god who watched over the welfare of their people. Similar teaching with regard to debt amnesties is also found in the Hebrew Bible with regard to 'sabbatical' and 'jubilee' years.[73] Before I examine this, and the role of the Temple in early Jewish economic history, the whole aspect of debt (in so far as it is connected with usurious lending) must first be considered, and especially the way in which it was perceived in the Hebrew Bible.

Debt actually plays only a small part in the Hebrew Bible, partly because it was not an important factor in primitive times, though it obviously became more so as Israel grew more civilised and life became more complex. That is not to say, however, that debt did not exist, it could come about in various ways. In an agricultural community the failure of the crops might lead to borrowing (Neh.5:3); a man might be involved in debt by becoming security for a friend (Pr.6:1); and in later times taxation for a native government or for the payment of tribute to a foreign

---

[72]*Encyclopaedia of Religion and Ethics, op. cit.,* p.550.

[73]See Deuteronomy 15:1-6; Exodus 21:2; 23:11; Leviticus 25.

suzeraign was a source of debt (Neh.4:10). As far as the Hebrew Bible is concerned debt always seems to have originated from such causes; it has little or nothing to say about the spendthrift who got into debt through laziness or extravagance. Moreover, commercial borrowing, which is a source of profit to the borrower, though known at a very early period in Babylon, e.g. in the time of Hammurabi, does not seem to have existed in ancient Israel.[74]

As far as the cost of borrowing, there is no certain and definite information as to the rate of interest. The clause in Neh.5:11, 'Restore . . . the hundredth part of the money,' has been understood to mean that interest was at the rate of one percent a month – twelve percent per annum, and that creditors were to forego their interest. More recent authorities read *mashsh'ath*, as 'interest,' instead of *me'ath*, as 'hundredth.'[75] Twelve per cent would probably be too moderate, the interest being determined mainly by the urgent need of the borrower. The consequences of debt, however, might be serious; loans were sometimes obtained on the security of land or houses and when the debtor could not pay the creditor took the property. Worse still, when there was no such security the debtor and his family might be sold as slaves (2 Kings 4:1-7; Neh. 5:4f.). It should be noted that slavery in Judaism was primarily a means of punishing thieves, or of providing a way for debtors to pay off their debts, since the penal system did not provide any form of imprisonment for these 'crimes.'[76]

---

[74]See *Encyclopaedia of Religion and Ethics, op.cit.*, p.555.

[75]*Ibid.*, p.555.

[76]Although it is true that ancient Judaism tolerated slavery, it sought in various ways, unparalleled in antiquity, to humanize it. It made sabbath rest mandatory for slaves as well as others (Deuteronomy 5:14) and, in the case of Hebrew slaves, limited the period of service to six years (Exodus 21:2). See D.J.Goldberg and J.D.Rayner, *The Jewish People: Their History and Their Religion*, (Penguin Books, London, 1989), p.308.

There was, of course, moral and religious significance to all this. Like other misfortunes, the distress which necessitates borrowing is sometimes regarded as judgment on sin (Deut. 15:6; 28:12,44), and it was one of the characteristics of the wicked man that he borrows and does not repay (Ps. 37:21). But usually the Hebrew Bible sympathises with the debtor and seeks to help and protect him. His position is regarded as the result of unavoidable misfortune. It is the duty of the prosperous man to help his poor neighbour in distress by benevolent loans, and it is not to be a matter of pure business (Deut. 15:7-11; Ps. 37:26, 112:5; Pr. 19:17). Necessities are not to be pledged, thus, the widow's ox, or her clothing, or a millstone are not to be taken in pledge, or pawn (Deut. 24:6, 17; Job 24:3). In fact, the Hebrew Bible does not regard with approval the practice of taking pledges (Job 22:6, 24:9).

In view of the fact that the insolvent debtor and his family might be sold as slaves, Exodus 21:2-11 was an attempt to give some measure of relief to the debtor by directing the emancipation of the Hebrew slave at the end of the seventh year, a 'sabbatical' law. This attempt is carried to an extreme in Deut. 15:1-6 which appoints a 'release' at the end of every seven years when all debts were to be cancelled – but not, it is interesting to note those of the stranger; again highlighting the differing internal and external policies to apply according to the law:

> "At the end of every seven years you shall grant a release. And this is the manner of the release: every creditor shall release what he has lent to his neighbour, his brother, because the Lord's release has been proclaimed. *Of a foreigner you may exact it; but whatever of yours is with your brother your hand shall release it.*" (Italics mine. Deut. 15:1-3, RSV)

The sequel shows what magnanimity the Deuteronomic writer demanded from his fellow countrymen when he wrote: "Beware that there be not a base thought in thine heart, saying, 'The seventh year, the year of release is at hand;' and thy eye be evil against thy poor brother, and thou give him nought." (15:9) There is, however, no evidence that the law was enforced, it is on the face of it impracticable. Indeed, the Deuteronomic writer himself seems conscious that he is only setting forward an ideal – this appears from 15:4. It has also been disputed as to whether in fact the 'sabbatical' year brought with it an absolute remission of debt, or merely a temporary suspension of the creditor's right to enforce payment.[77] It is interesting to note that the seventh year corresponded with the year in which the land lay fallow, in which case it may well have been extremely difficult for a debtor to repay his debt if the land was not being worked.

W.H.Bennett states with regard to this passage that we may set aside the AV, 'save when there shall be poor among you,' and adopt the RSV, 'howbeit there shall be no poor with thee,' i.e. no one shall need to borrow, 'for Jahweh will surely bless thee . . . if only thou diligently hearken unto the voice of Jahweh thy God, to observe to do all this commandment.' On the other hand if Israel disobeyed other commandments, so that there were poor, the nation was not likely to observe this particular ordinance – in either case it would be a dead letter, and so it seems to have been. Other less probable renderings have been attempted, 'howbeit there *should* be no poor in thee,' i.e. the nation should establish a social system which would make poverty impossible. The priestly 'law of jubilee' (Lev. 25, especially verses 10-12, 28, 30-31, 33, 54; and Lev. 27:17-18, 21, 24;) has a similar reference to the release. It provides that at the year of 'jubilee,' every fifty years, all land shall go back to the family to which it originally belonged, and that an Israelite sold for a slave through poverty shall be treated as a hired servant and released. As the loss of the family inheritance or of personal freedom was often due to debt, this law would

---

[77]P.Cleary, *The Church and Usury*, (Bloomfield Books, Suffolk, 1914) p.2.

have mitigated the unhappy consquences of what we should call bankruptcy. Here, again, this law, like that of the release, was a dead letter. Nevertheless, these laws are evidence of the anxiety of the legislators that neither an individual nor a family should be permanently ruined by insolvency.[78] And although, as Normon Solomon maintains with regard to the levitical regulations, it would be naieve to apply to the contemporary global situation rules which were addressed to one particular society in the first millenium BCE, yet "with careful, contextual reading, it may prove possible to extract certain basic principles on which we can build an approach to modern problems."[79]

Today, there is work being done at the 'Jubilee Centre' in Cambridge, England, an evangelical Anglican research body which produces informed work on current social issues, which has these sentiments at the heart of its operation. The work of Dr. Michael Schluter, as Director, is an innovative attempt at applying this Hebrew Bible teaching to our postmodern society. With co-author Roy Clements,[80] Schluter argues that today's society would do well to reconstruct ancient Israel's principles with regard to 'jubilee ethics,' in a number of ways.[81] They maintain that there is much to be learnt from 'kinship' institutions in the Hebrew Bible. Using the early Judaic period, as depicted in the Hebrew Bible, as a model, they define the

---

[78]*The Encyclopaedia of Religion and Ethics, op. cit.*, p.555.

[79]Normon Solomon, *'Economics of the Jubilee,'* a paper given for a Jewish-Christian Symposium on the Jubilee; World Council of Churches with the Ecumenical Institute, Bossey, May 1996.

[80]Michael Schluter and Roy Clements, *Reactivating the Extended Family: From Biblical Norms to Public Policy in Britain*, (Jubilee Centre Publications, Cambridge, 1986).

[81]Rushdoony similarly admits that the Sabbath and Jubilee years are central to a biblical ethic which calls for justice to all people – an ethic of freedom and responsibility. He maintains that they are types, as also the weekly Sabbath, 'of the restoration of paradise and the work of Christ.' See Rushdoony, *op.cit.*, p.249ff.

smallest recognised institutional kinship form as the '3-G' unit – the three-generational family, in which parents accepted their responsibility to look after grandparents who would live close by, not necessarily in the same house, but on the same plot of land. The clan, based on wider kinship ties also provided a further vital support-role for the 3-G family.[82] As I previously mentioned the concepts of 'kin' and 'clan' are difficult units to define in the light of our twentieth century understanding, but Schluter and Clements help to differentiate them as they appear in the Hebrew Bible at that time. They also, usefully, contrast this model with the modern West, where the family is defined as a '2-G' family – a two-generational unit. Unlike the '3-G' family, here, members are widely scattered and it is the state, rather than the adult children, who tend to look after the grandparents – although it must be pointed out that since this book was written in 1986, it is now not even the state who will take on this responsibility, and it would appear that under current social and economic policy the grandparents are left to sell up and fend for themselves. This, they see, as symptomatic of a decline in relationships in our society and suggest constructive ways in which policies might reactivate the extended family by, for example, the state giving financial incentives to the family to care for its own members, and the development of new house construction with 'clusters' suitable for extended family use.

Higginson argues that commendable as these recommendations are, it might be felt that what is being presented is an unduly romantic picture of what went on in the Hebrew agricultural economy, and conversely an overly jaundiced view is being

---

[82]An excellent comparison can be made by examining the study by Prof. Hugh D.R. Baker at the School of Oriental and African Studies, on the effects of modern change both internal and external on the lineage village of Sheung Shui, in the New Territories region of Hong Kong, viewed as both a self contained unit, and as part of a wider community. H.D.R.Baker, *Sheung Shui: A Chinese Lineage Village*, (Frank Cass and Company Ltd., London, 1968).

presented of what goes on in the modern industrial economy. With modern technological advancements families can still function meaningfully as extended networks even when, unfortunately, separated by distance – the close proximity of family is not always conducive to happy and supportive relationships as many tabloid headlines will attest. There is, of course, these days, the *necessity* to move when seeking employment, especially in areas of high unemployment, but unfortunately not everyone can afford the costs involved to do this.[83]

However, although there is some truth in these comments, I do believe that the concept of extended families supporting one another is something which is not only of great physical help, but also of immense psychological help. Where it has been inevitable for the family unit to separate, for whatever reason, the concept of 'relationism,' be it blood relation, or a sense of belonging in community, is of great importance. People need, as Howard Clynebell put it: 'a feeling of authentic love in dependable situations.'[84] Religion can provide this sense of the extended family in Jewish, Christian, or Islamic communities. In a secular environment it can be found in the local community centre, bingo hall, charity work, place of business, the list is endless, even, perhaps in the dole queue. (Indeed, in adapting in recent years structures within the workplace based less on an heirarchical structure and more on encouraging team work, one could suggest that the work place is succeeding as therapeutic community where the Church has now failed.) The significant ingredient is a common bond. From a theological perspective a faith bond represents a metaphysical and spiritual bonding which points beyond oneself, not just in terms of care for fellow humankind, but to a supreme deity which gives reason and purpose

---

[83]R. Higginson, *op. cit.*, p.103, 104.

[84]H. Clynebell, *Basic Types of Pastoral Care*, (Abingdon Press, New York, 1966).

beyond one's own particular selfish – even unselfish – gain. Hence, the pentateuchal teaching on the concept of usurious lending established, not only, a common economic bond, but also, a common spiritual bond between Jew and Jew, who were enjoined to grant interest-free loans to one another as an act of *chesed.*

Schluter and Clements also attach great significance to the fact that, as portrayed in the Hebrew Bible, each family had a plot of land. In the book of Joshua, chapters 13-19, the systematic sharing out of the newly conquered land, tribe by tribe, and clan by clan is described. In Leviticus 25, some movement in landholding was allowed, but, only the leasing of land for a limited time, because in the fiftieth year, the 'jubilee' year, everything was to be returned to its original owner. However, in advocating the principle of landownership for today, Schluter and Clements believe that every family should, as a right, be entitled to own a piece of property. There should exist a system of universal owner-occupation which might require the compulsory purchase of rented accommodation, or the instigation of a building programme specifically to assist those who are not owner-occupiers.

In the light of New Testament teaching, Higginson argues that land, too, loses its Old Testament theological significance. Jesus called disciples to leave all behind and follow him. They left all relations – and land – for Christ's sake and the gospel (Mark 10:29), and were to find their personal identity in him, not in their family plot. In the book of Acts those who possessed lands or houses sold them and brought the proceeds to the apostles so that they could be distributed to all those in need, the first signs of early Christian 'communism.' As time went on, and the parousia did not take place, the Church reverted to the more conventional pattern of people owning their own piece of property. This shows that eventually the practicalities of the time and situation can outweigh an initial theological interpretation.

It is interesting to note that one of the reasons frequently given for the fact that Jews ended up in the business of moneylending was that throughout the Middle Ages they were always being persecuted – expelled from countries, and debarred from owning land. There is a tacit assumption that if they had been permitted to own land they could have engaged in more 'ethical' commerce, and experienced a greater degree of security, both physical and financial. The debarrment from owning land, however, did not deter Jews from maintaining a high profile with regard to economic status and successful kinship relationships, and as I have already mentioned in Islamic countries and eastern Europe they were successfully engaged in farming activities. However, where their energies were employed elsewhere it was their sense of community, and special identity in the sight of God, which held them together. It would appear, in a peculiarly paradoxical way, that the Jews attained their economic success in the West by *not* owning land, although there were other contributing factors. With regard to the important stress that Schluter and Clements put on the idea of the universal ownership of land, however, if looked at in the light of the homeless, and the social status of some people at the end of the twentieth century, the concept of everyone owning a place to live, is one that should be whole-heartedly encouraged.

Thirdly, Schluter and Clements also believe that the long-term site holding of the '3-G' family and the clan would have encouraged the persistence of kin-based forms of economic activity. They do not find any evidence in the Hebrew Bible of economic activity being heavily concentrated in large cities or particular regions. Following on from this, in present day activities, Schluter and Clements wish to see active efforts made to promote the small family business sector. They suggest tax relief to equity earnings in firms belonging to members of a person's extended family, and they think there is a case for demerging some large companies, and for providing incentives to companies to open new plants in regions of high unemployment, thereby reducing migration out of the area. Within these rather impersonal institutions, there is an acknowledged fact that people do work more effectively in smaller, family-orientated, or kinship, groupings. It is a unit that works not just in terms of economic efficiency, or ease of communication, if all members of one particular activity are grouped together, but it gives to each individual a sense of responsibility, self-worth, and nurture in terms of team work. Christian Schumacher speaks and writes most effectively about this when he argues that to move towards theological 'whole' work, involves working in the small group which he suggests provides the 'optimum opportunity.'[85] It would also appear that there is a move toward an economy of entrepreneurial activity which will be maintained in the small group. Companies can, and are increasingly, using the small group concept, which cuts across departmental functions and lays stress on combining the necessary skills for the particular task in hand, to operate for the duration of its effectiveness and then re-group as necessary. This micro functioning in a macro organisation enlists the benefits of the 'kinship' system. Certainly it is the small-group mentality, and attitudes to community in terms of 'brotherhood,' which appear to have fostered Jewish economic success, as seen in the implementation of their internal economic policy, coupled with the Deuteronomic view of the 'other.' It is the kinship group within which Jews operate for the benefit not only of their community but also for themselves.

---

[85]Christian Schumacher, *To Live and Work: A Theological Interpretation*, (MARC Europe, 1987), p.52. I was also privileged to speak with Dr. Schumacher at a five-day conference I attended at Ridley Hall, Cambridge, on 'Faith in Business' – known then as the 'God on Monday' project, in Nov. 1992.

Finally, Schluter and Clements argue that the Hebrew Bible law provides a normative model of political economy, which is as relevant to an unregenerate society now as it was then; they are critical of those who restrict the usefulness of the Law to a few general principles as it fails to do justice to the richness of its details which they feel are worthy of close attention and emulation today:

> "Looking at the Old Testament Law from the perspective of the quality of relationships as its primary goal, and family and kinship as its central institutions, provides many disparate laws with a centre of gravity, a unifying theme. From this perspective, the Old Testament Law can be seen to have a high degree of internal consistency. Thus, if Capitalism is a system organised in the interests of capital, and Socialism in the interests of society, then OT Israel's ideology might best be described as *Relationism* as this word points towards both the underlying goal of the quality of human *relationships*, and the institutions of kinship, as blood-relatives are often referred to as 'relations'."[86]

The Old Testament is to be a paradigm for a pattern of relationships between key institutions – family, kinship, community, state, and capital – which is to be replicated today 'in certain fundamental respects.' However, for Higginson, the paradigmatic correspondence between Israel's institutions in Biblical times and the ones today, be they concerned with First, Second, or Third Worlds seems too simplistic. Schluter and Clements move too directly from the Hebrew Bible economy to the present day, and neglect, as Higginson suggests,[87] the important role played by the New Testament as a *filter*, refining, reinterpreting, and revolutionising what is there in the Old.

---

[86]Michael Schluter and Roy Clements, *op. cit.*, pp. 20-21.

[87]Richard Higginson, *op. cit.*, p.103.

However, I believe that Schluter and Clements' discussion on the Hebrew Bible paradigm, in terms of 1) the 3-G family for support; 2) the owning of land for security; and 3) the small business enterprise for success, does emphasise the very important role of the Jewish 'brotherhood' mentality, and their specifically Jewish economic ethic which could provide a model for other communities today. And, although, as Higginson suggests, the New Testament *can* act as a 'filter' through which this may be interpreted for the present day – and, no doubt, for Christians it surely must – I think, from the *Judaic* perspective, as with an Islamic or, indeed, a Hindu, the initial blueprint established in the Hebrew Bible as a basic working structure upon which society could be modelled and moulded today, is one that should be allowed to stand on its own merit. One could equally cite pure historical development in order to interpret the differences between then and now, but I do not think that this is the issue in question. In establishing an Hebraic paradigm it is not necessary to rush immediately to the New Testament to see how that has been, or might be, re-interpreted, if it means ignoring the very obvious advantages that it possesses as standing in its own right. Since writing this particular book on reactivating the extended family, ten years ago, Schluter is the first to admit that the Old Testament paradigm has been criticised as a little too literalistic in its interpretation,[88] but the Centre is still very concerned with what, today, they term, 'the R factor' – relationism; and relational justice calls for a dynamic perspective in which people are seen not just as individuals but as members of communities who need to be treated with consideration and respect. Note should be taken of the tremendous service they have performed in redirecting attention to the Old Testament

---

[88]With reference to a meeting I had with Dr. Schluter on Nov.9th, 1995, and again on Feb.9th, 1996 at the Jubilee Centre in Cambridge.

as a source for social and economic ethics.[89]   The Jubilee Centre has also done
tremendous work as a pressure group on issues such as credit, and debt, especially
significant is their Research Paper on 'Families in Debt,' and as a centre actively
engaged on the cutting edge with regard to prison work, the judicial system, and the
health service, to name but a few areas of concern, their work should be followed
with the amount of care and attention it deserves. One other area in which they have
been actively involved is the issue of Sunday trading, and it is the nature of Sabbath
trading in the Temple to which I now return.

The Temple

As with the Babylonians, it is interesting, therefore, to find the Temple
operating in similar fashion for the Jewish people. The wealth held in the Temple
represented not only contributions to the religious authorities, but seems to have
served also as a repository for the state and royal treasuries – we see enemies of the
Jewish states making a point of robbing the national treasury including that held in
the Temple. It would seem that during the period of the first Temple the money was
primarily circulated in the form of shekels, that is by weight rather than by coinage.
There are no examples of Jewish coins of that period. But, in the period of the
second Temple, we find the evolution of a monetary system. Coinage seems to have
been introduced in the seventh century BCE, gold, silver, and copper were weighed
out and the quality checked; some of the names for weights were taken over as coin
names and early coins were simply pieces of metal impressed with a seal, they

---

[89]I am indebted to Dr.Schluter for the information he provided me with, and the insights he has given
me with regard to my research on these visits to the Jubilee Centre in 1995/6.

seldom weighed more than a shekel in gold or silver.[90] The Maccabean kings issued what are believed to be the first Jewish coins. A lengthy study of the economic history of the Jewish people which covers thousands of years and embraces most of the countries of the world is neither possible nor appropriate for this book. However, in this section it will be important, in trying to move toward a Judaic understanding of usury, to at least attempt to put into some perspective the effect of external pressures on Jewish economic life, and also to continue to demonstrate the continued existence of characteristic trends that are a direct outcome of specifically *Jewish* religious and ethical factors.

During the 'Tanakhik Period' (until 586 BCE), the eight centuries after the Jewish conquest of the land of Israel, Jews are believed to have enjoyed what might be considered a normal national existence. Almost all Jews lived in their own country until the latter part of the period. Both politically and economically the reigns of David and Solomon saw the country at its peak. Solomon had concluded treaties with many of his neighbours that led to increased international trade and internal prosperity spurred by extensive state construction. Even the division of the country into two separate monarchies – North and South, Israel and Judah – did not result in any severe economic dislocation, and despite numerous battles and wars at this time they did not seem to have seriously disrupted economic development. From accounts in the Bible one is able to infer the existence of a subsistence economy based primarily on small farms as well as markets in the larger towns, e.g. Ruth 1 and 2; Judges 9; Isaiah 5:8; Hosea 5:10; Lev.25:8-24.[91]

---

[90]*Handbook to the Bible*, ed. D. & P. Alexander, Lion Publishing, Tring, 1973, p.108.

[91]I am indebted to the work of Dr. Meir Tamari on Jewish ethics and economic life which I follow closely in this section and the next. At one point Dr. Tamari was Chief Economist, Office of the Governor of the Bank of Israel in Jerusalem, and taught economics at Bar Ilan University in Israel. See Tamari, *op.cit.*, pp.61-64.

According to Tamari, there is, however, no reason to doubt the existence of a more sophisticated economy in which Jews were also active – despite the agrarian nature of Jewish society in this period. It is true that it was non-Jews who played the major role in trade and commerce (and the Hebrew word for trader would seem to illustrate this, since Jews adopted the name of a non-Jewish tribe *Cana'ani* to describe those engaged in commerce – Proverbs 31:24) but there is reason to believe that Jews also played some role in the commercial life of this period:

> "Although there is little evidence at this time of any sort of real financial institutions existing in the land of Israel at that period, nonetheless there existed a royal treasury as well as a repository for tithes and offerings in the Temple (1 Kings 15:18; 11 Kings 12:19; 24:13). Furthermore, from the words of the prophets we know of the existence of a wealthy class (Amos 3:15; 5:11) – of moneylenders (Proverbs 28:8; Psalms 15), bankers, and merchants. (1Kings 10:14-15)."[92]

There was a highly developed social welfare system which provided for the needs of the poor and the weak in accordance with biblical law. Welfare institutions flowed from the fundamental Jewish attitude that a man's property does not belong to him alone but is held in partnership with God and with the community. Thus, it is essential to note that the complicated developed system of the Jewish welfare state was *never* a reaction to the Gentile world, but an institution that was firmly entrenched in Jewish life from the very beginning of Jewish existence. Equally entrenched were Jewish moral standards for economic behaviour. The prophetic tirades against usury, false weights and measures, dilution of the currency, and non-

---

[92]*Ibid.*, p.53.

observance of the sabbatical and jubilee years, reflect, just as present day moral and ethical comment reflects, the accumulation of cultural and social mores.

The Mishnaic and Talmudic period (586 BCE to 500 CE) differed radically from the previous era in ways which affected the economic life of Jews, both directly and indirectly. In the latter part of the first Temple, Jewish communities developed in Babylon, Egypt, and Asia Minor, and thereafter the dispersion continued; now there existed this widespread Jewish 'Diaspora' – which eventually grew larger than the Jewish settlement in the Land of Israel. It still remained, however, the major centre of Jewish life for some eight or nine centuries after the destruction of the first Temple and the subsequent loss of independence in 586 BCE. A mass expulsion of the Jewish people to Babylon accompanied this destruction, while some fled to Egypt and the countries of Asia Minor. A small 'remnant' was allowed to return under the Persians, and so a new Temple and Jewish settlement arose, However, aided by the persecutions of Herod, and the destruction of the second Temple by the Romans in 70CE, which brought an end to Jewish political independence, and, finally, the unsuccessful Bar Kochba revolt, the Diaspora did become far larger than the Jewish community in Israel itself. By the third century CE, large communities were to be found throughout the Roman Empire and beyond, extending to Yemen, Saudi Arabia, India, and the Slavic countries. Jews were thus integrated into the sophisticated economies of the various empires within which they lived, so that both the scope and character of their society changed.

During this period of history the economy of the ancient world was characterised by extensive foreign trade, a breakdown of national and cultural barriers, and the sophistication of consumer gooods. Relatively long periods of peace encouraged economic activity. As a result, Jews, both in Israel and the Diaspora, were increasingly engaged in many economic activities. The basis of agriculture still remained the small farms but now they produced goods also for the export market. Judaism never had any religious or ethical objections to buying and selling goods for profit, so this diversification into trade was simply a result of changed economic opportunities, *not* a result of any ideological change – nor something forced on Jews by a hostile world.[93]

The dissemination of religious education which characterised the whole of this period also played an important part in the retention of Jewish ethical and moral teachings as the ideological framework for economic behaviour. The redaction of the oral Mosaic law into writing, first, in the form of the Mishnah and then later in the Talmud, together with this learning meant that all aspects of Jewish religious life, including economic activity, continued to be regulated and conducted within the framework of the Torah; and despite the loss of political independence following the destruction of the second Temple in 70 CE and the ever-growing worldwide dispersal of the population, the ability of Jews to communicate with one another created a framework for continuity in communal living and common religious behaviour in economic as in other spheres.

Many historians and sociologists either take this communal coherence and ease of communication for granted, or tend to view it as merely a social defence mechanism – the reaction of a minority group to a hostile world, taking the form of a sub-culture replacing the physical and political homeland. It would be naive to ignore these factors but it is absolutely essential to understand the religious element involved here. Rather, what we have, as Tamari suggests, is a development that flows basically and primarily from fundamental Jewish philosophy and religious practices:

---

[93]See Tamari, *ibid.*, pp.64-68.

> "The concept of a Divinely chosen national entity demanding mutual responsibility; the existence of a common language for study and prayers; and the existence of a national memory integrated into religious observance are fundamental to Judaism and predate the exile."[94]

The welfare system, interpreted in the light of religious obligation, was so deeply rooted in Jewish life and practice that it was able to cater even to the needs of a large, non-agrarian, and mobile population, living under conditions of recurrent warfare, expulsion, and slavery. During the days of the second Temple, Jews from distant lands sent to Jerusalem both their obligatory offerings to the Temple, and their sons to study in the academies of Jerusalem. Once again, the Temple served as a repository for charitable gifts and for tithes. Coins of different denominations, issued by various rulers and states throughout the then known world, were brought to the temple treasury as part of the tithes of Jews, both from the land of Israel and the Diaspora. This medley of coinage, together with the financing of international trade, led to the development of *money-changing* as an important part of the Jewish economy. In New Testament times there were three different currencies used in Palestine. There was the official, imperial money (Roman standard); provincial money minted at Antioch and Tyre (Greek standard); and local Jewish money which may have been minted at Caesarea; money for the Temple (including the half-shekel tax) had to be paid in the Tyrian coinage, the two drachma piece, not Roman. It is not surprising that money-changers flourished.[95] There were, therefore, money-changers in the Temple who dealt in foreign currency and Israeli currency of different denominations, for example, this money-changing is shown in Matthew

---

[94]*Ibid.*, p.68.

[95]*Encyclopedia of the Bible*, ed. P.Alexander, (Lion Publishing, Tring, 1978), p. 241.

21:12 when: "Jesus entered the Temple of God and drove out all who sold and bought in the temple, and he overturned the tables of the money-changers and the seats of those who sold pigeons. He said to them, "It is written, 'My house shall be called a house of prayer'; but you make it a den of robbers." See also Mark 11:15, where the temple cleansing is also depicted at the beginning of Jesus' ministry – whereas in Luke 19:45 it comes at the end, after Jesus has ridden into Jerusalem on the donkey.

These passages show that as well as buying and selling in the Temple, money-changing was also going on – an important sign of Jewish economic activity from a very early time. The money-changers also accepted deposits from private individuals and subsequently *lent* these sums to various people. *Here* can be seen the birthplace of moneylending Jews. The expansion of international trade as well as the sophistication of internal trade during this period of the second Temple led to the rapid development of a Jewish banking system

Already in the Talmudic period the Jewish economy included involvement in moneylending, and in many countries of the Diaspora, Jewish merchants and bankers seem to have made their first appearance. The main function of Jewish banking at this time was the exchange of coins and the accepting of deposits for safety and investment. It was often linked to the function of buying and selling goods, and the Mishnah employs the term *shulchani* for both a banker and a merchant.[96] We find in the Mishnah, of course, a clear elaboration of the forbidding of interest, so that it seems that the major banking functions were the lending of money free of interest on the basis of pledges – rather like pawn-broking, except that

---

[96] *Baba Metzia,* chapter 3.

it was interest free, and the providing of capital to joint ventures in which the provider participated in the risk.[97]

At the same time as the rabbis accepted money as a means of exchange, they also accepted the economic role of 'near money' – that is, goods or financial instruments, as distinct from currency, that serve as a means of payment. Debtors were allowed to pay their debts in kind by the Talmudic authorities where the debtor had run out of cash. Rav Ashi maintained that 'near money' implied unmovable property, since chattels (which here included slaves and promissory notes), were considered actual money; and Rav Yani maintained that commodities can also serve as money, so the spices of Antioch are like 'near money,' along with such goods as camels, cloths, sacks, and ropes of specific geographic areas.[98] It was an acknowledgement and throw-back to the pre-coinage, bartering system. Of greater importance was the rabbinical distinction between metals, such as gold, silver, and copper as commodities, and their role as a means of payment, as these definitions are fundamental to the halakhic treatment of interest – the whole network of halakhic rulings exists in order to ensure that the way a man accumulates wealth is neither morally damaging nor physically harmful to his fellow-men. It must also be in accordance with the norms of God-given Torah morality, even when these run counter to the accepted practice of the particular society in which Jews might find themselves. It must be remembered that Judaism is not an economic system – the purpose of halakhic rulings throughout the ages was to minimize injustice and promote maximum public welfare. Already, therefore, in the Talmudic period, discussions reflecting legal decisions regarding everyday business transactions

---

[97] *Ibid.*, chapter 5.

[98] M.Tamari, *op. cit.*, p.163.

involved an increasingly complex and diversified use of money in all its forms throughout the Jewish economy; this economy already, therefore, included involvement in moneylending and banking.

The Development of 'Jewish Economic Life' in Both the Christian and the Islamic World from Medieval to Modern Times

Here I will examine the way in which the Judaic religious teaching with regard to the concept of usury was allowed to operate, if at all, within the different societies of Christianity and Islam during the medieval period, and how relevant it is today within Jewish communities.

It has already been suggested that during this period of history, the economy of the ancient world was characterised by extensive foreign trade, a breakdown of national and cultural barriers, and the sophistication of consumer goods, which resulted in Jews, both in the Middle East and the Diaspora, becoming increasingly engaged in various economic activities. Although the small farms still remained the basis of agriculture, farming now produced goods also for the export market, and diversification was taking place in other spheres. There is evidence of Jewish wine, spices, and perfumes, and perhaps textiles being exported to the corners of the Roman Empire. Jewish basket weavers, fishermen, and sailors were to be found in Babylon; and a variety of guilds of Jewish artisans were to be found in Alexandria.[99] As already emphasised the diversification into crafts, trade, and banking, therefore, was *not* a result of any ideological change, nor something forced on Jews by a hostile world; Judaism *never* had any religious or ethical objection to buying and selling goods for profit, and so this result was simply that of changed economic

---

[99] *Ibid.*, p.66.

opportunities. It was only *later on*, in their efforts to earn an honest and reputable livelihood, that the would be Jewish trader became shackled by the kings and princes of medieval Europe who were the real arch usurers of their day.

> "The rate of interest charged by the Jewish moneylenders was excessively high. But they were forced to this course by the pitiless rapacity of the governments as well as by the inhuman laws then in vogue which put the severest restrictions upon the Jews . . . In England, Spain, and many other European countries he was absolutely forbidden by law to follow most of the trades and handicrafts which were open, without question, to all other citizens; and, when, in rare instances, freedom was given, it was penalized and embittered by the imposition of special taxation. The Church left the Jews nothing to do except to deal in money or second-hand clothing."[100]

However, the completion of the Talmud saw the beginnings of commercial and social correspondence between widely separated Jewish communities. This facilitated international trading, commerce, and finance, based as these are on interdependence, trust, and compatible, if not common, legal structures.

From the sixth century CE it becomes necessary to divide Jewish economic history, and the effect of its teaching on usury, into two main strands: the Jewry of Europe, and that of Spain, North Africa, and the Middle East. European Jewry lived under the conditions of medieval Christendom and its particular economic realities, whereas the latter lived under Muslim rule, in countries with a radically different economic system. It must be stressed that the basic tenets and premises of Judaism remained the same, so that today, after over a thousand years of separation, the religious differences between Ashkenazi (Eastern European) and Sephardi (Spanish,

---

[100] J. Abelson, in *Encyclopaedia of Religion and Ethics, op. cit.*, p.557/8.

Italian, North African, and Middle Eastern) Jews are marginal. Nevertheless, the realities of differing economic systems made their mark in many different ways. As Tamari remarks:

> "Although Islam, like Christianity, forbade taking interest, Islamic oral law provided a mechanism for banking and credit, so there was no necessity to create a special class of largely Jewish moneylenders. At the same time, the mosques, because of the egalitarian nature of Islam and its lack of clearly defined clergy, never assumed the same economic functions as the Catholic Church of medieval Europe. The mosques served neither as major landowners nor as depositories of wealth, so that there was very little religious incentive for economic discrimination against Jews. Furthermore, Islam, while opposed to non-believers, provided for their existence within the body politic, so that the Jew did not have to exist as a chattel of the church or the crown. Naturally, in periods of persecution Jews suffered; their property would be looted and their business destroyed. Yet expulsion, relegation to a special economic status, or existence on the periphery of the economic world were never major features of the Moslem world as they were of Christian Europe."[101]

It is, however, necessary to point out that within Islam the bulk of the revenue of the religious institutions was derived from private charity, principally in the form of permanent endowments of land and other immovable property by a deed of 'restraint' known as *waqf*. The property so restrained was removed from all further transfer of ownership and in theory valid in perpetuity. Such endowments (pl. *awqaf*) had been created from the earliest centuries of Islam by governors or private persons for the benefit of mosques, *madrasas*, convents, and charities of all kinds.[102]

---

[101]M. Tamari, *op. cit.*, p.69.

[102]See H.A.R.Gibb and H.Bowen, *Islamic Society and the West*, (Oxford University Press, London, 1957), chapter xii *"Religious Endowments (Awkaf),"* pp.165-178.

A further point to be mentioned is that throughout the Islamic world society came to be divided simply into believers and infidels, Muslims on the one hand and *Dimmis* on the other. By the terms of a contract (*dimma*) with the *Dimmis*, a Muslim ruler would guarantee their lives, liberties, and to some extent property, and allow them to practice their religion. In return the *Dimmis* paid a special poll tax and suffered certain restrictions such as a *Dimmi* man may not marry a Muslim woman but a Muslim man may marry a *Dimmi* woman. *Dimmis* were also obliged to wear distinctive clothing so that they would not be confused with true believers, and they were forbidden to ride horses or carry arms. As far as Jews were concerned by the fifteenth century the conditions under which they were allowed to live in the Ottoman Empire contrasted so strikingly with those imposed on them in various parts of Christendom that this period saw a large influx of Jews into the Sultan's domain, especially after persecution in Bohemia, Austria, Poland, and Spain.[103]

Jewish economic life, therefore, tended to develop parallel to the economic fortunes of the countries in which they lived, for example, with the explosion of world trade that characterised the later Middle Ages in Europe, North Africa and the Middle East, Jews of the Muslim world became intimately involved in both trading and financing; however, with the eventual discovery of the New World and the seaway around the cape of Good Hope to the Far East the economic importance of the Mediterranean world declined. The countries of Western Europe gradually became mercantile powers, and ultimately the major industrial nations. This led to a general economic decline in the countries of the Muslim world and the stagnation of Jewish communities, and large pockets of poverty-stricken and relatively underdeveloped Jewish communities became the norm in North Africa and the

---

[103]See *ibid.*, chapter xiv *"The Dimmis,"* pp.207-261.

Middle Eastern countries, although at the same time, individual Jews continued to play an important role in the shrunken commerce of these countries.[104]

In the eighteenth and nineteenth centuries, the European colonial powers increased their trade with Far Eastern markets and Sephardi Jews played an important role in the resulting expansion. Jews also played a major role in the banking and commercial activities of Egypt, Syria, Iran, and Hong Kong; and the Europeanisation of the countries of North Africa and the Middle East at the beginning of the twentieth century was accompanied by the growth in a substantial mercantile and professional class as the economies of these countries developed. The weakening of restrictive Muslim practices that was encouraged by the colonial powers, primarily France, made this development easier and quicker. Today, at the close of the twentieth century, a rebirth of Islamic fundamentalism is also having its effect, but I shall consider this in more detail later.

A Judaic understanding of usury, therefore, whether traced through the Islamic or European world, is to be seen in the light of an understanding of the spirit of capitalism which, I argue, is based primarily on this Judaic ethic, and that is, if, as Tawney defined it,

> "capitalism means the direction of industry by the owners of capital
> for their own pecuniary gain, and the social relations which establish
> themselves between them and the wage-earning proletariat whom
> they control." and if, "by the capitalist spirit is meant the temper
> which is prepared to sacrifice all moral scruples to the pursuit of
> profit."[105]

---

[104]M.Tamari, *op. cit.*, p.71.

[105]R.H.Tawney, *op. cit.*, p.93.

By these definitions I would maintain that Deuteronomy 23:19-20, lent itself to both these very things; not, as I have argued in respect of the internal economics of the Jewish community vis-a-vis the Jew/Jew economic relationship i.e. that one shalt not lend upon usury to thy brother, *but,* in terms of the *nokri*, the stranger. The external economic relation encourages pecuniary gain through the transaction of moneylending; and hand in hand with that does go the 'capitalistic spirit' if defined in terms of sacrificing, or trading, internal economic moral principles for the external economic, and sometimes unscrupulous, pursuit of profit. As Max Weber points out:

> "In order that a manner of life so well adapted to the peculiarities of capitalism could be selected at all, i.e. should come to dominate others, it had to originate somewhere, and not in isolated individuals alone, but as a way of life common to whole groups of men. This origin is what really needs explaining."[106]

The argument follows that barred from owning land, serving in the army, and other occupations, Jews, had of necessity to be based in this occupation, from which Christians were forbidden because of their religious injunction against taking interest; but the major flaw in this argument seems to be the existence of Jewish bankers and moneylenders established in the Muslim world where the economic basis of Jewish life was not as restricted as in Christian Europe. Tamari argues that it is true that Islam and Christianity forbade the taking of interest, but this does not seem to have been of as great importance as commonly understood.[107] In Islam there existed an oral law which provided an escape clause whereby interest became legally possible; and although there did exist a moneylending class in the Muslim world, this

---

[106]Max Weber, *op. cit.*, p.55.

[107]M. Tamari, *op. cit.*, p.167.

did not prevent Jews from, again, becoming equally successful in that sphere, nor did
it stop them becoming farmers, either, as there was not the same restriction on
owning land in these countries, as in other places:

> "Even in the Christian world, the restriction was not as absolute as the
> apologists would like us to believe. First the Italians and then the
> Hanseatic cities of Germany, together with minor sects in France and
> Spain, became involved in moneylending from the period of the
> Crusades – this despite the Church ruling against the charging of
> interest."[108]

There were also other factors at play which encouraged Jews to engage in the
moneylending profession. I.Agus argues that it was Jewish initiative and
entrepreneurial ability that led to an involvement in the banking services needed to
finance the growth in both local and international trade during and following the
Crusades.[109] This trade, together with the growth of national entities, provided a
demand for funds and assets which Jews were able to supply because of their
international connections and cultural development, established over a great period
of time. The feudal system had arisen due to the breakdown of Roman law and
peace, the decline of international trade, and the necessity for subsistence farming
which made agriculture the prime economic activity, and land the major force of
production:

> "Another aspect of feudalism was that it organised military, political
> and judicial power on a local basis. Not the Empire as in Roman
> times, or the nation as in modern times, but the barony, or the manor
> was the unit of power. Feudalism was a confession of the

---

[108]*Ibid.*, p.166.

[109]I.Agus, *The Heroic Age of Franco-German Jewry*, (Block, New York, 1969).

disintegration of the Empire and the extreme weakness of the State. Over against this disintegrated secular society of feudal barons and knights, each with an outlook limited to his province or his manor, stood the pan-European Church organised from Rome, as centralized as secular society was decentralized, and, therefore, if for no other reason, its master."[110]

When the Germanic tribes converted to Christianity, the Catholic Church became the unifying factor which transcended local and tribal loyalties. Feudalism was predicated on this international concept of Christendom. Jews, therefore, had no place in the economic heirarchy of a united Christian Europe; Church law restricted the Jewish role socially, economically, and physically. As Jews were not able to bear arms or own land they had no part in the feudal heirarchy. However, despite their exclusion within the feudal hierarchy, Jews were frequently invited to settle in a city or state when their presence was considered economically beneficial. Invariably their success brought in its wake anti-Jewish legislation, persecution, and often, expulsion. The ideological necessity for the Church to persecute Jews because of the rejection of their messiah, together with the jealousy of Christian leaders and financiers, made such persecution and expulsion a constant in European history. As outsiders Jews made convenient scape-goats for social, political, and economic troubles when they appeared. This pattern basically characterised Western Europe until the French revolution, and Eastern Europe until the end of the nineteenth century. At the same time the economic factors that produced feudalism in Christian Europe further emphasised the special position of Jews in that society – the most

---

[110]G.M.Trevelyan, *History of England*, (Longman, London, 1973), p.159.

obvious example being this gradual emergence of Jews as the moneylenders of Europe.[111]

I would conclude that it was a synthesis of specifically Jewish traditions, originating in the Temple, and developed over two thousand years of Diasporan exile, plus their precise religious teaching, together with the logical reaction to economic opportunities, and the external pressures which were brought to bear on Jews in exile that led them into the role of moneylending. This is not to deny the fact, though, that Jews were also engaged in other activities such as trade (wholesale and retail), textiles (manufacturing and trading), diamonds, jewellery, and consumer goods; as well as the liberal professions of medicine, law, science and education. At the same time that banking and commerce were major Jewish economic occupations, the separation of Jews from agriculture, crafts, and manufacturing was not as complete as is often imagined.

It was in the post-Talmudic period, after 500 CE, that diversified financial activities became increasingly important for Jews. Within the Qur'an is contained an allegation of Jewish moneylending and usury,[112] and Jews were actively involved in all the financial aspects of the Muslim world. But it was the Crusades which brought about the establishment of Jews as bankers and moneylenders, first in Western Europe and then in Eastern Europe. In England their role was so important that special records were kept of their debtors. However, the Jewish influence was short-lived, and towards the end of the thirteenth century, in 1290, Edward I called in Italians to take the Jews' place even prior to their expulsion.[113] The first general

---

[111]See Tamari, *op.cit.*, Chapter Four.

[112]Surah *Al-Nisa,* 4:158 ff.

[113]G.M.Trevelyan, *op.cit.*, p.220.

charter of privileges granted to Jews in Poland in the mid-thirteenth century refers to them as moneylenders; and their role in Germany was perhaps longer and more important than in any other European country starting in the later Middle Ages and lasting until modern times. Since World War II, throughout the Western World, heavy industry has declined and that of service industries and high technology industries has risen and Jews have played an important part in both scientific and industrial aspects, as well as continuing their well established role in banking and financial services.

However, having deliberated on the fact that Jews were highly successful economically, one of the most intriguing questions of Jewish history is the *source* of the wealth which enabled Jews to engage in banking – where did the money come from? I have argued that it was not just because Jews were barred from owning land that led them into moneylending, but it did actually account for the fact that it was the main stimulant to their holding assets in liquid form, land being the major form of capital in feudal Europe. These liquid assets provided the basis for their financial activities. An added incentive to liquidity was the constant expulsion and persecution of Jews which was so characteristic of Europe, especially after the tenth century. Liquid assets such as jewels, coins, or promissory notes could be easily hidden, and transferred without causing severe losses. However, this only explains *why* Jews kept their wealth in liquid form, and not *where* the wealth came from.

The major factor was the important role played by Jews in local and international trade, at first in the countries of the Near East and North Africa, and later, in medieval Europe. The international trade of medieval Europe was primarily of two types: the East-West flow between Europe and the Middle East, and the North-South trade between Northeastern Europe and the countries of the Baltic Sea and the Mediterranean. Jews were active and important in both trade currents, as they were able to bridge the gap between Christian Europe and the Muslim countries. Jews were nominally accepted by both in large numbers. The profits on international trade, especially in luxury goods, slaves, weapons, and jewellery, were exceedingly high. This made trade feasible despite constant losses from thieves and piracy. It was this trade which provided the funds for the Jews' subsequent investment in moneylending and banking. It can be noted that this is not a specifically Jewish phenomenon. One non-Jewish example is the financing of the industrial revolution in England in the eighteenth century by means of the accumulation of profits in the preceding centuries from international trade; and, in the twentieth century, the experience of the Chinese in South-East Asia is another example of the development of a financial community from a trading one. The Parsi also played the same role in the Indic World as Jews played elsewhere, and showed the same elasticity and initiative as Jews in using their special skills and experience to good effect in a variety of circumstances.[114]

This, naturally, assisted the Jews in becoming early capitalists. In contrast to the view of Jews as radical or socialist, historical facts point to their rapid advancement through the capitalist system to become a predominantly middle-class group. That, I believe, was due, largely, as a result of the Deuteronomic teaching on usury, which enabled Jews to make profit from the 'other.' However, it must also be noted that throughout the Jewish Diaspora there has always existed a Jewish working class, after all, no large concentration of people can exist solely as a mercantile or financial class. In those countries in Western Europe where legislation prevented Jews from owning land, farming was not a Jewish occupation; but in Islamic countries and in Eastern Europe, Jewish farming, as I have pointed out, did exist.

---

[114]Toynbee, *op.cit.*, p.121.

Furthermore, the autonomy enjoyed by most Jewish communities necessitated a substantial bureaucracy, and most communities also employed watchmen, market officials, and bookkeepers. The occupational distribution of Jews was typically far from stereotyped.

Because of this adherence to the Deuteronomic teaching on usury Jews were able to bridge the gap between Christian Europe and the Muslim countries; and, internally, despite the anarchy and danger which prevailed in feudal Europe, they were able to exploit a cohesive Jewish communal network to facilitate their trade. The existence of documents, for instance, issued to travellers by Jewish communities asking other communities to protect them and assist their members, together with the provision of community-operated hotels, contrasts strongly with the jealousy and antagonism which existed between the Christian citizens of different towns and loyalties. This autonomy enjoyed by the Jewish communities resulted in an extended legal system that provided the Jewish merchant with protection against defaults in debts and compensation for broken contracts on the part of his fellow Jewish traders. Endogenous Jewish moral, ethical, and religious principles provided a kinship network of trust and responsibility without which the banking system, or the system of international trade in which Jews played an important part, would have been impossible.

The modern economic history of European Jewry has to be viewed in the light of the political emancipation which followed the Napoleonic Wars. Political, religious, and legal restraints were gradually relaxed and then ultimately abolished. This process began in Western Europe in 'The Age of Enlightenment' (*Die Aufklarung*) which covers roughly the eighteenth century. The motto of enlightenment was *Sapere aude* – 'Have courage to use your own understanding.' According to Immanuel Kant writing in 1784 'enlightenment' was man's coming of age. It was man's emergence from the immaturity which caused him to rely on such external authorities as the Bible, the Church, and the state to tell him what to think or do. Governments were now said to derive their authority from the governed rather than appointed by God with inalienable rights to govern. Kant wrote at a point midway between the American and French Revolutions. The classic documents with concepts of life, liberty, and the pursuit of happiness (American), and freedom, property, security, and the right to protect oneself from violence (French), with their allusions to God, represent a middle stage between the traditional Christian view of the state and modern secular democracy at the beginning of the nineteenth century.

> "Calvin had seen the state as a divinely appointed instrument for the protection of law and order, the maintenance of morals, and the promotion of true religion, all based on the Word of God. The enlightened view of the state did not dismiss God altogether. In general enlightened thinkers adopted a deistic view of God, acknowledging his existence as Creator but leaving the conduct of life to man and his reason. The enlightened view of the state acknowledged the deity but proposed essentially humanistic goals for society, insisting that both the ends and the means should be determined by reason acting in accordance with nature."[115]

Also underlying this was was the idea of the social contract put forward by Thomas Hobbes in the seventeenth century and restated by John Locke and Jean-Jacques Rousseau who saw society based on an implicit social pact that combined freedom with just government in the interests of the majority. By the beginning of the nineteenth century Enlightenment had given way to idealism in philosophical thought (and classicism and romanticism in the arts) and its confidence in man's innate goodness and rationality seemed increasingly misplaced as the French

---

[115]C.Brown in *The Evangelical Dictionary of Theology*, (Marshall Pickering, Hants., 1985), p.355.

Revolution took its course and the Napoleonic Wars plunged Europe into turmoil. The process of political, religious, and legal emancipation for Jews, therefore, was only finalized throughout Europe after World War I. This participation in the economic development of the modern world occurred simultaneously with a decline in the power of Jewish communities. The easing of anti-Jewish pressures was obviously an important factor in this decline, but it was the rise of secularism and its assimilation which proved the major factor. It undermined the authority of the halakhic value structure and, hence, the legislative framework that had given the community so much of its power. Communal authority was increasingly restricted to the sphere of religious activity, and social welfare and the regulation of economic activity was left to secular (non-Jewish) society. Limitations on economic activity on account of religious study and observance became matters solely of individual, voluntary judgment, even though many orthodox Jews have continued to submit both to the Jewish Codes and to the rulings of the rabbinical courts, so that religious rulings regarding economic activities have continued throughout the nineteenth and twentieth centuries down to the present day.[116] Responsa today ruling on wages, labour conditions, strikes, interest, repayment of loans, competition etc., provide evidence of a continued religious involvement in economic matters that are applied to a much wider set of problems. Certain inbred attitudes remain and the Jewish religious and cultural heritage continue to affect Jewish economic life, even though no longer expressed in communal existence but rather as individual voluntary acts.

In modern economic life in Israel today the concept of usurious lending is still a consideration. Two reasons are given for its justification from the Deuteronomic point of view of lending to the stranger at interest. From a theoretical economic

---

[116]See Tamari, *op.cit.*, p.77.

point of view, it has always been acknowledged that interest contains two elements: a time factor and an element of risk. The supplier of the money is unable to use that money for as long as the loan is operative. By extending the loan he is losing an alternative use of his money in other ventures. It is for this loss of freedom, therefore, that the lender will desire to be paid. Basically, he is being paid interest for waiting to receive back his money. Furthermore, any loan, like any investment, contains an element of risk. It is possible that the debtor may not be able to pay the interest, or pay back the loan on time, or at all. It is not always easy from an accounting or economic point of view to determine whether the interest charged is payment for risk or a payment for the use of money for a specific period, and obviously within every type of loan transaction the degree of risk varies with the individual or institution concerned.

However, in time, a standard form of legalisation of interest was established known as *hetter iskah*, meaning the permission to form a partnership. A deed known as *shetar iskah*, drawn up and attested by two witnesses, stipulated that the lender would supply a certain sum of money to the borrower for a joint venture. The borrower alone would manage the business and he would guarantee the lender's investment against all loss. He would also guarantee to the lender a fixed amount of minimum profit. The deed would also contain a stipulation that the borrower would be paid a nominal sum as a salary, as well as an agreement on the part of the lender to share the losses. In order to render this loss-sharing agreement inoperative, provision would normallly be made for such loss to be proved by particular, mostly unobtainable, evidence. The amount of the capital loan plus the guaranteed minimum profit would be recoverable on the deed at the stipulated time it matured.[117]

---

[117]*The Jewish Encyclopedia, op. cit.*, p.388.

In the course of centuries this form of legalising interest has become so well established that nowadays all interest transactions are freely carried out, even in compliance with Jewish law, by simply adding the words *al-pi hetter iskah* (according to *hetter iskah* i.e. the permission to form a partnership). The prohibition on interest has lost all practical significance in business transactions, and is now relegated to the realm of friendly and charitable loans.

The establishment of Israel as an independent political entity raised some new moral issues, however, with regard to the effect of monetary policy. The new element introduced by this political independence was that, after many centuries (from the second Roman uprooting in 135 CE to 1948 CE there was no such thing as a Jewish state) Jewish policy had to act as an initiator of economic policy. In the past Jews did not have control over the public purse, so that they could not determine the course of monetary policy, interest rates, and the allocation of credit. Halakhic authorities had had to deal primarily with legal issues between individual Jews which arose out of monetary policy initiated by Gentile governments. In the State of Israel, however, these same authorities now had to deal with that monetary policy itself and with whether such a policy conflicted with Jewish law, and to adjudicate transactions between one Jew and another in light of that policy. Under Mosaic law a Jew is forbidden to exact interest from his brother, and in particular a poor brother, as is shown in the passages quoted from Exodus and Leviticus. He has a religious obligation to lend his fellow Jew money in the form of an interest free loan, since the lender is in reality only a trustee of his own wealth. On the other hand, the debtor, too, has religious obligations. There is the important concept of an unconditional obligation to repay the loan, which has implications not only in the sphere of credit, but also for many aspects of a modern economy. How, therefore, would the Israeli state proceed to implement its monetary policy? Would it be in terms of halakhic law, or more expedient rulings?

In fact, the Israeli economy chose the second alternative and it serves as a clear example of a system whereby the waiving of creditors' rights, and delayed payments, became an integral part of the economic system, certainly not in accordance with halakhic principles. As Chief Economist at the Office of the Governor of the Bank of Israel in Jerusalem, Meir Tamari sheds some illuminating insight into this situation. According to Tamari,[118] the new state utilised subsidised loans and cheap government credit to stimulate agriculture, manufacturing and tourism, in order to finance the absorption of large-scale immigration and a heavy defense burden. In view of the lack of accumulated private capital this made eminent sense, and in most Western countries today, the state uses selective economic intervention to foster its social and political aims. Unfortunately, this blanket government intervention in the capital and money markets led to the establishment of firms on the basis, not of their economic efficiency, but rather their ability to implement the socio-political policies of the state. These firms, therefore, tended to become white elephants and needed large sums of public funds to bail them out in order to prevent unemployment and macro-economic problems. Within a short time this government policy of intervention to prevent business failure or bankruptcy became an integral part of the capital market structure. This in turn encouraged the further establishment of inefficient firms, squandering public money. The subsidised credit and loan capital were not always used for the purposes for which they were granted. This system, in fact, bred a certain immorality regarding the use of public money as well as the economic waste involved.

---

[118]Meir Tamari, *op. cit.*, p.173.

In a state run according to Jewish law, however, as Tamari points out, the halakhic treatment would have been different. Here, we would have seen how justice and mercy, but, above all, communal responsibility as well as mutual assistance, is viewed with regard to the whole concept of moneylending where usury is forbidden. One might argue that as the creditor is no doubt wealthier than the debtor that he should waive his right to repayment. This would be an act of mercy. However, to insist that the creditor do so makes him assume a responsibility for the welfare of his debtor over and above the obligations imposed on him by the *mitswah* of the interest free loan. The creditor may decide to do so as an act of *chesed*, but to *obligate* him to do so would be to obscure the conceptual differences between these two religious precepts. To deny the lender his money on the basis of the need of the debtor is to blur the demarcation between justice and mercy which is such an important element in Judaism. The community does always have a definite obligation to try and solve the social and economic problems of the debtor, and the creditor as a member of that community shares in that duty, but, justice demands repayment of loans made as acts of righteousness. The halakhic authorities insist that, if necessary, the debtor be compelled to divest himself of his assets in order to pay back his loan. He would be left with only religious articles, food, clothing, and necessities for a certain period of time. This may seem to be cruel and stern, but it has to be viewed within the Jewish framework of mutual assistance, of individuals acting beyond the demands of the law, and an age-old record of communal responsibility – the whole aspect of 'brotherhood' as either giver or receiver, and the internal economic policies which that entails.

However, in the State of Israel today, despite its early economic policies, the free loan exists as a parallel banking system. There are large public free loan societies as well as those organised by a particular synagogue, or even as a form of private initiative.[119] The free-loan societies lend money not only to their members but to the general public, assumedly their fellow Jews, usually without means tests or other questions about the purpose of the loan or the financial status of the applicant. All that is asked of the borrower is the requirement that operates within Jewish law, that some guarantor will pay should the borrower default. The free loan has never been envisaged as a form of consumer protection but always as an act of righteousness, to provide people with loans for any purpose. This facility is not available to those outwith the community. It would appear that the Deuteronomic principle is still alive and operating today.

Conclusion

A Judaic understanding of usury must be viewed in the light of its sources in the Hebrew Bible. These are primarily found in the law books of the Pentateuch, in the books of Exodus, Leviticus, and Deuteronomy. The Deuteronomic teaching, moving from law-code to covenant-code, provided a 'Deuteronomic double standard,' in so far as allowing interest-free loans to operate between Jew and Jew, but forbidding them between Jew and '*nokri.*' The teaching, no doubt, was formulated to protect a small and vulnerable community as they moved into their 'promised land.' Because of this teaching, however, two different economic systems arose within the Jewish community: one, internal which, with the prescription of interest-free loans between Jew and Jew, fostered the concept of 'brotherhood'; and the second, external, which, with the proscription of interest-free loan between Jew and foreigner, promoted the concept of, what Emmanuel Levinas describes as, the

---

[119]*Ibid.*, p.171.

'other.'[120] This also facilitated a quest for gain, and a development of the spirit of capitalism, as profit accrued from the interest paid on loans.

From very early days, beginning in the Temple, Jews were engaged in money-changing which led to moneylending. As agricultural activity increased products were produced for sale, and as world markets opened up and trade increased, the Jews became very active in this sphere. Their wealth increased due also to their entrepreneurial skills. This success was a factor in persecution and expulsion from the lands which they occupied, having no land to call their own from the second century CE. Therefore, because of an accumulation of a number of factors – their wealth, their skill, their debarrment from owning land, their initiative, their atavistic moneylending characteristic developed from the Temple days, and their religious teaching, they became among the leading moneylenders of Europe. Jews did not have a problem with accumulating profit but, in religious terms, their main concern was their stewardship of it. Their religious system fostered a responsibility to the poor of their own community, and they were obliged to give gifts of money as, *chesed*, acts of loving kindness within the concept of righteousness. Developed by their religious identity was also a strong sense of community which stayed with them throughout persecution, even up to the present day. However, over time, in the non-Jewish world, the response to social and economic issues became for modern Jews a matter of private and individual choice, in which one could feel free to observe all, some, or none, of the rituals of Judaism, including those which addressed economic behaviour. It is not surprising, therefore, to find that a distinctly Jewish pattern of economic life does not in fact exist for many Jews in the Western world, any more than does a Jewish pattern of behaviour in other

---

[120]See footnote 4 on Levinas in my conclusion.

fields. This does not detract from the fact that for over two thousand years the concept of usury has been an important issue in the economic development of Jewish life. I have argued in this chapter that the religious teaching with regard to the Deuteronomic exemption which allowed the Jew to accept interest on a loan from a foreigner, was paramount in establishing a specific model of 'Judaic economic man.' However, it was the 'horns of the dilemma' of the Deuteronomic double-standard with which the Christian Church struggled. It posed a threat to the professed universalism of Christianity, as I shall discuss in the following chapter. To the Christian, whose vision of morality was rooted in the 'Brotherhood of Man' under the 'Fatherhood of God,' the Deuteronomic double standard for the 'brother' and the 'other' appeared paradoxical, mysterious, and vicious.

Chapter Two

Toward a Christian Understanding of Usury

The Christian Attitude to Old Testament Law

Does the Old Testament law have any function for the Christian believer? How is the teaching on usury found in the Torah to have any influence on the New Testament Christian? From an Old Testament perspective it seems natural, as John Goldingay points out, for an examination of Old Testament interpretation to include consideration of how the law ought to influence behaviour. After all, the law functions in connection with judgment because firstly it expresses the will of God, the Creator, which he expects his creatures to obey simply because they *are* his creatures. Secondly, it expresses the will of God, the Redeemer, which he expects his people to obey because they are his people. "Israel's hope of salvation is of a day when the law will be obeyed (cf. Jer.31:31-34), perhaps of a day when a new law will be given, but not of a day without law."[1]

St. Paul has a complex attitude to the law. The law puts a Christian believer in a state of anxiety because s/he cannot fulfill it, but the gospel releases the believer from this anxiety. The person who believes in Jesus Christ is free from the law (Romans 7:6) – the law is replaced at the heart of the believer's relationship with God by Jesus himself. At the same time Paul describes the law as 'holy, just, and good' (Romans 7:12); it is God's gift in connection with the old covenant (Romans

---

[1]See John Goldingay, *Approaches to Old Testament Interpretation*, (Apollos, Inter-Varsity Press, Leicester, updated edition,1990), p.47ff.

9:4-5). However, it does not follow if for example one looks at the church in Corinth, that all Christians know by inspiration what things they ought to do, or even to do them if they do know. Paul, therefore, emphasizes the nature of the reponse to God's grace which Christian discipleship requires. Jesus is the end of the law but not the end of commandment, and under the new covenant, as under the old, disobedience brings disaster. This attitude appears also in St. Matthew's gospel which will have nothing to do with 'legalism' but whose real enemy is antinomianism. Matthew's gospel pictures Jesus as revealing the true meaning of the Torah and calling his disciples to put it into practice.

However, Jesus' attitude to the law has also complex strands in it, further complicated by scholarly disagreement as to how far his own words can be distinguished from the development of the gospel tradition and the work of the evangelists and redactors:

> "It is a matter of scholarly debate whether Jesus' teaching should be seen as an exposition of the law, or a penetration to its implicit inner principles, or a radicalizing of it, or a replacement of it for the new age, or an independent revelation of God's will which does not relate very directly to the law's concerns."[2]

One aspect of Jesus' attitude is to treat the law as very far from God's final word with regard to the expectation of his people, and to add his own teaching to it. Sometime his teaching with regard to the law can be seen as a protest against the way the law has been interpreted or supplemented, or as a sharpening of the Torah. Equally, he shows concern to be prescriptive about the behaviour of those who wish to follow him, for example in the 'Sermon on the Mount.' He can also speak very

---

[2]*Ibid.*, p.49.

positively about the law in terms of determining his own conduct about 'what is written.' There is a tension in Christian terms between God's law and grace and man's behaviour.

As Goldingay also points out, in the Bible and in the Reformers there are two approaches to this. Both assume a soteriology of grace. One (characteristic of Paul and Luther) works with an ethic of contexts and avoids the trap of legalism. The other (characteristic of the Old Testament, Calvin and the Puritans) then works with an ethic of norms and is concerned that the person who belongs to God by grace does not fail to live responsibly before him. "Those who emphasize contexts tend to suspect those who stress norms of being legalistic, while those who emphasize norms tend to suspect those who stress contexts of being antinomian – despite the fact that even the most orthodox ethicists have recognised that nearly every rule has its exceptions."[3] These two approaches, therefore, need to be held in tension if neither is to fall into the other two positions.

New Testament Christians, therefore, are reminded of the demands of the Old Testament law. And while Christians are not going to take the Old Testament law as God's final word on behaviour it seems equally clear that, even in the light of New Testament scripture and the teachings of Jesus Christ and the interpretations of Paul and other New Testament writers, it would be odd for them simply to ignore it as a possible source of guidance for decision making over the way of life God expects of his people.[4]

---

[3]*Ibid.*, p.50.

[4]*Ibid.*

New Testament Sources

In the New Testament the scope of the Hebrew Bible, appropriated in Christian terms now as the 'Old' Testament, is widened in two ways. Firstly, according to Paul Mills, the qualification for a loan is widened from the teaching in Deuteronomy 15:8 with regard to anyone who needs to borrow, to that of anyone who *wants* to borrow (Matthew 5:42); and, secondly, the emphasis is shifted in a universalistic way from lending to only 'brothers' (Deuteronomy 23:19) to lending to anyone, including enemies, and at the same time expecting nothing in return.[5] This universalistic argument is attached to the reading of Luke 6:34,35 (verses peculiar to Luke[6]) which can also vary in interpretation according to translation:

> "Give to him who begs from you, and do not refuse him who would borrow from you." (Matthew 5:42; RSV)

> "And if you lend to those from whom you hope to receive, what credit is that to you? Even sinners lend to sinners, to receive as much again. But love your enemies, and do good, and lend, expecting nothing in return." (Luke 6:34, 35a; RSV)

Some controversy has arisen with regard to the actual understanding of 'to receive as much again' and 'lend, expecting nothing in return,' the interpretation of which will reflect differently on lending practice. For example, as Mills points out:

> "An alternative rendering of the final phrase could be 'lend, without hoping to receive any return' – a translation which employs an idiom known to be current from at least the fourth century. In the context of v.34, this could either mean that lending was to be undertaken

---

[5]Paul Mills, *"Interest in Interest: The Old Testament Ban on Interest and its Implications for Today,"* (Jubilee Centre Publications Ltd., 1993). See also *"The Ban on Interest: Dead letter or Radical Solution?"* (Cambridge Papers, Volume 2, Number 1, March 1993).

[6]*Peake's Commentary on the Bible*, eds. Matthew Black and H.H.Rowley, (Van Nostrand Reinhold (UK) Co. Ltd., Berkshire,1962), p.830.

without any thought of a pecuniary return in the form of interest or it could speak of lending without any thought of recovery of the principle from the inception of the loan. The 'loan' would then effectively become a gift . . . Marshall[7] however, argues that 'receiving the equal amount' cannot refer to the extension of a loan with no thought of repayment because this is indistinguishable from a gift. Rather, he suggests that the phrase refers to receiving offers of loans in return. Some sort of equal treatment through reciprocal loans must then be the meaning of 'receiving a return' in v.35. The contrast is drawn between 'sinners' who lend to each other in the hope of being able to call on a return favour in the future and the obedient disciple who lends without entertaining such selfish motives."[8]

It is, however, interesting to note in the RSV Interlinear Greek-English translation of the New Testament that these verses run thus:

"And if ye lend from whom ye hope to receive, what thanks have ye? even sinners to sinners lend that they may receive back the equal things. But love ye the enemies of you and do good and lend nothing despairing i.e. despairing not at all (other ancient authorities read 'despairing of no man')."[9]

Although these verses can be seen in terms of *attitudes* to lending (and, equally, the attitude to whom one is lending i.e. the 'enemy'), and not to the concept of usury as such, it is possible to read an injunction against the Deuteronomic principle into them. From a Judaic perspective, in the light of the teaching in Deuteronomy 23:19-20, in which the Jews were 'allowed' to lend at interest to the foreigner, Jesus could be reminding the disciples of this by asking what credit is it

---

[7] I.H.Marshall, *The Gospel of Luke*, (Paternoster Press, Exeter, 1978).

[8] Mills, *op. cit.*, p.7.

[9] A.Marshall, *The RSV Interlinear Greek-English New Testament*, (Marshall Pickering, Hants., 1968), p.251.

to a Jew if he lends to those from whom he hopes to receive, i.e. not only the principal, but interest as well? Everyone in a defined kinship group would lend expecting to eventually receive back that which they had lent, even as Gentiles would; but how much better would it be to lend and expect nothing in return? However, this does not deny the *possibility* of receiving something back – they might be pleasantly surprised if they do not lose hope in human nature. It has also to be remembered that this teaching was made in the light of a predominantly agricultural and/or small business society (Jesus was, after all, a carpenter) where borrowing itself would be frequent enough, not so much on a commercial basis, but more of a loose and personal kind, as between friend and friend, kinsman and kinsman, 'sinner' and 'sinner.' It should also be noticed that although interpreters take this passage to reflect the lending of money, it is not specifically mentioned, and in an agrarian community, or one of small trade, could equally reflect the lending of tools, seed, livestock, help etc. which was no doubt common practice.

Finally, it has to be seen in the context of that which precedes it. In Luke's gospel this passage immediately follows the teaching referred to as 'the Beatitudes' and 'the Woes' – the ones who will be blessed are balanced by the condemnations that will befall the rich and full. It also follows the 'Golden Rule,' and most importantly it is linked in the previous verses to loving and doing good. It is not just about 'lending expecting nothing in return,' but more specifically it states: "Love your enemies, and do good, and lend, expecting nothing in return." There are three injunctions about how to behave toward one's fellow men, be they friend or enemy, and in all things they are enjoined to 'despair of no man,' or 'expect nothing in return.' It is, therefore, in my opinion, a passage that can be invoked to support the concept of interest-free loans, even gifts, not to those to whom it is easy to give, but to those to whom one would rather even not. It does transcend the brother/foreigner distinction in Deuteronomy in terms of loving one's enemy, doing good, and lending with a generous spirit, the reward for such lending being spiritual rather than monetary – encouragement toward an open-hearted charity.

The ethic of lending, therefore, is adequately covered by the general principles established by Jesus in this passage from Luke's gospel. There is no call to deal with usury as an economic or commercial factor as there later is for the prophet, Muhammad, himself a trader; and from the above reading of Luke 6:34,35a, Jesus is not calling for an interest-free economy as such, but for interest-free loans to be made in specific cases in a generous spirit, not to the needy as one might expect, but to the 'enemy' (who presumably would be needy, but the inference is different) with the expectation of receiving nothing in return, although this is not to deny the possibility of a return at some later date.

A further, very important point to be noticed, however, is that universality is a common theme in Luke's gospel. Luke was probably a Gentile, or at least a Hellenistic Jew, and both of his books (Luke and Acts) are slanted towards the Gentiles. He shows that the gospel is universal, that Jesus has broken down the barrier between Jew and Gentile and inaugurated a world-wide community in which the old inequalities between slaves and freemen, men and women, no longer exist – as also brother and foreigner. He also modifies peculiarly Jewish expressions and allusions to Jewish custom in order that Gentile readers may better understand – something that appears to be taking place in this passage from Luke 6.[10] Luke thus

---

[10]For example, "Woe to you, scribes and Pharisees, hypocrites! For you are like white-washed tombs" (Matt.23:27) derives from the Jewish custom of whitewashing grave stones to make them clearly visible so that no one would unintentionally contract ceremonial defilement by brushing against them. Luke paraphrases in order to get rid of the distinctive custom, but keeps the essential thought: "Woe to you! For you are like concealed tombs, and the people who walk over them are unaware of it" (Luke11:44). See R.H.Gundry, *A Survey of the New Testament*, (Zondervan, Michigan, 1981), footnote 18, p.92.

portrays Jesus as a cosmopolitan Saviour with broad sympathies and one who mingles with all sorts of people, in fact, whereas Matthew concerns himself more with Jesus and the Kingdom, Luke concerns himself with Jesus and the people, a point which is aptly expressed in this particular text.

The only occasions where Jesus does specifically refer to banking and interest are in the similar/parallel parables of the talents (Matthew 25:14-30) and the ten minas[11] –one mina was equivalent at that time to about three months' wages (Luke 19:11-27), but it is alluded to more in casual phrases rather than the heart of the teaching. In both parables a master calls his servants and deposits varying amounts of money with each of them in order that it may be put to work whilst he is away. In both parables one servant (the one with the least money) is so frightened of his master as a 'hard' man that he just keeps the money for fear of losing it, and thus only returns the principal lent. Both of the masters chastise this servant, not, as it might appear, because he did not bank the money and then could have at least claimed the interest owing, but that he had idly not put his 'talent' to good use. (A talent was not a coin but a weight, and it is interesting that in modern day interpretation the same word is used to denote peoples' 'gifts.') In fact, the servant is condemned out of his own mouth. He did not bank the money because he thought the master a 'hard' man who 'gathered where he did not sow,' but this is exactly what a 'hard' man would have expected him to do. The reason he did not bank the money, therefore, was because he was lazy and not a trustworthy steward of his master's property. The story also becomes an exposé in the eyes of 'liberation

---

[11]A 'mina' was equivalent to 50 shekels, and weighed approximately 500 grms; a talent was equivalent to 60 minas and weighed 30 kg. See *Encyclopedia of the Bible*, ed. Pat Alexander, (Lion Publishing, Herts., 1978), p.241.

theologists' where the third servant becomes the hero of the hour because he refuses to follow his master's shady ways and stands up to him for his injustice.[12]

From a theological perspective, according to Barclay[13], it is obvious that the useless servant stood for the Scribes and Pharisees, and for their attitude to the Law and the truth of God. The servant wanted to hand back his talent to the master exactly as he had been given it. Equally the Scribes and Pharisees wanted to keep the Law exactly as it was; any change, any alteration, any development, anything at all new was anathema to them. Their method involved the paralysis of religious truth. There is much more than this to the parable, but this analogy gives insight into the thrust of the parable rather than the actual importance of depositing the money to collect interest. What is significant is the fact that this procedure is obviously widely accepted and established at this time. As Mills points out, Jesus' mention of putting money on deposit at interest may be a reference to the moneychangers at the Temple in Jerusalem who accepted money on deposit and possibly lent at interest to foreigners so as not to contravene the Mosaic Code – a point to which I referred in Chapter One.[14] Hence, the Old Testament prohibition on interest is not being set aside by the teachings of Jesus. The existence of the practice is acknowledged and castigated as reaping where one has not sown and gathering where one did not winnow.

There is little in the rest of the New Testament writings concerning debt or interest. Debt is used as a graphic example of the obligation that an individual owes to God because of his sins. The practice of debt cancellation is spiritualised to

---

[12]Richard Higginson, *Called to Account*, (Surrey, Eagle, IPS Ltd., 1993) pp. 27-29.

[13]W.Barclay, *The Gospel of Matthew*, Vol.2, (The Saint Andrew Press, Edinburgh, 1975), p.323.

[14]Mills, *op.cit.*, p.8.

illustrate God's grace in forgiving humankind (Matthew 18:27). The forgiveness of sin is likened to the cancellation of debt. At a more practical level Paul urges the Christians in Rome not to leave any debts outstanding especially in the payment of taxes (Romans 13:7,8), and the issue of debt and interest is discussed no further, apart from Christians being urged to avoid the need of being dependent on others outside of the Church (1Thess. 4:12). In the light of these sparse references to lending and interest in the New Testament, the Hebrew Bible injunctions would appear to be still of relevance to Christians, although to be interpreted in a spirit of generosity and love, not just for one's neighbour but also for one's enemy.

It is, therefore, on the basis of this Biblical teaching, both from the Hebrew Bible and the New Testament scriptures, that the Christian Church wrestled with the whole concept of usurious loans. The aspect of this struggle particularly pivoted on the Deuteronomic exception, established, as I have suggested, to protect and keep together a poor community with regard to its religious and ethnic identity and economic status whilst settling into an alien and hostile land. The writings in the New Testament equally implied that the ban on interest in the Hebrew Bible, which was not just a ceremonial injunction but the law, was still relevant and to be interpreted in the light of loving one's enemy. The result was that the general question of the Christian Church's attitude to the application of the 'Old Testament' law became a central issue. It led to much controversy in the early Church and beyond. Christians questioned why the Deuteronomic Code in 23:19,20 allowed the Jews to lend at interest to foreigners, contradicting the Christian universalistic teaching of brotherly love, which extended the concept of lending and expecting nothing in return, not only to one's neighbour but also to one's enemy.

The Patristic Position and the Early Church Councils

In Chapter One I tried to show how seriously the Judaic response to their religious law and teaching on the prohibition of usury was taken. Jews were enjoined to lend to each other as brothers without taking interest on a loan, but were permitted to lend at interest to the *nokri*, the foreigner.

Christians, however, were left in a more ambiguous position. The teaching in the New Testament scriptures on usurious lending is couched in more idealistic and universalistic terms in the light of loving not only one's friends, but equally one's enemy and neighbour. The problem that the Christians in the early Church faced (and still face today) was the fact that there was no specific guidance as to how they were to regard the taking of interest in the New Testament teaching, although, as has been seen, there was an oblique reference to it in Luke 6. The second problem was how to come to terms with what appeared to them a 'Deuteronomic double-standard' which allowed Jews to charge interest to the '*nokri*' but not to the '*ger*.' According to Christ's teaching loans were to be made in a spirit of love for one's enemy, as well as one's friend, with the expectation of nothing in return. In first century simple, Christian, fraternal communities, with a pervasive atmosphere of kindly charity, the hard bargainer for gain was an unwelcome intruder[15] – the personification of the spirit of the alien world without.

The early Church Fathers looked with severe disapproval upon usury. They may have been influenced in certain cases by classical Greek thought. In classical times the outright opposition to usury came from the philosophers and the moralists. Plato's contribution is surprisingly slight, his condemnation being based on the class

---

[15]See 'Usury (Christian),' *Encyclopaedia of Religion and Ethics*, ed. J. Hastings, Vol. xii, (T.&T.Clark, Edinburgh, 1921), p.550.

conflict it might engender, rather than on any deeper philosophical foundation, concerned as he was with an account of the ideal social structure and the origin of the city, then identical with the state.[16] The Roman philosophers were unanimous in their opposition on moral grounds. Two of the classical philosophers, however, must be singled out because of the subsequent significance of their teaching in the treatment of usury by Aquinas and his followers. These two are Aristotle, a Greek; and Seneca, a Roman. Seneca considered usury to be morally wrong because it involved paying for time and this became a vital element in Aquinas's analysis of prohibition. The incorporation of Aristotle's ideas, as I later discuss, was much more substantial, although, in fact Aristotle was not rediscovered until the twelfth century. The position in classical Greek and Roman civil law was, however, straight-forward. Solon (638-558BCE) was an Athenian law-giver who in a time of great economic distress cancelled outstanding debts and introduced some democratic changes, but although his laws did contain many provisions for the poor debtors, they did not prohibit usury nor did they impose maximum rates; and, although in theory usury was prohibited in Roman law, in practice enforcement was inoperative due to universal evasion, and debtor protection was achieved by the imposition of legal maximum rates.[17]

---

[16]See Eric Roll, *A History of Economic Thought*, [Faber and Faber Ltd, (1938), Fourth Edition, 1973], pp.27-31.

[17]See T.W.Taylor and J.W.Evans, "Islamic Banking and the Prohibition of Usury in Western Economic Thought," *Nat. West Quarterly*, Nov., 1987, p.16. According to George O'Brien, in Rome the 'Twelve Tables' fixed a maximum rate of interest, at probably ten or twelve percent. per annum, but which cannot be determined exactly because of the expression '*unciarum foenus.*' "The legal rate of interest was gradually reduced until the year 347BC when five percent. was fixed as a maximum. In 342BC interest was forbidden altogether by the Genucian Law, but this law, though never repealed, was in practice quite inoperative owing to the facility with which it could be evaded; and consequently the oppression of borrowers was prevented by the enactment, or perhaps it would be more correct to say the general recognition, of a maximum rate of interest of twelve percent. per annum. This maximum rate – the *Centesima* – remained in operation until the time of Justinian.

The determining factor, however, for the early Fathers was the Old Testament legislation and the general principles of the New Testament teaching, more especially a strained interpretation of Luke 6:35. They interpreted it in various ways, all in terms of prohibition. As John Dow remarks Tertullian, Cyprian, and Clement of Alexandria accepted the Old Testament precepts in Ex.22:25; Dt.23:19; Ps.15; and Ezek.18.8 as still binding on Christians. For Tertullian the prohibition of usury in the Old Testament was only a preparation for the Gospel demand to forgo the principal as well. Apollonius compared usury to a game of chance and Lactantius condemned it. In the fourth and fifth centuries it was even more vehemently condemned which suggests that the evil was increasing. Ambrose (c.340-397) stated that it added to the number of the poor and an entire work was dedicated to the theme of usury (*De Tobia*). Ambrose saw the practice of usury as possible only towards an enemy in war though even this concession was apparently only due to the interpretative difficulties of the text Deut.23:19-20. In this instance the Deuteronomic discrimination allowed Jews to take interest from the enemies of God's people, these being the original inhabitants of Canaan. The taking of interest therefore could be equated to an act of war. Although inherently evil in itself, killing, such as capital punishment or war, could be justified in certain circumstances, so too, could the taking of interest be regarded as an act of war against the enemy; 'where there is right of war, there is also right of usury.'[18] In other works his condemnation

---

Justinian . . . fixed the following maximum rates of interest – maritime loans twelve percent.; loans to ordinary persons, not in business, six percent.; loans to high personages (*illustres*) and agriculturists, four percent." George O'Brien, *An Essay on Medieval Economic Teaching*, (First edition: Longmans, Green and Co., London, 1920. Reprinted: Augustus M. Kelley, New York, 1967), pp.160-161.

[18]B.Nelson, *The Idea of Usury: From Tribal Brotherhood to Universal Otherhood*, (The University of Chicago Press, Ltd., London, 2nd edition, 1969), p.4.

of usury is absolute, including the cornering of grain and speculating on prices of agricultural products in times of famine, all considered as manoeuvres of usurers. The same condemnations appeared in the works of John Chrysostom. Jerome maintained that the prohibition in Deuteronomy had been universalised by the Prophets and the New Testament, as Christians had been enjoined to treat everyone as 'brother.' Augustine placed it in the category of crime, classifying usury as theft under the seventh commandment. Basil and Gregory of Nyssa denounced usurers as 'a breed of vipers that gnaw the womb that bears them.'[19] Basil's homily upon Psalm 15 was, in fact, the inspiration of much patristic thought. According to Mills, Basil denounced interest for increasing the poverty of the borrower and thereby reducing him at times to slavery or suicide; Gregory proposed that the 'offspring' money produced in the form of interest was unnatural as money was sterile.[20]

The standpoint of the Fathers, however, must not be explained as a mere narrow reading of Scripture. Their collective Christian consciences abhorred the exploitation of the defenceless and less fortunate. Throughout this period the practice of usury is regarded not as an economic but as a *moral* question. Indeed, with regard to the economic situation, the Fathers were only concerned with consumption loans to needy borrowers, as this was the only form of loan prevalent in the economic circumstance of the time. The concept of commercial loans had not yet arisen. Borrowing was still largely for the urgent personal needs of poor men, who were fit subjects not for exaction but for charity, or the opportunity to improve their own lot in life – very similar in that respect to the impoverished peoples of the

---

[19]See John Dow article "Usury (Christian)" *Encyclopaedia of Religion and Ethics*, ed. J.Hastings, *op.cit.*, p.550.

[20]Mills, *op.cit.*, p.11.

low income countries of today. The Christian conscience at this time was finely sensitive to the obligation of charity. Wealth was the gift of God, and men were but stewards: *dispensatores* not *possessores.*[21]

As the Church developed in power, especially after the conversion of the Emperor Constantine in 311 CE, antagonism against usurious lending gradually hardened into prohibition within the canons of the early church councils. At first only clerics were dealt with, who, as guardians of ecclesiastical property may have had practical difficulties and temptations. In the statute of the Council of Elvira (c.305) it stated that:

> "If any cleric be found taking usury, he shall be deposed and excommunicated. If, moreover, a layman be proved to have taken usury, and promise, on being reproved for it, to cease to do so and not exact it further he shall be pardoned; but that, if he persist in that iniquity, he must be cast out of the Church."[22]

The seventeenth canon of the Council of Nicaea, 325, reiterated this deposition for usurious clerics who 'in lending require their twelve percent';[23] by 345 at the Council of Carthage it was equally declared reprehensible in laymen[24] and this view was repeated by the Council of Aix-la-Chapelle in 789 under Charlemagne (742-814). It is important to note that the *Hadriana*, a collection of canons, was the most influential body of ecclesiastical legislation for Charlemagne's empire. In it is

---

[21]Hastings, *op.cit.*, p.550.

[22]"Canons of the Council of Elvira, c.305" in *A New Eusebius: Documents illustrating the history of the Church to AD 337*, ed. J.Stevenson, (SPCK, London, revised edition, 1987), p.291.

[23]*Ibid.*, ("Canons of Nicaea, 325"), p.342.

[24]Hastings, *op.cit.*, p.551.

contained the single most important document of the early Church on usury: the epistle, '*Nec hoc quoque*,' of Pope Leo I, the Great (440-461), a papal decree that categorically forbids clerics to take usury but also declares laymen who take it as guilty of seeking *turpe lucrum* (shameful gain). It is the most formal general prohibition of usury enunciated by supreme ecclesiastical authority before 1179.[25]

At the same time that the *Hadriana* appeared, the Christian teaching found expression, for the first time in history, in the *secular* legislation of the State. Citing Nicaea; '*Nec hoc quoque*'; the 'Apostolic Canons'; and the 'law of the folk,' the capitularies of Charlemagne forbade usury to everyone. That the State should ban usury for laity, as well as clergy, is an important event. Here in the formative age of medieval civilisation the rule with regard to usury is acknowledged by the secular power as obligatory on all Christians. From this time on both Church *and* State press the fight against usury.

Several times the Holy Roman Empire renews the basic prohibition; and the Nynweger capitulary of 806 gives the first medieval definition of usury – 'where more is asked than is given.' The Church also continues the battle by means of episcopal capitularies, for example, the Paris synod of 829 showed a wider use of biblical authorities, and the Synod of Pavia in 850 took the sharpest methods yet against lay usurers. In 889 an episcopal capitulary contained the first legislation referring to usury taken by means of a contract.[26] Similar sanctions were invoked

---

[25]J.T.Noonan, *The Scholastic Analysis of Usury*, (Harvard University Press, Massachusetts, 1957), p.15.

[26]*Ibid.*, p.16.

against usurers in England by the Council of Northumberland, Alfred the Great (849-899), and Edward the Confessor (1004-1066).[27]

Nevertheless, as Noonan maintains, although progress has been made in some way toward a prohibition on usury, the period from approximately 750-1050 C.E. is primitive. The positive contributions to date are such that the Holy Roman Empire has enacted the usury prohibition into the law of the land and there is much local legislation against usury by bishops, as well as a collection of biblical texts against usury; also, there has been the rejection of the defense that the usurer is entitled to a reward for helping the borrower productively. There is equally the recognition in a particular influential set of canons that recognises papal condemnation of usury which is applicable to laymen.[28]

However, although strong sanctions are laid only against clerical usurers, the papacy sponsors no general legislation on the subject. Usury itself is barely defined, and at no time is it said that usury is a sin against injustice. The generic category of usury remains *turpe lucrum*, and although the taking of usury *is* treated as a serious sin, it is denounced more as a form of avarice or uncharitableness. Around 1050, however, the Christian teaching upon the subject enters a second stage of development.

Introduction to the Medieval Period

One of the very interesting facts about Western Medieval economy with regard to usury, especially in the light of twentieth century practice, and the Islamic system, is that both are explicitly ethical systems, and the detailed parallels are very

---

[27]Mills, *op.cit.*, p.11.

[28]Noonan, *op.cit.*

close and often the practices are identical; there is some evidence, according to
Taylor[29], of common origins – this assumedly in the light of the influence of Jewish
teaching on Muhammad at Medina. This is an interesting point to bear in mind as
we examine the analysis of usury by the Scholastics in the medieval period. It will
be seen that both early Western Medieval economics and Islam prohibit usury
outright. However, later on, the prohibition evolves to exclude certain specified
returns. For example, what is eventually permissable is a return from a partnership
– provided the partner making the investment genuinely shares the risk; in both
practices there is evidence that prohibition is only justified on the distinction between
the fungible and the non-fungible,[30] as both reject 'time' as a justification of the

---

[29]Taylor and Evans, *op.cit.*, p.26.

[30]The definition of fungible and non-fungible items is not straight forward. The Roman law said that
the matter of loans was goods consisting in number, weight, or measure, that is goods which were
'fungibles': "by giving them we contract a credit; for they can be repaid by being returned in their
species rather than individual; and in other goods we cannot contract a credit, because one of these
cannot be repaid for another, if the creditor is unwilling." In the transfer of a fungible good
ownership is transferred and a loan contracted upon which it is illicit to profit; whereas, in the
temporary transfer of a horse or a house ownership is retained and profit is licit. All fungible goods
have a determined value. Natural fungibles like wheat have their value fixed naturally by their
quantity. Artificial fungibles like money have their value fixed by law. The stock scholastic
examples of fungibles were also 'consumptibles' i.e. consumed in their use e.g. bread, wine, oil, grain,
wood for fire, and according to Aquinas, money – in that one cannot receive back the same coins after
having exchanged them for goods. Money cannot bear fruit, its value is its use. However,
consumptibility in use depends on agreement as to the primary purpose of a commodity; fungibility
requires assent to a certain standard of quality. The usual scholastic examples of fungibility, grain
and oil, are not fungible unless a certain origin and certain age are first assumed. Fungibility is,
therefore, not simply a juristic way of saying consumptibility. For example even in an age of little
manufacturing there were examples of goods which were fungible but not consumptible in first use
– swatches of cloth; young pigs; wool for packing; and lead for ballast. However, according to
Noonan, the scholastics' imagination did not extend to them, or at least they failed to consider the
difficulty of applying the usury rule to loans of non consumptible fungibles. He suggests that in fact
St. Thomas was more careful than his contemporaries in distinguishing the limits of the natural law,
believing that the natural law taught the sinfulness of usury only in the case of goods consumptible
in use. If this is so, a large area of lending would be left outside the natural prohibition as he
conceives it. In this case it would be more appropriate to refer to the scholastic argument with regard
to 'consumptibles' rather then 'fungible' goods. See Noonan, *op.cit.*, pp.40; 57; 71; 391.

payment of interest. Clearly practice sometimes deviated from the principle, but not nearly as much as contemporary Western thought has done by apparently removing itself far from its own tradition – hence the gap between Western and Islamic banking systems today. It is in the light of this apparent contradiction, or *volte-face*, in Western theological thought that the medieval teaching on the concept of usury raises important issues to be addressed in the West today, especially if we compare modern banking methods and market economies in the Islamic world to those which operate in the West.

If we take 750 CE as the beginning of the specifically medieval development on usury, it is important to note that the Bible was not the single source of influence that determined medieval thought – indeed at this time only one Old Testament text was cited with any frequency and that was Psalm 15 because it admits no exceptions and because it was used by the first ecumenical council. Of as much initial influence were the writings of the Fathers against usury and the numerous condemnations of clerical usurers by earlier councils, as outlined briefly above. It was, thus, the combined weight of these authorities, and not a single authority, which influenced and was responsible for the early medieval position. In stating this, it is equally important, however, as Noonan points out, [31] to reject three hypotheses which are sometimes put forward to account for the medieval stand on usury.

One hypothesis sees it founded upon the doctrine of Aristotle, but Aristotle was not 're-discovered' in the West until the twelfth century, and by that time the medieval position was well established, and it became merely a simple auxiliary instrument of the usury prohibition in the hands of, for instance, St. Thomas Aquinas.

---

[31]I am greatly indebted to the work of J.T.Noonan in his book 'The Scholastic Analysis of Usury.' It is the most comprehensive survey of this period from which I quote in this section.

Secondly, a perhaps more reasonable assumption is that there was a causal link between the scholastic usury theory and the economic conditions of the time. This was the case in the sixteenth century when economic pressure to modify the usury theory clearly triumphed, but the sixteenth century was a commercial, humanistic age, in which economic rationalism was already of importance. The early Middle Ages, by contrast, were neither commercial, nor humanistic. People were inclined to accept a bare theological rule simply because it was a theological rule – and to apply it in all its bleakness. No doubt, the facts that the economy was almost completely agrarian, and that borrowing was nearly always for consumption, contributed toward the emphasis upon the doctrine in the ninth century. (The European economy in the ninth century was strikingly similar to the Judaic economy in which the Mosaic law on usury was first applied). Perhaps the sudden zeal with which the usury legislation was welcomed in this period may be partially understood as a last ditch effort to save the small free farmers from absorption by the larger landholders, who were usually the lenders. It was in the twelfth century in Italy as trade revived, that the papal efforts to suppress usury became most strenuous. By the thirteenth century when the Italian city states were already in an early stage of capitalistic development the scholastic analysis of usury began. On the whole, at this time, most scholastic authorities were motivated by theological considerations than economic facts.[32] That is not to deny, however, that there would not have been a rule in the shape that it took, with the dominance it achieved, if economic conditions were not partially to justify it, conditions after all were still receptive to a ban on usury, but the conclusion to be reached is that the relation between the scholastic theory of

---

[32]Noonan, *op.cit.*, p.13.

usury and the economic conditions of the time is an indirect rather than a direct causal connection.

The third hypothesis which can also be dismissed is that the usury prohibition was related to the Church's own interests, but many churches and monasteries were heavily endowed, the higher clergy were also generally men of wealth with money to invest or loan, and the papacy itself often had large idle sums of money on deposit in banks. There was, therefore, ample temptation in the medieval period for the Church to change the usury prohibition *in favour* of investors, bankers, and creditors, as the Church itself could have hugely benefitted. But instead, the Church insisted on a law which convicted of sin its most trusted emissaries and many of its highest dignitaries. Therefore, at the beginning of the medieval period the evidence of the usury prohibition ran counter to ecclesiastical economic interest, for the usury law was first applied and worked most heavily against the monasteries. It is important to note, as Noonan maintains, that it was the authority of the actual Church, which stood at the head of all later developments on the concept of usury, rather than a biblical text in itself, or Aristotle's teaching, or economic conditions.[33]

From approximately 1050-1175 the Christian teaching on the subject of usury entered a different phase, possibly because of a general development in learning enabling a more detailed knowledge of the Fathers and a greater understanding of the concept of usury, and also a revival of trade. As commerce grew, it soon became clear that usury on business loans, through which borrower-merchants made themselves profits, had to be viewed in a different light. As commercial loans were different to consumption loans, how were they to be viewed? As a result of this commercial activity in the late eleventh century writers began to see the lending at

---

[33]*Ibid.*, p.14.

interest as a sin against justice. The first medieval writer who quoted St. Augustine as having canonical authority upon the subject, classifying interest as theft under the seventh commandment, was St. Anselm of Lucca. Anselm's classification of usury as theft is an influential precedent. It was followed by Hugh of St. Victor, Peter Comester, and Peter Lombard, whose 'Sentences' were of such importance in directing later medieval thought. A restriction which also began to emphasise the unjust character of their acquisition was made by Ivo of Chartres who pointed out that usuries as stolen goods, following St. Augustine, may not be given as charity.

In 1139 the Second Lateran Council, composed of a body of bishops having the absolute authority of an 'infallible' ecumenical council, was the first to issue an explicit decree of universal prohibition against usury for all. It does not, however, say explicitly that usury is a sin against justice. In 1159 the legal form of the prohibition of usury began to approach its definitive shape with Gratian, a twelfth century Benedictine monk and the Church's greatest ever lawyer. His *'Concordia Discordantium Canonum'* is a collection of canons which, modified and revised, form a part of the law of the Church until the complete revision of canon law in the new Code in 1917.[34] In it usury – for the first time – is treated as a special subject; it is an authority which directly governed the scholastic writers throughout the medieval period. It is a probable proof of the growing importance of the subject with the growing influence of commerce. Its contents sum up the position on the question of usury arrived at by the beginning of the twelfth century: St. Augustine, St. Jerome, and St. Ambrose, as well as the Nynweger statute (under the erroneous title of the

---

[34]Peter de Rosa maintains, however, that although Gratian's *Decretum*, or Code of Canon Law was easily the most influential book ever written by a Catholic, it was peppered with three centuries of forgeries and conclusions drawn from them, with his own fictional additions. Of the 324 passages he quotes from popes of the first four centuries only eleven are genuine. See *Vicars of Christ : The Dark Side of the Papacy*, (Bantam Press, 1988) p.82.

Council of Agde), are all used to prove that usury is 'whatever is demanded beyond the principle.' *'Nec hoc quoque'* of Leo the Great is still the most general ecclesiastical condemnation of usury which Gratian can cite, and Psalm 15 is his only biblical reference. The inadmissibility of usurious gain as charitable offerings is reaffirmed, and Gratian particularly insists on the obligation of restitution, otherwise it is no more than theft.[35]

The climax of the early medieval campaign against usury is reached with the vigorous actions of two twelfth-century popes, Alexander III (1159-1181) and Urban III (1185-1187). Alexander III declared that credit sales at a higher price than cash sales should be considered usury – this was significant in the fact that it was the first extension of the usury prohibition to cases where the explicit form of the transaction is not that of a loan. He also declared that the Church could not dispense from the prohibition against usury even to raise money for such worthy causes as the ransoming of Christian captives from the Saracens. The reason being that usury is a crime detested by both pages of the Testaments. It is clear, therefore, that usury is not merely a matter of a simple ecclesiastical rule; it has not yet, however, said to be against the natural law. The Third Lateran Council over which Alexander presided in 1179, declares usury condemned by both Testaments, excommunicates and denies Christian burial to 'manifest usurers,' and prohibits the reception of offerings made by them. These strong measures were confirmed by Urban III. In a letter which becomes the decretal *Consuluit*, he cites Luke 6:35. The immense importance of this citation can hardly be exaggerated. For the first time in the entire tradition, a specific command of Christ is authoritatively interpreted by a pope as prohibiting usury.

---

[35]Gratian, *Decretum Gratiani*, Part II, Causa 14, Q.4, in *Corpus juris canonici*, ed. E.Friedberg, (Leipzig, 1879-1881), and cited in Noonan, *ibid.*, p.19.

Luke 6:35 will stand, effectively unquestioned, as an absolute divine prohibition of gain from a loan until questioned by Dominic Soto in the sixteenth century. Not only that, but the papal use of it by Urban III is of equal importance. Where a lender intends to receive gain from a loan, whether it has been stipulated or not, the lender is guilty of 'mortal usury' because this is prohibited by Luke 6:35. Again and again scholastic writers will refer to this biblical text and to the Pope's application of it to show that intention to gain will constitute usury.

The Scholastic Interpretation

In this particular case, I am defining the 'scholastics' as those men in the medieval period who were the acknowledged intellectual and moral leaders of all of Europe for several hundred years. Obviously no account of scholastic thought can be exhaustive but, in this case, at this time, the scholastic field in which the authors worked, within a common tradition and constantly referring to each other's work, is a fairly easy one in which to determine which authors were representative, influential, original, or astute. The scholastic interpretation of the usury analysis, however is the result of the interaction of many forces, it has a religious origin and religious authority controls much of its development. It is Western man's first try at an economic theory, and the theory's tools are legal concepts. It is from this time on that the ideal of justice, as opposed to charity or greed, underlies every statement of it. The scholastic analysts attempt to regulate the cost of credit with these clumsy tools. For three centuries some of the best minds of Western Europe engage in an idealistic effort to frame the intellectual and moral conditions under which credit might justly be extended. People such as Robert of Courcon, William of Auxerre, Hostiensis, Giles of Lessines, St. Thomas Aquinas, St. Bernardine, St. Antoninus all felt that usury was a pressing problem and devoted their arguments against it. They sought to define distinctions between it and lawful profit and to investigate the nature of money and value. The theoretical structure they erected was not a consistent piece but it did encourage risk-sharing investment and charity to the poor. However, to simplify, to find a neat, consistent, logical pattern, to teach a single lesson or draw a universal prescription is not possible. As Noonan points out:

> "It is clear that almost all the historical errors about the scholastic analysis of usury theory arise from a single failure: a failure to consider the theory broadly enough, to take into account either the multiple character of its foundations, theological, economic and legal, or the multiple aspects it presented in practice, particularly the aspects under which it encouraged the growth of interest titles and above all the use of alternative methods of credit besides the loan."[36]

On their own initiative, the scholastic authors developed the contracts of irregular deposit, insurance, annuity, and bills of exchange. These are all essentially *medieval* discoveries, and they are directly nurtured by the necessities of the usury theory.

However, the scholastics were primarily disciples of the Roman law. Economics in their view was always secondary. Neither economics nor law, however, are at the origin of the scholastic theory – originally and primarily it is a *theological* creation. That usury is a sin was a dogma of the Catholic Church. It was because it was part of the content of Christian revelation that the prohibition of usury became the object of detailed, rational exploration; therefore, throughout the scholastic treatment of it ecclesiastical authority plays a dominant role. It is the effort of scholastic writers to explain, to expand, and to apply the positive teaching of the Church which results in the natural-law analysis of usury. They do not rely on

---

[36]*Ibid.*, p.407.

authority, or revelation, or Roman law alone, but they make a determined effort to rest their case against usury on the nature of man and the nature of things in themselves, whilst at the same time they try to determine what forms of credit are naturally lawful and just – a point which is often neglected. Another main attribute of the scholastic's approach was their casuistry – the kind of examination of moral principles on a case-by-case basis – which if there is any criticism to be applied to this method was that, in fact, they did not put forward enough cases and they tended to re-examine the classic situations too often.[37]

Of course, one might argue, that in the rational development of the scholastic theory of usury, theology still dominates reason. As Noonan questions, does not the Church decide *a priori* what the scholastics must then prove *a posteriori*? Undeniably the scholastics are all either theologians or canonists, starting their investigations with an awareness of the teaching of the Church, and therefore, their opinions will not surely run against her positive determinations. Indeed, in the medieval period many flimsy or, indeed, fatuous arguments were seized on to support 'rationally' what the author knew he was bound by authority to believe; equally, many medieval theologians anxious to preserve the effectiveness of the dogmatic rule, arbitrarily rejected interest titles and contracts which later scholastics would find lawful. However, there did develop a sound analysis of usury and a valid, if narrow and technical, case against it. At the same time, it is in the medieval period itself that the theory of legitimate interest and alternative methods of credit originates. The rules of the Church were more often the result, rather than the cause, of the scholastics' reasoning, and usury analysis developed not only from a study of

---

[37]So Noonan, *ibid.*

the sources of revelation, as would a purely theological analysis, but also from a consideration of the demands of natural justice in concrete economic circumstances.

If we now consider the period from 1150-1450, among the first pioneering theologians writing on the subject of usury from the perspective of natural law is William of Auxerre (1160-1229), deacon of Beauvais. Probably no scholastic writer on usury before St. Thomas Aquinas is as influential as he is. He made five contributive arguments to the discussion of usury: he declares that usury is against the natural law; teaches that it is intrinsically evil; makes an important distinction between the absolute and conditional voluntariness of the debtor; gives a general rule for detecting frauds on the usury laws; and produces a new argument on the sinfulness of selling time. Each proposition will become incorporated in the general medieval teaching on usury.[38]

As the thirteenth century develops, so too, does the intellectual life of the Church, particularly fostered by the intensive study of theology encouraged by the two great new orders, the Dominicans and the Franciscans. This, however, adds surprisingly little, at this time, to the analysis of usury, although we shall find wordy warfare between the various orders concerning usury in the fifteenth and sixteenth centuries. Their one substantial contribution, however, was to introduce Aristotle into the argument, and this was expanded upon by St. Thomas Aquinas (1225-1274). Partly because of his general theological pre-eminence – he was a Dominican and a teacher at the University of Paris and various Italian universities, and partly because of the intrinsic weight of his arguments, St. Thomas holds a special place in the development of the usury theory, and the importance of his opinions cannot easily be exaggerated.

---

[38]Mills, *op.cit.*, p.15.

However, before turning to the work of this great theologian, it is important to consider the work of two great canonists, Pope Innocent IV and his friend, Cardinal Hostiensis. The difference in the approach to usury by the scholastic canonists and the scholastic theologians can best be observed through their different roles, as both were servants of the Church, guided by its teaching of the Gospel, the natural law, and the canons. The canonists, however, were concerned mainly with solutions valid for the external forum of the Church and the administration of the law; fitting their commentaries to the canons, they made no comprehensive attempt to reconcile the canons or produce a synthesis. The theologians, on the other hand, were focusing mainly on the confessional, and are at once more systematic, more logical, and often more severe.

At the same time, therefore, that the theologians were repeating the old arguments to prove the injustice of usury and Aristotle was offering new support to their proofs, these two eminent canonists, whose opinions were to carry much weight in canon law, attempted a revolutionary departure from the tradition of the past two hundred years. Sinibaldus Fliscus was a native of Genoa and elected Pope as Innocent IV in 1243. Henry of Susa, Cardinal Hostiensis, had taken his doctorate in Roman law at Bologna and studied canon law at Paris. In 1261 he became a cardinal and archbishop of Ostia. Their opinions on usury reflect a much more acute understanding of the issues than that of the famous theologians of the new orders.[39]

Innocent ignores the old arguments completely offering no comment on them. He develops entirely new arguments of his own to show usury to be a social evil, but he in no way suggests its injustice. His main argument is that usury is prohibited because of the evil consequences that follow from it. For example, if usury were

---

[39]See Noonan, *op.cit.*, pp.48-51.

permitted then all the rich people would rather put their money in a secure fixed-interest loan than invest in agriculture. This would mean that only the poor would be left to do the farming and then they would not have the tools and animals with which to farm, and famine would result. This argument may seem a little naive or exaggerated at first in twentieth century culture, but the experiences of agricultural communities such as ancient Greece or China offer considerable corroboration. Two further arguments maintained that usury resulted in poverty for the debtor, and the taking of usury stimulated a spirit of greed. His main thrust appears to show the uncharitableness, not the injustice of usury; not once does he even say that usury is unjust. This attitude is a startling departure from the tradition of the hundred years before him.

His influence on Hostiensis is clear. Hostiensis' chief argument against usury is the familiar one that ownership of a loan has passed to the debtor, and although he adds the thought that there is no use of a loaned good without its consumption, he does not develop this argument and it is left to St. Thomas Aquinas for its decisive presentation. He does however go on to cite the Pope verbatim, and in so doing seems implicitly to agree that usury is a sin of uncharitableness or avarice, or is a social evil, but is not against justice. This mature abandonment of the old grounds by Innocent and Hostiensis is especially significant. It might have been thought that when two such highly placed authorities abandon the contention that usury was against natural justice, the Roman canonists might have considered a general revision of the theory. But if this was contemplated no more was heard of it, and while the canonists hesitated, the theologians continued to maintain steadfastly that usury was, first and foremost, a sin.

St. Thomas Aquinas and the Aristotelean Theory

In his *Politics*, Aristotle discusses two kinds of wealth-getting: 'the economic' and 'the acquisitive.' The economic is explained as part of the management of a household; it is the obtaining of the natural goods which are necessary to live well and it has a natural limit in the natural needs of man. Natural needs, however, lead to natural barter, and then money has to be introduced, by law, as the measure of such exchanges. But once money is introduced another part of wealth-getting, i.e. retail trade, arises. Exchanges now shift from being made to satisfy simple needs, to making money. Here, runs Aristotle's argument, there is no natural limit to the desire for money. As man's desire for wealth is unlimited, the accumulation of money becomes his end. Even in itself, however, retail trade for money is unnatural, because its end – the acquirement of money – is unnatural; and what is worse is that men seek to gain at the expense of each other. But of all kinds of trade, the most unnatural and the most justly hated is usury, because usury not only seeks an unnatural end, but misuses money itself. Money was intended to be used in exchange and not to increase at usury. It is the unnatural breeding of money from money. Aristotle's objections to usury are, thus, based on the alleged purpose of money, and more broadly on the alleged purpose of retail trade – it is only a particular objection based on a larger opposition to all pecuniary gain from commercial transactions.[40]

However, in the translation of the *Politics*, available to both St. Albert and St. Thomas, William of Moerbeke, rendered the Greek term for retail trade as '*campsoria*' – a term with the specific meaning of money-changing. Thus, instead of being presented with a condemnation of all retail trade, which in any event

---

[40]See Aristotle, *Works*, (tr. B.Jowett, William Benton, Chicago, 1952).

medieval theologians would not have accepted, the early scholastics found in Aristotle only a condemnation of traffic in money. As they themselves were already suspicious of the *campsores* they found this highly natural. Aristotle's case against usury, therefore, which rests largely on his case against *all* trade, is accepted by St. Thomas as simply a case against those who make money from money – in any event a highly specialised and suspect group.

The incredible influence of St. Thomas Aquinas has been so great in the history of the Church from the thirteenth century that something of his background is necessary. Thomas Aquinas (1225-1274) was an Italian theologian and Doctor of the Church, born at Roccasecca, near Aquino, in Italy. He was inducted into a Benedictine monastery at the age of five but later was forcibly removed by his family and enrolled at the new secular University at Naples (1239) where he joined the Dominicans. Sometime after 1245 he began studies under Albert the Great at the Convent of St. James in Paris, and in 1248 Aquinas and Albert started a school in Cologne. Aquinas returned to Paris in 1252 to teach at the university, and from 1259-1268 he taught at the papal *Curiae* in Italy, where he met the translator, William Moerbeke. His final years were spent in Naples, teaching in a Dominican house. He died at Fossanova on the way to the Council of Lyons in 1274. Although his influence for a time waned, he was canonized in 1326, made a Doctor of the Church in 1567, commended for study by Pope Leo XIII (*Aeterni Patris*) in 1879 and declared the official teaching of the Catholic Church.[41]

Although he is credited with some ninety-eight works (nine of which are of doubtful authenticity), St. Thomas Aquinas never wrote a general treatise with regard

---

[41]*Evangelical Dictionary of Theology*, ed: W.A.Elwell, (Marshall Morgan and Scott Publications Ltd., Hants., 1984), p.1090.

to usury.   Treatments of usury are scattered throughout his works.   When commenting on the *Sentences* of Peter Lombard he used as his first and principal argument the Roman law point that in a *mutuum* (loan) ownership is transferred.   If A borrowed money from B his ownership over it was absolute; it was more than *possessio* it was *dominium*.[42]   The process of exchange had the quality of a sale, and to sell an article and then charge for the use of it was unjust.   He was still, however, seeking in the natural law for other grounds against usury.   He introduces a second argument which he takes from Aristotle but with two highly interesting divergences:

> "All other things from themselves have some utility; not so, however, money.   But it is the measure of utility of other things, as is clear according to the Philosopher in the *Ethics* V:9.   And therefore the use of money does not have the measure of its utility from this money itself, but from the things which are measured by money according to the different persons who exchange money for goods.   Whence to receive more money for less seems nothing other than to diversify the measure in giving and receiving, which manifestly contains iniquity."[43]

The first divergency is that while Aristotle's text cited by St. Thomas declares that the value of money is determined by the goods for which it is exchanged, St. Thomas ignores this and fastens upon the statement that money is a measure.   This will be for St. Thomas the essential definition of usury.   Two consequences, therefore, result from this: one is that the goods for which money is exchanged are not considered in his analysis of money itself.   In particular, changes in the supply of natural goods affecting the purchasing power of money are not considered.

---

[42]Hastings, *op.cit.*, p.551.

[43]See Noonan, *op.cit.*, p.52.

Secondly, money, thus formally considered, is conceived as having only one constant, fixed value – its legal face value.

This consequence leads to the second divergence from Aristotle. Aristotle had objected to usury because it was a distortion of the *purpose* of money, which is that money has a fixed natural end. St. Thomas, therefore, is entirely original in basing his objection, not on the final cause, but on the formal nature of money. If money is a measure, with a fixed value, deliberately to value it differently at different times is to distort unnaturally its formal *character*. The purchasing power of money may change due to fortuitous circumstances, such as the increase in natural goods, and since this is not due to the holder of money, there is no moral fault. But the holder of money who himself sets out to produce variations in the value of money is guilty of diversifying the measure. This is St. Thomas' own argument and not Aristotle's. Of course, as Mills points out:

> "As with the simplistic sterility argument, the ability to maintain a fixed value of monetary units only exists in an economic system which uses a metallic currency for money whose value is not being deliberately altered by agents within the system (e.g. a government that is debasing the currency). Once 'money' becomes an abstract concept of a right of purchasing power over goods embodied in paper currency or drawing rights at banks, it becomes far more difficult to maintain a fixed value for a unit of money since supply can be highly volatile and determined by the complex interaction of many agents."[44]

However, Aquinas' major argument against usury goes further. This is based on his observation that money is a 'consumptible':

---

[44]Mills, *op.cit.*, p.14.

"In those things whose use is their consumption, the use is not other than the thing itself; whence to whomever is conceded the use of such things, is conceded the ownership of those things, and conversely. When, therefore, someone lends money under this agreement that the money be integrally restored to him, and further for the use of the money wishes to have a definite price, it is manifest that he sells separately the use of the money and the very substance of money. The use of money, however, as it is said, is not other than its substance: whence either he sells that which is not, or he sells the same thing twice, to wit, the money itself, whose use is its consumption; and this is manifestly against the nature of natural justice."[45]

The notions that money does not bear fruit, and that its value is its use, are firmly implanted in Roman law. It is Roman law that most clearly sets forth the conception of goods consumptible in use, in treating of bequests of money and goods such as wine, oil, and grain. Aquinas' argument, however, appeals beyond the law to nature, and shows that the law is simply the formulation of the nature of things. St. Thomas points out that some goods are naturally destroyed in their use. Their use and value are thus essentially identical with their substance. Other goods, such as a house, a horse, a book, a garment etc., are not essentially consumed by their use (although Aquinas does admit that a house may deteriorate through use, but this is strictly '*per accidens*'). Money, according to Aquinas is formally a measure – its value is determined by its face-value as a measure. It is therefore a consumptible: its substance must be changed or 'alienated' in order to use it; in the same way, when wood is used for fuel its form is 'alienated' although one will receive from its use a good of equivalent worth in the form of heat. When coins are borrowed, they are only of use if they are exchanged for goods. Hence, a lender of coins can expect the

---

[45]*De malo*, Q.13, art. 4c cited in Noonan, *op.cit.*, p.54.

borrower to repay the exact value of the coins, but he cannot receive back the exact same coins that were originally lent. Aquinas' case rests finally then on the metaphysical rather than legal grounds. It is the real distinction between accidental and essential change which forms the foundation of his reasoning.

The concept of money outlined above is central to later theories on usury. Money is the mean between two terms of a sale but it can never itself be the term of a sale. As already pointed out, to sell money would be to give it two simultaneous different characters. The legal sameness of money at any given time had to mean that its value was the same at any time. Only the formal character of money should be considered in determining the justice of a contract involving money. This was the necessary assumption that St. Thomas and the schools in general made as the principal argument against usury.

In itself, therefore, the loan of money did not justify a charge for its use. The scholastics were, however, ready to face the logic of facts and to make allowance for special cases. In due course the custom sprang up of admitting compensation on various extrinsic grounds.

If bargains were not kept a delay in payment might inflict serious loss. Was there to be no compensation? In time the lender was allowed to fix a fine to be paid if the bargain was not kept, the *poena conventionalis*, and this fine was often as high as the amount of the original debt. This sum presented the difference between the creditor as he actually was, and as he should have found himself had the bargain been kept – hence the name *interest* – 'that which is between.' As the civil law had allowed the defaulting debtor to be imprisoned or even to become a slave, this money payment may have seemed a milder solution. However, it is worth pointing out, that *poena* in itself is not a case of interest in the strict sense, as it was intended vindictively rather than as a compensation – to punish negligent or fraudulent deferment of payment due. On the other hand it was a step nearer to acknowledging delay by the debtor in repaying a loan as an entitlement to interest payment.

It is very important to point out, in the light of this, that the concept and the term 'interest' are derived from the Roman law. *Interest is never thought of as payment on a loan.* It is the 'difference' to be made up to a party injured by the failure of another to execute his obligations. Interest is purely compensatory, and it is accidentally and extrinsically associated with a loan. In fact, at no time in the first century of analysis is a general theory of interest developed. The canon law deals with particular cases, the canonists comment on these individually, and the theologians mention the same individual cases or treat the problem of interest in their answers to objections to the usury prohibition. General principles are noted only as they arise in particular situations. The early recognition of interest is thus strictly limited to individual cases where the writers have seen that the lender has actually suffered damage.

Usury Prohibition: But Is There a Right to Interest?

The acceptance of 'interest' so far, has only involved fault on the part of the debtor and actual delay in the repayment of a loan. Did the original law concept of *interesse*, as the 'difference' due to failure to fulfill an obligation, prohibit the admission of such payment without any failure on the part of the debtor? The right to interest would have been of little consequence if it had been restricted to cases where the debtor was at fault after a loan had been given him, yet such was the original conception of interest. The scholastics would have to take a huge step to admit that interest might be due from the *start* of a loan. To do this seemed to many of them to abandon the foundation for the usury prohibition, the normal gratuitousness of a loan, and it was certainly to go well beyond the Roman notion of *interesse.* But the leap was finally taken.

Two further titles which eventually won approval by the scholastics as licit for compensation from the beginning of the loan were *lucrum cessans* and *damnum emergens.* By handing money over to another the lender deprived himself of the gain he might have made in various ways (*lucrum cessans*). Aquinas disapproved of this as a basis of claim, a future gain being regarded as too hypothetical. It was selling what did not exist and, in all probability, might never exist. Although by the fifteenth century this plea had gained wide acceptance, it was not so in the early scholastic period. The first hundred years contain no recognition of *lucrum cessans.* It is Hostiensis, in a much later work, *Commentaria super libros decretalium,* who is the first author to give unmistakable and full approval to a case of *lucrum cessans,* although he does insist that the merchant's principal motive must be a charitable one and that he will not be allowed to lend habitually. For the very first time the honest business man is given lawful reason for charging beyond the principal even though his debtor is in no way at fault. This authoritative canonist's recognition of pure *lucrum cessans,* however much restricted in its practical conditions, is of the greatest importance.

The theologians, however, are unmoved by Hostiensis' opinion, and continue in the tradition of Aquinas. Giles of Lessines allows interest only in delay, and in his long discussion of usury he never mentions the possibility of interest due from the beginning of a loan. Scotus is as adamant against interest of any kind from the beginning of a loan as is St. Thomas in *De malo.* The first theologian, as distinct from a canonist, to admit interest without fault by the debtor seems to be Astesanus who cites Hostiensis as his authority.[46] At the same time that he admits *lucrum cessans*, Astesanus allows the equivalent of *'damnum emergens.'* Another real expense capable of proof for which the scholastic allowed for compensation was seen in the light of someone who had lent his money but was compelled himself to borrow at a high rate of interest through the failure of a debtor to repay. This was known as *damnum emergens.* In the case of Astesanus it was interpreted in a rather convoluted way to refer to the cities of northen Italy, who, faced with great financial needs, had instituted a new method of financing themselves, unknown to the rest of Europe. They sold shares in the public debt to their citizens under compulsion and then paid a moderate interest on them. Although the sales were, in fact, more in the nature of a capital levy than a loan, the morality on receiving interest on them was debatable. Astesanus held, in direct contradiction to his teacher, Alexander Lombard, that the interest is licit compensation for damages experienced. He stressed the fact that the loans were compulsory, and that the receipt of the interest is licit only as long as the bondholder would rather have his principal back than receive the interest. However, the battle for interest was by no means won on the strength of a few theologians and the authority of Hostiensis, and throughout the fourteenth century the interest titles are frequently disapproved, for example by Joannes Andreae, Buridan, and Henry of Hesse. By the end of the fourteenth century, therefore, the opinion of the theologians and canonists would still seem to be against *lucrum cessans*, but in the fifteenth century *damnum emergens* does become more commonly accepted because of the need to justify the financial practices of the Italian city states.

By 1400 the controversy over the licitness on the forced government loans had become a hot issue. For a century the forced loan had been employed by the

---

[46]*Ibid.*, p.119.

governments of Venice, Genoa, and Florence, the leading 'capitalistic' communities of Europe. The Florentine handling of the loan was usually taken as the model for theological discussion. It is an important issue because it defines more clearly the growing distinction between the concept of usury, i.e. the voluntary seeking of profit from a loan, and that of interest, seen as compensation for the foregone gain, and due only in default.

The loan was organised in the form of a government fund called a *mons*. Every lender was given a share in the *mons*, and these shares were the object of trade. No date was set for the redemption of the shares, and annual payments were made as 'gift and interest' to the bondholders. In Florence the payments were reduced from fifteen percent in the thirteenth century, to ten percent and finally to five percent in the creation of the *novissimus mons* in 1390. The Franciscans, led by Francis of Empoli defended this important civic institution. The Augustinians, led by Gerard of Siena, and others, attacked it, and were first supported by the Dominicans. The victory of the Franciscan viewpoint prepared the way to the general acceptance of interest from the beginning of a loan; the arguments of Laurentius de Ridolfi in 1403 are outlined below, and they are substantially the same as those of his Franciscan predecessors and successors, and the views he opposes are the typical Augustinian ones.

The position of the opposition of the *mons* was based on the fact that, theoretically, interest was due only in default, and any interest paid as due from the beginning of a loan is usury. Therefore the State was guilty of promoting usury, and the creditors were guilty of taking usurious profit. Those in favour pointed to the compulsory nature of the loan, and the meagerness of the interest paid. Usury was the *voluntary* seeking of profit from a loan. Where it is forced there can be no will to profit, and where the profit is only a mere five percent the possibility of realising a true profit is absent. In fact, by the conscription of their capital a great hardship was enforced on people for which they should be compensated. A similar comparison could be drawn with the new superannuation scheme employed by the Australian government, whereby the workers contribute five percent of their earnings to a superannuation scheme in order to draw a pension when they retire; the government contributes a further three percent, and from 1997 the employer also has to contribute three percent. Agencies dealing with the poorer elements in society object to this blanket payment from the less well off as crippling. The difference is, of course, that this scheme is designed to benefit the worker in the long term, but it equally benefits the government in the short term providing much needed capital in which to invest in the economy etc. Likewise, compensation for *lucrum cessans*, the gain foregone by the merchants, who were the principal bondholders, should also be forthcoming. The higher rates of profit available elsewhere made it evident that no one would willingly choose the city's bonds as good investment. The payment of *lucrum cessans* would not be that of the payment of profit to a usurer, but, rather, some measure of recompense to those seriously affected by lending in this compulsory fashion. Where usury was acknowledged by the Franciscans was in terms of a lender who, though forced, *preferred* lending and receiving interest, to keeping his money without interest, and thereby committed a sin; equally, if after the loan has been made by a coerced lender, the lender changes his mind and prefers the interest to getting his loan back, he commits usury. To legitimate the premise that interest *is* due from the start of a loan was the reply that the city is like a debtor in perpetual delay as it set no date for the redemption of the bonds. If interest in delay is licit, so it is in this case, where the delay is without limit. By supporting the licitness of the *mons* as a policy, as well as directly by his arguments for the licitness of interest compensation, Laurentius is defending the case of *lucrum cessans* and *damnum emergens.* After his exposition on the case interest on the *mons* is generally admitted. This means that by the beginning of the fifteenth century, in one large area of lending, recognition of the right to interest from the beginning of a loan has been won. The overall result of all this was that once delay was recognised as a reason for compensation, the practice easily sprang up of lending gratuitously for a short period and charging for delay beyond that period. This was but a step from the modern methods of calculating interest.

Another extrinsic title which won its way to approval was that based on the risk, e.g. in maritime ventures, that the sum borrowed would not be restored *(periculum sortis).* It is the risk assumed by a lender when he agrees not to hold his debtor for the capital if through some misfortune he fails. It is the kind of risk borne by a partner or insurer, for the Middle Ages offered two other modes of investing money: rent charges, and partnership, comparisons of which with the present day will be made later. Besides understanding the objections raised against usury, and the distinction made between usury and interest, it is equally important to understand the contracts which were allowed as licit, in order to fully comprehend the usury theory. If the objections to the loan contract are considered out of context it would appear to effectively bar any profit from pecuniary investment; any practical development of commercial credit; or any capitalistic management of finance.[47] However, there were other investment opportunities recognised as lawful by the scholastics, and it is only in considering these, in conjunction with the already discussed arguments for and against the prohibition of usury, that an overall opinion on the general significance of the usury theory can be achieved.

---

[47]See Noonan, *op.cit.*

Contracts: The *Societas, Foenas Nauticum,* and *Census*

The scholastic discussion on the *societas*, or partnership, is important not only in showing the wide area open to investment capital, but also in its use of the fundamental concepts of the usury prohibition, which, as we have seen, were based on ownership, the sterility of money, and risk. The most telling point is that operations which are indistinguishable from a loan are analysed from another standpoint and found licit.

The *societas* was a normal form of commercial organisation throughout the Roman world, and it is in the form given it by Roman law that it enters the thought of the scholastics. It is the union by two or more persons of their money or skill for a common purpose, usually profit.[48] It is an inflexible rule of the *societas* that one partner cannot have the opportunity of having all the profit while his partner bears only the responsibility for the loss. However, if one partner contributes a great deal more to the union than the other, it is possible that he could be freed from responsibility for the loss, while his partner bears all the responsibility and gets only a part of the profit. Although it would appear that a partnership in which one partner is entirely freed from the risk of losing his capital is indistinguishable in effect from a loan, the Roman law treats a loan as formally distinct from this contract. The *societas* is mentioned in a theological context in the eleventh century by Ivo of Chartres as a contract distinct from a usurious loan, and the *Glossa ordinaria* says simply that if one invests money with a businessman, contracting a partnership so that the risk is shared by both, then the contract is licit. Thus, without analysis or debate, this contract – so enormously important to commerce – is recognised; and what is to be the principle for the next three hundred years is laid down: *assumption*

---

[48]See Noonan, *op.cit.*, Chapter vi. p. 133 ff.

of risk distinguishes the capitalistic investment in a partnership from a loan. The *societas* or variations of it (such as the *collegantia* or *accomendatio*) were common in eleventh century Venice and twelfth century Genoa. The almost complete lack of theological comment upon these arrangements would seem to indicate that the conscience of the day readily accepted the capitalistic *societas* as a different matter from usury, and easily saw the distinction. This contract had become essential to the life of business.

At the same time a contract in many ways similar to a partnership was being used by Italian commerce in defiance of the rule that it was sinful to gain from a loan. The enterprising financiers of the active Mediterranean ports such as Venice, Marseilles, Barcelona, and Genoa had not been content with the simple *societas*. The *foenas nauticum* had been revived, with a subsequent papal decretal on the subject. In this contract money or goods are loaned to a shipowner, the creditor assuming the risks of his debtor while the money or goods are actually at sea. If a shipwreck occurs and the property is lost, the debtor will not be liable in any way to return the loan. Once the voyage is completed, however, the borrower trades at his own risk, and if he loses the loan through commercial misfortune, he must still repay the lender. The Roman law permits the creditor to charge double the legal rate of interest for the time he actually runs the risk at sea as 'the price of peril.' The *foenus nauticum* is, in fact, half a loan and half a partnership. The Roman law, however, does not assimilate the case with partnership, but treats it strictly as a kind of licit usury. The canonists and scholastics follow the sharp discrimination between it as a loan, and the normal partnership.

However, in 1237, Gregory IX issued the decretal *Naviganti*. According to Noonan, it is:

"By any standard . . . the most important single papal decree on the usury question with the exception of those containing the basic prohibition itself."[49]

The issue in point was that considered in the first sentence which read: 'One lending a certain quantity of money to one sailing or going to a fair, in order to receive something beyond the capital for this that he takes upon himself the peril, is to be thought a usurer.' Thus was created a great problem for the analysis of usury. As Noonan points out, the decretal appears to reject incidence of risk as the criterion of ownership, because, although the investor takes the risk of capital upon himself he is still considered by the Pope to be a lender, i.e. one who has transferred ownership of his goods to a borrower. To deny that the incidence of risk was the index of ownership was to leave no way of discriminating between the licit *societas* and any illicit loan, because in each case money was given by a capitalist to a trader or worker and returned to him with a profit. If the difference between the two cases did not consist in the different risks run by a partner and a lender, there was no other difference between them:

"If the implication of the apparent meaning of *Naviganti* were worked out, one would be forced to conclude that every investment of money at a profit with another person would be usury, whatever form the investment took. *Naviganti* would seem to strangle commerce at its roots."[50]

Against the commercial usage of the time, it would seem improbable that a wholesale condemnation of all money investments was not intended by the decretal. In using the term 'loan' and with reference to the salient feature of *foenus nauticum*

---

[49]*Ibid.*, p.136.

[50]*Ibid.*,p.138.

i.e. the creditor's assumption of the risk, *Naviganti* is assumedly striking at the revival of the sea-loan contract current at cities such as Genoa.   Considering the length of time the *societas* proper had been accepted by everyone it is difficult to believe that any condemnation of it could have been meant. However, the task of the usury analysts with regard to this particular decretal is still debated in the sixteenth century, and we shall readdress the issue later on. At this stage, in the mid fifteenth century, at the end of two hundred and fifty years' discussion of the *societas* it is still held, as it was in 1200, that where an investor runs all the risks of his partner, he has not loaned to him at usury, but has retained ownership and is entitled to profit. But all the great problems posed by the acceptance of the *societas* for the usury theory have remained unanswered. Why is risk used as the criterion for ownership? If it is the criterion, how is *Naviganti* completely valid? Why are the use and ownership of money distinguished in a *societas* and not in a loan? In fact, the early scholastics were working with two different theories on money, risk, and ownership, one of which they applied to loans, the other to partnerships.

According to one theory, money was sterile, risk was no title to profit, ownership was the same as use in consumptible goods. In the other theory, money produced a surplus value, risk became the grounds for a reward, and ownership was determined not by the identity of use and ownership, but by the assumption of risk:

> "Probably the greatest single difference in the two theories was in the treatment accorded to money, and this difference arose from money in loans being considered formally as a measure, while in partnerships money was tacitly identified with the goods it buys and not considered in its formal character at all . . . There was practical justification for the different approaches taken. In the partnership the rate of return was normally closely related to what the capital earned.

In a loan there was no assurance that a lender's profit bore a fair relation to the productive power of his capital."[51]

In any event, the distinctions as drawn, left a wide field open for investment in business. The attempted control of the high interest rates of the *foenus nauticum* is quite sound evidence that the policy of the prohibition went beyond just the control of consumption credit. Here commercial credit was regulated. The willingness to accommodate the *societas*, however, reflects a general belief that the usury prohibition should not eliminate commercial profit, and this belief was ultimately the basis for confining the usury rule to a narrow set of situations. In the Middle Ages, the *societas* made risk-sharing investment a substantial form of capital-rewarding enterprise.

Just as the *societas* was the most usual contract for capital investment in commerce or animal husbandry, so the *census* was the normal form of investment in land, and the regular instrument of State credit. The *census* was of immense importance in providing a licit opportunity for investment in credit. Like the *societas*, it must be seriously considered, in order to obtain a more balanced picture of the economics of this time, which are often portrayed as extremely restrictive with regard to finance because of the restrictions the scholastic usury theory placed upon it. In discovering what made investment in a *census* licit, and what distinguished it from usury, the basic concepts of ownership, risk, and the sterility of money which played a part in the discussion of the *societas* must be abandoned. The important concepts here are sale, time, and right. The development of these, although not so closely involved in the usury theory as the other set, do, however, tend toward the adoption of an analysis which, if not contradictory to the usury theory, at least offers

---

[51]*Ibid.* p.152.

an alternative to it which would make the usury theory dead in practice. This alternative is not formally adopted by the medieval scholastics, but the elements of it are assembled by them and are made ready for their use by their sixteenth century successors.

A *census* is an obligation to pay an annual return from fruitful property. No English word interprets it precisely, even 'annuity' does not necessarily imply that the annual return is based on a fruitful good. Most interestingly, in light of what has gone before, the buyer of a *census* is in a lender's role because he provides the money, and the seller is a debtor because he binds himself to the annual payments. For once, the contract is unknown to the Roman law. Its growth may have been in part due to the ban on profitable loans. When it was first used, the return on the *census* was generally paid in real fruits, but as the money economy developed, payments of fruit were converted into annual installments of cash. Was, therefore, such a transaction any different from a loan? The standard answer was that it was a sale – but if it was a sale, what was sold? It was Henry of Eutin, who declared that the *census* is the purchase of a right to money. The right is bought, he maintained, only for the sake of the money to which one is entitled. Nevertheless, it is the *right* and not the money which is bought. The acceptance of the *census* as the sale of a right to money meant that the contract could be ruled by the laws relating to the just price, not by the usury prohibition; the 'just price' was first employed by Roman law and declared that a seller is entitled to recovery of the 'justum pretium' from a buyer who has taken advantage of him, unless what was given him was at least half the just price. The *census*, therefore, was defined as *not* an exchange of money for money to be returned in time, but an exchange of two present goods, cash and the right to cash. Much confusion reigned over this particular issue, and it raises opinion later on. At this point, however, the acceptance of *census* actually provided large avenues for lawful investment in credit, in contrast to the prohibition on usury which would appear to inhibit it, if not deny it altogether. These three contracts, therefore, provided investment opportunities recognised as lawful by the scholastics, and allowed pecuniary profit for commercial enterprise, but they did not address the concept of lending to the poor, nor the acceptance of the idea of lending as a profession, as did the usury prohibition. These ideas were addressed, however, in the later Middle Ages, with the acceptance of the *montes pietatis.*

Montes Pietatis

The medieval usury doctrine discouraged the small-loan business. Public lending to the poor was absolute usury, and the *societas* and the *census* had provided no effective alternatives for achieving the same result. To accept lending as a profession would be to make a radical break with the past – this break came with the acceptance of the *montes pietatis*; and with it came not only a belief that lending could be a livelihood, but the acceptance of the *montes,* which were pawnshops, also led to the acceptance of much of the structure of institutional banking and a charge for the institutional obligation of being in a position to lend.

Throughout the Middle Ages public usurers had to be tolerated as a necessary evil, though not approved or encouraged. The Third Lateran Council had excommunicated 'manifest usurers,' which applied to the professional lenders who made usury their business. These professional moneylenders were pawnbrokers who made loans for consumption purposes to the poor at high rates. Their usual rate of interest was forty three and a half percent per annum. Some states had positively licensed these moneylenders and participated in their profit through heavy license fees, but the Council of Vienne, in 1317, declared that in so doing the rulers of the States brought excommunication upon themselves, too. This, however, did not prove to be an effective deterrent; often the State would direct its chief efforts toward eliminating the competition of unlicensed usurers.

The men who were public usurers were usually, as I noted in Chapter One, the Jews. They were, of course, unaffected by excommunication. According to the Fourth Lateran Council, they were to be boycotted commercially by Christians and were to be held to make up to the Church the taxes on Christian properties which had come into their possession through usury. These provisions do not seem to have been followed. The Jews did not feel bound by the canon law and so they entered the business and did so because few Christians would openly compete with them. This traffic was deplored by the theologians, not because they were damned anyway, but because it was immoral and unnatural.

However, one group of Christians was an exception to the general Christian avoidance of open usury. These were the lombards, men chiefly from the hill towns of northern Italy, such as Asti and Chieri. Originally, and generally, the lombards were also Lombards, but not all Lombards were lombards. The proper noun 'Lombard' seems to have become the common noun 'lombard,' a term designating any public Christian usurer. They spread throughout Europe even more successfully than the Jews, and for some reason, showed a strange insensitivity to ecclesiastical and social censure. Both lombards and Jews and other open moneylenders were generally hated by the poor, whom they exploited, and considered social outcasts by the rest of the community. From the viewpoint of the poor and from that of the rulers there was an urgent need to find a substitute for the Jews and the lombards; in fact, in many places in the fifteenth century there was a strong anti-Semitic tinge to the feeling against operators of the small-loan business. Therefore, the questions asked were these: if the demand for credit was licit, was there no legitimate way of supplying it; and if the need for it was so great, could not its cost be lowered, and could it not be furnished by the Church?

In 1461, Hermolaus Barbarus had been sent to Perugia as papal governor and had found the city's statute authorising the Jews to take limited usuries in the city a direct infringement of canon law, incurring excommunication for a governor in enforcing it. He therefore abolished it, but then had been left with the problem of finding some way of meeting the needs of the poor for credit. To fulfill these needs he instituted the first *mons pietatis*, and the institution spread throughout Italy with amazing rapidity.

A *mons pietatis* was a public pawnshop, regularly financed by charitable donations and run not for profit but for the service of the poor. It had to charge a small fee for its care of the pawns and for administration costs. In Italy this fee usually amounted to about six percent, in comparison with approximately the thirty-two to forty-three percent charged by the public usurers. From the very beginning the *mons* met theological opposition on the grounds that it was an institution making a business out of lending at usury. However, in 1467, Paul II approved the constitution of the original Perugian *mons*, and successive Popes approved the *montes* in other Italian cities. The Franciscans fully supported the institution, and a great Franciscan preacher, Bernardine of Feltre, became its special apostle and travelled throughout Italy attacking Jewish moneylenders and pleading for the *mons* as the remedy for usury. Some *montes* founded by the Franciscans originally loaned entirely gratuitously, but in 1493, Bernardine convinced a general council of the order that the only way of preserving them was to charge interest; therefore, a mandatory interest charge was made by all the Franciscan establishments. At the end of the fifteenth century, there were eighty *montes pietatis* in Italy – a growth which in itself shows the necessity of their work.[52]

It was such a momentous break with the past that there was, inevitably, further protest, and, in fact, it became an issue between the orders. While the Franciscans championed the *montes pietatis,* the Dominicans almost everywhere attacked them as usurious. Theological disputes over the *montes* became a public scandal. In 1516 a papal bull intending to settle the matter was placed before the Fifth Lateran Council, an ecumenical council, presided over by Leo X, the first Medici Pope. With only one dissent, the bull *Inter multiplices* was accepted by the Council. The *montes* were allowed to levy moderate interest, provided their object was to cover working expenses and not to make a profit. The Church which had resisted usury in the interests of the poor was now compelled to allow moderate interest to an institution which existed on behalf of the poor.

Accordingly, several sixteenth century pontiffs authorised particular *montes* to accept deposits and pay interest upon them in compensation for the *lucrum cessans* suffered by the depositors. The strict rules for *lucrum cessans* set out by the popes were not kept, and by the middle of the sixteenth century it became common practice to accept the deposits of anyone who wished to invest and to pay five percent on them. From this time on, then, a good number of the Italian *montes* were 'mixed' *montes* – institutions not financed purely by charity, but by private investment. Gradually they came to lend to businessmen at eight or ten percent, as well as to the poor. These secular mixed *montes* were not like a commercial banking system, for they did not create credit, but their structure was substantially similar to that of savings banks, financed by deposits and lending at interest to all. Navarrus was the

---

[52]See P. Cleary, *The Church and Usury*, (Bloomfield Books, Sudbury, 1914), p.106ff.

first influential canonist to try to justify this finance, and by the end of the sixteenth century the idea of a lending institution charging interest for its services has been overwhelmingly accepted. Unquestionably, the virtual unanimity of assent to it by theologians after 1516 is to be ascribed to the force of the conciliar decree. Yet the natural law argument, based on *damnum emergens*, and on the right to charge for assuming the obligation to loan played a great part in winning rational consent to the institution. Inevitably, the acceptance of charitable lending institutions leads to the acceptance of non-charitable lending institutions, and, as the first kind are allowed to charge for their services and pay their employees' salaries out of interest, so are the second. In this way, with the acceptance of the *mons pietatis*, professional lending becomes accepted. The theologians and the canonists, while formally maintaining the usury prohibition, seem to have, paradoxically, left no limit to the possible gain on a loan licit in practice – the sole proviso is that the gain be realised by the indirect means of putting money into a lending business.

Contractus Trinus

The controversy on the triple contract in the sixteenth century also shows forces moving towards the admission of interest. A capitalist class was emerging, a process that was aided by the large profits made by traffic in Indulgences for which the Church itself was responsible. The powerful banking house of the Fuggers of Augsburg was behind John Eck who championed this method of investment at the University of Bologna in 1515, and John Major (or Mair) argued with cogency in its favour. Three different contracts with three different persons were allowed: a contract of partnership; a contract of insurance against loss of capital; and a contract of insurance against fluctuation of profit. Could a merchant make all three contracts with just one man? That meant that his capital was guaranteed, so was a fixed return. Was this usurious?

What, in effect, was happening here was the modification of the later scholastics' acceptance of the application of insurance to the contract of *societas*. This application struck at the one practical test of usury – the criterion of the incidence of risk; and at the same time, it led indirectly to a clear abandonment of the thesis of the sterility of money. Thus toppled two great pillars of the usury theory. In judging all economic areas neither 'doctrine' had been upheld consistently in the Middle Ages, but each had been maintained strenuously in connection with the usury rule. In the triple contract both were rejected in relation to usury analysis, and the usury theory was seriously altered. It opened the way for legitimizing nearly all transactions involving the extension of commercial credit, and turned largely on the morality of insurance.

Insurance first developed in the fourteenth century in Mediterranean ports as the best means of securing risks in maritime currency; property insurance was not a contract used by Roman law, and the early Middle Ages were equally unfamiliar with it. By the end of the century, however, property insurance, in which an owner transferred the risks of his property to an insurer, for a fee, had become familiar to all the commercial cities of Italy. *Naviganti* is no objection, for that deals with a sale of risk associated with profit on a loan. Thus without any important opposition whatsoever, the insurance of property was accepted by the theologians. Only one obscure late fifteenth century writer seems to have sensed the peril that the acceptance of insurance posed for the usury theory. This is John Consobrinus, who, in a short treatise, *De justitia commutativa*, published in 1494, forthrightly attacked marine insurance as usurious:

"This contract is usurious on both sides, because each one intends to place himself in gain and the other in loss . . .[Also] he [the insurer] sells for 50 pounds, what is not his own, nor can be, because it is of God alone to preserve the ship. Therefore, he does a great injustice to God . . . Whence briefly I say that every lucrative contract which does not depend on a man's industry or diligence or on his own property is illicit and usurious . . . It is indeed licit to a man to expose his things at his own peril, but not at the peril of another: because never does the risk pass to some other person, except in those things in which passes the ownership."[53]

Here is a very explicit statement of the theory of the identity of risk and ownership, which the early scholastics had made essential to the application of the usury prohibition. Despite mistaking the insurer's function, Consobrinus, better than any famous authority, grasped what the theological approval of insurance would do to the usury theory. But he was not an influential writer, and the common opinion at the end of the fifteenth century stood clearly for the licitness of property insurance. Indeed the only reason for rejecting it would have been in order to save a portion of the speculative reasoning behind the usury theory – condemning a just contract for the sake of a debatable theory. Consobrinus alone proposed to treat matters from this viewpoint.

The acceptance of insurance, however, was balanced by the rejection of guarantee, and it is over this that the controversy of the triple contract evolved. Guarantors, of course, had been frequently used on loans, and their right to damages had long been recognised. In 1400 Laurentius de Ridolfi had proposed for the first time the right of a guarantor to charge a flat rate of two percent for his services. He claimed that the charge was not for the loan proper but for the sake of the guarantor's credit. However, at the same, defending the contract in principle, he advised all to

---

[53]Noonan, *op.cit.*, p.203.

abstain from it. St. Bernardine indignantly repudiated the contract of guarantee at two percent as a clear attempt to make a profit from a loan; and St. Antoninus said the contract was a simple fiction, in which the guarantor and the original lender were identical, so that the lender collected usury in the form of the fee for the guarantor.

The arguments concerning the 'Triple Contract' are dealt with in great detail in Noonan's work, and it is not the nature of this book to outline the minutiae. However, in moving toward this Christian understanding of usury it is important to be aware of the arguments as they arose for and against its usage, and also, the way in which other contracts which involved a usury principle were accepted as licit transactions, as we have noted with regard to the acceptance of the *societas, foenus nauticum*, and *census*.

No one up to 1485 had related insurance to investment contracts in such a way that the effect upon the usury theory was evident. In that year Angelus Carletus de Clavasio, vicar-general of the Franciscans, wrote the *Summa angelica de casibus conscientiae*, in which he discussed the investment in a partnership using the incidence of risk to distinguish a usurious loan from a true partnership. Angelus maintained that it is usury if you put your money in a partnership, your capital is guaranteed by your partner, and he pays you an additional reward at his discretion. But Angelus adds that you could insure your capital with a third party and still licitly take your profit from the partnership. The debate now centered on the authority of the dead medieval writers who condemned a riskless partnership and the ingenuity of the living later writers who defended it. The early scholastics had unanimously maintained that the capitalist's reward in a partnership came as fruit from the use of money. Evidence of his responsibility for risk was not his title to payment, but simply ownership. When the risk criterion disappeared, i.e. in a risk-free partnership, it became evident that in the partnership money was to be treated as fruitful, and the old theory was unable to deny that this might be done. Although there were new attacks on the contract, on new grounds, most of the prominent scholars after 1485 were in favour of it, with strong support coming from the newly founded University of Tubingen, for example, Gabriel Biel, and his pupil Conrad Summenhart.

Although Summenhart defended vigorously the justice of the triple contract and so may be considered a believer in its essential lawfulness, having answered objections by a highly abstract analysis of what is meant by 'nature,' he, nevertheless, holds that at the present time it is sinful, as such use is against charity. What he did not attempt personally, his pupil John Eck did.[54] Eck had become lecturer in theology at the University of Ingolstadt outside Augsburg, a city with a particularly intense interest in finding licit means for safe investment. At this time Augsburg was the leading financial city of Germany, and stimulated by a prosperity boom in minerals, was threatening Florence for the financial leadership of Europe. In 1514, Eck taught at the university that the guaranteed contract was licit. The merchants were jubilant. The learned were dismayed at the publicity. The bishop forbade any further discussion, and Eck was insulted by many as a scandal monger. In 1515, partially financed by his friends the Fuggers – the most prominent commercial and banking house in Augsburg having already captured the papal banking business from Florence, and blessed by the papal nuncio, Eck set out to defend his thesis at the centre of canonist learning, Bologna. He disputed for five hours before the full university and was generally favoured by the jurists, but the humanists at Nurenburg, avowed enemies of Augsburg and scholasticism, at once spread the rumour that Eck had defended usury at Bologna. Despite his short connection with the triple contract and the lack of any definitive outcome to his

---

[54]*Evangelical Dictionary of Theology, op.cit.*p.340.

efforts on its behalf, Eck is of great importance to the history of usury, for he made the triple contract known to all the learned world of Europe and to the merchant bankers of his time. He defended the contract under the name of the 'five percent contract,' the popular name for it in Germany taken from the fact that the net return to the capitalist partner was currently five percent. At the same time he is the first author to describe the transaction as involving three contracts instead of two: the original contract of partnership; a second contract of insurance of the principal, in which insurance is given in return for an assignment of the future probable gain from the partnership; and a third contract by which an uncertain future gain is sold for a lesser certain gain.[55] The third contract had not been specifically considered in the discussions of Angelus de Clavasio and Summenhart, and is essentially a guarantee of a fixed interest return. Thus, the triple contract becomes the standard form of the operation, and *'contractus trinus'* becomes its standard theological description. As to the qualifications with which he would safeguard its use, Eck insists that it be done only with a merchant, for an actual business purpose; the investor has the intention not of lending or profiting on a loan, but of entering a lawful and true partnership; the merchant agrees to the insurance clauses perfectly freely; and a just price be paid for the insurance, but not of usury. At that present time, five percent seemed a reasonable return to the investor, leaving enough in the way of compensation to the merchant for his insurance services. There was an immediate reaction to Eck's theses in theological circles. The faculty of theology at Paris, was asked for its opinion, but for unspecified reasons remained silent. But, its dean, the Scottish theologian John Major, offered an unhesitating assent to the arguments of Eck and Summenhart. He added only that it was not advisable to preach on the contract to

---

[55]Noonan, *op.cit.*, p.209.

merchants. His arguments, however, in terms of casuistry and the *Naviganta*, are worth considering here. Of even greater import, is to understand Major (or Mair), as a person who bridged the gap between the old scholastics and the new Reformers.

The Casuistry of John Major

Major was a transitional figure: "his nominalism afforded him some footing in a world no longer comfortable with older systems."[56] He has been proposed as 'the last scholastic' by John Durkan, who also writes, "If we think of scholasticism as the old learning, then Mair is its last distinguished representative . . . Yet Mair cannot be written off as a representative of the old learning, because circumstances forced him to gradually come to terms with the new situation in the world of learning."[57] Major looked at the present and anticipated the future; as the world expanded local cultures and practices needed new directives, and tradition, failing to provide sufficient insight, became less influential.

In 1530, John Major responded to a group of Spanish merchants living in Flanders who asked the University of Paris to address the moral licity of certain commercial practices. One question concerned risk. Was it licit to receive payment for assuming the risk that another runs? The point Major addressed concerned maritime insurance. If one is paid a fee, is one obliged to pay the owner the worth of the cargo of the ship if it is lost at sea? Major used the scholastic method, in response to the problem, by presenting two common objections: the insurance is both useless, and prohibited. Major asked, can the captain of a ship hire out this task of

---

[56]J.F.Keenan, "The Casuistry of John Major: Nominalist Professor of Paris (1506-1531)," (*The Annual of the Society of Christian Ethics*), p.208. I am very grateful to Dr. Ian Torrance for drawing my attention to this paper and providing me with a copy of it (October 24, 1993).

[57]John Durkan, "John Major: After 400 Years," (*The Innes Review* 1, 1950), pp.131-157.

protection, or should the captain reserve the task of guaranteeing the cargo's safety himself? After all, the insurer does not prevent possible loss of cargo, a sinking ship will sink whether insured or not, therefore insurance is useless in that respect. Major's response did not address the state of the cargo but the psychological state of the shipping merchant. His worry would be allayed that at least if the cargo is lost, its worth is not. By providing the insurance, the agent is, in effect, entering into a partnership in which the worries and the worth of the cargo are equally born by agent and owner alike.

In examining positive law, Major noted that the law has no injunctions against maritime insurance, only conditions for when it would be fraudulent; and in examining *Naviganti*, he wrote that, there the Roman Pontiff did not prohibit maritime insurance, per se, but rather usury, which prohibits receiving a fee from a loan. However, in line with his argument, he maintains that the insurance agent does not receive a fee for a loan, but rather for his share in the partnership and for the service he provides by underwriting the cargo and sharing in the anxiety. A usurious contract is different, then, from a contract of maritime insurance.[58]

A second case which Major turned his attention to in response to the Spanish merchants from Flanders, concerned *cambium bursae*. This was a development from the old *lucrum cessans*, which had received some limited support in the late fifteenth century. In the sixteenth century the interest in the concept grew. Now its proponents asked not whether a fee can be received for a singular loan, but whether an entire business or way of life can be instituted based upon the premise of *lucrum cessans* – fee for the loss of potential profit. This gave rise to the *cambium bursae*, the institutional expression of *lucrum cessans*. Could a merchant take up

---

[58]Keenan, *op.cit.*, p.211.

moneylending as a way of life? This is not the first time that the merchants had asked the theology faculty for resolution of moral matters in economic affairs.

These merchants, however, were not, as Keenan puts it: "unethical Neanderthals seeking a lenient judgment to legitimate their money-making. Rather they were interlocutors with the Parisian faculty as well as benefactors for many students attending the university."[59] Religious students from Paris travelled to different cities from England to Flanders searching for funds to continue their studies, they were known as 'Lenten appeals,' and they received support from these merchants. A significant reason why the Church revised its teaching on usury was precisely because conscientious Christians were involved in financing.

Major legitimated *lucrum cessans* by referring to the case of the blacksmith. If he borrows a blacksmith's anvil, hammer, and other items, he leaves him not only without the tools of his trade, but has also deprived him of the profit he might have made in using them. Therefore, in returning the instruments it is legitimate to pay him for the loss of profit he would otherwise have made. Thus, Major distinguished usury, a profit for the loan itself, from compensation for the profits that were lost by the lender. In another case study he also invokes charity to commend the action. Not only was *lucrum cessans* permitted, it could be morally superior. With these insights, Major examined *cambium bursae*, using the scholastic method to engage possible objections.

An objection concerning social utility is countered with the fact that if there was no loan there would be no commerce. The main objection argued that if *cambium bursae* is licit, then there will be less commerce because potential

---

[59] *Ibid.*, p.213.

merchants will prefer to be lenders. Major responded with another case, which is worth repeating in order to follow his logic:

> "Socrates is planning on attending six fairs, one every two months, for the next year. But before he leaves for the first, Plato presents him with a plan, through which a loan will enable him to go to the first fair and Socrates can stay at home for the first two months and make the same profit through the loan. Later Cicero comes with the same proposal for the next fair, and after him John, and others. As a result, Socrates is no longer a merchant, but a lender, yet six others have become merchants because of Socrates' good turn. Thus the practice of *cambium bursae* leads to more not fewer merchants."[60]

Major's final verdict, however, is quite surprising in the light of his line of argument for he states that: 'the case is illicit; such a state of life is dangerous and dishonest, and needs to be rejected by all prudent men.'[61] Major refused, in the name of prudence, to develop this occasional practice into an institutional one. Though he rejected the simple *cambium bursae*, later in his *Commentary on the Fourth Book of the Sentences*, he upheld the licity of the complicated triple contract, which eventually became the paradigm for licit financial loans. The *cambium bursae* did not sufficiently distinguish a loan's profit from a loss's repayment, nor underline the required partnership for legitimate financing. On the other hand, the triple contract, proposed by Summenhart and Eck, embodied the necessary distinctions. Major had added that prudence cautioned against preaching the charge to merchants, but as Keenan points out, the concept of 'prudence' itself had changed from the earlier scholastic use:

---

[60]*Ibid.*, p.214.

[61]John Major cited in Keenan, *ibid.*, p.214

"Prudence, then in this context is considerably different from prudence in the writings of the other, earlier scholastics. In Aquinas, for instance, prudence is the virtue that all persons engaged to perfect the moral virtues interior to the agent . . . to set limited goals for the agent's own growth. But in the sixteenth century, prudence sought to perfect not one's own internal nature but rather the external conduct of society."[62]

Equally, Major, writing as a nominalist, denied universals, and without universals, the nominalist theologians of the sixteenth century published commentary on the more specific and codified *Sentences* rather than attempt a synthesis like *Summa Theologiae.* "Codes, not world views, were being shaped at this time."[63] Indeed, their prudential decisions were not intended to inform the masses but their habit of making new rulings with greater frequency in the sixteenth century was one of keeping the laity reliant on ecclesiastical authority for decisions of conscience.

Just as important as John Major's opinion, if not even more important, was that of Thomas de Vio, Cardinal Cajetan, who was elected general of the Dominican order in 1508, and created a cardinal in 1517; he was one of the chief champions of the papacy in the troubled years of the beginning of Lutheranism. His opinion on the triple contract was sought by an abbot of Ulmer, Conrad Koellin, who was disturbed by Eck's preaching. Although he maintained that the contract should not be introduced because it would open the way to the cloaking of usury, where the custom of using it prevailed, he would tolerate it. It would be preferable to loans at 'manifest' usury. Moreover, what he would condone as licit, was if the second and third contracts were entered into separately and independently from the partnership contract, and with the aim only of freeing the investor from care and fear of fraud.

---

[62]*Ibid.*, p. 218.

[63]*Ibid.*, p.217.

He challenges neither the notion of riskless ownership of an investment, nor the fertility imputed to money in the partnership.

Thus with no real opposition by the leading theologians of the early sixteenth century, the triple contract was proposed and popularized but its conflict with some of the earlier scholastic assumptions led to doubts among those inclined to a strict adherence to early theory. The practical character of these doubts is well illustrated by the history of the 'five percent controversy' and the Jesuits.

The 'Five Percent Contract' and the Jesuits

Forty years after Eck's bold defence of the 'triple contract,' in 1560, the Society of Jesus, a new and vigorous reforming order, arrived in Augsburg, under the leadership of St. Peter Canisius. They were appalled by the corruption of the clergy, and the immorality of the townsfolk and they were also particularly struck by the general and open practice of usury in the form of loans at 'five percent.' Canisius refused to absolve those taking the five percent in confession. In 1567, Francis Borgia, the Secretary-General of the Jesuits, wrote to Canisius saying that Pope Pius V had been consulted by the Jesuits on the triple contract bringing a five percent return, and that the Pope, speaking as a private theologian, had declared this licit. The Pope's approval was not to be publicized, lest it encouraged avarice.[64] This is the first official mention of the triple contract as a way of solving the difficulties caused by the five percent contract. In 1571, Menginus, another Jesuit in Germany, wrote to the Jesuit procurator, pleading for advice on the five percent contract, declaring that 'other religions concede it, turning the whole populace from us.'[65] In

---

[64]*Ibid.*, p.213.

[65]*Ibid.*, p.214.

1573, the second Roman commission gave its report, and on receiving it, a congregation of Roman Jesuits adopted an important series of resolutions. A simple loan at five percent was illicit; a number of alternative contracts and titles to interest were licit – among these was the triple contract. This approval is the first decisive evidence of the crystallization of official Jesuit thought in favour of the contract. In April 1581, after much intervening debate, a Congregation of the Jesuits meeting in Rome substantially affirmed the teaching of the 1573 Congregation that a simple five percent loan was usury, but the triple contract was permissable. Therefore, after almost thirty years of experiment and uncertainty in a principal banking city of Europe, the Jesuits had become wholly committed to the defense of the contract, and henceforth, were its advocates.

Before 1586, there had been no positive papal intervention on the triple contract. Then, in that year, Sixtus V issued the bull, *Detestabilis avaritia* – detestable avarice, proclaiming that men had used the honest name of *societas* as a pretext for their usurious contracts. This was done by giving money or animals to a merchant, business man, or agricultural worker, in the name of a partnership, but actually with the provision that their capital be always safe and that the so-called partner run all the risk. This was solemnly condemned and the penalties against usurers and moneylenders would be invoked if the practice continued. It appeared to be a decisive blow to the triple contract. However, it failed to have an effect for two reasons. One was that the bull was seen as purely positive legislation, not a declaration of the divine or natural law, and purely positive legislation lapses, according to the principles of canon law, if it is not received by the subjects of the positive law. Since the bull was nowhere received it had, insofar as it was perceived as positive law, no force whatsoever. Alternatively, there were those who thought that the bull insisted too much on its basis in divine law to be taken as purely positive, and that it merely prohibited contracts of partnership which were 'naturally usurious.' Since the triple contract was not 'naturally usurious' it was, therefore, argued that the bull left it untouched. In a private response to a question on the bull, Sixtus V himself declared that he had only condemned what the doctors condemned, which was widely interpreted to mean that he did not condemn the triple contract. Cardinal Toledus, a close advisor of the Pope, continued to publish a work in which the triple contract was not condemned, and in 1602 the Sacred Rota declared that insurance contracts made separately from the partnership contract were not affected by the bull. In the eighteenth century, Pope Benedict XIV declared that the use of the triple contract was only 'less congruous' to the intention of the bull. Thus, neither by the common opinion of the theologians, nor by authority itself was the interpretation supported that the bull definitely outlawed the triple contract.[66]

In the late sixteenth and early seventeenth centuries, the most representative authorities on economic morals and the triple contract were again the Jesuits, a fact which reflects the intellectual status that the new order had attained. There were three Jesuit thinkers who were considered the authorities at the height of the development of the usury theory: Louis Molina (1536-1600); Leonard Lessius (1554-1623); and John de Lugo (1593-1660).

In theological circles Molina is chiefly known as the author of Molinism, a subtle metaphysics of the relation of free will and grace, but he equally had a remarkable knowledge of contemporary economics. In his treatment of usury he produced the treatise, *De justitia et jure*, which appeared in 1593-1597, and was to be relied on by both men of law and of business throughout Catholic Europe. With regard to the triple contract Molina accepts the standard arguments and notes the

---

[66]*Ibid.*, p.221.

prevalence of the contract in Portugal. Merchants like it because they are freed from the trouble of satisfying a suspicious partner that he is getting his full profit; and widows find it advantageous. He is not sure enough of his arguments, however, to rest his case on the partnership contract, and, therefore, he adds that even supposing a true loan is effected, the investor can take a profit under the title of *lucrum cessans*. Molina's advocacy of *lucrum cessans* as a justification for the transaction may be considered either as a tacit repudiation of the defense of the contract in itself and, thus, a regression in liberality; or, as a brilliant suggestion of the proper way of legitimizing all business loans without the cumbersome and curious procedure of the triple contract, and thus a step forward in the practical tolerance of business finance. In any event, his suggestion was not generally adopted until two hundred and fifty years after his day.

Like Molina, Lessius, a Belgian Jesuit who taught theology at Louvain and became familiar with the economic life of Antwerp, perhaps the leading financial city of the age, found the triple contract a popular and necessary device and the common theological teaching in its favour. Some Belgians oppose the triple contract as being of great spiritual harm and confusion to the people, and to the temporal loss of the community. Lessius counters this with the reply that the contract is for the good of souls because it leads men from usury, and is for the temporal good, as it benefits wards and widows, whilst at the same time providing capital to the merchants at a low cost. Lessius is the first theologian, however, who maintains that the investor may refuse to invest unless the merchant enter both insurance and partnership contracts at once. Rather than any specific advance in theory, therefore, but by this stated recognition of the investor's right to insist on the insurance, plus an acceptance of a high rate of return to the capitalist, together with an insistence on the contract's spiritual and temporal benefits, Lessius is the most liberal writer to date on this contract; it is a way of reaching a sound commercial result.

Lugo, a Spaniard who spent twenty-two years teaching theology in Rome, and was made a cardinal in 1643, as an economic moralist is subtle, comprehensive, and exhaustive in analysis. St. Alphonsus has described him as the greatest moral theologian after St. Thomas. He uses all Lessius' arguments in the contract's favour, stating that the common opinion is for it. He adds one theoretic refinement in answer to the objection that ownership is transferred and a loan made because the investor is secure against any injuries to his investment. Lugo replies that whether the merchant carries out the agreement or not, he will be bound to pay the investor, so that the investor will suffer no direct harm by the neglect of his right; but this does not destroy the fact that he has a right and consequently remains owner, and not lender, of the property. The leading scholastic moralists of the golden age of usury analysis, therefore, support the triple contract. As Noonan maintains:

> "Lugo's refinements are the nice speculations of a theorist; Molina is shrewder and on stronger ground; Lessius shows the contract's easy application to business practice. All three are witnesses to the need for this intricate analysis as a way of justifying commercial credit."[67]

During the centuries, however, in which the scholastic theory was undergoing extensive modification at the hands of the scholastics themselves, a powerful movement was developing in European intellectual centres to abandon the scholastic theory altogether. As the fate of the scholastic theory in modern times and modern evaluations of it were to be largely influenced by this new movement, it is

---

[67]*Ibid.*, p.225.

appropriate to consider what other influences were around during the sixteenth century. As Noonan points out, the practical differences between the developed scholastic theory and the new theory of usury are not, perhaps, very great; but the theoretical differences are substantial.

The Non-Scholastics: Calvin – a Counter theory?

The yoke of authority was broken by the Reformation – perhaps it is not surprising that in the freer atmosphere of Protestantism the binding strictures on usury should be cast off. This did not take place without some opposition, however. Martin Luther preached eloquently against the practice, feeling keenly as a son of the people the oppression at the hands of the nobles and the rich city merchants which eventually led to the peasants' revolt. There was also his Christian fury against the Jewish usurers who ensnared his fellow-believers, and his zeal for moral reform tended to swing him back to the strictest standards of the early Church Fathers. In 1540, he called on ministers to preach against usury. However, he did concede that where the participants were not poor, rent charged on land and interest that compensates for actual loss (*damnum emergens* and *lucrum cessans*), provided the charge is moderate, could be allowed. It was left to Calvin, however, to open the flood gate, and that without any such intention on his part. His standpoint was actually the same as his contemporaries.

The Reformers were no longer bound by the canon law, although they were still bound by a vigorous tradition of Christian opposition to usury. John Calvin (1509-1564), the Protestant leader to make the most notable contribution to a new theory, abandons the detailed analysis of the scholastics to urge one general principle – follow the 'Golden Rule.' Accordingly usury must be re-defined. It is sinful only if it hurts one's neighbour. Biting usury which sucks the life blood of another while the usurer runs no risk will always be condemned by God's law; but a modest profit on a loan under any circumstance is by no means forbidden. The only arguments against taking profit on a loan are drawn from Scripture. Of these, Calvin maintains that Luke 6:35 had been twisted from its real sense. It merely commands generous lending to the poor. Jesus merely wished to correct the vicious custom of the world whereby men readily lent to the rich who could pay back, and not to the poor. Deut. 23:19 was political. The passages in the Old Testament are to be interpreted as requiring only the observance of charity and equity toward the poor, or, if they are to be interpreted more strictly, they still may be considered only as positive political law appropriate for the Jewish economy, but no longer binding today.[68] As for Aristotle's argument that money is sterile, Calvin has only contempt for it: when money buys a field, from which is yielded a yearly revenue, money then bears money. Interest also proceeds from money as naturally as rent from a field or house.

However, at the same time that Calvin attacks the general usury prohibition, he is not giving it indiscriminate approval, nor will he condone it as a trade; moderate usury is necessary for business, but it would be better if all usury were abolished. He lays down several important reservations: the taking of even moderate usury should never be made one's occupation; all habitual usurers are to be expelled from the church of God and the well-ordered state; usury is never to be taken from the poor; it should never exceed the legal limit and often should not even be as great; the word of God, and not custom, should guide the lender; the lender should have no greater profit from the loan than the borrower; and ministers of the gospel, if they must make investments, should lend only to merchants and in such a way that their profit is not

---

[68]Jean Calvin, "Consilia, De ususris," in *Opera,* Vol. X.cols. 248-249.

certain.[69] Calvin wrote to Ecolampadius his guarded opinion. He hesitated to make any concessions, feeling that on the one hand, to condemn usury altogether was to impose stricter restrictions than even God himself desired, and on the other hand, that if he yielded an inch, some would take a mile. And exactly what he feared happened.

Even though Calvin is not enthusiastic about taking usury, indeed he makes a strong attack on the interest titles allowed by the scholastics, a world eager for commercial freedom found it convenient to drop Calvin's qualifications, while his concessions were seized on as an authority for a new standard. Calvin, therefore, does mark a new approach to the usury problem in two ways: firstly, in denying an absolute divine prohibition on all usury; and, secondly, in suggesting that money be identified with the goods it buys. This last point is the essential theoretical one, but it is only suggested, not developed, in Calvin. It is interesting to note that Calvin has often been regarded as the father of capitalism, mainly because Max Weber based some of his assumptions on the growth of the Protestant ethic and the spirit of capitalism on Calvin's teaching on predestination and election. However, I think this is somewhat misguided with regard to Calvin's actual views. The doctrine of justification by faith is much more at the real heart of Calvin's teaching, as Reid points out. Prosperity is not a sign of an individual's election or sanctification on the part of God. A person is justified through *faith* in Christ. Good works do not produce faith, but faith will produce good works. A believer surrenders his or her life in service to God – for God's glory, which may result in the person becoming wealthy. If s/he does become wealthy it is a gift from God, but if s/he does not become wealthy it is not a sign that s/he is not in grace. God gives his gifts as he wills.

---

[69]Noonan, *op.cit.*, p.366.

"Prosperity is no sign of election or of sanctification. In fact, Calvin
is constantly warning against the seduction of riches. His comments
on Ezekiel 18:7-9 make this very clear, although he is by no means
anti-business. His constant contention is that those who become rich
have a responsibility for the poor. So often those who dislike Calvin
contend that he taught that if one were poor it was because of laziness
which is a sin. But this is far from the truth. Calvin held that people
might be impoverished for various reasons and those who had more
were under obligation to help."[70]

Calvin's doctrine of 'calling' was quite different from that of the Middle
Ages. The medieval thinkers applied calling or vocation to those entering the
priesthood and the religious life, but the Reformers applied it to all human living and
activity – God calls each individual into a certain occupation in life, whatever that
might be. This, according to Weber, opened the door to individualism – long before
Thatcherism. Since man was not dependent on the church, a priesthood, or any other
aid to salvation, but solely on the sovereign electing will of God, he could think of
himself only as an individual, and therefore all his actions would be individual. As
an individual he must work out his own election, that is, his salvation, in and through
his calling. This formed the basis for the Puritan ethos as held by the Puritans in
England, New England, and Holland in the seventeenth century. They were very
self-disciplined, hard-working, and rational in their approach to their 'calling,'
without taking time off for leisure or personal enjoyment. The result was, in
Weberian terms, a 'worldly asceticism,' that furthered the accumulation of money.
Weber maintained that Calvin took the view that the money could not be spent for
personal enjoyment or luxurious living, but must be employed productively in

---

[70]W. Stanford Reid, "Jean Calvin: The Father of Capitalism," (*Themelios*, January, 1983), p.23. I am
very grateful to Dr. Michael Schluter for providing me with a copy of this paper (Nov.9th, 1995).

businesses to increase one's income, and therefore one's capital. At the same time he believed that the Puritans kept wages as low as possible in order to gain a better profit, and that the poor were poor because of their wasteful habits and laziness, and therefore charity for the poor was not to be dispensed with any freedom or generosity. It was thus out of this attitude and perspective on life that capitalism developed in the Industrial Revolution and has come down to our own time,[71] – although now the religious aspects of the ethos have disappeared and it is simply a mad rush for money.

However, Weber completely misrepresented Calvin's thinking on the poor. The plan which Calvin worked out in Geneva for a diaconate to take care of the poor and the sick makes this very clear, as also the fact that Calvin insisted that employees must be given proper and adequate wages. What Weber does not take account of and which, I believe, is of significant importance, is that Calvin had taught that it was not wrong to receive a moderate rate of interest (5%) on loans which were used for business so that money could be lent to others. Calvin, therefore, as Tawney maintains,[72] opened up the way for the taking of interest – although with reservations that were conveniently swept aside – which in turn led to the development of finance capitalism in a way that could not have happened during the Middle Ages. The medieval theory had held that whilst labour was all right for a Christian, commerce was morally dangerous. However, the period from the Reformation down to the opening of the eighteenth century was a period which, while seeing a great extension of business and commerce, also saw a growing separation between religion and

---

[71]Max Weber, *The Protestant Ethic and the Spirit of Capitalism*, (tr. Talcott Parsons, Unwin University Books, London, 1930),pp.79-92; 98-128.

[72]R.H.Tawney, *Religion and the Rise of Capitalism*, Penguin Books, Middlesex, 1922), pp.111ff.

business practice. It would seem that the later seventeenth century capitalists were men who were more influenced in their operations by business expediency than by religious or ethical principles. The economic expansion which had begun by 1500, then began to develop even more rapidly with the invention of the steam engine, and new methods of spinning and weaving and other technological advances which required more capital and skilled labour. The outcome was the Industrial Revolution, which laid the basis for the contemporary economic development and its concurrent problems.

It is not within the remit of this book to detail the causes which brought about the rise of capitalism. However, I would maintain that it had existed in an embryonic form since the day of the Temple, and I would equally maintain that the teaching with regard to usury was also an important aspect of its development. By the sixteenth century Calvinism undoubtedly played a part – although in the case of his teaching on the usury question it was only through a misrepresentation of his views, and it was in the light of this misreading that 'Calvinism' provided a sense of freedom from the old, often disregarded Roman Catholic strictures. With its stress on one's direct responsibility to Christ as King, it tended to give its adherents a greater sense of freedom and independence from the control of the institutional church. They could act according to their consciences, but this encouraged individualism at a cost to the spirit of community. At the same time Calvin emphasized that the Christian must be honest and fair in all his economic activities. Indeed, it is equally important to note that, according to Troeltsch, Calvin's views could as easily be interpreted as a blueprint for socialism as for capitalism, had not other factors entered the picture.[73]

---

[73]E. Troeltsch, *The Social Teaching of the Christian Churches*, (Vol.2, tr. O. Wyon, Allen and Unwin, London, 1931).

It was not surprising, therefore, that when the theologian had given way to the usury principle, the jurist was ready to rush in and establish the case. Charles du Moulin (Molinaeus, 1500-1566), a distinguished French lawyer, is the first Catholic writer to urge the licitness of moderate usury. He demolished with meticulous detail the old arguments of the canonists, although he is careful not to oppose the Church itself. Though his book was placed on the Index, it was freely republished and circulated widely, especially in the Netherlands, where Reformation principles were spreading and commerce was developing. The hardiest defense of usury yet undertaken was made in 1630 by a Calvinist classicist, Claude Saumaise (Salmasius, 1588-1653). While Calvin had been reluctant to admit usury of any kind, and Molinaeus had at least forbidden it on loans to the poor, Salmasius enters a ringing defense of the most despised of all usurers, the licensed, public moneylenders who drew their profits from the poor. His works are principally directed against the illogic of the Calvinist communities which would not condemn usury outright, but which persisted in excluding professional usurers from communion.[74]

His general position is that selling the use of money is a business like any other business. If it is licit to make money with things bought with money, why is it not licit to make money from money? The seller of bread is not asked whether he sells to a poor man or a rich man, why should the usurer? The moneylender performs a very useful service, as does anyone who provides a means for meeting a great public need, and since he is licensed by the State, he must therefore have the State's approval. The question to be asked was: is there any law against usury? Salmasius argues that in the Bible it is true that Jews were forbidden to take usury from any

---

[74]Noonan, *op.cit.*, p.370.

other Jew, poor or rich. But its prohibition was political, and given chiefly because Jews were united in a blood brotherhood. After the destruction of the Jewish state, argues Salmasius, it no longer held. As for the gospel, Jesus Christ means to teach nothing of civil polity or economic transactions. The only ecclesiastical law against usury that Salmasius knows of is the papal law, and why should anyone obey the Pope? In Salmasius, all religious scruple against usury is brushed aside, and the secular law alone sets a limit to profits.

Up to the middle of the eighteenth century, however, no Catholic author had been able to expound the Calvinist theory of the licitness of moderate usury without his orthodoxy being challenged. Now Scipio Maffei, a Veronese count and a friend of the reigning Pope Benedict XIV issued a defense of usury based on the Calvinist position. His main theses had all been stated before in Calvin, Molinaeus, and Salmasius: the Old Testament prohibited usury only from the poor; the New Testament simply required one to be charitable in a general way; the Fathers and Councils only condemned excessive usury; the only usury condemned by any law is usury that hurts one's neighbour; money is not sterile but the instrument of business, and therefore fruitful; loans at interest are necessary for commerce; and the State not only tolerates, but actively enforces, loans at usury; usury is already permitted by the personal *census*, the triple contract and *lucrum cessans*, which are understood broadly to include the loss of all future investment opportunity. The natural law argument, Maffei asserts, is that ownership passes in a loan, but he denies that this happens. The lender is still the owner because he can still bequeath or donate the value of the loan. He alienates only the physical quantity, not the value of the money.[75] Therefore, if the lender is still the owner, he can collect rent, as any owner does on property given to another for use.

There are, therefore, as Noonan points out, three great theoretical differences between the scholastic and the non-scholastic positions. The scholastics assert that all usury is condemned by the divine law, while their opponents assert that only uncharitable or illegal usury is condemned. The scholastics analyze the loan contract on the basis of the equality of the objects exchanged, while their opponents consider the person of the parties to the loan, and the benefits they subsequently receive. The scholastics treat the chief object of loans – money, as bare cash, while their opponents identify it with capital.[76]

According to Noonan, under certain economic conditions, these theoretical differences might lead to substantial practical differences, but here they do not, mainly because the scholastics teach that the divine and the natural prohibition of usury is only on profit taken without just title on a loan contract, and they are able to find a multiplicity of titles and contracts by which profit may be received. For example, compensation for a lender's lack of use of his money in an expanding economy becomes identical with paying him for the use of his money. Actually the developed scholastic theory and its critics agree in approving the same act, and their only real and common opponent is the early scholastic theory with its arbitrary restrictions. There is, however, a difference in connotation and attitude between the scholastics and their opponents. The scholastics begin with a general prohibition and find the exceptions; their opponents begin with a general permission and make restrictions. There are also still reservations and restrictions on the scholastic side.

---

[75] *Ibid.*, p.373.

[76] *Ibid.*, p.375.

They had not as yet approved the full development of the interest titles to the general right to charge for the lack of the use of one's money, although the implicit personal *census* and implicit triple contract came to the same thing. At this stage, however, it would be perhaps impossible to think of a transaction involving the extension of credit at a moderate profit which could not have been justified in terms of the revised scholastic analysis.

The Usury Position 1700-1850

An overview of the development of political economy in the first half of the eighteenth century on the question of usury, or interest, as it is now referred to, will be dealt with, in order to move toward an understanding of the Christian perspective advocated by the 'Victorian Christian Socialists' from the middle of the nineteenth century.

Economic thought in England developed briskly in the first half of the eighteenth century. The economic writings of David Hume (1711-76) are important as a synthesis of economic thought prior to Adam Smith. In his essay *'Of Interest'* (1752) Hume began by stating the well-accepted doctrine that a low rate of interest was the surest sign of the flourishing state of the country's trade. He went on to show as William Petty (*"Political Arithmetick,"* 1690; *"Sir William Petty's Quantulumcumque Concerning Money,"* 1695), John Locke (*"Some Considerations of the Consequences of the Lowering of Interest and Raising the Value of Money,"* 1691) and Dudley North (*"Discourses upon Trade,"* 1691) had done before him, that a low rate of interest was a cause not an effect and, therefore, joined them in opposing state regulation of interest:

> "But he went further than Locke by rejecting the view that a low rate of interest was the result of an abundance of money, although he

admitted that both occurred together. Among the factors which determined the rate of interest he distinguished first of all, as North had already done, the supply and demand of borrowers and lenders. A high rate of interest would, he thought, be caused by 'a great demand for borrowing' and 'little riches to supply that demand.'"[77]

Hume's recognition of self-interest and the desire for accumulation as the driving force of economic activity in his time helped to establish him as one of the foremost exponents of the new economy and an important pre-Smithonian economist. With regard to the whole question of charging interest, Adam Smith, when he wrote *"The Wealth of Nations"* (1776), did not feel it necessary to discuss the issue of whether interest should exist or not, but what the legal maximum should be:

"In a country, such as Great Britain, where money is lent to government at three percent and to private people upon a good security at four and four and a half, the present legal rate (five percent) is as proper as any for, if a higher legal maximum was permitted, the greater part of the money which was to be lent would be lent to prodigals and projectors, who alone would be willing to give this high interest."[78]

Smith recognised that if a free market in loans was allowed to exist by the state, inefficiencies would arise through loans being concentrated upon the over-

[77]Eric Roll, *op.cit.*, p.120.

[78]Adam Smith, *An Enquiry into the Nature and Causes of The Wealth of Nations*, (1776) eds. R.H.Campbell and A.S.Skinner, (Clarendon Press, Oxford, 1976, Volume 1), p.357.

optimistic or over-indulgent. This argument was subsequently denied by Jeremy Bentham.[79]

By 1780, therefore, the scholastic theory and the counter theory, approaching the usury problem from different theoretical viewpoints, agree in approving the common practice. The scholastic theory is stated in stern negative rules which can still cause doubt for the more scrupulous lender. However, in 1787, a recommendation which would have been no less acceptable to the major critics of the scholastics, than to the scholastics themselves, was made by Jeremy Bentham in a series of letters. It is a plan for a repeal of even the legal limit on usury, and although it had no effect on the scholastic theory in any way, it is a landmark in calling for the most complete abandonment of the old Christian prohibition of usury as well as the scholastic theory.

Bentham takes Salmasius' position that moneylending is a trade like any other, and from this basis argues logically that there is no more reason to suppose that the legislature should determine the proper price of money than it should determine the price of other goods. The government, he assumes, should stay out of business. 'Let every man be free to make his contracts as he will, and if a sane man prefers to pay usury to going without a loan, let him do so without hindrance of the law.' The law as it is, protects no one, but raises the cost of money by exposing lenders to an additional risk and prevents the poor from being assisted. The sources of this foolish and ancient law, Bentham adds, are not hard to discover: a Christian opposition to temporal prosperity; an anti-Semitic distrust of Jewish methods; an ignorant reverance for Aristotle's maxim that money is barren; and a worldly love

---

[79]Paul Mills, *op.cit.*, p.23.

of present pleasure and hatred for the abstemious lender.[80]   These four motives combined to set in motion the whole formidable machinery against usury, vestiges of which still plague Britain today. Bentham dismisses all scruples against usury; usurers are men as honest as other tradesmen. It was entirely inappropriate for the state to intervene and set an artificially low price. The effect of usury laws which fixed a maximum legal rate was that in areas where the regulation could not be enforced, particularly in loans to the poor, actual rates would be forced up to compensate for the risk of prosecution. Bentham maintained that people should not be deprived of the opportunity of paying any rate of interest they saw fit if they need to borrow.

In a series of decisions between 1822-1836, the Holy Office, the Roman congregation charged with the supervision of Catholic doctrine and morals, ended all doubts and practical difficulties by publicly decreeing that the interest allowed by law may be taken by everyone, although both before and after the Holy Office decrees there is considerable theoretical controversy. However, the licitness of the rent of money as a fruitful good, at least in production loans, is asserted. The title of the civil law is revived. The biblical and conciliar prohibitions of usury are explained as prohibitions only of excessive usury and Calvin, Molinaeus, and Maffei become the new authorities. The scholastic defenders of the new theory assert that only in its terms can the general permission to take interest be understood and modern commerce be justified. On the other hand, the champions of the old theory reassert the familiar arguments against all usury, pointing out that the general permission to

---

[80]J. Bentham, "Defence of Usury, 1818," (in *Economic Writings,* ed. W. Stark, G. Allen and Unwin, London,1952), pp. 9-13; 47; 53; 96-106.

take interest can be understood as an extension of the title of *lucrum cessans*, and need involve no adandonment of the old principles.[81]

In the early nineteenth century, partly because of the disruption of the French Revolution and partly because of a general lack of interest in scholastic philosophy, competent scholastic theologians were rare, and great scholastic theologians were non-existent. Consequently, no commanding figure arose to defend the old theory, although since all the weight of traditional authority was on its side, it was still generally accepted. But facile and persuasive writers were urging its abandonment and the acceptance, in greater or lesser degree, of the theory of Calvin and Maffei.

The first of these works pleading for a substantial change in theory is the *"Dissertations sur le pret-de-commerce,"* published by William Cesar, Cardinal de la Luzerne, in 1822. Luzerne attempted to show that no dogma of the Church is at risk by admitting moderate profit on loans to business men and the rich. Pointing out that the marks of a dogma of Catholic faith are that it is defined by a pope or council, or taught universally and with more unanimity by the theologians, he makes an extensive review of papal, conciliar, patristic, and scholastic teaching on usury. This investigation establishes to his satisfaction that the only dogma that can be said to exist on usury is that excessive or oppressive profit on a loan is evil. As to the business loan, he demonstrates that distinct condemnation of it is confined to the scholastics of the thirteenth through to the fourteenth centuries, and by all the tests of dogma, such transient and local opinion cannot be elevated above the rank of positive law. He ascribes the medieval position to the economic conditions of the time, to the tyranny of Aristotle, and to the ignorance of the Fathers. Luzerne's

---

[81]Noonan, *op.cit.*, p.377.

analysis of the origin of the scholastic view, according to Noonan,[82] is not very adequate, and his analysis of the decrees on usury of the medieval Councils is open to dispute, but his is the most successful effort yet to show how part of the old usury prohibition could be treated as positive law without compromising any dogma, and his work thus removed one of the most serious objections to the new theory.

An equally influential and even more enthusiastic advocate of the new theory was the canon, Mark Mastrofini, a member of the papal court, His work, *"Discussion sur l'usure,"* written in 1828 was generally received with admiration in Rome. The work is simply a forceful presentation of the theses sustained by Molinaeus and Maffei. Its most original part is its formulation of their theory in terms of money's 'applicability' – by which Mastrofini means both the power of being able to use money and its actual use. This applicability is separate from money itself and may always be charged for. A worker cannot be asked to work for nothing simply because he is idle. Similarly, nor can a lender with idle funds be asked to surrender their applicability freely. Rejecting the old theory completely, Mastrofini still admits, indeed argues, that he asks for nothing new in practice. *Census,* he says, is simply the term used in Germany for a loan at a profit. The triple contract, the exchange business, and *lucrun cessans* are dependent for their justice on the licitness of renting the use of money.[83]

A little later, in the middle of the century, Francis Funk, a German theologian, and distinguished ecclesiastical historian, also put the weight of scholarship at the service of the new theory. Funk took the position that money in one economy might be considered fruitful, and in another, sterile. In the Middle Ages, he argued, the

---

[82]*Ibid.*, p.383.

[83]*Ibid.*, p.384.

feudal and guild systems restricted the opportunity for investment; ownership of the land was ruled by feudal agreements, while the labour supply was either in feudal vassalage or controlled by the guilds. At the same time, commerce was hampered by war, thieves, and both national and municipal trade barriers. In this static world where land and labour were frozen and capital accumulation difficult, money had no mobility. It could not be freely exchanged for productive goods. It could, therefore, not be considered the equivalent of fruitful capital. Borrowing was usually for consumptive purposes, and the borrower's need gave a lender with idle cash the opportunity to exploit him. The general usury prohibition was based on these general conditions. (Undoubtedly, a small capitalistic class would have had a right to profit on their loans, and their right was destroyed by the general prohibition, but law is made for what happens generally, and here the majority were protected.)

Funk explains the change in practice by a change in economic circumstances. Law, either moral or statutory, which regulates economic activities is necessarily preceded in time by the activities regulated; certain general moral principles are changeless, but their application in particular laws depends on the economic pattern of a society. Such a particular law as one concerned with usury, therefore, does not remain abstractly motionless, but develops with economic changes. Yet as the economic changes must first occur before a change in the law is appropriate, there will always be a natural lag between economic development and modification of the law – as the economic structure of Europe changed, money became capable of widespread fruitful employment, and the Church altered the law to meet the new conditions. The exceptions broadened into general permission, so that with regard to usury, when loans became generally available for production and money was considered fruitful, the Church allowed the taking of interest. Therefore, it is the change in economic circumstances which explains the change in practice, whilst the only dogmatic principle involved is that it is sinful to exploit one's neighbour. This principle remains unaltered, though differently applied in different conditions. However, whilst Funk defends medieval practice, he condemns medieval theory. The early scholastics had protected the needy borrower, but they were right for the wrong reasons.

They proceeded legalistically, using the abstract forms of the Roman law without examining either the economic significance of these concepts or the moral essence of the usury law. Fortunately their theoretical deficiences led to no practical errors, but the proper theoretical approach is set out in the new theory: abandon the legal technicalities of contracts and titles; adopt one general moral principle that no contract should injure an impoverished neighbour; and always consider the economic purpose of a loan.[84] There is neither scriptural nor natural reason for opposing this new approach. The Bible is seen to disapprove only exploitation of the poor. Where money is lent for productive purposes it should be considered a productive good and lawfully rented. The pillars of the old theory no longer stand. The right to interest taken in its old form with the conditions required by the scholastics would not justify many of the economic operations of the present day which are advantageous to everyone, according to Funk, and therefore should be abandoned. The transference of ownership in a loan is a determination of positive, not natural, law, and the sterility of money is no longer true. There is, however, one proviso: when a borrower borrows for consumptive purposes, he is in need, and the money lent is not productive, therefore to charge him for the loan is sinful usury, but Funk's whole attitude implies that the case of pure consumption credit is rare. Money is normally productive, and the rent of it as a fruitful good is licit.

---

[84]F.X.Funk, *Zins und Wucher*, (tr. and referred to in Noonan, *ibid.*, p.386.)

In the face of many defections from the scholastic theory, however, a very able, presentation of the old theory was made at the beginning of the twentieth century by Joseph Ernest Van Roey, then a young theologian, and later cardinal-primate of Belgium, in *"De justo auctario ex contractu crediti."* He vigorously objected to the confusion of money and real capital made by the sponsors of the licitness of the rent of money. The object of a money loan, he stated, is money, not real capital, and to treat a loan as the rent of real capital is a fundamental error in theory. The consumptibility of money, not its productivity, is at the heart of the old analysis, and money's consumptibility is unchanged by its subsequent exchange for real goods. According to Van Roey, modern practice may be understood not as the rent of money, but as the universal claiming of *lucrum cessans.* In the economy of the day, he maintained, every holder of money can employ it profitably, and thus to forego money's use in a loan gives every lender a right to interest. Although practice has changed with economic change, the scholastic principles, which are part of Catholic doctrine, remain unchangeable and equally good in their new application.[85]

However, at the turn of the century, no such firm declaration for the old theory is to be found elsewhere, but rather, a statement of doctrine on usury syncretistic in its approach and reconcilable with either the old or new theory. Thus Adam Tanquerey, a French author of a popular theological textbook, taught that money was, in his day's economy, virtually fecund and could be rented at a profit because the lender always suffered *lucrum cessans* – a statement of the case that in effect combines the two theories. The German Jesuit, Jerome Noldin, declared that money was today readily substitutable for fruitful goods, and therefore anyone surrendering its use deprived himself of an estimable good; here, again, the appeal

---

[85]Joseph Ernest Van Roey, *De justo auctario ex contractu crediti,* (cited in Noonan, *ibid.,* p.389.)

is equally to *lucrum cessans* and to the fecundity of money. At the same time the new theory of usury won a clear victory when the tendency became general to reject the old claim that Luke 6:35 was a strict precept forbidding all profit on a loan, and to take it as a counsel of perfection only.[86]

A final formal step in the acceptance of general interest-taking occurred with the issue in 1917 of the new *Codex iuris canonici*. This replaced all earlier collections of canon law and became the sole statute book of the universal Church. The many complicated responses, decrees, and bulls on usury of the old canon law are now summed up in a single rule:

> "If a fungible thing is given someone, and later something of the same kind and amount is to be returned, no profit can be taken on the ground of this contract; but in lending a fungible thing it is not itself illicit to contract for payment of the profit allocated by law, unless it is clear that this is excessive, or even for a higher profit, if a just and adequate title be present."[87]

Apart from the revival of speculation about the legal title, the Code did not affect usury theory; as two American Jesuits, T.L.Bouscaren and A.C.Ellis, pointed out, the canon 'states implicitly that in modern times there is always present in such a loan some just reason for demanding the legal rate of interest . . . The canon, however, deliberately avoids determining what these just reasons are, leaving that to Catholic moralists and economists to determine.'[88] The canon itself speaks of legal

---

[86]Noonan, *ibid.*, p.390.

[87]*Codex iuris canonici,* Rome 1920, c.1735.

[88]Noonan, *op.cit.*, p.391.

interest which may be excessive and hence immoral, so that it is clearly implied that the law by itself does not create a right to interest.

At the beginning of the twentieth century, therefore, in moving toward a Christian perspective on the usury issue, the general state of opinion remained substantially with syncretist presentations of the usury theory. The usury rule, sapped of its vitality in modern economic conditions, is not abandoned, but so limited in the likelihood of its applicability that profit on credit transactions is made the norm, and usury the exceptional case of unjust exaction. As for canonist doctrine itself, as Roll points out, its teachings were steadily weakened with commercial expansion until it was faced with the complete collapse of its power to regulate economic life.[89] After the Reformation the Church was no longer able to stand in the way of the growth of commercial capitalism, and whether Protestant and Puritan doctrines were themselves conducive to the development of the capitalist spirit is an area of discourse, already much debated, which is not totally relevant to this book. I have maintained that it found its embryonic form as a result of the Judaic teaching on usury. What is important is that the harmony between Church dogma and feudal society, between theological and economic thought, responsible for the all-embracing quality of the Canon Law, came to an end with the decline of feudal society. This harmony had enabled the institutionalized Church, with its spiritual and secular power, to claim the right to order the whole of human relations and conduct on this earth as well as to provide the precepts which would lead to spiritual salvation. But:

> "Canonist thought was essentially an ideology, in economic matters it was an illusory representation of reality. It was successful so long as the conflicts of reality had not become very acute. With the

---

[89]Eric Roll, *op.cit.*, p.53.

sharpening of these conflicts, the antithetical elements in this ideology were seized upon by the contending parties, and the original universal character was lost . . . A separation was effected by which religious dogma ceased to represent an analysis of existing society as well as a code of conduct . . .Though attempts were again to be made to introduce ethical elements into the main stream of economic thought, it remains henceforth independent of religion. The foundation for a secular science of economy was laid."[90]

As Trevelyan sums it up – in the Middle Ages men thought and acted corporately. The place of every man was fixed by his place in some community – manor, borough, guild, learned university, or convent:

"The villein and the monk scarcely existed in the eye of the law except through the lord of the manor and the abbot of the monastery. As a human being, or as an English subject, no man had 'rights' either to employment or the vote, or indeed to anything beyond a little Christian charity. The unit of medieval society was neither the nation nor the individual but something between the two – the corporation."[91]

Only in the later age of the Renaissance and the Reformation, after the emancipation of the villeins had shattered the economic system on which the feudal world rested, was it possible to take another step forwards to personal freedom. Then indeed many of the medieval corporations went down before the omnipotent State on the one hand and the self-assertive individual on the other. The monastries and orders of the friars disappeared from England, and the town corporations and guilds saw their more important functions divided between the individual and the State. But

[90]*Ibid.*, p.53.

[91]G.M.Trevelyan, *History of England*, [Longman Group Ltd., London, (first edition1926) 1973 edition], p.212.

some medieval institutions survived unimpaired. The secular clergy, the lawyers and the universities adapted themselves to the service of the new nation, and the 'House of Commons,' where the 'commons' or 'communities' of the realm were represented, became the chief organ of the national life.[92]   Important as these developments were, however, it never deterred attempts to address the thought of the Church on economic issues in terms of justice for the poor.

It is necessary, therefore, to focus finally on the efforts of social Christianity to engage in an appraisal and practical theological application of the usury issue during the last one hundred years. This has been interpreted in terms of low-cost credit and debt finance, especially with regard to justice for the poor, and in providing the means for both individual and collective economic improvement within communities. It was marked, originally, by experimentation in 'associationism' and the development of 'co-operative banking.' For the Christian Church the horns of the Deuteronomic dilemma have been blunted, and the *spirit* of Luke 6:35 has replaced it: "But love ye your enemies, and do good, and lend, hoping for nothing again." (RSV) An incarnational theology was developing where Christ was seen to be in all human beings, as all human beings were in Christ. This symbolized 'Christian economic man' at the turn of the century.

Christian Socialism: 'Unsocial Christians and Unchristian Socialists' – Experiments in 'Associationism' and Co-operative Banking

In moving toward an understanding of the concept of usury within the Judaeo/Christian tradition, it has been necessary to take into account the multiple character of its foundations: theological, economic, legal, political and social, as well

---

[92]*Ibid.*, p.213.

as the multiple aspects it presented in practice, especially the aspects under which it encouraged the growth of interest titles and above all the use of alternative methods of credit besides the loan. From 1450-1750 the analysts engaged in an attempt, mainly with the use of legal concepts, to adjust the letter of the old law to changed economic circumstances, and with the growth of trade to adopt a new willingness to consider the commercial lender's viewpoint. The theoretical structure they erected was not a consistent piece but it encouraged risk-sharing investment and charity to the poor. It was within this structure at the end of the nineteenth century that 'Christian socialism' evolved as an early response to the forces of urbanisation and industrialisation in Great Britain.

With the acceptance of the modern day understanding of 'usury' as an exorbitant rate of interest, and 'interest' itself accepted into the fabric of economic life, the usury debate has evolved into the issue of how to incorporate the principles of low-cost credit and debt finance, and the concept of justice, into the structure of poverty stricken communities and societies of the disadvantaged. That is not to deny, however, the possibilities for the existence of an interest-free banking system, according to theological principles, and I shall examine this in my next chapter. I conclude this chapter with an analysis of how the practical application of the 'usury' issue, as it is now perceived, has been employed by social Christianity within the previous one hundred years in Great Britain, particularly in terms of 'associationism' and co-operative banking methodology, and posit the question: where do we go from here?

As far as the Christian socialism of the nineteenth century in Great Britain is concerned, its answer lay in its view of humanity, and an incarnational theology. Its broad Christian humanitarianism was related to a belief in Christ as immanent in the world, and in eternal life as relationship with him. Theological learning was important and the great prophet of the new attitudes was an Anglican clergyman, Frederick Maurice. "The truth is," he observed, "that every man is in Christ; the condemnation of every man is, that he will not own the truth."[93] There were no reservations about Maurice's doctrine of humanity and it unified all the Christian socialists of the century behind a liberating appraisal of the possibility of the betterment of mankind.[94]

The 'Christian Socialists' of Victorian England produced a radical departure from the received attitudes of the Church both in their religious and their social contentions, although their 'socialism' was not especially either 'political' or 'Socialist.'[95] In 1848 Maurice met with Charles Kingsley, also an Anglican clergyman, and John Ludlow, a lawyer, to plan a Christian response to the events of the Chartism of the day, the revolution in France, and anxious to promote 'associationism,' co-operative enterprises, as a means of releasing working men from the effects of the economic competitive system. Symptomatic of this origin was the group's description of themselves as Christian socialists. The title emerged when Maurice was discussing with Ludlow a new series of tracts for working people:[96]

> "We must have something special to tell them, or we ought not to speak. 'Tracts on Christian Socialism' is, it seems to me, the only title which will define our object, and will commit us at once to the

---

[93]Frederick Maurice, *The Life of Frederick Denison Maurice*, (Macmillan, London, second edition,1884), volume 1, p.155.

[94]Edward Norman, *The Victorian Christian Socialists*, (Cambridge University Press, 1987), p.7.

[95]*Ibid.*, p.1.

[96]It is interesting to note that at this time the majority of working people, if they were Christians, belonged to the non-conformist chapels rather than to the established church; thus, while religion helped to hold society together, it also mirrored and perhaps reinforced class structure.

conflict we must engage in sooner or later with the unsocial Christians and the unchristian Socialists."[97]

Co-operative enterprise had in fact preceded the 'Christian Socialists' – there were the experiments of Robert Owen in the 1830's, and the Rochdale Pioneers in 1844. Robert Owen was a Welshman who worked in Scotland. He was born in 1771 and in 1800 he bought the New Lanark cotton mills near Glasgow, and as a capitalist entrepreneur ran them profitably, paying good wages and establishing a miniature 'welfare state' with education for the children, medical care, housing and welfare benefits. It marked a radical departure from *laissez-faire* capitalism. Owen challenged capitalism on four fronts: its industrial organisation; by a visionary community; through a trades union movement; and through a consumers' organisation. All that survived of Owen's schemes was the co-operative movement – an organisation that bought goods wholesale, retailed them to its members at prevailing prices, and distributed the profits to consumers in proportion to their purchases. His followers founded the Rochdale Co-operative Society.[98]

It is well known that *consumer* co-operatives originated in Britain with the first co-operative store started by the Society of Equitable Pioneers in Toad Lane, Rochdale in 1844. It is not so well known that it was the pioneers' intention to earn a surplus from the store and use it to promote *production* co-operatives. They launched a textile mill, the Rochdale Co-operative Manufacturing Society in 1854, but this fell victim to its own success. It put shares on the market to raise money for expansion and was bought up by outsiders. By the turn of the century there were

---

[97]Quoted in *Social Christianity*, ed. John Atherton, (SPCK, London, 1994), p.13.

[98]See John Vaizey, *Revolutions of our Time: Social Democracy*, (Weidenfeld and Nicholson Ltd., London, 1971), pp.20-25.

about one hundred worker co-operatives in Britain, but they were the poor relations of the movement. They were outnumbered by the consumer co-operatives, and at a congress in the 1880's a proposal that these should give membership rights and shareholdings to their own employees was rejected. It was left to Mondragon in Spain to create, many years later, a joint co-operative of consumer and workers. The model of this movement I address in my conclusion.[99]

By the early 1850's Edward Vansittart Neale (a rather enigmatic and introspective nephew of William Wilberforce) was emerging as the most important figure within the Christian Socialist Movement. The ideals preached by Owen had already generated a considerable amount of activity in the North of England, and while Neale and his friends struggled to establish self-governing workshops in London, co-operative stores were almost effortlessly multiplying within the industrial areas of Lancashire and the West Riding of Yorkshire. Northern co-operators followed the lucrative example of the Equitable Pioneers in Rochdale. Their retail store successfully attracted member-customers by providing them with periodical dividends proportionate to purchases. Neale was almost alone among the 'Christian Socialists' in appreciating the economic and social significance of this development.[100] His vision was that co-operative stores by acting collectively could serve as practical foundation stones upon which to build a movement capable of changing the mode of production:

---

[99]Hans Wiener with Robert Oakeshott, *Worker-Owners: Mondragon Revisited*, (Anglo-German Foundation, London, 1987), p.56.

[100]Philip Backstrom, *Christian Socialism and Co-operation in Victorian England: Edward Vansittart Neale and the Co-operative Movement*, (Croom Helm Ltd., London, 1974), p.3.

"If the stores continued to multiply, formed wholesale centres, and synchronized their individual efforts by joining together in a broadly based co-operative union, they would, in effect, be creating a great new market of their own while accumulating enormous profits. The implications were obvious: given possession of both the necessary capital and a controlled, reliable market, they could launch producers' co-operatives with full assurance of success. Private enterprises, lacking those advantages, would be gradually squeezed out of existence, unable to compete."[101]

This was Neale's vision, but he knew that it could never materialise in the absence of central co-ordinating institutions serving practical functions. He, therefore, played a most prominent part in building up the main federal organs which constituted the heart of the modern Co-operative Movement: the Co-operative Wholesale Society (CWS), the Insurance Society, the *Co-operative News*, and especially the Co-operative Union. He also initiated a banking society – the Co-operative Freehold Land, Building and Investment Society. Neale had found the establishment of 'people's banks' by Dr.Schulze-Delitzsch, firstly in Germany then also in Austria, Italy and Belgium, initially appealing. These organisations, like co-operatives, were originally designed to enable the working classes to accumulate their own capital for use in the establishment of self-governing workshops and other co-operative associations. However, Neale did agree that people's banks, as well as co-operative stores, would prove inadequate if taken as ends in themselves – if labourers failed to use them as a means to implement larger ideals. Co-operative banks would promote voluntary union for self-help, and when universally applied Neale's view was that this principle was capable of bringing about permanent social reform. Banks and stores served a valuable intermediate function by facilitating the

---

[101]*Ibid.*, p.3.

accumulation of a 'collective fund' that could 'convert capital from the master of labour into its servant.'[102] Neale worked towards establishing uniformity by bringing together the many separate co-operative associations under common operating procedures and constitutional rules. In terms of the usury issue, this is seen as an attempt to provide low-cost banking facilities and profit-sharing for member/customers.

It is an interesting point that in his biography on Neale, Philip Backstrom concludes that just as Owen may be referred to as the father of co-operative ideology in Britain, so Neale should take his rightful place as the father of 'Co-operation.' However, he was surprised by one fact. He did not expect to find information to detract from the popular view that British Co-operation was an exemplary Victorian working class movement which had always been unquestionably democratic. Backstrom found, however, that he had to take a thoroughly revisionist position. It was perplexing to discover that the familiar models used by historians when forming concepts about 'working class' men and movements could not be readily applied to Co-operation, indeed, although the working men were the primary patrons and dividend-receiving members of the co-operative stores, it is questionable whether the overall efforts of the co-operative consumers actually added up to a 'working class movement' at all. Was the average co-operative store, in fact as well as theory, a successful example of working class democracy?

Shortly before his death Neale realised that Co-operation's central organisations, painstakingly devised to bring about social change, were unsuited to the task. The stores had hoped to accumulate capital for use in advancing the cause of Socialism, the objective being the establishment of utopian communities:

---

[102] *Ibid.*, p.61.

"But burgeoning wealth generated indifference and their original ideal was soon reduced to rhetorical cant, while reality came to be enumerated more crudely in terms of pounds, shillings and pence: it is common knowledge that Co-operation was so successful as a consumers' movement that most of its leaders abandoned their community building socialism to become shopkeeping capitalists . . . the CWS became a self-perpetuating bureaucratic machine which was economically conservative and ideologically inflexible, and within the shadow of its narrowly materialistic influence the entire Co-operative Movement was gradually transformed into a great impersonal business enterprise."[103]

Perhaps this outcome was inevitable. As Backstrom points out, within the context of socialism's economic model a working man is unique only in his productive functions; as a consumer he loses his special class identity and his objectives are almost certain to reflect the prevailing mode of production in society. John Ludlow had predicted as early as 1851 that it was dangerous to place too much emphasis on the co-operative store, predicting that when the old co-operative spirit was lost, and the middle man had finally been eliminated, 'the opposition of interest between producer and consumer would be exhibited in its naked form.'[104] By the late 1870's most of the important committee men in the Northwest were thoroughly indoctrinated with the idea of the bourgeoisie, and it is difficult to establish the degree to which the working masses themselves were speaking through the medium of the Co-operative Movement. It is a rather sad indictment that Neale and his idealistic friends, the 'Christian Socialists,' who were perjoratively called 'individualists' and described as anachronistic and utopian, were in reality the

---

[103]*Ibid.*, p.6-7.

[104]Quoted in Backstrom, *ibid.*, p.7.

authentic heroes of the working class. Their failure as 'Christian Socialists' within the Co-operative Movement was in fact a great loss, and by the 1870's was not, by then, in any sense an expression of 'Christian Socialism.'

However, the spirit of 'social Christianity' and 'co-operation' lived on and this model of enterprise was in time exported to almost every country in the world. It now takes many forms with widely-differing applications. I shall return to this model in my conclusion, but to suggest that a co-operative is simply just another type of business is to miss the whole point, because if the sole objective is to maximise return on capital invested, there is no reason to form a co-operative. It could be said that co-operatives exist simply out of enlightened self-interest; but equally, they are democratic organisations specifically committed to generating wealth for the benefit of their members – and therefore, the wider community, by conducting their affairs with total integrity. The preoccupation with members' interests and involvement distinguishes co-operative enterprises from other forms of associations. Co-operation arose from the need of the people to help themselves and each other because neither the state nor the market could, or would, supply what they wanted on acceptable terms, if at all. In that respect co-operatives are 'bottom-up' organisational structures as opposed to the 'top down' hierarchy of conventional businesses, and in the beginning they were imbued with Christian socialist ideals.

Early 'Christian Socialism' was rooted, therefore, as Maurice had maintained, in fundamental beliefs about God and his relationship to humanity; and although Neale has been described as having discarded for a time a religious basis, there was a sense that for his entire life he clung to the warmer pietistic fervour and socially dynamic side of Evangelicalism with "a sense of oneness with God, an inner harmony, and a deep belief in the Messianic promise of a new Millennium."[105] Neale's vision had been to end the injustice of divisive individualism in favour of communitarianism, and although the first stage of Christian Socialism finished sharply in 1854 its influence was so great that it provided a stimulus and continuity to social Christianity across a gap of twenty years running into the 1870's to 1890's, a period marred by deep economic recession.[106]

The re-emergence of organised radical 'Christian Socialism' owed much to the achievements of Stewart Headlam and his Guild of St.Matthew (1877-1909). His creative sacramental socialism stimulated the interpretation of the immanence of God through contemporary realities:

> "Accordingly, baptism became the means of entry into the greatest democratic and egalitarian society in the world, and 'the mass was the weekly meeting of a society of rebels against a Mammon-worshipping world order.' So the secular was used to interpret Christianity, rather than a version of socialism chosen to fit it. The development of incarnational theology was continuing apace. From Maurice's belief that all people were in Christ, and the consequence of making no distinction between sacred and secular, Headlam sought to seek the illumination of God's purposes through such secular means as socialism and the London County Council's education policies."[107]

For Headlam and his colleagues, the Church was expected to live the life of brotherhood as an agent of enabling society as a whole to express the same. The

---

[105] *Ibid.*, p.24.

[106] In fact the concept of 'unemployment' was first used in the 1870's – see M.B.Reckitt, *Maurice to Temple: A Century of the Social Movement in the Church of England*, (Faber, London, 1947), chapter 5.

[107] John Atherton, ed., *op.cit.*, p.17.

strong reaction against *laissez-faire* capitalism as competition and individualism was still a formative influence, but the emphasis was increasingly on working within the existing system. It was an exercise in its modification rather than its transformation. The clarification of Christian social reform took place, therefore, in relation to changes in the wider context, for example, 1889 saw the disruption of the great dock strike, but also witnessed the publication of two influential books. *"The Fabian Essays"* reflected the belief that Socialism was but the next step in the development of society; and *"Lux Mundi"* expressed a powerful Christian engagement with the contemporary context. Focused on the incarnation, and the fruit of 'the Holy Party,'[108] it tried to relate traditional Christian belief to advances in science, philosophy and biblical criticism for the Catholic faith. There also arose in the same year the Anglican Christian Social Union which again, based on incarnational theology, sought to apply the moral truths and principles of the Christian religion to the social and economic difficulties of the time. Denominations had their own Christian socialist organisations, such as John Clifford and the Baptist's Christian Socialist League (1894-98) and the Friends Social Union of 1904. By the 1900's, therefore, the Christian socialist critique was lodging itself effectively enough in the mind of the Church. Compared with 1850 it was a remarkable change, and symbolized Maurice's concern to 'socialize' the Church.[109]

From the end of World War I to the end of World War II the tradition of Christian social reform in Britain was affected in substantial ways by dramatic theological developments on the European continent and the United States, in a

---

[108]The Holy Party began to meet in 1875, and included Henry Scott Holland and Charles Gore. It continued to have a summer working retreat until 1915. The subtitle of *"Lux Mundi"* was "A Series of Studies on the Incarnation." John Atherton, ed., *ibid.*, f.n.28, p.46.

[109]*Ibid.*, p.19.

period which was dominated by a great economic depression and by international crises marking the rise of fascism and Stalinism. The influence of the neo-orthodoxy of Karl Barth and Emil Brunner, and the theological realism of Reinhold Niebuhr and John Bennett, gradually replaced the optimism of early Christian socialism with a more realistic understanding of power, sin, and the associated importance of justice.

During the 1940's and 1950's, set in the context of the growth of the Welfare State and social market economy, and the cold war between the two competing ideologies of capitalism and communism, social Christianity made little progress in Britain. Biblical theology, the reform of canon law, the promotion of local church worship and community, and the increasing moral absorption with international, military, and personal issues, diverted attention from matters of political economy. The late 1960's and 1970's, however, witnessed a decisive change of climate as Keynesian economics[110] and the corporate state ran into the major problems of high unemployment and inflation, and public finance. It was during this period that the first credit unions were set up in Britain – in 1964 in Wimbledon in England, and in Drumchapel in Scotland in 1970.[111] Credit unions are co-operatives. The setting up and running of community credit unions is governed by two Acts of Parliament: the Industrial and Provident Societies Act of 1965 and 1978, and the Credit Union Act of 1979. Credit unions are self-help organisations which are established to provide loans at low rates of interest to the poor. They are significant structures for providing

---

[110]Keynesian economics' main policy implication is that government fiscal policy is needed to restore full employment whenever the economy shows signs of settling down into equilibrium with substantial unemployment. See R.S. Lipsey, Positive Economics, (Oxford University Press, Oxford, 1989), p.696

[111]See *The Community Credit Union Handbook*, p.4. I am very grateful to Ms. Jackie Burns working for the social strategy unit in Aberdeen for providing me with this material.

low cost finance, addressing the concept of 'usurious loans' in the modern age. I therefore consider their potential in greater detail in my conclusion.

The arrival of Margaret Thatcher in 1979 as leader of neoconservatism in government, challenged this postwar consensus of welfarism and Keynesian economics. 'Thatcherism' provoked the Churches into a sharper defence and elaboration of the social reformist interpretation of modern trends; and official church opinion on social affairs, in denominational and ecumenical bodies, has continued to be dominated by Christian social reformism. The 1980's reports *"Faith in the City"* (Anglican), *"Mission Alongside the Poor"* (Methodist), and *"Just Sharing"* (Church of Scotland) exemplify this approach.[112]

The renewed interest in social Christianity can be found in the writings of Ronald Preston and his Christian comment on complex economic and social issues. His social comment on the contemporary context is characterized by discerning judgments advocating a mixed welfare-state economy which avoids the grave deficiencies of *laissez-faire* capitalism and state socialism. He argues strongly against moving directly from the Bible or natural law. Instead he advocates the use of a more indirect way of promoting a reciprocal relationship between Christian insights and empirical trends. His development of middle axioms symbolizes this commitment.[113]

---

[112]John Atherton, ed., *op.cit.*, p.21.

[113]'Middle axioms' was a term first used by J.H.Oldham in 1937. They have been interpreted in various ways. Ronald Preston argues that "The formulating of middle axioms is the central task of practical theology . . . if it is to be coherent in understanding the historic situation of modern Christianity and its practical implications . . . Middle axioms, however, are not concerned with universal situations but with current ones; and in a descending order of particularity from global to national, regional and local situations . . . Is it possible for the churches to provide some guidelines based upon some broadly agreed interpretation of the many and confusing movements, crises and causes which jostle in the public forum? . . . If churches co-operatively wish to develop middle axioms in any area they must get together a group of people from relevant disciplines and from those

It is within this definition of 'middle axioms,' therefore, that I turn to examine the religious teaching found within the Islamic tradition on usury, in order to see if an empirical investigation of another theological discipline could provide a different economic model in the market place concerned with justice for the poor. If the concept of 'usury' as exorbitant interest is so readily accepted in the West now, and the use of interest as a legal entity is built into the law,[114] is there any banking or economic system which could implement the Judaic and early Christian notion of interest-free loans with a view to a fairer redistribution of wealth, or wealth creation, and help for the poor? Can, for example, the ethical teaching in respect of usury of another great monotheistic religion – Islam – provide a paradigm for the rest of the world to adopt as we move into the twenty-first century with its concept of Islamic Banking facilities? How has this tradition responded to the teaching on *'riba'* in its Holy Scripture: the Qur'an?

---

who have practical experience of the issues . . . to work on the matter . . . It is possible that as a result of this co-operative work broad agreement may be reached in suggesting in what direction it is possible to foster change, whilst those who agree on this may differ on the precise policies by which it should be fostered . . . We need not prescribe precisely how it should proceed, or expect an agreed terminology . . . The essential point is that it moves from the relatively more certain ground of faith, and 'principles' derived from it, to the less relatively certain ground of empirical analysis and evaluation of 'facts' and trends; and that it attempts to lessen the relativity by seeking by co-operation a consensus at the middle level . . . This procedure roots social theology firmly in the realities of the world today. Indeed one of the advantages of a continuous process of developing them is that it forces the churches to keep up to date." See Ronald Preston, *Church and Society in the Late Twentieth Century: The Economic and Political Task*, (SCM Press, London, 1983), appendix 2, pp.141-156.

[114]In the UK under the Consumer Credit Act of 1974, it is legal to charge any rate of interest as long as it is not proven in court to have been extortionate in the circumstance.

Chapter Three

Toward an Islamic Understanding of Usury

'*Riba*': Qur'anic Sources and Definitions

This chapter will address the problem – in so far as one defines it as a 'problem' – of the prohibition on usury to be found in the Qur'an, the 'Holy Book' of the third (chronological as opposed to hierarchical) great monotheistic tradition – that of Islam. Here, usury is called '*riba*[1],' and is unequivocally forbidden. How this is interpreted within the Islamic tradition, in terms of the 'brother,' i.e. the Islamic community (*ummah*), and also in terms of the 'other' (non-Islamic community) will be discussed. The premise that Islam may be able to offer an alternate form of finance, a workable solution in terms of supplying *riba*-free banking facilities to present day communities, will also be explored, in order to work toward an Islamic understanding of the concept of 'usury' as interpreted at the time of Muhammad, throughout the history of Islam, and in the context of present day Islamic society and its place in the world.

The prohibition of *riba* appears in the Qur'an in four different revelations. The Qur'anic sources are quoted below in the order in which they appear in the Qur'an, but, chronologically, Surah xxx.39, is the first of these revelations, and is dated to the Meccan period, six or seven years before the *hijrah*, when Muhammad was still living among a trading community. It emphasized that while interest

---

[1]The word '*riba*' is derived from the root r.b.w., meaning to increase, grow, or augment.

deprived wealth of God's blessings, charity increased it. The second revelation, Surah iii.130, experienced in Medina, around the second or third year after *hijrah*, enjoined Muslims to keep away from *riba* if they desired their own well-being; and the third, Surah iv.161, is also dated to the early Medina period, most probably revealed in the fourth year after *hijrah*.[2] It severely condemned *riba*, in line with its prohibition in the previous scripture, and it placed those who took it in juxtaposition with those who wrongfully appropriated other people's possessions. The fourth revelation, Surah ii.275-280, (verses which belong to the last months before the death of the Prophet, Muhammad[3]) severely censured those who engaged in *riba*. It established a clear distinction between *riba* and trade, instructing 'believers' to take only the principal amount due, and forego even this in the case of a borrower's hardship:[4]

> "Those that live on usury (*riba*) shall rise up before God like men whom Satan has demented by his touch; for they claim that trading is no different from usury. But God has permitted trading and made usury unlawful. He that has received an admonition from his Lord and mended his ways may keep his previous gains; God will be his judge. Those that turn back shall be the inmates of the Fire, wherein they shall abide forever. God has laid His curse on usury and blessed alms-giving (*zakat*) with increase. God bears no love for the impious and the sinful. Those that have faith and do good works, attend to their prayers and render the alms levy, will be rewarded by their Lord

---

[2]See Muhammad Asad, *The Message of the Qur'an*, (Dar al-Andalus, Gibraltar, 1980), p.100.

[3]See p.194 below.

[4]See J.Schacht in *Encyclopaedia of Islam, Volume III*, eds: M.Th.Houtsma; A.J.Wensinck; E.Levi-Provencal; H.A.R.Gibb; W.Heffering. (E.J.Brill, Leiden; Luzac & Co., London. 1936), p.1148; and also M. Umer Chapra, *Towards a Just Monetary System*, (The Islamic Foundation, Leicester, 1985), p.56.

and will have nothing to fear or to regret. Believers have fear of God and waive what is still due to you from usury, if your faith be true; or war shall be declared against your God and His apostle. If you repent you may retain your principal, suffering no loss and causing loss to none. If your debtor be in straits, grant him a delay until he can discharge his debt; but if you waive the sum as alms it will be better for you, if you but knew it. (Surah Al-Baqarah ii.275-280)

"Believers, do not live on usury (*riba*), doubling your wealth many times over. Have fear of God, that you may prosper." (Surah Al-Imran iii.130)

"We forbade the Jews good things which were formerly allowed them; because time after time they have debarred others from the path of God; because they practice usury – although they were forbidden it – and cheat others of their possesssions." (Surah Al-Nisa iv.161)

"That which you seek to increase by usury (*riba*) will not be blessed by God; but the alms (*zakat*) you give for His sake shall be repaid to you many times over." (Surah Al-Rum xxx.39)[5]

The Qur'an, therefore, contains some passages which condemn a practice called in Arabic, '*riba,*' which generally signifies increase, growth, excess, rise etc., but in the Qur'an the word *riba* is referred to in a specific context. In the pre-Islamic period the word *riba* was used conventionally to identify a class of business transactions, and the common feature of these was that a fixed amount was required over the principal due.[6] It is, therefore, the Arabic word for the pre-determined return on the use of money which is forbidden, and although, literally, it means 'increase' or 'profit,' technically it has come to mean 'usury' or 'interest,' and, generally, it

---

[5]N.J.Dawood, *The Koran*, (Penguin Books, London, revised translation, 1990), pp.40; 53; 77; 286.

[6]Waqar Masood Khan, *Towards an Interest-Free Islamic Economic System*, (The Islamic Foundation, U.K. and The International Association for Islamic Economics, Islamabad), 1985, p.24.

means any unjustified increase of capital for which no compensation is given. The term *riba*, however, is used in the *Shari'ah* – Islamic law – in two senses. Islamic jurists have classified *riba* into two types: the usury of debts: *riba al diyun*; and the usury of trade: *riba al bai'* – also known as *riba al-fadl*.

The usury of debts was an established practice amongst Arabs during the pre-Islamic period. It may arise in two situations. Firstly, as an excess over and above the amount of principal loan which is incorporated as an obligatory condition of giving the loan and in this situation is known as *riba al diyun*. Secondly, an excess amount is imposed over and above the amount of principal loan if the borrower fails to pay the principal on the date due. Thus, more time is allowed for payment in return of the excess amount, and if the borrower fails to pay again, a further excess amount over the principal, usually the double of the first excess, is imposed, and so on. This kind of usury may occur through debt or trade and is known as *riba al nasi'ah* – the usury of delay.[7] The prohibition of *riba al nasi'ah* essentially implies that the fixing in advance of a positive return on a loan as a reward for waiting is not permitted by the *Shari'ah*; only where there appeared an element of risk, was the concept of *riba* allowed, and that only in accordance with the principles of justice laid down by divine law:

> "It makes no difference whether the return is a fixed or a variable per cent of the principal, or an absolute amount to be paid in advance or on maturity, or a gift or service to be received as a condition for the loan. The point in question is the *predetermined positiveness* of the return. It is important to note that, according to the *Shari'ah*, the waiting involved in the repayment of a loan does not itself justify a

---

[7]*Elimination of Riba from the Economy*, (published by the Institute of Policy Studies, Islamabad), 1994, papers and proceedings from a workshop held at the Institute of Policy Studies in April, 1992, p.341.

positive reward . . . However, if the return on principal can be either *positive* or *negative* depending on the final outcome of the business, which is not known in advance, it is allowed provided that it is shared in accordance with the principles of justice laid down in the *Shari'ah*."[8]

The importance of the aspect of positive or negative return on the principal will be discussed later in the context of Islamic banking principles. However, apart from the usury of debt, Islam also addresses the problem of usury of trade. It wishes to eliminate not merely the exploitation that is intrinsic in the institution of interest, but also that which is inherent in all forms of dishonest and unjust exchanges in business transactions. These are extensively identified in the teachings of the Qur'an and the *sunnah* (custom sanctioned by tradition, particularly that of the Prophet, Muhammad, enshrined in *hadith*), and they are encompassed under the generic term, *riba al bai*,' which, as has already been noted, is also known as *riba al-fadl*. This is the second sense in which *riba* has been used, and which was also practised by the Arabs in the pre-Islamic period. It is encountered in hand to hand purchase and sale of commodities and covers all spot transactions involving cash payment on the one hand and immediate delivery of the commodity on the other.[9] This will be discussed in more detail further on, what is essentially being required, however, and is important to note, is that justice and fair play are demanded in all transactions, and anything that is received as 'extra' by one of two parties to the transaction is *riba al-fadl*. Justice can be rendered only if the two scales of the balance carry the same value of goods.

---

[8]Chapra, *op.cit.*, (f.n.3), p. 57.

[9]Chapra, *ibid.*, p.58.

The development of the modern-day definition of usury in terms of exorbitant or oppressive interest rates, as opposed to the initial scholastic definition of any increment, whether excessive or moderate, beyond the principal of a loan, was noted within the Judaeo/Christian tradition. In Islam a similar problem arises, with regard to definition, as to whether *riba* refers to interest or usury. There is still disagreement on this issue. A report in 'The Economist' (1996) stated that in Egypt the newly appointed 'Grand Imam,' Sayed Tantawi, as former 'Grand Mufti,' had declared that payment of fixed interest on bank deposits was lawful in Egypt, whereas the late Grand Imam, Sheikh Gadd-al-Haqq said it was usury and forbidden.[10] Kurshid Ahmad maintains that as far as Islam is concerned it has laid down very clear criteria:

"There cannot be any economic or *Shari'ah* justification for confining riba to usury and excluding interest from its jurisdiction. As far as economic analysis is concerned there is no technical difference between interest and usury. Whether we look upon the phenomenon from the demand side of economic analysis or the supply side, the rationale developed in economic theory for interest and usury are the same. If it is a reward for waiting or time-preference, there cannot be any differentiation between interest and usury. If the question is examined from the productivity approach, again there cannot be any differentiation against the two. That is why whatever differentiation has been introduced in the literature comes mostly on moral grounds alleging that one is high and exorbitant (usury) and the other is low and as such reasonable, and secondly that usury deals with loans to the poor for consumption purposes while interest deals with profitable

---

[10]In the late 1980's this had resulted in thousands of Egyptians rushing to invest in 'Islamic' savings schemes, most of which turned out to be pyramid scams and destitute investors are still trying to get their money back. The good intentions of 'islamisation' do not, unfortunately, always result in good practice. See *The Economist*, April 13th, 1996, p.57.

commercial advances. There is no economic substance in any of these excuses."[11]

With regard to the differentiation between consumption and production loans, it has been argued that at the time of Muhammad, *riba* transactions were mainly for consumption purposes demanded by the poor, and, therefore, the production loans prevalent in the present financial system cannot be treated as *riba*, as debt financing for business capital is the outgrowth of industrialisation and as such was non-existent at that time. However, as Waqar Masood Kahn points out, historical evidence amply demonstrates that production loans were made during this period, and were even known in Babylon and ancient Egypt; nor is it logical to argue that only the forms of *riba* which existed in the time of Muhammad should be prohibited as this would have the implication of granting legitimacy to several unanimously agreed prohibitions in Islam. For example, in the Qur'an, the word '*khamr*' is used for the prohibition of alcohol. *Khamr* was a special kind of alcoholic drink made out of grapes, but in Arabia, all kinds of alcoholic drinks were referred to as *khamr*, and as such there was no dispute in applying this injunction to all kinds of alcoholic drinks, since the essence was to prohibit the use of all things that intoxicate.[12] Similarly, the essence for the injunction of *riba* is that it is unjust for a lender to demand a fixed return over the principal loan, irrespective of what happens with the loaned money. Thus, in the ensuing discussion, the terms '*riba*' and 'interest' will be used interchangeably, and the definition of a specifically Islamic banking system will be based on the Qur'anic

---

[11]Khurshid Ahmad, "*Elimination of Riba: Concept and Problems,*" a paper from a workshop held at the Institute of Policy Studies in April, 1992, Islamabad, Pakistan, collected in a book entitled *Elimination of Riba from the Economy, op. cit.*, p.38.

[12]W.M.Kahn, *op. cit.*, p.27.

assumption that a payment or receipt of interest is categorically forbidden – unlike the Judaic interpretation which allowed for the Deuteronomic exemption toward the 'foreigner.'[13]

However, although the word *riba* itself may be understood to mean usury/interest, what it actually meant in practice is a different matter. Unlike the Judaic understanding of usury which was accepted to be the, even minimal, payment of interest on a loan at whatever the accepted rate, in Islam, despite the above definitions, what *riba* was, exactly, is a more complicated issue. The earliest mention of the term and concept of *riba* in the chronology of Qur'anic revelation occurs, as I noted, in Surah xxx.39. As Muhammad Asad points out, although in a linguistic sense *riba* denotes an 'increase' of, or an 'addition' to a thing over and above its original size or amount, in the terminology of the Qur'an, *riba* signifies any 'unlawful addition' by way of interest to a sum of money or goods lent by one person, or a body of persons, to another, but Islamic scholars have not yet reached an absolute agreement on its definition which "would cover all conceivable legal situations and positively respond to all exigencies of a variable economic environment." He further maintains that according to the uncontested evidence of Ibn Abbas the passage condemning and prohibiting *riba* in legal terms (Surah ii.275-281) was the last revelation received by the Prophet, who died a few days later, hence the Companions had no opportunity to ask him about the *Shari'ah* implications of the injunction. Umar ibn al-Khattab is reliably reported to have said:

---

[13]See Chapter One: "Thou shalt not lend upon usury to thy brother; usury of money, usury of victuals, usury of anything that is lent upon usury: Unto a stranger thou mayest lend upon usury; but unto thy brother thou shalt not lend upon usury: that the Lord thy God may bless thee in all that thou settest thine hand to in the land wither thou goest to possess it." Deuteronomy 23:19-20 (Authorised Version of the Old Testament).

"'The last [of the Qur'an] that was revealed was the passage [lit., "the verse"] on *riba*; and, behold, the Apostle of God passed away without [lit., "before"] having explained its meaning to us.'"[14]

Strictly, as already noted, the word means 'increase,' but, according to Rodinson, it does not appear to signify mere 'interest' in the sense in which we use this word today, nor in the Judaic understanding, but rather, "the doubling of a sum owed (capital and interest, in money or in kind), when the debtor cannot pay it back at the moment when it falls due."[15]

The interpretations given to the word, therefore, have been varied. At first, it seems, *riba* was understood to mean the exaction of any interest when money or foodstuffs were lent – *riba al nasi'ah,* which comes from the root *nasa'a,* which means to postpone, defer, or wait, and refers to the time that is allowed for the borrower to repay the loan in return for the 'addition' or the 'premium.'[16] Subsequently, the definition was made more precise, in the *hadith,* through complex logical deductions and external influences, until, in general, it was taken to mean *any advantage* accruing to one of the contracting parties in the sale or barter of precious metals or foodstuffs. Only perfect equivalence between what is supplied by both parties is permissable – *riba al-fadl.* The difficulties involved will be seen when I examine how the various Islamic traditions tried to determine the legal implications and interpretations of the term *riba,* and the way in which *hiyal,* or tricks, were invented to get around it. *Riba* is still very much a Qur'anic concept which Islamic

---

[14]Muhammad Asad, *op.cit.,* see n.268, p.62; n.35, p.622.

[15]Maxime Rodinson, *Islam and Capitalism,* (Allen Lane, Penguin Books Ltd., London, 1974. Translated from the first publication in France by Editions du Seuil, Paris, 1966), p.14.

[16]Chapra, *op. cit.,* p.57.

banking attempts to interpret in the market place today, and this will be discussed later in the light of its historical development, and in moving toward an Islamic understanding of *riba* as we move into the twenty-first century. According to Asad, "every successive Muslim generation is faced with the challenge of giving new dimensions and a fresh economic meaning to this term which, for want of a better word, may be rendered as 'usury.'"[17]

It has been argued that within the surahs of the Qur'an, these various passages which prohibit *riba* seem sometimes to be aimed at the Muslims, sometimes at the Pagans, and sometimes at the Jews and Christians (the Jews are also blamed for breaking their own laws forbidding usury – surah iv.161) and it might also be thought that the prohibition of *riba* in Islam was due to a wrong attitude toward wealth amongst the rich merchants of Mecca, but Watt maintains that the polemic in the Qur'an against the practice called *riba* is directed solely at the Jews in the early years at Medina.[18]

According to Watt, a reconstruction of the situation would be that Muhammad, in his first years at Medina, was nominally in alliance with the Jews, but when he eventually appealed to them for contributions, either to support poorer emigrants until booty came in, or, more likely, for military preparations, most of the Jews refused, or said they would lend money at interest. Muhammad understood that it was contrary to their Jewish law to lend at usury to co-religionists, but, what is significant, is that in his eyes Jews and Muslims *were* co-religionists ('brothers'). The Jews, therefore, ought to make outright contributions to his cause or, at least, loans without interest, which, of course, with this interpretation would be in

---

[17] Asad, *op.cit.*, n.35, p.623.

[18] W. Montgomery Watt, *Muhammad at Medina*, (Clarendon Press, Oxford, 1956), pp. 296-298.

accordance with the Deuteronomic principle. In this way the very question of usury developed into an aspect of Muhammad's quarrel with the Jews about the recognition of his own prophethood.[19]

However, Watt's interpretation does not stand up to casual reading of the relevant passages in the Qur'an, as Rodinson remarks.[20] It is obvious that Surah iv.161 is aimed against the Jews, and it is arguable that Surahs xxx.39 and ii.275-280 may also be pointed in that direction, but they could equally refer to Christians or Pagans. Surahs ii.275-280 and iii.130 specifically exhort believers to refrain from the practice of *riba*, and therefore it could be assumed that they were addressing Muslim practice, although Watt would maintain that once the connection between usury and the Jews has been established, it would be natural to regard the threat of war against believers who take usury as equally directed against Jews. Surah xxx.39 would appear to make more sense if it was seen in terms of reminding the Muslim of God's curse on usury and his blessings bestowed on alms-giving. The surahs written in Medina, however, as Watt maintains, and with regard to *riba* it would appear to be the majority of them, would be more likely to be aimed at the Jews because of their influence and prevalence there,[21] but there is no indication that they

---

[19]M. Watt, *Ibid.*, p.297.

[20]Maxime Rodinson, *op.cit.*, p.250.

[21]W. Montgomery Watt maintains that "in Medina Jews and pagan Arabs were settled side by side. There were also quite a number of Jewish tribes settled at oases in Arabia and in the fertile parts of southern Arabia, either refugees of Hebrew race or Arab tribes which had adopted Judaism. There were apparently practically no Jews in Mecca" W. Montgomery Watt, *Muhammad at Mecca*, (Oxford University Press, London, 1953), p.19. According to Patricia Crone it would appear that there may well have been Jews in Mecca at the time of the Prophet; she writes that Jewish traders settling in, or trading with, Mecca are also mentioned in connection with predictions of the Prophet: "A Jew settled in Mecca for trade at the time of the birth of Muhammad, whose future prophethood was well known to him (Ibn Sa'd, *Tabaqat*, 1, 162; the version cited in Mawardi, *A'lam*, p.153, omits the trade)." Patricia Crone, *Meccan Trade and the Rise of Islam*, (Blackwell, Oxford, 1987), n.29, p.139.

were exclusively so, and in general it would appear more appropriate to interpret them in the light of Muhammad addressing his new following.

In the time of Muhammad, in the highly developed trading system of Mecca,[22] transactions with a fixed time limit and payment of interest, therefore, formed an essential element, as did speculations of any kind. A debtor who could not repay the capital, be it goods or money, with the accumulated interest, at the time when it fell due, was given an extension of time in which to pay, but at the same time the sum was doubled, this is clearly referred to in Surah iii.130. In Surah xxx.39 the Qur'an contrasts *riba* with the obligation to pay *zakat* but without directly forbidding it. The express prohibition follows in Surah iii.130 and is, as we noted, intensified in Surah ii.275-280. The Qur'an regards *riba* as a practice of unbelievers and demands as a test of belief that it should be abandoned. The whole idea underlying the prohibition of usury was that all believers were brothers and therefore ought to help one another financially as well as in other ways: for example, al-Ghazali writing in the late eleventh century CE, maintained that as well as material assistance and personal aid, the duties of brotherhood in Islam also extended to holding one's tongue, or, paradoxically, knowing when to speak out; forgiveness; prayer; loyalty

---

[22]In her book (*ibid.*), Patricia Crone deconstructs the theories about the nature of Meccan trade which the writings of W. Montgomery Watt have made conventional i.e. his explanation of the rise of Islam in terms of the moral and social crisis precipitated by the success of Meccan trade and the violence which this new commercial way of life was doing to traditional tribal values. Crone suggests that Islam should not be thought of at all as a function of Meccan trade but might be better understood as a nativist movement, "a primitive reaction to alien domination" in which "Muhammad mobilised the Jewish version of monotheism against that of dominant Christianity and used it for the self-assertion, both ideological and military, of his own people." See also: Daniel A Madigan, "Reflections on Current Qur'anic Studies," (*The Muslim World*, Vol. LXXXV, No. 3-4, July-October 1995), p.361.

and sincerity, and the relief from discomfort and inconvenience.[23] However, with regard to the prohibition of *riba,* this teaching came at a time when a different class structure was developing in the Arab world itself, which would have far-reaching moral, social, economic, and political implications for a tribal society. At the time of the Prophet, as Malise Ruthven points out, the political economy of the Arabian peninsular was based on a few trade-based city-states under the control of Bedouin aristocrats, and equally, transactions of a fixed time limit, with a payment of interest, were an essential part of the old Meccan trading system; under this aegis a different social and economic structure was beginning to develop, and Muhammad's preaching, therefore:

> "represented a protest against some of the social and moral implications of the system which were developing at that time, particularly the emergence of social stratifications and a differential class structure – the old tribal loyalties were, on the whole, giving way to a newer division between rich and poor."[24]

As Montgomery Watt also points out, by the time of Muhammad there had been no readjustment of the social, moral, intellectual, and religious attitudes of the community, especially with regard to its economic situation. In the rise of Mecca to wealth and power at this time we have a movement from a nomadic economy to a mercantile and capitalist economy. The tendency to individualism and away from tribal solidarity was fostered in Mecca by the circumstance of commercial life. There

---

[23]Muhtar Holland, (translator), *The Duties of Brotherhood in Islam – Translated from the Ihya of Imam Al-Ghazali,* (The Islamic Foundation, Leicester), 1975.

[24]Malise Ruthven, *"The Evolution of Islamic Principles in Relation to Financial Dealings: An Historical Perspective."* A paper from a conference report on 'Islamic Banking,' London, September, 1984, p.3.

was an interesting new phenomenon in Mecca – the appearance of a sense of unity based on common material interests. If we are to look for an economic change correlated with the origin of Islam, then it is here that we must look.[25] Although Patricia Crone's proposed theory is an interesting one in terms of Islam being a nativist reaction to alien domination, it would appear difficult to discount the enormous effect the economic situation in Mecca was having at this time, whether its successful trading was due to spices, incense, luxury goods, or, indeed, leather.[26] It can be noted also at this point that the concept of '*ummah*,' which will be discussed later, in trying to theoretically level out the rich/poor divide in terms of equality and social justice would, in fact, threaten tribal loyalties even further as a Muslim would owe his allegiance to the *ummah* and not to the tribe. A similar disturbing phenomenon exists within Islam today with regard to the divided loyalties of the modern-day Muslim between the *ummah* and the nation-state:

---

[25]W. Montgomery Watt, *Muhammad at Mecca, op.cit.*, p.19.

[26]Patricia Crone contends that the Meccans carried on a largely local trade in humble products, not luxury goods, and that the commodities most often associated with Meccan trade were leather in various forms – clothing, animals, and miscellaneous foodstuffs, upon which she finds unlikely that the Meccans could have founded a commercial empire. However, John W.Jandora argues that Crone's assessment derives from consideration of relative value, and the factor of demand should have been taken into consideration. Meccan fortunes may well have derived from trade in hides, skins, and other animal parts. From the end of Abraha's reign (ca. 570 CE) to the beginning of the *hijra* (622 CE), the Sassanid and Byzantine empires were at war from 572 to 591 and from 606 to 616. During these periods of conflict the demand for leather would have considerably risen as it was used for a wide variety of military equipment, such as: rawhide thongs, scabbards, saddles, saddle bags, bridles, horse armour, belts, straps, fasteners, bow cases, shields, jerkins, and body armour – including lamellar cuirasses, cheek and neck guards, and greeves. Items made of horn also included body armour, corselets, and bows. Any sustained surge in demand, therefore, could easily have led to an increase in wealth overall, some growth in population, and a bigger distinction between rich and poor. It is likely that traditional values and ethics were compromised or abandoned by many, and thus would emerge the very conditions which are reflected in the Qur'an. See John W.Jandora, "The Rise of Mecca: Geopolitical Factors," in *The Muslim World,* (Vol. LXXXV, No. 3-4, July-October, 1995), pp.333-344.

"This analogy between the pre-Islamic tribal system and the present nation-state system is a disturbing phenomenon for the Muslim activist. One Muslim activist calls the present system worse than the pre-Islamic system because the present system is organised and the pre-Islamic Arabian system was not centrally organised."[27]

This inherent tension faces Muslim tribesmen in today's Muslim state. The Pathans, divided between Afghanistan and Pakistan are a good example. When asked about his identity, Wali Khan, the symbol and leader of Pathan identity, replied:

"'First I am a Pathan because I have been so for thousands of years; then I am a Muslim, which I have been for about one thousand three hundred years and, third, I am a Pakistani, which I have been only for the last forty years or so.' Ethnicity, religion, and nationality – in that order; the chronological sequences of his identity are thus summed up. The modern state has sapped the tribal system of its vitality . . . nothing disintegrates tribalism as much as the arrival of the first electric pole or the first government-controlled school. Tribalism exists as a whole or not at all."[28]

Justice, however, in economic terms consisted for the Qur'an in forbidding a type of gain that was particularly excessive – *riba.* The fact that the usurer profits from a person's need in order to exploit him justified the prohibition. The Prophet, Muhammad condemned *riba* in the most unambiguous words during his farewell pilgrimage to Mecca:

---

[27]Abdullah al-Ahsan, *Ummah or Nation? – Identity Crisis in Contemporary Muslim Society,* (The Islamic Foundation, Leicester), 1992, p.99.

[28]See Akbar S. Ahmed, *Postmodernism and Islam,* (Routledge, London, 1992); Wali Khan quoted on p.133.

"He who has a pledge let him return it to him who entrusted him with it; all usury is abolished, but you have your capital. Wrong not and you shall not be wronged. God has decreed that there is to be no usury and the usury of Abbas b. Abdu'l-Muttalib is abolished, all of it."[29]

At the same time, there existed in Islamic terms, *zakat*. Part of the product of taxes and gifts (*zakat*) collected by the head of the community was to go towards helping the poor; to hospitality; to the ransoming of prisoners; and perhaps to grants or loans to the victims of certain disasters or circumstances of war. Usury was the very antithesis of *zakat*; as Surah xxx.39 states: "That which you seek to increase by usury (*riba*) will not be blessed by God; but the alms (*zakat*) you give for his sake shall be repaid to you many times over."

'Zakat' – One of the 'Five Pillars' of Islam

The whole concept of *zakat* is an extremely important one in Islam as it constitutes the third of the 'Five Pillars of Islam.' The Arabic term *zakat* is also difficult to translate: etymologically, the root signifies 'purification' and in this sense the word has taken on the meaning of almsgiving. The link between purity and almsgiving is equally biblical as can be seen in the Christian Gospel of St. Luke: "But give for alms those things which are within; and behold everything is clean for you." (Lk.11:41, RSV). However, the almsgiving in the Islamic tradition has become quasi-official and regulated by all kinds of laws. Originally, *zakat* was not gathered or distributed via formal institutions during the early Meccan period as Muslims were few in number and living in a society hostile to their beliefs; it was left to an

---

[29]A. Guillaume, *The Life of Muhammad: A Translation of Ishaq's Sirat Rasul Allah,* (Oxford University Press, London, 1955), p.651.

individual's conscience to give *zakat* privately to assist the poor. However, following the *hijrah* to Medina, the task of *zakat* was revealed to the Prophet, Muhammad, more as a command (Surah ii:110) than merely advice (Surah xxx:39). By the second year the Prophet had defined the basic rules, the forms of wealth covered, and who should pay and receive *zakat*. Thus for those who possessed the financial means (*nisab*), *zakat* had evolved from a voluntary practice to an institutionalized, socio-religious duty.[30] *Zakat* implies the rightful and legal claim of the poor against the rich: charity, which is also an obligation placed on the rich by Islam must be paid, in addition, according to conscience. In this sense, *zakat* can be compared, but not equated, with the Judaic notion of *chesed*, which was equally not charity but an act of loving kindness, associated with righteousness, payable, however, unlike *zakat*, to either rich or poor in time of need. This legal principle that the poor have a right to part of the property of the rich is, however, stronger than just an appeal to the generosity of those with possessions.

The Qur'an teaches that it is good to give alms publicly, but to give them in secret is better (Surah ii.271); elsewhere the word 'right' is used formally: "Give their right to the near of kin, to the needy, and to the wayfarers.'" (Surah xxx.38). Surah Al-Insan (lxxvi) is a eulogy to acts of generosity, while Surah Al-Muddathir (lxxiv.38-56), on the contrary, consigns anyone who has refused to feed the hungry to hell.

As *zakat* is an annual wealth tax, rather than income tax it is not payable unless a Muslim has amassed some capital. The scale of payments, fixed by the tradition – *hadith*, varies according to the type of property held, starting with a basic

---

[30]See Abdallah al-Shiekh, "Zakat" in *The Oxford Encyclopedia of the Modern Islamic World,* (ed. J.Esposito, Oxford University Press, 1995), vol.4, p.366ff.

rate of one fortieth of the individual's total capital, including savings, jewels, and land; or as defined in the twentieth century: "two and a half per cent of capital, capital reassessed annually at current market prices, plus income, minus expenses including living expenses and minus any debts if there are any."[31] There are also special categories, thus, it was provided that 10% should be given of the revenue of fields watered by rain, and 5% of those with artificial irrigation. Oil is not mentioned, but, today, in oil-rich Muslim countries like Saudi Arabia individual liability for *zakat* can in theory be enormous, but the actual amount paid may be purely nominal. The money must be paid out of a sense of duty, on pain of punishment in the after-life. Even in oil-rich Brunei – where *zakat* is the only tax – there is no system of accounting.

At present, many Muslims consider that state taxation, part of which is directed towards the same social ends as *zakat*, has replaced it. The principle of *zakat* had lapsed except in very traditionalist countries like Saudi Arabia, or practiced amongst Muslims who observed the law strictly. However, the present fundamentalist movement with its return to the Muslim law and revivalist attitude, has restored the *zakat*, and in countries in which *zakat* is not officially collected by the State, committees have been created which are skilled in collecting it and redistributing the aid. *Zakat* is now applied in Jordan, Saudi Arabia, Malaysia, Pakistan, Kuwait, Libya, Iran, and Sudan.[32]

Experiences in its implementation vary. For example, the application of *zakat* in Pakistan was based on the Zakat and Ushr Ordinance of 1980, which took effect

---

[31]Ibrahim Kamel, *"Money Management and General Trading Under Islamic Banking Procedures,"* paper from the report on a conference on Islamic Banking, London, 1984. p12.

[32]Abdallah al-Shiekh, *op.cit.*, p.368.

in 1981, after the introduction of President Zia ul-Haq's islamization programme in 1979. The *zakat* is assessed annually on all income or assets in excess of two thousand rupees (approximately two hundred dollars) and deducted directly from bank accounts and other financial assets, such as investment shares, annuities, and insurance. Critics have questioned government intervention with regard to collection and distribution of what was perceived as a personal obligation before God, not the State, and the Shi'i minority community, which has its own legal system, objected to the application of Sunni law. The government did, therefore, amend the *zakat* ordinance to exempt those who believed that compulsory deduction of *zakat* was against their school of law, but not before it had proved a divisive measure.

In Sudan, *zakat* became an official compulsory Islamic duty based on government legislation in 1984. In 1989 the Islamic National Salvation government came to power and the *zakat* system entered a new phase. The Zakat Law of 1990 built on previous experience but added a much larger vision to the role of *zakat* in society, especially with regard to its collection and distribution. There are still problems to be faced, however, in terms of the relation between the *zakat* and the secular tax system, and whether the *zakat* should in fact be applied to the means of production which the 1990 act had included in terms of agriculture, livestock, factories, modes of transportation, trade goods etc. These recent efforts, however, are considered as the beginning of a long road toward the ideal *zakat* application.[33]

Timur Kuran questions whether it is, in effect, even possible. *Zakat*, he maintains is essentially a redistribution scheme similar to those operating throughout the world, except that it is a far less comprehensive system, and rather regressive. The main problem, according to Kuran, would appear to be the Islamic economists'

---

[33]*Ibid.*, p.369.

attachment to the particular rates and exemption limits, often in kind, set out by the early Muslims in seventh century Arabia: for example, a person who owns up to twenty-four camels pays one goat for every five camels. In any contemporary society, even an undeveloped one, a substantial portion of the national product comes from the service sector, manufacturing, and communication. Therefore, although *zakat* on certain livestock, grains, and fruits may be specified with great care and may very well reduce inequality in an agricultural economy, to implement a *zakat* scheme into a modern Islamic economy today would place the burden on low-income peasants, and virtually none on shipping tycoons, industrial bosses, and bureaucrats. This is also shown in the case of the *'nisabs'* for silver and gold – 52.5 tolas (21 ounces) for silver, and 7.5 tolas (3 ounces) for gold, exactly the levels stipulated by the Prophet, Muhammad. According to Kuran (writing in 1984) this means that each member of an Islamic economy can hold roughly two hundred dollars' worth of silver, and eleven hundred dollars' worth of gold without paying *zakat*, as it is paid only by people whose holdings exceed the minimum *nisab*.[34] The problem could be solved by implementing a value added tax on the differing products and services but most religious authorities would object to such an innovation as it negates the concept of *zakat* as specifically defined in Qur'anic stipulations.

The basic teaching of the Qur'an is that all worldly wealth is unclean unless it is used in the service of Allah and Islam, and 'the Book' is full of warnings of the terrible fate awaiting those becoming rich through 'usury,' or failing to share their wealth with other Muslims. The rich man may only 'purify' his wealth, which he is

---

[34]Timur Kuran, "The Economic System in Contemporary Islamic Thought: Interpretation and Assessment," (*The International Journal of Middle East Studies*, Vol. XVIII, 1986), p.145.

then free to enjoy with the blessing of Allah, by paying *zakat*. In this context, therefore, it can be understood why the exacting of *riba* was prohibited.

In an era of socialist societies the theoreticians of Islam may, therefore, refer to the *zakat* in order to justify the intervention of the state or the community in the sharing of riches. The fact that the poor in Islam have rights over the property of the rich could lead governments to redistribute property in the public interest, although it is equally affirmed that the right to private property remains unaffected. According to Jomier, some apologists even go so far as to say that "the *zakat* made Islam a socialism before socialism."[35] It is an interesting assertion to make especially in the light of the debate with regard to whether 'Islam' was an obstacle to *capitalist* development. I will address this argument later. However, as far as the teaching on *zakat* is concerned, the Qur'an recalls the rights of the most disadvantaged, and *zakat* was a way of gaining these rights for these people by fostering this strong sense of community. There are, however, problems in the present day as the scope of *zakat* in its original form is far too restrictive for its intended purposes. It serves as a major redistributive function only in a primitive agricultural economy resembling that of seventh century Arabia. The pitfalls of instituting the traditional system of *zakat* in a contemporary economy can be seen in a country like Malaysia which collects *zakat* from paddy-producing agricultural households – eighty-eight percent of which lie below the poverty line, while exempting most property owners and wage earners for whom no explicit allowance is made in the traditional sources of Islam.[36] This is an

---

[35]Jacques Jomier, *How to Understand Islam,* (Les Editions du Cerf, Paris, 1988; SCM Press, Ltd., London, 1989.) p.62.

[36]See Kuran, *op.cit.* p.145: an empirical study by two Malasian economists, Ismail Muhd Salleh and Rogayah Ngah (*"Distribution of the Zakat burden on Padi Producers in Malaysia")* showed that the recently imposed *zakat* scheme actually accentuated inequality.

anomaly which must be addressed, but it is not easy. Alternative redistribution schemes could be implemented which might drastically reduce the level of income inequality, but this would be to ignore the religious element of *zakat* which still retains an intrinsic altruistic function in fostering ideals of justice and community. In a large community, relying on voluntary redistribution alone will not overcome the problem of poverty; charity must be supplemented by obligatory taxes. I will suggest further on that Islamic banking in terms of non-usurious, risk-sharing partnerships might prove an alternative, or supplementary, solution in providing sufficient credit for the poor in low income countries in order to improve their circumstance and that of a community.

This concern for community, as with the Judaic concern, but with a different connotation in the Islamic world, is bound up with the whole concept of *ummah*, which in turn is related to the concept of 'Unity' or *tawhid*. To move toward an Islamic understanding on the prohibition of usury – *riba*, it is essential, therefore, to comprehend not only this idea of the 'purification' of self, and wealth, as expressed by *zakat*, but also to understand the force of the concept of community, or *ummah*, and the obligations which bind one to it and in it. This is totally expressed in the Islamic concept of unity – *tawhid*, that God is One.

'Tawhid' and *'Ummah'*

As a religion which was revealed to the Prophet, Muhammad, nearly fourteen hundred years ago, Islam continues to base itself on what is in the nature of things, concentrating particularly on the Divine nature itself. For this reason Islam is based from beginning to end on the idea of 'Unity' – *tawhid*, for God is One. According to Seyyed Hossein Nasr:

"It is, in fact, emphasised so much that for a non-Muslim it seems as a pleonasm, a kind of excessive reiteration of something which is obvious. But to the Muslim the idea of unity does not just mean the assertion that there is only one God sitting in heaven instead of two or three. No religion could convert a quarter of the population of the globe . . . with just such a simple idea. Unity is, in addition to a metaphysical assertion about the nature of the Absolute, a method of integration, a means of becoming whole and realising the profound oneness of all existence. . . Every manifestation of human existence should be organically related to the *Shahadah, La ilaha ill' Allah*, which is the most universal way of expressing Unity. This means that man should not be compartmentalized either in his thoughts or actions. Every action, even the manner of walking and eating, should manifest a spiritual norm which exists in his mind and heart."[37]

Traditionally, *tawhid*, an Arabic term meaning literally 'making one' or 'unifying,' was recognised as a fundamental doctrine of Islam by early theologians even though the word is not mentioned in the Qur'an.[38] Its popularity as Islam's defining characteristic is a modern development as its meaning and implication is one that has undergone continuous revision, most dramatically in the contemporary era, especially in the work of Iran's Ayatollah Ruhollah Khomeini (1902-1989) where *tawhid* came to represent revolutionary Islam, and has emerged as a powerful symbol of unity – divine, spiritual, and sociopolitical. It was the Hanbali jurist, Ibn Taymiyah, who shifted the emphasis of *tawhid* from the early theologians' defense of divine unity against dualists and trinitarians, to that of sociomoral issues; and in the nineteenth century he enjoyed some renewed popularity among the Wahhabiyah. But the modern importance of *tawhid* did not begin to emerge until 1897 when a full

---

[37]Seyyed Hossein Nasr, *Ideals and Realities of Islam,* (The American University in Cairo Press, Egypt, 1989), p.29.

[38]Tamara Sonn, "Tawhid" in *The Oxford Encyclopedia of the Modern Islamic World, op.cit.,* vol.4, p.190.

discussion of its implications was published by the Egyptian reformer, Muhammad Abduh. *"Risalat al-tawhid"* was an attempt to reintroduce the classic issues of Islamic theology. However, by the mid to late twentieth century *tawhid*, as an organising principle of human society, had become for many Islamic reformers a rallying point. In the 1960's *tawhid* was proclaimed the underlying principle of all true religion by Sayyid Qutb, the ideologue of the Muslim Brothers and executed in 1966 under the Nasser regime in Egypt. In 1982, Ismail al-Faruqi, a much travelled Islamic scholar and activist born in Palestine in 1921 and governor of Galilee in 1945 (and murdered in 1986), claimed that *tawhid* was the core of all Islamic religious knowledge, "as well as its history, metaphysics, esthetics, ethics, social order, economic order, and indeed the entire Islamic world order."[39]

Tawhid, therefore, expresses itself on the social plane in the integration of human society, which Islam has achieved to a remarkable degree; and, politically, it manifests itself, as Nasr maintains, in Islam's refusal to accept as the ultimate unit of the body politic anything less than the totality of the Islamic community, or *ummah.*

The term *'ummah,'* therefore, often translated as 'Muslim community,' designates a fundamental concept in Islam. It has often been used to express the essential unity of Muslims in *diverse* cultural settings. In Qur'anic usage – the word occurs sixty-four times – the connotations of community and religion do not always converge, so that it is found referring to an unrestricted group of people (xxviii:23); the followers of prophets (x:47); a group of people adhering to a specific religion (v:48); a misguided group of people (xliii:33); a stated period of time (xi:80); as well as an order of being (vi:38). However, there is also a sense in which the concept of

---

[39]*Ibid.*, pp.190-198.

the *ummah* refers to an ideal state, an original all encompassing unity that is always invoked but never completely recovered. Surah x:9 reads: "People were once a single *ummah*, but they differed (and followed different ways). Had it not been for the word proclaimed by your lord before, their differences would have been resolved." This rudimentary concept of *ummah* is complemented by the narrower concept of the *ummah* of believers. This is the 'medium *ummah*' (ii:143), which is qualified as 'the best *ummah* evolved for mankind, enjoining what is good, forbidding what is wrong, and believing in God." (iii:110). This specific *ummah* – the followers of Muhammad, shouldered the central role in the fulfillment of this mission after him. It was during the period of the first four 'rightly guided' caliphs after Muhammad's death, that important Islamic ideals were actually conceived; these included the principles of the unity of *ummah*, the *ummah* as the ultimate source of political authority, and the related principles of the unity of political leadership and the unity of the land of Islam. By the end of the second century of Islam this unity was corroborated by an Islamic cultural tradition, and although the differences between the civil and religious notions of *ummah* have parallels in *hadith*, it is the *hadith* literature that provides the concept of *ummah* with its more precise and focused meaning.[40]

Traditionalists and *hadith* scholars argued that Islam could only be preserved by safeguarding the unity of the *ummah*. Therefore, the standard legal formulations of the classical period defined it as "a spiritual, nonterritorial community distinguished by the shared beliefs of its members."[41] This had legal consequences.

---

[40]See Ahmad S. Dallal, "Ummah" in *The Oxford Encyclopedia of the Modern Islamic World, op.cit.*, vol.4, p.268.

[41]*Ibid.*, p.268.

One expression of the treatment of the *ummah* as a legal entity resulted in the distinction in Islamic jurisprudence between religious obligations that fall on individuals and other obligations that the *ummah* shoulders collectively as one unit.[42] During the classical period, therefore, the literature viewed the *ummah* as a socioreligious reality with legal and political importance, and from the third century of Islam it also conferred a distinguished status on the Arabs within the larger *ummah* of Muslims. Arabness as a cultural identity had a unique and organic link to the religious, political, and social identity of the Islamic *ummah*. As Hourani points out, in the history of Islam, and indeed in its essential structure, the Arabs had a special part:

> "The Qur'an is in Arabic, the Prophet was an Arab, he preached first
> to Arabs, who formed the 'matter of Islam,' the human instrument
> through which the religion and its authority spread; Arabic became
> and has remained the language of devotion, theology, and law."[43]

---

[42] A *fard al-kifayah* (lit. 'duty of the sufficiency') defines a communal responsibility, and was one of the major vehicles used by jurists to talk about society as a collective entity. By the time of al-Shafi'i (d.820) the doctrine was accepted. In principle, if some religious obligation belonging to the category of *fard al-kifayah* is not fulfilled within a community of Muslims then all have collectively sinned. By the eleventh century CE the *fard al-kifayahs* constitute a compendium of religious and moral obligations. Although the *fard al-kifayah* is normally acknowledged as a collective duty it can in some cases be discharged by an individual. A remarkable feature is that a Muslim may have his or her obligation or duty discharged by someone else and an interesting corollary is that, likewise, another Muslim can be punished for someone's neglect. *Fard al-kifayah/fard al-ayn* take the places in moral discourse of the concepts of public and private spheres. In recent Muslim literature these concepts have been equated with the notion of social responsibility, although there are other categories which equally describe the fact that there is no domain of behaviour bereft of moral assessment: *wajib* (obligatory), *mahzur* (proscribed), *mubah* (neutral/permitted), *mandub* (recommended), and *makruh* (reprehensible). They may prove important concepts for those seeking the restatement of Islamic social doctrines at the end of the twentieth century. See A.Kevin Reinhart, "Fard al-ayn" and "Fard al-kifayah" in *The Oxford Encyclopedia of the Modern Islamic World, op.cit.*, vol. 2. pp1-3.

[43] A. Hourani, *Arabic Thought in the Liberal Age 1798-1939*, (Oxford University Press, London, 1962), p.260.

This social and linguistic identity was seriously challenged under the pressure of European colonial encroachment on Muslim domains, and Islamic resistance movements defending the *ummah* emerged throughout the Islamic world. The earliest forms of nationalism in the Islamic world, including non-Muslims among them, appropriated the concept of *ummah*. This might disrupt the political unity of the *ummah* for a time, but it did not challenge the theoretical authority of the concept. However, beginning in the 1960's, Arab nationalists began to speak in favour of a complete separation of religious and national identities, indeed, as Islam had expanded and embraced the non-Arab world, it could no longer be held together by its 'Arabness.' There existed Arabs who were non-Muslim, and Muslims who were, equally, non-Arab, although the recitation of the Qur'an in Arabic can still maintain the vestiges of unifying 'arabness.' Islamists argued that loyalty to the Islamic *ummah* negates any other loyalty to ethnic, linguistic, or geographical identities, even though, as we have already noted, this can create personal conflict.[44] In contemporary political discourse today, the idea of the Islamic *ummah*, carries with it, therefore, the notion of the nation-state with which it is competing, in the sense that, as Aziz al-Azmeh points out: "The word *ummah* denotes the nationalist conception of the nation, as well as the Islamic community which would necessarily denote, for 'the people,' the civil community which binds their social universe."[45] The political and legal expression of the idea may have been curtailed with the

---

[44]See quote by Wali Khan, p. 201.

[45]Aziz Al-Azmeh, *Islams and Modernities*, (Verso, London, 1993), p.70. See also the whole of Chapter 3, "Arab Nationalism and Islamism," pp.60-76.

gradual secularization of public life, but as a source of social identity it still persists in the Islamic world.[46]

What, perhaps, is more important in terms of *ummatic* versus nationalist identity, is not so much the tension between them, but their mutual interdependence and the constructive assessment of three significant characteristics with regard to the *ummah* as formulated by the Prophet, and as distinguished by Abdullah al-Ahsan. These elements, he maintains, must be addressed by the contemporary Islamic revivalist movements as a way of coming to grips with the rich history of Islam. They are: the ideology of change from *jahili* to monotheism; the role of the *ummah* in history – prescribing what is good and proscribing what is evil; and the unity of the Islamic direction of prayer.[47] As Tarik Hamsi al-Azami equally points out, the ideological dimension of all Muslims takes them beyond their nationalistic, ethnic, and linguistic divisions; enjoining what is good and forbidding what is evil gives them a universal humanistic identity; and the unity of their direction in prayers, i.e. toward the *Ka'ba* in Mecca, unites all Muslims despite sectarian, or nationalistic, differences.[48]

There is, therefore, a crisis in *ummatic* identity in the twenty-first century. Social, political, economic, and intellectual changes surrounding the Muslim world since the nineteenth century causes not only the Muslim, but the rest of the world to ask: Can the Muslim develop an Islamic concept of citizenship that meets the

---

[46]Ahmad S. Dallal, *op.cit.*, p.270.

[47]Abdullah al-Ahsan, *op.cit.*, pp.1-27.

[48]Tarik Hamdi al-Azami, "Religion, Identity, and State in Modern Islam," (*The Muslim World*, Vol.LXXXIV, No.3-4, July-October, 1994), p.335.

conditions of the Modern World, and, if so, does that make the concepts of *ummatic* and nationalistic identity mutually exclusive?

As Hourani points out, the link between human beings in pre-Islamic society was that of natural relationship, based on blood or analogous to that which was based on blood – it was the solidarity of the clan or tribe, *asabiyya.* The link, however, between the Muslims in the *ummah* was a moral link, a common obedience of the law, an acceptance of the reciprocal rights and duties laid down in it, and mutual support and exhortation in carrying it out. In the Muslim *ummah* power was a delegation by God (*wilaya*) controlled by his will and directed to the happiness of Muslims in the next world even more than in this.[49]

> "For the moral imagination of Muslims, the early centuries of Islam have always been a compelling drama in three acts: the early days of the prophet and his immediate successors, the golden age when the *umma* was what it should be; the Umayyad period when the principles of the Islamic polity were overlaid by the natural human tendency towards secular kingship; and the early Abbasid age when the principles of the *umma* were reasserted and embodied in the institutions of a universal empire, regulated by law, based on the equality of all believers, and enjoying the power, wealth and culture which are the reward of obedience."[50]

In later ages this period of history served as a norm both for rulers and ruled as a lesson of what God had done for his people. It also provided material for reflection on the moral problems of the corporate life of the *ummah* in, for example, the struggle for the caliphate between Ali and Mu'awiya, then between Umayyads and Abbasids, and the breach between Sunnis and Shi'is. Today the difficulty of

---

[49] A.Hourani, *op.cit.*, p.7.

[50] *Ibid.*, p.7.

embodying God's will in the life of society is seen in this tension between the *ummatic* identity versus that of the nation state. According to Lawrence, nationalism is doubly wrong because it is an idea imported into Muslim countries from nineteenth century European state systems, and because it asserts that ultimate loyalty of the individual is to the nation – right, or wrong:

> "Nationalism resurrects the kind of tribalism or *jahliya* that Muhammad opposed and which early Muslims, temporarily, overcame. In its stead there should be a patriotism that seeks the benefit of all states of society and of Muslims everywhere, i.e. patriotism should replace the *qawmiya* (or ethnocentrism) of one group with the *wataniya* (or solidarity) of all groups as equal participants in the Islamic *ummah.*"[51]

Also in its stead Lawrence maintains that there should be emphasis on the general welfare of all Muslims – *maslaha*, exercised on behalf of the believers against the prevailing ignorance *(jahliya)*. *Maslaha* can be defined as public welfare – "the establishment of legal principles recommended by reason of being advantageous."[52] According to necessity and particular circumstances, it consists of prohibiting or permitting a thing on the basis of whether or not it serves a 'useful purpose.' Traditionally it had been no more than a rule for the interpretation of texts. In explaining the Qur'an and *hadith*, the jurist should assume that God's purpose in making his revelation was to promote human welfare, and therefore the interpretation best suited to this purpose should be chosen. Muhammad Abduh, a devoted student of al-Afghani and Mufti of Egypt in 1899, however, made *maslaha* a rule for

---

[51]Bruce Lawrence, *Defenders of God*, (I.B.Tauris & Co. Ltd., London, 1990), p.216.

[52]Abdul Rahman I Doi, "Maslaha," in *The Modern Encyclopedia of the Modern Islamic World*, *op.cit.*, vol.3, p.63.

deducing specific laws from general principles of social morality. General principles must be applied to the specific problems of social life by human reason, but, since these problems change the application must also change. What was important was that the guiding rule at any time was to be the general welfare of mankind at that time. Coupled with that idea was the second principle of *talfiq* – the notion that in any particular case a judge could choose that interpretation of the law, whether it came from his own legal code or not, which best fitted the circumstance.[53] This principle was further developed by Rashid Rida. *Maslaha* had been a subordinate principle, a guide in the process of reasoning by analogy rather than a substitute for it, but for Rida it becomes itself the positive principle of decision, replacing analogy:

> "What Rashid Rida is saying in fact is that there is and can be no *ijma*, even that of the first generation, in matters of social morality; or, in other words that the Muslim community has legislative power. The rulers of the community have not only the executive and judicial powers, they can legislate in the public interest. Thus there can be a body of 'positive law' (*qanun*) subordinate to the *Shari'a* in the sense that if there is conflict it is the latter which is valid, but otherwise independent and with a binding force which derives ultimately from the general principles of Islam."[54]

In other words, having rejected the old conception of *ijma*, he introduces a new one – the *ijma* of the *ulama* of each age, as an organised body and a legislative rather than a judicial principle working by some sort of parliamentary process. In 1897 Rida left Syria for Egypt, and in 1898 he published a periodical in Cairo called '*al-Manar*,' which he continued to publish more or less regularly until he died in

---

[53]See Hourani, *op.cit.*, p.152.

[54]*Ibid.*, p.234.

1935. It served as an organ of reform according to the ideas of Abduh, and into it were poured his reflections on the spiritual life, his explanations of doctrine, endless polemics, his thoughts on world politics, and the great commentary on the Qur'an – *Tafsir al-Manar*. For Rida, a distinguishing sign of Islam was that it had created a single community – not simply a Church, a body of people linked by faith and worship yet separated by their natural charateristics, but a community in every sense:

> "The long history of the caliphate, the spread of a common culture, and many centuries of mingling and intermarriage, have created an *umma* which is both a Church and a kind of 'nation': it is held together by unity of religion, of law, by equality and mutual rights and duties, but also by natural links, and in particular that of language, since Arabic is the universal language of devotion, doctrine, and law wherever Islam exists."[55]

Therefore, if we conceptualise Jews and Christians as worldwide communities – and in this sense they become 'the other' existing beyond the range of ummatic 'brotherhood' although, in a pluralist society, sharing mutual cross-reference points – we must also admit that Muslims belong to a single, coherent *ummah*: "The *kehilla*, the church, the *ummah* – each does exist. Each has points of cross-cultural identification and transnational loyalty." To speak of communities that relate to the scripture of Qur'an, Torah, Bible, "with any honest recognition of ethnic, linguistic, geographical diversity . . . is to admit the persistence of de facto pluralism, whatever the monotheistic creed or unifying mandate of scripture."[56] The unity of the *ummah*, therefore, is a moral and religious unity which does not prevent its division into national states, and, therefore, differing national identities; indeed, as

---

[55] *Ibid.*, p.229.

[56] B.Lawrence, *op.cit.*, p.231.

Mohammed Arkoun would maintain,[57] it is a fallacy to assume a uniform 'Islam' although Islam has become the supreme bond as opposed to nationality, and it is the *shari'ah* which remains to give unity to the Muslim congregation or *ummah.*

The *Shari'ah*

Why is it, that the Muslim bows toward Mecca, or the *Ka'ba*, in prayer?[58] It is because there exists in Mecca, in the house of God, a black stone. In the Islamic tradition this stone, the black stone of the *Ka'ba*, which 'fell from heaven' symbolises the original covenant made between God and man – the *al-mithaq*. The idea of covenant is an aspect of religion often forgotten in modern times but it is essential in Islam, as it is in Judaic terms. In Judaism, however, the covenant is made between God and his chosen people, the people of Israel, whereas in Islam it is made between God and man as such, and not a particular race or tribe.

---

[57]See M.Arkoun – an Algerian Islamic scholar and writer, b.1928, and one of today's leading Arab Muslim intellectuals. Arkoun is involved in the sensitive task of recasting and reinterpreting the classical religious, legal, and philosophical traditions through a sophisticated hermeneutical system inspired by contemporary Western critical methodologies. The '*Lectures du Coran*' (2nd. edition, Tunis, 1991) is a work that brings together various studies ranging from close readings of Qur'anic surahs to an essay on Islam and politics. See also "Arkoun, Mohammed" in *The Oxford Encyclopedia of the Modern Islamic World, op.cit.*, vol.1, p.139.

[58]According to Jandora, it would seem possible that the sanctuary around the *Ka'ba* might have had a considerable effect on the growth of the settlement in Mecca. However, there is no evidence apart from Islamic canonical history for the existence of a sanctuary of great renoun or antiquity. The Islamic canon itself does not reveal much about the sanctuary before Quraysh settled in its environs about the mid fifth century CE. and this approximate dating is derived from counting back five generations (thirty years each) from Muhammad to his ancestor Qusayy, who supposedly brought Mecca under the control of Quraysh. It maintains that the *Ka'ba* was founded by Ibrahim and Isma'il (Abraham and Ishmael of the Hebrew Bible) and was subsequently controlled by Amaliq, Jurhum, and then Khuza'a who were in turn displaced by Quraysh. There is no evidence that the Meccan sanctuary itself, in contrast to Arafat and Mina nearby, was an object of pilgrimage prior to Islam. See Jandora, *op.cit.*, p.333.

"To accept the Divine covenant brings up the question of living
according to the Divine Will. The very name of Islam is intimately
connected with this cardinal idea. The root '*salama*' in Arabic, from
which *Islam* is derived, has two meanings – one peace, and the other
surrender. He who surrenders himself to the Divine Will gains peace.
The very idea of Islam is that through the use of intelligence which
discerns between the Absolute and the relative one should come to
surrender to the Will of the Absolute. This is the meaning of Muslim:
one who has accepted through free choice to conform his will to the
Divine Will."[59]

In a particular sense, therefore, 'Islam' refers to the religion revealed through

the Qur'an, but in a more general sense it refers to religion as such. According to

Nasr some Muslim sages see three different levels of meaning in the word 'Muslim.'

Firstly, anyone who accepts a Divine revelation is a 'Muslim' in its most universal

sense, be they Muslim, Christian, Jew, or Zoroastrian. Secondly '*muslim*' refers to

all creatures of the universe who accept Divine law in the sense that they conform to

the unbreakable laws which the Western world would call the 'laws of Nature.'

Thirdly, there is the highest meaning of Muslim which applies to the saint. The saint

is like nature in that every moment of his life is lived in conformity with the Divine

Will, but his participation in the Divine Will is conscious and active whereas that of

nature is passive. However, as Malise Ruthven points out, a Muslim, in the primary

sense, is one who has made a voluntary act (one cannot undertake Islam on behalf of

another) of self-surrender or 'existential commitment' to God and his Prophet and the

'subjective correlative' of Islam in this primal sense is *iman* or faith:

"Just as the Muslim is one who has surrendered his whole being to
God, the *mumin* is one who is characterised by an unwavering faith
in him. Generally the two words are interchangeable; however,

---

[59]Nasr, *op. cit.*, p.27

where 'Muslim' acquires the secondary meaning of one who is formally or outwardly a member of the Islamic community, but not necessarily a believer in terms of inner conviction, *iman* and *mumin* acquire the added force of committed belief/believer."[60]

Islam, then, is a universal concept that comprehends persons and the universe about them and lies in the nature of things, concentrating particularly on the Divine nature itself, expressed in the concept of *tawhid.* Unity is, in addition to a metaphysical assertion about the nature of the Absolute, a method of integration, a means of becoming whole and realising the profound oneness of human existence, socially expressed in the concept of the *ummah*; and totally incorporated in the *Shari'ah,*[61] and it is here that the teaching on *riba* was further expounded in the light of this Islamic understanding of both *tawhid* and *ummah.*

The *Shari'ah*[62] is Divine Law, in the sense that it is the concrete embodiment of the Divine Will according to which people should live in both their private and social life. It is the ideal pattern for the individual's life and the Law which binds the Muslim people into a single community. I shall consider this in more detail here, because it is essential to comprehend the all-embracing nature of the *Shari'ah.* The whole concept of usury, or *riba*, within the Islamic banking system even today, is so inextricably tied up with the religious significance of the *Shari'ah* that it is important, especially for Christians and secularists with a Christian background, to appreciate

---

[60]Malise Ruthven, *Islam in the World,* (Penguin Books, London, 1984/91), p.128.

[61]Nasr, *op.cit.*, pp.27,28.

[62]From the root *shara'ah* – to 'introduce,' 'enact,' 'prescribe.' *The Concise Encyclopedia of Islam,* eds. N.Drake and E.Davis, (Stacey International, London, 1989), p.361. Also: 'the road to the watering place, the clear path to be followed; as a technical term the canon law of Islam.' – *The Shorter Encyclopaedia of Islam,* eds. H.A.R.Gibb and J.H.Kramers, (E.J.Brill, Leiden, 1974), p.524.

its role. I particularly mention Christians because a Jew who believes in Talmudic Law can understand what it means to have a 'Divine Law' whereas for most Christians such an understanding comes with difficulty, precisely because in Christianity the 'Divine Will' is expressed in terms of universal teachings such as being charitable, but not in the concrete laws as specified with their religious connotation within the Talmud and *Shari'ah,* for the Jew and the Muslim respectively. This is apparent if we examine the Christian understanding of the concept of usury in terms found in Luke 6.[63] Rather than a concrete law it reveals the concept of a universal teaching which created problems in the Church for centuries, not least, of course, was Christ's admonition: "Think not that I have come to abolish the law and the prophets; I have come not to abolish them but to fulfil them." (Matt. 5:17; RSV). In early Christianity this resulted in much discussion with regard to the understanding and interpretaion of the Judaic law.

The idea of Divine Law in Islam, therefore, is traditionally expressed by the word *shari'ah,* but it can also be expressed by the word *fiqh* which originally meant understanding of the law in the broad sense. This specialist usage emerged at about the same time as the first juristic literature, in the late eighth and early ninth centuries (CE):

> "All efforts to elaborate details of the law, to state specific norms, to justify them by reference to revelation, to debate them, or to write books or treatises on the law are examples of *fiqh.* The word connotes human and specifically scholarly activity. By contrast, *shari'ah* refers to God's law in its quality as divine . . . Practitioners of *fiqh* try to discover and give expression to the *shari'ah.* For

---

[63]See Chapter Two: "And if you lend to those from whom you hope to receive, what credit is that to you? Even sinners lend to sinners, to receive as much again. But love your enemies, and do good, and lend, expecting nothing in return." (Luke 6:34; 35a. Revised Standard Version).

Muslims, the *shari'ah* evokes loyalty and is a focus of faith; *fiqh* evokes at best respect for juristic scholarship and for a literary tradition."[64]

The word *shari'ah* itself is derived etymologically from a root meaning 'road,' as with the Hebraic *halakhah* of the Gemara. It is of great symbolic significance that both the the Divine Law and the Spiritual Way, or *Tariqah*, which is the esoteric dimension of Islam, are based on the symbolism of the way or journey. The *Shari'ah* by considering every aspect of human action thus sanctifies the whole way of life for the Muslim and gives religious significance to what may appear as the most mundane of activities. In Islam the embodiment of the Divine Will is not a set only of general teachings but of concrete ones. Not only is man told to be charitable, humble, or just, but the *Shari'ah* contains the injunctions of the Divine Will for every particular situation in life; whereas, as I have suggested, in Christianity the Divine Will is expressed not in concrete laws but in terms of universal teachings such as being charitable, loving, forgiving, repenting, etc.

As Nasr points out, the difference between the conception of Divine Law in Islam and Christianity can be seen in the way the word canon (*qanun*) is used in the two traditions.[65] In Islam it has come to denote a man-made law, in contrast to the *Shari'ah* or divinely inspired law: in the Christian West the opposing meaning is given to this word, i.e., in the sense that canonical law refers to laws governing the ecclesiastical organisation of the Catholic and Episcopal churches, and has a definite religious connotation. Christianity, as such, therefore, had no Divine legislation of

---

[64]See N.Calder, "Law," in *The Oxford Encyclopedia of the Modern Islamic World, op.cit.*, vol.2, p.450.

[65]Nasr, *op.cit.*, p.94.

its own, in the way that Judaism or Islam had. Christianity had to absorb the Roman Law in order to become the religion of a civilisation. The Roman Law became absorbed into the Christian perspective and 'Christianised' once this religion became dominant in the West.

In this respect it is worth noting that Patricia Crone makes the point that the *a priori* case for a Roman and/or provincial component in Umayyad law is also very strong, and given that it was Umayyad law which the scholars took as their starting point for the creation of the classical *Shari'ah*, there may in principle be residues of this component anywhere in the classical system.[66] She also concludes that the genetic make-up of Islamic law might thus be hypothetically summarised:

> "The tribal legacy of the invaders in conjunction with Jewish concepts provided the Muslims above all with the capacity to reshape, though Jewish law certainly and tribal law possibly contributed raw material too. What they reshaped was essentially provincial practice. This practice contained elements of Roman law in Syria and Egypt, just as it contained elements of Sasanid law in Iraq; and Roman law certainly, and Sasanid law probably, entered the Shari'a as a result."[67]

P. von Sivers also makes the point that both caliphal dynasties of the Umayyads and the Abbasids sought to consolidate their power through

---

[66]Patricia Crone and Martin Hinds also point out in *God's Caliph*, (Cambridge University Press, Cambridge, 1986) that: "We should like to stress that the Umayyads concerned themselves with all aspects of the Shari'a, not merely with the law of war, fiscality and other public matters as Schacht believed to be the case. There is no sense in early Hadith that the Umayyads should be invoked as authorities on public rather than private law; on the contrary, they regularly lay down rules regarding marriage, succession, manumission and the like. It is only when it comes to ritual law that they practically vanish from the material (with the exception of Umar II) . . . The almost total absence of Umayyad caliphs from early Hadith on ritual law is thus likely to mean that it was in this field that their legal competence was rejected." p.53/54.

[67]Patricia Crone, *Roman, provincial and Islamic law*, (Cambridge University Press, 1987), p.16; 99.

caesaropapism – 'a policy of claiming divine sanction for the caliphate and imposing doctrinal unity on the empire,'[68] which by c.712 CE stretched from Iberia to northwest India. However, during the formative period of c.750-1050 CE, caesaropapism was rejected by the religious scholars who had been engaged to devise the desired doctrines and in 1063 the caliph pronounced Sunnism – the scholars' anticaesaropapist version of Islam, as the official orthodox religion. And contrary to widespread contemporary opinion, as von Sivers points out, original Islam – that is, the scholarly Sunnism shaped during this period – did not fuse religion and state. The Sunni scholars maintained that their rulers had to be good Muslims but at the same time they adamantly opposed caesaropapism.

Religion to a Muslim is essentially, therefore, the Divine Law which includes not only universal moral principles but details of how man should conduct his life and deal with his neighbour and with God. It guides man towards an understanding of the Divine Will by indicating which acts and objects are from the religious point of view obligatory, duty (*wajib, fard*); which are meritorious or recommended (*mandub, mustahabb*); which are forbidden (*haram*); which reprehensible, disapproved (*makruh*), and which indifferent (*mubah*).[69]

Some may object that accepting the *Shariah* totally destroys human initiative but this is to misunderstand the inner workings of the Divine Law. Human initiative is required in selecting what is in conformity with one's needs and living according to the Divine norm as indicated by the *Shari'ah*, and a person is free to choose whether to obey or not. It may be a question of obeying one's own individual

---

[68]P. von Sivers, "Islam in the Middle East and North Africa," in *The Oxford Encyclopedia of the Modern Islamic World, op.cit.*, vol. 2, p.255.

[69]See Joseph Schacht, *An Introduction to Islamic Law*, (Oxford University Press, 1964), p.121.

conscience devoid of 'religious' consideration, i.e. it may, at best, be only possible to say that we cannot know whether God exists or not, in which case it may be difficult to obey because of religious doubt – not the doubt of which Kierkegaard speaks, i.e. 'it is difficult to have faith, because it is difficult to obey,' but the honest, rational and relative doubt of an intelligent, enquiring mind. On the other hand, one may choose to obey because one truly believes that the Divine Law is eternal and transcendent, and that which one wishes to obey. It, thus, acts as a strict religious moral framework within which one chooses to orientate oneself ethically, or pay the price for breaking the Law, which in fundamental Judaic and Islamic terms relates to a law which does not differentiate between the religious and the secular. The *Shari'ah* is, ideally, for Islam the means of integrating human society; it is the way in which man is able to give religious significance to his daily life and to be able to integrate this life into a spiritual centre.[70]

---

[70]In essence all of the *Shari'ah* is contained in the Qur'an. It contains the principles of all the Law which were explained and amplified in the prophetic *Hadith* and *Sunnah*, which together constitute the second basic source of Law. These in turn were understood with the aid of the consensus of the Islamic community (*ijma*). The concept of *ijma* has always implied the concensus of those qualified in matters of Law, the *ulama*, combined with an inner interaction with the whole of the community, whose results are only felt gradually. Finally, these sources of Law were complemented by analogical human reasoning (*qiyas*) where necessary, i.e. to use human reason to compare an existing situation with one for which legislation already exists. There was therefore a gradual process by which the Law became established in its external form, and made applicable to all areas of human life. This process was completed in about three centuries during which the great books of law in both Sunni and Shi'ite Islam were written. The four important schools of Sunni law, the Malikite, Hanafite, Shafi'ite and Hanbalite, that constitute the accepted schools of *Shari'ah* to the present day, thus came into being in the third Islamic century. In the Shi'ah world its formation of the Law goes back to the fifth and sixth Imams, especially the sixth Imam Ja'far al-Sadiq so that Twelver Shi'ite Law is often called Ja'fari Law. In Twelver Shi'ism those who have obtained a high state of proficiency in the science of the Law and possess the other traditional requirements become *mujtahids*, that is, those who practice *ijtihad* or exercise their opinions in questions of Law. They are living interpreters of the Law who interpret it in the absence of the Imam and in his name. Every Shi'ite believer must follow a living *mujtahid* whose duty it is to apply and interpret the Law from generation to generation – not to change the Law to suit the convenience of men but to face and solve every new situation and problem in conformity with the teachings of the *Shari'ah* to newly arisen problems. For the Muslim the fact that the Divine Law was explicitly formulated in its final form after several stages does not

The Divine Law is comprised of branches depending on the particular aspect of life with which it is concerned. Some of the traditional scholars have divided it into two branches, one dealing with acts of worship (*ibadat*), and the other treating of transactions (*mu'amalat*).[71] This classical division has led certain modernists to the conclusion that the first part of the *Shari'ah* can be preserved while the second can be secularised or at least changed as one sees fit. However, according to the *Shari'ah* there is no way to separate completely what concerns the relation between man and God from man's relation to other men. Such acts of worship as the congregational prayer, or fasting, have a definite social aspect and involve the whole of the community; equally, how one deals in the market place directly affects the quality and intensity of one's worship.

In the domain of economics the *Shari'ah* contains both specific instructions and general principles. It, therefore, legislates certain forms of taxation such as *zakat*, and for the Shi'ah also *khums* (one-fifth). In a more general sense the economic teachings of the *Shari'ah* are based on the respect of private property whilst, at the same time, opposing an extreme concentration of wealth in the hands of a single person or group. *Riba* is specifically forbidden; the paying of *zakat* itself

---

in any way diminish from its Divine nature and the immutability of its injunctions. See Nasr, *op. cit.*, Chapter iv. Development of the law within the schools depends on two major hermeneutical principles. The synchronic principle required that any formulation of the law, at any time, must be justifiable by reference to revelation; the diachronic principle, which was equally important, though frequently overlooked, required that participants in a school tradition preserve loyalty to the tradition by taking into account the interpretative achievement of older masters, i.e. the law had to be justifiable by reference to the continuity and established identity of the school. Modern historians have not generally accepted the traditional accounts of the origins of Islamic law and have produced an important alternative account associated with the names of Ignacz Goldziher; Joseph Schacht; and John Wansbrough. See "Law," in *The Oxford Encyclopedia of the Modern Islamic World,* vol. 2, *op.cit.*, p.450ff.

[71]*Ibid.*, p.106.

has the function of 'purifying' one's wealth. Wealth is also to be distributed among the rest of the members of society through the 'Muslim public treasury' – *bait mal al-muslimin.*[72] Of all the aspects of the *Shari'ah* its economic teachings are perhaps those that have been least perfectly realised throughout Islamic history, but they have always stood as the ideal to be reached. The general spirit of the teachings contained in the *Shari'ah* is deeply ingrained in the economic life of Muslims; and, although specific forms of taxation may not have been followed by those who object to them, and non-shari'ah taxes may have been levied, the general economic principles of the *Shariah* have been realised to a great extent throughout history among traditional merchants and in craft guilds.[73]

These concepts, implicit and explicit within the *Shari'ah*, therefore, have a profound influence on the Islamic understanding of the concept of usury. Contrasted with the rule of *zakat*, the concept of *riba* is seen to be exploitative of those least able to afford to repay loans let alone any interest accrued; the concept of *ummah* symbolises the Islamic understanding of the sense of community expressed in its totality within the confines of an Islamic world. The concept of *tawhid*, that God is One, is equally expressed in man's striving after wholeness and integration, not only with self, but in community, and in the obligations which that entails in providing for the poor. At the same time Islam acknowledges a profit motive as acceptable to God if this wealth is 'purified' by sharing it. Islam regarded interest as exploitative (*zulm*), and prohibited it not only among Muslims, but also between Muslims and non-Muslims; in fact, with regard to *riba*, according to Kurshid Ahmad, "Islam wants

---

[72]*Ibid.*, p108.

[73]The guild shaykh contributed to the administration of the city and it was through his intermediary that a certain number of taxes were levied on the craftsmen and traders. See Andre Raymond, *"The Role of the Communities (Tawa'if) in the Administration of Cairo in the Ottoman Period,"* in *The State and its Servants*, ed. Nelly Hanna, (The American University in Cairo Press, 1995), pp.32-43.

to build a just economic order for the well-being of all human beings: a new model for mankind."[74]

The Historical Development of the Islamic Teaching on *'Riba'*

That the rigid prohibition of usury in Islamic law only developed gradually is clear from many traditions.[75] What was generally understood in the earliest period as the *riba* forbidden in the Qur'an, seems only to have been interest on loans, chiefly of money and foodstuffs, and anything that goes beyond this is to be regarded as a later development. The reason for such prohibition is said to be the fear of *riba*, or the recognition that there is no tradition of the Prophet relating to this. Muhammad is said to have re-iterated this prohibition at his farewell pilgrimage, and the principle passage in Surah ii relating to this is the latest in the whole Qur'an, which the prophet could not expound before his death. Therefore, while the existence of the Qur'anic prohibition of *riba* has never been doubted, the difference of opinion that finds expression in tradition regarding the relevant facts is continued in the earliest stage of development of Islamic law.

With the death of Muhammad authoritative direction as from on high abruptly ceased. In all religious communities professional theologians are to be found defining what a person must believe and do in order to live as a faithful member of his 'church.' In Islam these duties are defined perhaps even more meticulously than in the Jewish Talmud, and to a far greater extent than any ordinary European would suppose possible, although, of course, in these secular times great latitude in some of these matters is common among many Muslims, as with many Jews or Christians.

---

[74]Kurshid Ahmad, *"Elimination of Riba: Concept and Problems,"* from a paper in *Elimination of Riba from the Economy, op. cit.*, p.47.

[75]J. Schacht, *Encyclopaedia of Islam, op. cit.*, p.1148.

Readers of the Qur'an will perceive that although the laws which govern Muslim custom, *sunna* – 'beaten path' – are foreshadowed there, they will look in vain for the details which make these customs into formal rites and rules of behaviour. To find the underlying authority for these rules one has to go to the books of tradition, *hadith*, which recall the action or speech of the Prophet, Muhammad – although, in fact, what he is reported to have said and done are not always the same. Exactly when records of the deeds and the words of the Prophet were first written down we do not know, even early tradition is at variance on this point. Some say that the Prophet authorised the writing of his sayings; others assert that he forbade it. It is certain, however, that several small collections of traditions were assembled in Umayyad times. It is not the remit of this book to discuss the minutiae of the growth of the tradition, although it is extremely interesting, and for a very useful study in the chronology, provenance and authorship of early *hadith* see G.H.A.Juynboll.[76] However, in order to move toward an Islamic understanding of usury, certain traditions will be discussed with regard to the formulation of the interpretation of the concept of *riba* as it appears in them.

Hadith Interpretation

As the result of a lengthy process, *al-hadith* or Tradition, came to be considered second in authority to the Qur'an. 'Tradition' was an account of what Muhammad said or did, or of his tacit approval of something said or done in his presence. At first, there was no collected body of traditions, it was only gradually as new problems arose that the need of a subsiduary authority was felt – as the demand for traditions increased, the supply grew to meet it. When books of tradition came

---

[76]G.H.A.Juynboll, *Muslim Tradition,* (Cambridge University Press, Cambridge, 1983).

to be compiled the traditions had two necessary criteria: (i) the chain of authorities (*isnad,* or *sanad*) going right back to the source of the tradition, and (ii) the text (*matn*).[77] The ninth century (CE) was the time when the important classified works – *musannaf* – were compiled; six of these works eventually took precedence over others and came to be considered the most authoritative. These were the *Sahihs* of al-Bukhari (d.870) and Muslim ibn al-Hajjaj (d.875), followed in importance by the *Sunan* works of Abu Da'ud (d.889), al-Tirmidhi (d.892), al-Nasa'i (d.915) and Ibn Madja (d.887);[78] both contain details of religious observance, law, commerce, and aspects of public and private behaviour, and the *Sahihs* contain biographical material and Qur'anic commentary. It is in all these works that comments on usury are found, and in theory the traditions of al-Bukhari and Muslim are all considered sound, whereas those in other books have varying degrees of worth, although that is not to say that there have not been criticisms made even of some of al-Bukhari's and Muslim's traditions. As there was no official body to commission the books of Tradition they had to make their own appeal to the community and by the tenth century (CE) the collections of al-Bukhari and Muslim were fairly generally recognised, with the others gaining recognition over a longer period of time. Although other books were also compiled they did not command as much respect as the 'six books.' It might be noted that all the works quoted so far were recognised by Sunnis. The Shi'is have books of their own, accepting only traditions traced through Ali's family – to support the claim of the Shia.

---

[77]*The Encyclopaedia of Islam – New Edition*, Volume III, ed. B.Lewis; V.L.Menage; Ch.Pellat; J.Schacht. (E.J.Brill, Leiden; Luzac & Co., London; 1971), p.24.

[78]Andrew Rippon, *Muslims – Their Religious Beliefs and Practices,* Volume I, The Formative Period, (Routledge, London, 1990), p.37.

In time criticism of the traditions developed for various reasons. It was claimed that much was fabricated. Seemingly impeccable *isnads* were attached to the most extraordinary traditions by the storytellers – *kussas* – in order to astonish the common people and to receive payment for their stories. Others spread false doctrines, or, at the other extreme, the very pious invented traditions to exhort men to live righteously. Some were accused of carelessness in transmission or of being inaccurate in old age. Eventually traditions were divided into *sahih* (sound), of which there were seven grades, the first of which were those given by al-Bukhari and Muslim. *Hasan* (good) were considered not quite so strong but were necessary for establishing points of law, and the remaining two categories were *da'if* (weak) and *sakim* (infirm).[79] The early grammarians, though they dare not say that the *hadith* were not authentic, asserted that the Arabic in which they were written was so bad that they could not be shown to transmit the actual words of Muhammad, even though they doubtlessly conveyed the same meaning.[80]

The criticism of traditions was very detailed, showing how seriously the work was undertaken, and one recognises the genuine effort made to clear away what was false. It is not the remit of this work to remark on whether a tradition was genuine or not, merely to note the criticism of it in the words of Robson, and to show how as accepted tradition it applied to the Islamic teaching on the concept of usurious lending:

> "Professor J. Schacht has argued cogently that *isnads* grew as time passed, and so legal traditions which belonged to a later period were eventually traced back to the Prophet. While one does not feel

---

[79] *The Encyclopaedia of Islam – New Edition, op. cit.* p.25.

[80] A.Guillaume, *Islam,* (Penguin Books, London, 1954), pp.91/92.

justified in explaining away the whole body of Tradition on these lines, it it quite clear that much material coming from a later date has been attributed to the Prophet, and this makes it very difficult to find a satisfactory criterion by which one may recognise what is genuine. Material which accumulated within a certain circle may often have seemed to a later generation to have come from a Companion who settled in the area, and by a natural process to have been attributed to him with the assumption that he had the Prophet as his authority. One result of Western criticism is that we must be chary of accusing men like Abu Hurayra of inventing many traditions, for they probably heard and transmitted very little of what they are reputed to have told."[81]

The books which collected together what were considered genuine *hadith* reports, served as the theoretical basis for Islamic law, and in the beginning the laws concerning usury, or *riba*, were very complex indeed. It must be remembered that the Qur'an consists mainly of broad and general propositions as to what the aims of Muslim society should be. The so-called legal material constitutes essentially the bare formulation of the Islamic religious ethic, so that fairness and good faith in commercial dealings, and incorruptibility in the administration of justice, are all enjoined as desirable norms of behaviour, rather than legal structures of rights and duties. The same applies to the precept of *riba* which is more particular, and peculiarly Islamic, in its terms – it is simply declared to be forbidden (*haram*) but no indication of the legal incidents of the practice is contained in the Qur'an. The primary purpose of the Qur'an is to regulate the relationship of man with his Creator rather than his fellows, so that while the legislator sees the consequences of wrong-doing in the light of sanctions enforced by human agency, the Prophet would see it in terms of fault in the sight of God. For those who were pledged to conduct their

---

[81] *The Encyclopaedia of Islam – New Edition, op. cit*, p.27.

lives in accordance with the will of God the Qur'an itself did not provide a straightforward code of law. This necessarily would pose problems. Usury – *riba* – had simply been prohibited, but what would be the effect in practical terms of the essentially ethical standard imposed by this measure? As Coulson remarks:

> "It is hardly too cynical to suggest that the potential lender or borrower might be at least as interested in the effect of his dealings on his pocket or his person as he would be in the prospect of eternal damnation"[82]

And, according to Schacht, it is clear from many traditions that the rigid prohibition of usury in Islamic law only developed gradually; what was generally understood in the earliest period as the *riba* forbidden in the Qur'an seems, as I have already intimated, only to have been interest on loans, chiefly of money and foodstuffs, and anything beyond this was a later development.[83] The crucial question, much debated in modern scholarship, might be asked as to when did Muhammad emerge as being the source of authority for the community? Equally, when did the notion of the 'local tradition' as basis for legal practice become supplanted by the *sunna* as second only to the Qur'an? Important though these questions are, the exact dating of these facts is not essential for this exposition. What is of historical importance is that these developments took place over a period of time so that by the ninth century CE both were in place.

---

[82]N.J. Coulson, *A History of Islamic Law*, (Edinburgh University Press, 1964), p.17.

[83]See J. Schacht in *Encyclopaedia of Islam*, (Riba), *op. cit.*, p.1148.

The 'Schools of Law' with Regard to *Riba*

During the last decades of Umayyad rule, in the middle of the eighth century CE, pious scholars grouped together to form the early schools of law; and when the Umayyad dynasty was finally overthrown the Abbasids came to power in 750 CE and two streams of anti-Umayyad criticism, political and legal, converged.

Although the Umayyads had become very unpopular, it must be remembered that under them vast territories were being conquered. Amid the pressing problems being created by incessant wars, the financing of the empire, the different languages spoken in the conquered countries, and the settling of the hordes of land-hungry Arabs, it would be foolish to expect that a code of law could be drawn up, or, if it were drawn up, administered systematically in the circumstances that prevailed. So, although, as Coulson points out, discontent was fostered by the complaints of the Persians and other non-Arab converts (*mawali*) against the racial discrimination of the Arab dominion, and was exploited by those who wished to seize power for themselves,[84] Guillaume contends that one could not but admire the Umayyads in so far as:

> "The system that had sufficed to guard the right to a few sheep or camels had to be transformed before it would suffice to adjust the rights and claims of a tribe of millionaires."[85]

Indeed, what is pertinent, is that prior to the advent of Islam the unit of society, as already mentioned, was the tribe, a group of blood relatives who claimed descent from a common ancestor and who owed their allegiance not merely to a

---

[84]N.J.Coulson, *op. cit.*, p.36.

[85]A.Guillaume, *op.cit.*, p.93.

nominal leader but to the tribe as a whole. The tribe was bound by a body of unwritten rules which had evolved along with the tribe itself; their source lay in the will of the whole community, even though they may have been initiated by an individual. The Arab tribes who accepted Muhammad as the Prophet and spokesman of God regarded themselves as constituting a new kind of group – *ummah* – wherein the bond of common religious faith transcended tribal ties, even if fragmented – unlike Judaism which maintained its tribal identity within its diasporan communities; and the Qur'an, consisting mainly of broad and general principles as to what the aims and aspirations of Muslim society should be, was essentially the bare formulation of the Islamic religious ethic. In time, this was augmented by the Islamic schools of law and the *hadith* traditions which established rules of conduct, especially with regard to *riba*. The nature of this report is to examine the traditional teaching from the early, classical, schools of law with regard to their teaching on usury, but it is worth noting that today the 'living law schools' equally have the task of evaluating modern social life and modern legal thought from an Islamic angle to determine which elements in traditional Islamic doctrine represent, in their view, the essential Islamic standards. As Schacht remarks:

> "The situation in which the modernist lawyers of Islam find themselves resembles essentially that which prevailed at the end of the first and at the beginning of the second century of the hijra. Islamic jurisprudence did not grow out of an existing law, it created itself; and once again, it has been the modernist jurists who prepared, provoked, and guided a new legislation. It had been the task of the early specialists to impose Islamic standards on law and society . . . it still casts its spell over the laws of contemporary Islamic states: in the states of traditional orientation, such as Saudi Arabia, as the law

of the land; and in the states of modernist orientation as an ideal influencing and even inspiring their secular legislation."[86]

The earliest schools were geographically defined, they were congories of scholars who lived in the same city, often making a livelihood as merchants and shopkeepers and discussing law in their spare time. Early legal schools were found in Iraq: Kufa – the Hanafis; the school of Sufyan al-Thawri; the Zaydis, a Shi'ite sect; the Imamis or Ithna-ash'aris, 'Twelver Shi'ites'; and the Isma'ilis, dissident Imamis, and are known from the works of Qadi Nu'man. This is interesting because they based themselves on Imami law taken from Kufa, whereas most extant Imami doctrine has been filtered through Qumm, the second Shi'ite centre. At Basra there were the Ibadis, a subset of the Kharijites. In Syria there was the school of Awza'i; and in Medina – the Malikis; the Shafi'is; and the school of Layth b. Sa'd, an Egyptian who studied in Medina. Mecca and the Yemen did not produce a classical school. Other schools consisted of the Hanbalis; the Zahiris; and miscellaneous schools such as the Jaririyya founded by Tabari. Although at first sight the doctrines of all these schools are very similar, there are important differences, and the most important ones are not those between Sunnis and non-Sunnis, but rather those between the Kufan and Basran schools on the one hand and the Medinese and later schools on the other. One finds, according to Crone, that the Hanafis, the Ibadis and the three Shi'ite schools regularly form one bloc, perpetuating the legal tradition of the old Iraqi schools, while the Malikis, Shafi'is and Hanbalis form another.[87]

The Sunni Muslims today, therefore, are distributed among four surviving schools of law, the Shi'is having their own schools. The first, chronologically, is the

---

[86]See J.Schacht, *op.cit.*, chapter 15, "Modernist Legislation," pp.100-111.

[87]P.Crone, *Roman, provincial, and Islamic law, op.cit.*, p.19ff.

Hanafite, named after Abu Hanifa (d.767), the founder of the Iraqi school. It was the official school of the Ottomans and is widespread in Turkey, and today followers are centred in Iraq, the Indo-Pakistani sub-continent, China, and Lower Egypt; broad-minded without being lax, the school likes to appeal to reason. The second Sunni school is the Malikite, after Malik ibn Anas (d.796), the founder of the Medina school and the author of the first comprehensive law book to survive – the *Muwatta*. His school, today, is predominant in West Africa and Upper Egypt, and completely dominant in North Africa, and its followers constitute the most homogenous body in the realm of Sunni law; it stresses a broad appeal to the principle of general utility, evoking among some people the idea of the 'common good.'[88] The third is the Shafi'ite, named after Muhammad Ibn-Idris al-Shafi'i (d.822), the outstanding figure in Muslim jurisprudence and a powerful and forceful thinker. His succeeding influence on generations was very great, and his school is represented today in Lower Egypt, Syria and southern Arabia, from whence it spread to Malaysia, Indonesia and

---

[88]The concept of the 'common good,' which may be compared to the idea of 'public welfare' in Islam – *maslaha*, in relation to economic interests is a very interesting one. John Atherton remarks that it was Adam Smith who, in fact, recognised the importance of *self-interest* as the basic motivator in the economy. 'It is not from the benevolence of the butcher, the brewer, or the baker, that we expect our dinner, but from their regard to their own interest. We address ourselves, not to their humanity but to their self-love.' In pursuing that interest privately and competitively, the consequences served the 'common good,' whether intended or not. In other words 'the individual is in this, as in many other cases led by an invisible hand to promote an end which has no part of his intention . . . I have never known much good done by those who affected to trade for the public good.' This approving acknowledgment of the relationship between self-enrichment and public good represented a fundamental break with medieval and biblical authority, and Atherton states that today 'the common good, with its overtness of undue political interference in economic life and private choice, may no longer be an appropriate concept for Christian social thought.' Indeed, he states that 'even that fine 'gathering' concept of the 'common good' must be foregone if we are to do justice to the survey of the market economy and its Christian responses. It is too closely associated with the liberal and other responses, and is too suggestive of a Christian synthesis, a Christian overview of the world. Even a provisional framework appears too close to the concern for a Christian map, and its inability to reflect the changing complexities of an increasingly plural world.' See J.Atherton, *Christianity and the Market* (SPCK, London, 1992), pp.41; 256; and 265.

East Africa; this school attempts to combine tradition and the consensus of the Muslim community (rather than the consensus of individual scholars), and results in a broad recourse to reasoning by analogy. Finally there are the Hanbalites, followers of Ibn Hanbal (d.855). He was intensely conservative in the matter of the *hadith*, and intolerant and fanatical with regard to a Muslim's duties and responsibilities – he was alleged never to have eaten watermelon because he was not in possession of any Prophetic precedent on the subject. He rejected human reason in any form as a source of law i.e. the *qiyas* as arguments by analogy, and insisted that each and every legal rule could only find its requisite authority in the divine revelation of the Qur'an and the practice or example of the Prophet. He collected in his work, the *Musnad*, more than eighty thousand *hadiths*. For centuries his school has been diminishing and it never succeeded in gaining any real territorial dominion until its tenets were adopted by the Wahhabi movement in the eighteenth century, so that today the Hanbali school is the official law of Saudi Arabia.[89]

The legal scholars were publicly recognised as the architects of an Islamic scheme of state and society which the Abbasids had pledged themseleves to build. Under this political sponsorship, therefore, the schools of law rapidly developed. During the eighth century (CE) of the many schools of law which flourished at this time those of Medina (Malik) and Kufa (Hanafi) were to prove the most important and enduring.

It is interesting to note that none of these schools treated the lending of money at interest as a criminal offence, so that enforcing payment in a court of law did not, in fact, constitute a problem. The literalistic Hanbalis ruled that repayment of a usurious loan could not be enforced because it was against the Qur'anic

---

[89]A.Guillaume, *op.cit.*, p.102.

teaching; similarly, the Malikis and Shafi'is adopted the position that a contract which was thus rendered illegal could not be enforced under the Law; only the Hanafis enforced the repayment of the principal which they regarded as a gratuitous loan, but they could not enforce the debtor to pay the interest.[90] Paradoxically, with its strict adherence to a literalistic legal interpretation of the Qur'anic teaching, the Hanbalis actually allowed for more innovation, proscribing only that which was actually forbidden in the Qur'an itself.

It was at this stage, c.770 CE, however, that opposition to the generally accepted legal method in the early schools materialised. According to Coulson, its distinguishing feature was a rigidly doctrinaire approach both to the substance of the law and the jurisprudential basis on which it rested. The doctrinaire group advocated a strict and much more meticulous adherence to Qur'anic norms than did the scholars who were prepared to accept current legal practice into their scheme of law unless an explicit principle of the Qur'an was violated.

With regard to the teaching on *riba*, therefore, the doctrinaire group, with their rigid interpretations, ruled that the barter of certain commodities – gold, silver, and certain foodstuffs – against a commodity of the same species was only permissable when the offerings on both sides were exactly equal in weight or quantity and when delivery on both sides was immediate. Former Medinan doctrine had allowed the exchange of gold ore against a smaller weight of gold coinage, the difference covering the cost of minting; but to the doctrinaire group this constituted *riba* and was thus prohibited:

> "This approach naturally resulted in the law of the doctrinaire group assuming a highly negative character, in essence if not in form, to the

---

[90]M.Ruthven, *op.cit.* ("The Evolution of Islamic Principles in Relation to Financial Dealings"), p.5.

degree that it lost touch with practical needs and circumstances. It is difficult to see any point or purpose in a transaction where 'Umar takes 20lb. of Zayd's wheat in exchange for 20lb. of his own wheat in the same session."[91]

However, although on the surface it appears hard to understand why anyone would want to exchange a given quantity of gold or silver, or any other commodity against its own counterpart, what is essentially being required, as Chapra reminds us, is justice and fair play. The price and the counter value should be just in all transactions where cash payment – irrespective of what constitutes money, is made by one party and the commodity or service is delivered reciprocally by the other.[92]

Under the influence of the doctrinaire opposition the current doctrine in the early schools was gradually modified and many of the stricter rules advocated by the opposition, such as those concerned with *riba*, won a general acceptance. There was a growing tendency to claim the authority of the prophet for it and to express it in the form of a tradition. From the years 770-800 CE the reasoning of individual scholars, local consensus, and the reported precedents of Muhammad lay in uneasy juxtaposition.[93] This stage of legal development is mirrored in the first written compendium of law produced in Islam – Malik's *Muwatta*.

Malik recognised the general prohibition against *muzabana* contracts, the barter of unripe fruits on the tree against the same species of dried fruits, but at the same time he recognised the validity of the barter of *ariyya,* or unripe dates on the palm, against dried dates. In connection with *riba*, tradition mentions various

---

[91]N.J.Coulson, *op. cit.*, p.42.

[92]Chapra, *op. cit.*, p.59.

[93]Coulson, *op. cit.*, p.43.

antiquated forms of sale of special kinds, like *muhakala, mukhabara, muzabana*, etc. which concern the exchange of different stages in the manufacture or development of the same thing, or of different qualities, and which are forbidden. An exception is made, obviously because of its undeniable practical and social necessity, of what is known as *arriya* – fresh dates on trees intended to be eaten, which it is permitted to exchange in small quantities for dried dates.

Although, as already stated, the Qur'anic prohibition of *riba* has never been doubted, the difference of opinion in the tradition continued in the earliest stage of the development of Islamic law. Indeed, numerous traditions forbade *riba* without defining it more closely.

> "Unanimity prevails, however, with regard to the main lines of the limitations to be imposed upon the exchange of goods capable of *riba* (*mal ribawi*). It is only permitted if transfer of ownership takes place at once and, so far as goods of the same kind are concerned, only in equal quantities. In the case of a loan it is forbidden to make a condition that a larger quantity shall be returned without regard to the kind of article. Gold and silver are generally regarded as *mal ribawi* (only exceptionally are coins of small denomination included)."[94]

In the schools of law the following goods are expressly mentioned in addition to gold and silver as bearing the prohibition of *riba* at their exchange: wheat; barley; dates and salt (sometimes also raisins, butter and oil). According to the Hanafis gold and silver represent examples of the class of things defined by weight (*mawzun*) and the four other things those sold by measure (*makil*). According to the Malikis and Shafi'is, gold and silver represent the class of precious metals and the four other things the class of foodstuffs. A more plausible explanation is that all six

---

[94]*Encyclopaedia of Islam*, (Riba), *op. cit.*, p. 1149.

commodities were used as money in and around Medina, particularly among the bedouins, and therefore, *riba al-fadl* would be involved in the exchange of any goods against cash or any commodity which is used as money.[95] The more staple the food item or the greater its need for sustaining life, the greater the injustice inflicted in an unfair exchange. In that respect the use of money could help reduce the possibility of an unfair exchange. A strict view held that even the exchange of the same quantities of the same thing, especially of precious metals, was *riba,* whereas an old interpretation stated that there is no *riba* if the transfer of possession takes place at once. This perception of *riba,* however, is in connection with exchange or barter – *riba al-fadl*. The prohibition of *riba al-fadl* was intended to ensure justice and remove all forms of exploitation through unfair exchange and to close all backdoors to *riba* because in the *Shari'ah* anything that serves as a means to the unlawful is itself unlawful. Riba in a loan, *riba al nasi'ah*, exists not only when one insists upon the repayment of a larger quantity, but if any advantage at all is demanded. Even exchange (*suftadja*) is sometimes actually forbidden because the vendor, who is regarded as the creditor, reaps the advantage of avoiding the cost of transport. This did not prevent the spread of this arrangement in the Arab middle ages, however, and its influence on European money-changing.[96]

The importance of the prohibition of *riba* which deeply affected every day life, and the growing requirements of commerce, gave rise to a number of methods of evasion. From the standpoint of the law there is nothing formally to object to against some of these, and therefore they are given in some of the law books and expressly said to be permitted. The Shafi'is, and later, Hanafis, have recognised such

---

[95]Chapra, *op. cit.*, p.59.

[96]*Encyclopaedia of Islam* (Riba), *op. cit.*, See *Riba* – pp.1148-1150.

methods of evasion, whereas, the Malikis and the Hanbalis reject them.   The
recognition of these methods of evasion is not contrary to the strict enforcement of
the prohibition in the *fiqh*.   Their line of argument is based not only on their formal
negative rejection of deduction by analogy but also on their positive estimation of the
intention underlying the evasions.

One of the oldest transactions of this kind is the 'double contract of sale'
(from one of its elements it is called *bai al-ina*).   The way in which it operates is that
the moneylender sells to someone who wants to borrow money at interest, something
against the total sum of the capital and interest which are to be due at a fixed date,
and at the same time he buys the article back for the capital, which is at once handed
over.[97]   This transaction was taken over in medieval Europe under the name of
mohatra.[98]   Another method of evasion consists of handing over to the creditor the
use of a thing as interest by a fictitious agreement to sell or to pledge.   All these
practices are still in use and in spite of the prohibition of *riba*, moneylending is a
flourishing business in most Muslim countries, and fifty per cent is often regarded
as moderate interest.   However, with regard to the *hadith* and the schools of law,
there have been, in the late twentieth century, serious attempts amongst Muslims to
take Qur'anic principles seriously in the conduct of some moneylending business,
and, in particular, within the context of the phenomenon known as 'Islamic Banking,'
however that is defined, and this will be discussed in a later section.   One of the most

---

[97]For example: The moneylender will sell to the borrower goods to the value of £40 plus £10 interest,
and the date to repay the £50 will be agreed on for some future date.   At the same time the
moneylender buys back the goods for the capital value of £40 which is immediately handed over to
the borrower.   The £50 is then repaid at a later date as agreed.   The borrower has a capital advance,
and the moneylender has his money returned plus interest at a future date.   Ostensibly the article is
sold at a first-hand purchase price and bought back at a lower second-hand rate.

[98]*Ibid.*, p.1150.

interesting aspects for me as a theologian is that it appears to be the only religion at present engaged in a serious attempt to practically apply its moral and ethical scriptural teaching with regard to the concept of usurious lending within the context of the market-place i.e. a global free-market economy.

In parts of the Islamic world pious Muslims have always been conscious that a direct breach of the prohibition of *riba* is a deadly sin, and to this day, they not infrequently refuse to take bank interest. In the light of this, therefore, in the modern era, banking systems have developed which take seriously the prohibition of *riba* in the Qur'an. It is, in this respect, to the development of what might be termed an 'Islamic economic system' to which I now turn, incorporating as it does not only economic activity but ethical considerations based on economic and social justice.

The Development of 'Islamic Economics'

According to the doctrine of *tawhid* there is no strictly mundane sector of life. In every field of human activity, action, including economic action, has a spiritual dimension so long as it is in harmony with the goals and values of Islam. It is these goals and values that determine the nature of the economic system in Islam, and a proper understanding of them is essential for a better perception of it. It is only in the comprehension of the concepts of brotherhood and social justice, *tawhid* and *ummah*, already discussed with regard to the Qur'anic teaching on the prohibition of *riba*, that the development of a specific Islamic economic system can be understood. Although by no means complete, these goals and values can be defined as: economic well-being within the framework of the moral norms of Islam; universal brotherhood and justice; equitable distribution of income; and freedom of the individual within the context of the social welfare.[99] Islam is not devoid, as we have seen, of positive assertions about economic reality, and, therefore, it is theoretically possible to replace non-Islamic economic value judgements by Islamic ones. As Kurshid Ahmad remarks: "Economics is not as innocent of value judgments as we are often led to believe, nor can it ever be."[100] And, although one might argue that it is not possible to have meaningful *Islamic* economics, any more than we can have Islamic mathematics or Islamic atom physics, this book is maintaining that distinct and meaningful Islamic economics is possible with particular regard to the Islamic teaching on *riba*. Equally, it can be admitted that several areas of economics, such that they are, cannot be different whether given an Islamic framework or any other – such as first and second order conditions for achieving a given amount of production with minimum costs, given factor prices, and a production function.[101] How an 'Islamic economic system' developed, and is defined, however, can be deduced from an historic overview.

In an article entitled "*The Muslim Scholars and the History of Economics: A need for Consideration,*" Abbas Mirakhor addresses the theory of 'the Great Gap.' This, according to Joseph Schumpeter in his 'History of Economic Analysis' (1954), existed for five hundred years before the epoch within the Christian European tradition of Thomas Aquinas and the Scholastics,[102] the implication being that for that

---

[99]Muhammad Umar Chapra, *Objectives of the Islamic Economic Order,* (The Islamic Foundation, Leicester), 1979, p.6.

[100]Khurshid Ahmad, *Studies in Islamic Economics,* (International Centre for Research in Islamic Economics, King Abdul Aziz University, Jeddah; The Islamic Foundation, Leicester), 1980, p.4.

[101]*Ibid.,* p.5.

[102]The 'Scholastics' can be defined as those men in the medieval period who were the acknowledged intellectual and moral leaders of Europe for several hundred years. The Scholastic interpretation of

period nothing was said, written or practiced which had any relevance to economics. The question which Mirakor poses and addresses, however, is: how were the Scholastics able to compose such a relatively large body of thought regarding economic matters in the thirteenth, fourteenth, and fifteenth centuries?

> "The more one studies the economic ideas of Islam, the economic writings of the Muslim writers who preceded the Scholastics, the economic processes and institutions existing in both the Muslim East and the Muslim West in the seventh through fourteenth centuries, the more sceptical one becomes of Schumpeter's "the Great Gap" and the disregard of historians of economic thought of the contributions of Muslim scholars in the development of economic thought and institutions in the thirteenth, fourteenth and fifteenth centuries."[103]

Mirakhor further maintains that the works of, for instance, Udovitch, Labib, Tuma, and Hassan Uz-Zaman, have all shown that ideas regarding fiscal policy, monetary policy, and institutions, credit and credit instruments, price determination and price policy, market and market regulation, commodity exchange, monopoly, government budgets, supply and demand, checking and saving accounts, rudiments of banking institutions and procedures on the formation of partnerships and 'commenda' *(mudharaba)* contracts, as well as usury, had all developed in the world of Islam in the first two and a half centuries of its life. By the ninth century CE many of these ideas had appeared in writing in the form of *Fiqh* Manuals. Between the ninth and fourteenth centuries authors from the Islamic East, such as Ghazali, Ibn Al-

---

the usury analysis within the Christian tradition was the result of the interaction of many forces but it had a religious origin and religious authority controlled much of its development. It was Western man's first attempt at an economic theory, from this time on the ideal of justice, as opposed to charity or greed, underlies every statement of it. It was originally and primarily a *theological* creation.

[103] Abbas Mirakhor, "The Muslim Scholars and the History of Economics," *The American Journal of Islamic Social Studies*, Volume 4, Number 2, Dec. 1987, p.249.

Ukhuwa, Kai Ka'us Ibn Iskander, Nizam Al-Mulk, Ibn Abi'ar-Rabi, Al-Farabi, Ibn Sina, Nasir Al-Din Tusi and Al-Diwwani, as well as those from Muslim Spain with whom the Scholastics were familiar, such as Ja'afar Al-Dimishqi, Ibn Bajja (Avempace), and Ibn Rushd (Averroes), had dealt with economic ideas on taxation, market regulation, usury, permissable economic behaviour, wages, prices, the division of labour, money as a medium of exchange, coinage price fluctuations, and finally ethical prescriptions regarding observance of the 'mean' in economic behaviour.[104] The economic writings of Ibn Khaldun in the fourteenth century have a wide range of discussions on economics including the subjects of value, division of labour, the price system, the law of supply and demand, consumption and production, money, capital formation, population growth, public finance, and trade cycles. Khaldun discussed the various stages in economic progress through which societies pass and he also noticed, in the Keynesian sense, the importance of the demand side, particularly government expenditure, in avoiding business slumps and maintaining economic development.[105] He was, according to Mieczkowski, in some respects ahead of the founder of economic science Adam Smith.[106]

The writings of the Greeks became available to Muslim scholars in the middle of the ninth century, but the extent of the knowledge of economic behaviour in medieval Islam was far greater than that, and much of what is important in this

---

[104]*Ibid.*, p.250.

[105]Kurshid Ahmad, *op.cit.*, p.261; and see also Aziz Al-Azmeh, *Ibn Khaldun*, Chapter Two, "The Problematization of History," [The American University in Cairo Press, Cairo, 1993 (Routledge, London, 1982)], pp.92-101.

[106]Bogdan Mieczkowski, *"Ibn Khaldun's Fourteenth Century Views on Bureaucracy,"* Islamic Social Sciences, Vol. 4, Number 2, December 1987, pp.179-199.

corpus of economic ideas had its origins in the first two and a half centuries of Islam. Mirakhor continues to explain how the transmission of Islamic economic thought to the Scholastics took place, and how, in fact, the Scholastics borrowed from this. He also maintains, and shows, that to search for Islamic ideas on economics one must begin with the primary documentary source, the Qur'an. This lays great emphasis on economic justice as the foundation of social justice, and as required by the axiom of unity, social and economic justice require a simultaneous adjustment in all aspects of economic life:

> "Muslims are told to earn and enjoy wealth, and economics becomes the substantive base of the Islamic social order and is invested with a unique moral quality. A Muslim engaged in the act of production is engaged in a form of worship, *Ibadat.*"[107]

Hence, the economic behaviour is teleological in that its ultimate aim is God (in the same way that *tachlis* operates within a Judaic framework) and the 'Islamic Community' has a central position in the Islamic social arrangement. Within the economic ideas of the Scholastics, Mirakhor concludes that many concepts in the field of money, credit, partnership, market and market forces, arguments against usury, theory of value, and other ideas found their origin in the Muslim East. The fact that many sources of Islamic economic ideas were available to the Scholastics only serves to strengthen this argument – especially with regard to the effect of the writings of Averroes on Aquinas. The Qur'an is known to have been translated into Latin twice, once by Peter Cluny, d.1156, a copy of which was available to St.Thomas, and again by Robert Ketton and Hermann of Dalmatia.[108]

---

[107]Mirakhor, *op. cit.*, p.253.

[108]M. Watt, *The Influence of Islam on Medieval Europe,* (Edinburgh University Press, 1972), pp. 60-71.

Although the Qur'an and the *Sunnah* prescribe how the economic life of the community should be regulated (for example, with regard to the acquisition and disposal of private property; the method of purchase and sale of goods; the redistribution of wealth through various forms of taxation and almsgiving; the borrowing and lending of money; the provision of care and protection for the poor and needy; and the procedure of bequeathing wealth and property), there does not exist, however, as M.Shaghil points out, any compendium or consolidated picture of the principles on which economic life is to be patterned in order to be in conformity with the tenets of Islam. "The requisite information has to be pieced together, analysed and interpreted to present a unified account of what may be euphemistically called Islamic Economics."[109] I would agree with this, but what Shaghil goes on to offer in the name of 'Islamic Economics,' however, is, according to T.Torrance:

> "an extreme type of collectivism involving 'demonetizing the economy' and 'dispensing with the market economy.' (p.44) Even the product market, at the retail level, is to be centrally planned entailing ration coupons for food, clothing, etc. . . . Shaghil's approach, with total planning from the centre even at the micro-economic level is not, and has never been, used even in the USSR. As an idea it is as unworkable as anything can be and I find it quite surprising to find such a notion advocated in the name of Islam!"[110]

Unworkable as his ideal Islamic economy would appear to be, it is at least an attempt to address an economic system which in Shaghil's opinion presents an

---

[109]M.Shaghil, "Islamic Economics; A View," *Journal of the West Asian Studies Society,* 1986, p.12.

[110]Letter to Prof. J. Thrower from Prof. T.Torrance dated 22/4/88, Department of Economics, Aberdeen University. I am very grateful to Professor Thrower for providing me with this information as well as various journals.

hypothetical model of an economy consistent with the highest principles of Islam. For instance, in discussing the 'demonetizing of the economy,' he is no doubt reflecting the fact that in the Middle East the monetarisation of transactions has been a relatively recent phenomenon, and, even today, many people do not use banks. As Wilson points out:

> "In other Third World societies there were no moral objections to the replacement of barter with cash and credit transactions. Due to the Islamic code of ethics, however, there has been popular resistance to modern financial developments in many parts of the Muslim world ... although most people no longer regard paper money as being un-Islamic, the use of cheques, commercial bank credit and other banking instruments is viewed with suspicion by many devout Muslims."[111]

Shaghil's ideas, however, are quite different from Tahir's, who, in outling Islamic budgetary policy (with regard to Malaysia), is quite happy with market-oriented arrangements provided that particular outcomes do not offend too strongly on matters such as Islamic ideas of welfare and income distribution:

> "From one viewpoint the system ('Islamic economics') apparently shares two of the essential features of Western capitalism: freedom of enterprise and the right to private ownership. But these feature are reinforced by a concern for economic justice and the general welfare of the community. . . . In modern Western societies the individual's sense of responsibility is, to a considerable extent, diminished by state control of the public services . . . In Islamic societies, the state or the ruler cannot relieve the individual of his duties imposed by certain injunctions explicitly shown in the Qur'an (xxiv.55)."[112]

---

[111]Rodney Wilson, *op. cit.*, p.182.

[112]Hailani Muji Tahir, *Islamic Budgetary Policy in Theory and Practice*, (Ph.D. Thesis, Aberdeen University, 1988). p.504.

This system is reminiscent of the social welfarism of Judaic practice but just as the concept of moneylending, albeit to the 'other,' was condoned in Judaism and gave rise, as I believe, to an early form of capitalistic enterprise (atavistic almost from the beginnings of money-changing in the Temple), it is perhaps this very same concept which has been a stumbling-block, in capitalistic terms, to its development within Islam. To uphold the Qur'anic injunction against *riba* was to foster the notion of *ummah* and 'brotherhood' in socialistic, rather than capitalistic terms. To remain within the Qur'anic prohibition, Islamic economics ingeniously had to invent ways in which a specific banking system could operate within its Qur'anic remit.

It is equally important to remind ourselves, however, that the kind of utopian, ideal society envisaged in Islam for mankind, or for that matter homogeneity within the Judaic diasporan communities, in so far as an economic structure and pattern is concerned, does not, in fact, exist (except perhaps symbolically, or loosely), anywhere in the Islamic, or Judaic, world. The whole concept of 'utopianism' which philosophically and politically shook the Western world to its roots during the last two centuries, is, however, now affecting the Islamic world profoundly – although the idea of unilateral progress rejected in the West is now being rejected by Islam. Islam has had its descriptions of the perfect state of society in works such as those of Farabi, describing the 'virtuous society' – *al-madinat al-fadilah,* or the texts of Shihab al-Din Suhrawardi who refers to the land of perfection as the *na kuja-abad* - the 'land of nowhere': utopia.[113] Utopianism usually seeks to establish a perfect social order through purely human means. However, Nasr maintains that within the realm of Islam, the *Dar al-Islam* – as opposed to the *Dar al-Harb,* the 'realm of war,'

---

[113]Seyyed Hossein Nasr, *Traditional Islam in the Modern World,* (Kegan Paul International Ltd., London, 1987), p.107.

or those lands not under Muslim rule – the Muslim is always aware that if there were to be a perfect state it could only come into being through Divine help. He points out that this has prevented, until recently, the kind of utopianism present in modern European philosophy from growing upon the soil of Islamic thought:

> "Hence, although the idea of the cyclic renewal of Islam through a 'renewer' (*mujaddid*) has always been alive, as has the wave of Mahdism which sees in the Mahdi the force sent by God to return Islam to its perfection, Islam has never faced within itself that type of secular utopianism which underlies so many of the socio-political aspects of modern thought. It is therefore essential to be aware of the profound distinction between modern utopianism and Islamic teaching concerning the *mujaddid* and the modern reformer, who usually, as a result of his feeble reaction to modern thought, can hardly be said to have brought about the renewal of Islam."[114]

But this is to deny at least two concepts. One is that an Islamic construct of utopianism, even whilst denying any Western influence, is not necessarily devoid of secular implication, if not intention, e.g. as self-styled *wilayat al-faqih* (the guardianship of the jurist), Khomeini's political doctrine was conducted exclusively in terms of traditional Islamic discussions with hardly any reference to Western or Western-inspired politico-ideological notions. However, while he drew on traditional sources and forms of reasoning, he reached very novel conclusions which were only possible and plausible on the assumption – implicit in Khomeini's work – of secular and utopian ideas within a modern nation-state and its peculiar form of politics, such as democracy, equality, liberty, and social justice, albeit clothed in Islamic terms.[115] Secondly, it could be argued that the renewal of Islam might

---

[114]*Ibid.*, p.107.

[115]Sami Zubaida, *Islam, The People and the State: Political Ideas and Movements in the Middle East*, (I.B.Tauris, London, 1989/1993), p.3;13.

manifest itself just as convincingly in terms of adherence to the Divinely inspired Will and Law of the Qur'an and the *Shari'ah*, implemented by the *ulama*, whilst waiting for the Mahdi to return Islam to its perfection. There are those who, like Rida, in any event, rejected Mahdism.

In the development of an Islamic economic system in the present day – or, as some would maintain, an 'Islamising economy,' in the sense that in an Islamic society it is felt that all of its institutions should operate in accordance with Islamic principles, or be encouraged or compelled to do so, the question is: what does this demand? Is it to be economic development with a view to 'catching-up' with the industrialised countries of the West? Or, does it demand total socio-economic reconstruction in the light of a basically different model – an Islamic model – with its own set of assumptions, ideals, and growth-path, something that would be unique and value-specific?[116] If the solution is the latter, and this book is addressing this possibility within the framework of Islam's underlying economic ethic with regard to *riba*, how can this ethical principle, which I have so far addressed in theological and historical terms, fit into an economic system designed for a community in the twenty-first century, with not only constraints imposed within secular societies, but also within Islamic societies themselves?

A.E.Mayer points out that from the 1960's onward the barriers which formerly divided the doctrines of schools of law and Shi'is and Sunnis became more permeable and Muslims began to produce theories that eluded traditional categories especially with regard to the application of Islamic precepts to issues such as macroeconomic principles. In this area the traditional prohibition of *riba* was

---

[116]Khurshid Ahmad, "Economic Development in an Islamic Framework," a paper from *Studies in Islamic Economics, op. cit.*, p.171.

reinterpreted as a principle that required the elimination of interest charges. Among those writing on the subject was an Iraqi Shi'i cleric Muhammad Baqer as-Sadr (1931-1980).[117]

Although, as I have remarked, a large body of literature can be found within the Islamic world with regard to economic issues, including that which filled Schumpeter's 'Great Gap,' as Chabli Mallat points out, by 1960 it had produced no consistent reflection in the field let alone a general theory of economics; indeed the reliance on Ibn Khaldun from which to draw an Islamic theory of economics was a confirming sign of the apparent dearth of material. This is why the works of Muhammad Baqer as-Sadr in banking and economics are significant. Against a classical background where the discipline of economics did not exist, Sadr wrote two serious and lengthy works on the subject: *'Iqtisaduna'* (Our Economics) and *'al-Bank al-la Ribawi fil-Islam.'*

The premise on which Sadr bases his whole method of *Iqtisaduna* derives from the distinction between doctrine and science, in which *madhhab* (doctrine, school) is defined as the way a society pursues its economic development and addresses its practical problems; and *'ilm* (science, knowledge), is defined as the science which explains economic life and the links between economic facts and the causes and factors which determine them.[118] Most of *Iqtisaduna* is devoted to the exposition of an Islamic distributive system deriving from the injunctions of Islamic law in the economic field. There is a need to establish methodologically the intimate

---

[117]Ann Elizabeth Mayer, "Law: Modern Legal Reform," in *The Oxford Encyclopedia of the Modern Islamic World*, *op.cit.*, vol. 2, p.471.

[118]See Chabli Mallat, *The Renewal of Islamic Law*, (Cambridge University Press, 1993), p.121 ff.

connection between law and economics, and the precise role of the *Shari'ah* in the discovery of the discipline of Islamic economics.

Iqtisaduna consists of three parts. The first two parts are critiques of the capitalist and socialist systems and operate negatively by presenting counter arguments to classical theories. The third part deals with Sadr's concept of an Islamic economy. Against capitalism, therefore, Sadr's argument rests on the criticism of the emptiness of the concept of liberty when applied to an economic exchange between unequal parties; against socialism Sadr develops an argument against the Marxist overemphasis on the class struggle, and its unrealistic prescriptions against the basic, and natural, instincts of economic self-interest in mankind – as exemplified by Adam Smith. Islamic economics is introduced as a general egalitarian reading of the principles with regard to the concept of property in a predominantly agricultural context.

The bulk of Islamic economics analysised by Sadr, therefore, forms the concept of distribution, and the book separates 'distribution before production,' which introduces the concept of need and the notion of labour, and 'distribution after production,' which is concerned with the distribution of 'productive wealth.' The thrust of *Iqtisaduna*, therefore, is based on the ways in which Islam has organised distribution to maximise the economic wealth depleted by man's exploitation of economic resources.[119]

Sadr draws a number of conclusions with regard to law and economics within Islam. Firstly, he considers Islamic economics as a *madhhab*, a doctrine, not a science, *'ilm*. It shows the way to follow in the economy, and does not explain the

---

[119]See Chabli Mallat, "Sadr, Muhammad Baqir Al-," *The Oxford Encyclopedia of the Modern Islamic World, op.cit.*, vol. 3. p.450ff.

way economic events occur. These two areas, according to Sadr, must be clearly separated in the approach to Islamic economics. Such a discipline simply does not exist – there is in Islam nothing resembling the writing of thinkers like David Ricardo or Adam Smith. Further, Sadr maintains that Islamic economics is based on the idea of justice; thirdly, Islamic law is the preferred way to Islamic economics; and finally, Islamic economics is based on discovery not formation – the Islamic methodology premised on the prohibited-permissable paradigm laid out by the Qur'an requires inferences drawn from the superstructure which is the law to the infrastructure i.e. the economy.

According to Mallat, Sadr's contribution is remarkable, not least in respect of the fact that he was neither an economist nor a banker: "He was the only scholar able to produce a comprehensive text which could draw on the 'economic' texts of the classical *fiqh* treatises as well as on the sources of Marxist and capitalist traditions available in Arabic, and surmount that pyramid of constraints with some measure of success." He has overcome two basic hurdles. The first can be described in terms of sources, i.e. the most interesting side of Sadr's research appears in his emphasis on *fiqh*. In the absence of a discipline of economics in classical Islam, the complexities and riches of the *Shari'ah* as elaborated in the work of the jurists, and not as a direct extrapolation from a *hadith* or a Qur'anic verse, renders Sadr's exercise different from most other endeavours in the field; and, secondly, when Sadr writes that Islamic economics is not a science, he weakens perhaps some of the 'legitimacy' of the field, "but he does not set as a goal an impossible Holy Grail of truth for a nascent and uncertain discipline."[120]

---

[120]Mallat, *The Renewal of Islamic Law*, *op.cit.*, p.187.

Most of *Iqtisaduna,* therefore, is devoted to the exposition of an Islamic distributive system deriving from the injunctions of Islamic law in the economic field. Sadr introduces a detailed critique of Marxist socialism and Western capitalism before proceeding with a presentation of his own alternative system, derived from his distinction between *madhhab* and *'ilm.* Unlike Islam, Marxism claims the scientific method and adopts as its central economic thesis the position that "any development in the operations of production and its modes is accompanied by a necessary development in social relations in general, and in the relations of distribution in particular."[121] For Islam, according to Sadr, this is incorrect. There is no necessary connection between these two elements, and against Marxism he proposes the recognition of two types of social need, which constitute legal spheres with different regimes:

> "Islam sees that man operates within two spheres: in the first sphere, man exercises his work on nature, and tries variously to exploit it and subdue it for the fulfilment of his needs. In the second sphere, man exercises his work over relations with other individuals in several areas of social life. The forms of production are the result of the first sphere, and the social systems (*anzima*) the result of the second sphere. Each of the two spheres – in its historical existence – was subject to many developments in the mode of production or in the social system, but Islam does not see a necessary connection between the development of the forms of production and the development of the social rules (institutions, *muzum*). It therefore believes that it is possible to conserve the same social system, with its functions and essence through the ages, whatever the differences between the various modes of production."[122]

---

[121] *Ibid.,* p.118.

[122] *Ibid.,* p.118.

Against capitalism, Sadr addresses the peripheral question of circulation (*tadawul*), an area in which injustice is created since money becomes a commodity for hoarding or using, not as a means to facilitate circulation but as an object of wealth per se. Capitalism severs money from its circulation use, and uses it for its own sake, whereas Islam restores the right balance by three essential prescriptions of the *Shari'a*: the payment of taxes (*zakat*) which directly deflects the propensity to hoarding; the prohibition of *riba*; and the discretionary intervention of the ruler. He argues for the need to establish methodologically the intimate connection between law and economics, and the precise role of the *Shari'ah* in the discovery of the discipline of Islamic economics.

Central to the legal perspective is the fact that distribution is identified as the area in which the central economic problem of society is generated. The two concepts which underpin this 'apparatus of distribution' (*jihaz at-tawzi*) are 'need' (*haja*) and 'labour' (*'amal*) together with a third element that of Islam's original view of property:

> "From the Islamic perspective, labour is the cause of the worker's ownership of the result of his labour. This private ownership based on labour is a natural drive of man to appropriate for himself the result of his work . . . In Islam, labour is the central concept from which property derives. All the forms of property must therefore be qualified. In this perspective property becomes 'a secondary element of distribution' and is always limited by a set of moral values and social interests established by religion."[123]

The essential social problem, injustice, is therefore 'explained' economically by Sadr in the context of distribution and the necessity of an interventionist role by

---

[123]*Ibid.*, p.120.

the state to ensure that social differences will not be so acute as to allow wealth to remain in the hands of the rich.

Iqtisaduna, however, has been subject to scathing criticism by Sunni scholars, who have put forward the Shi'i limitations of Sadr's theory. The most detailed criticism appears in two separate critical essays on *Iqtisaduna* published by Dar as-Sahwa in Cairo in 1987.[124] According to Mallat, the work of Yusuf Kamal tends to lose focus by easy generalisations, but in contrast Abdul-Majd Harak presents a systematic and well structured analysis.[125] Harak's major criticisms relate to land property and the role of labour in Islamic economics, and for both Kamal and Harnak all the mistakes in *Iqtisaduna* are rooted in Shi'i influence on Sadr. In Sunni *fiqh*, Harak argues, the principle is the sanctity and absoluteness of private property:

> "Sadr's theories are directly inspired from Socialist thinking adduced with a sectarianism which derives from the importance of the Twelve Imams in Shi'i law and theology. Similarly, the principle in labour law is the absolute freedom of an owner to have labourers work for him on the basis of a salary. 'Mere work cannot be considered as the sole justification in ownership.'"[126]

There was, indeed, a significant chasm between Sunni and Shi'i attitudes on the question of land ownership (notably for the *kharaj* category[127]), and it could be

---

[124]With reference to: Yusuf Kamal and Abdul-Majd Harak, "Al-Iqtisad al-Islami bayna Fiqh ash-Shi'a wa Fiqh as-Sunna: Qira'a Naqdiyya fi Kitab Iqtisaduna," *Islamic Economics between Shi'a and Sunni Fiqh: a Critical Reading of Iqtisaduna*, Cairo, 1987.

[125]See Mallat, *The Renewal of Islamic Law, op.cit.*, pp.143-146.

[126]*Ibid.*, p.144.

[127]The price of rent is called *kharaj*, and the land is consequently classified as *kharaj* land. There is no private ownership of *kharaj* land, it falls under public control. Sadr is careful to specify in this

argued that Sadr did not take this into account. Indeed, classical Hanafi authors like Quduri (d.428) draw an important distinction between *kharaj* and *'ushr* land and with regard to *kharaj* the element of private property, in contrast with Sadr's prohibiton, is dominant: "The main land in Iraq is *kharaj* [land] and belongs to its inhabitants (*ahl*) who can sell it and dispose of it at will."[128] However, as Mallat points out, the use of words like *kharaj*, *'ushr*, and *tasq* which convey a wide range of legal regimes and in any case tend to be obscure in the classical text, and the immense number of authors, of historical periods and variations, suggest rather that several economic systems can and will be derived by the modern Islamic seekers of 'correct economics':

> "The wide spectrum covered is characteristic of the possibilities offered by the legal tradition. It is much less a function of sectarian closed models (which would favour in Sunnism private ownership and the state cum Imam in Shi'ism) than a characteristic to be found *within* both Shi'i and/or Sunni *fiqh*. As the debate in Islamic Iran between the defenders of absolute private property and those who favoured state nationalisation and redistribution of land clearly shows, the non-sectarian dimension of the divide is profound. In Iran, the tenants and opponents of absolute private property are all Shi'is. *Iqtisaduna* is actually remarkable for the absence of any conspicuous Shi'i sectarianism in its analysis and sources."[129]

It is true that on the whole references to Shi'i jurists prevail in *Iqtisaduna* but as Mallat points out, Sadr draws freely on both Shi'i and Sunni scholars. Shafi'i,

---

regard that control in this case is different to nationalisation. State ownership of *kharaj* land is described as 'public' (*'amma*). See Mallat, *ibid.*, p.128.

[128]*Ibid.*, p.145.

[129]*Ibid.*, p.145.

Malik; Sarakhsi (Hanafi school), and Ibn Hazm (Zahiri school), as well as many of their disciples and followers, are all used by Sadr as authoritative sources; even the school most antagonistic to Ja'farism, the Hanbali school (in its Wahhabi-Saudi version), is drawn upon in the persons of Ahmad Ibn Hanbal and Ibn Qudama. In fact, the absence of sectarianism in *Iqtisaduna* explains the interest in Sadr beyond the strict confines of the Shi'i world. As Mallat also remarks, it is only a matter of time before Sadr, who was killed in 1980, gains the respect of all for a legacy which may or may not be agreed upon from an ideological point of view, but which can only be acknowledged as formidable in modern Islamic thought.[130] This is especially true, he continues, with regard to the law and the concept of interest-free banking within the development of an Islamic economic system. There is no tradition of economics in Islam. The texts from the Qur'an, the *Sunnah*, and the classical tradition (*turath*) must be questioned 'economically.' The search for a synchronic Islamic theory of economics and banking, as opposed to the diachronic work of the historian, has proved complex and difficult. The material drawn from legal treatise cannot be merely descriptive or explanatory, it must be able to perform in practice, whether in the state or in a bank. The seriousness of Islamic economics can only come from the rich and unique tradition of Islamic law; this is the only tradition which can offer conceptual tools which are properly 'Islamic.' The operation is, therefore, highly selective, but it is this particularly imaginative effort which makes for Sadr's originality. The Islamic economist needs "proficiency in classical legal texts, a practical and performing methodology, synthesis to bring about a comprehensive system, and innovation with the terminology."[131] Few scholars have

---

[130]Chibli Mallat, *The Oxford Encyclopedia of the Modern Islamic World, op.cit.*, p.453.

[131]*Ibid.*, p.186.

been able to meet all the requirements and Islamic economics is still at an early formative stage. This explains why a phenomenon like Muhammad Baqer as-Sadr is so noteworthy.

'Islamic Banking' and *'Riba'*

As Ausaf Ahmed remarks, it must be recognised from the outset in discussing Islamic banking in terms of an Islamic economic system, that Islamic banking is only one of several institutions of the Islamic economy, and it is neither a necessary nor a sufficient condition for the existence of an 'Islamic economy.' The mere presence of a few Islamic banking institutions will not make any economy any more Islamic than it might be at the present; for that to happen far-reaching structural changes and reforms would have to be carried out in almost all spheres of social and economic activities, and probably other new institutions would have to be created. Of course, countries more dedicated to the ideology of Islamisation in all spheres of its social, political, and economic order, would, perhaps, find the terminology more fitting. Banking activity, however, is only required when an economy has developed sufficiently to result in the separation of savers from investors, thus, in an undeveloped economy savers and investors may be the same people and the financial intermediation of a banking system may not be necessary. However, an Islamic economy no matter how primitive or advanced could never be permitted to practice *riba* and still remain Islamic. It could also be noted that commercial banking is not the only way to organise financial activities on a non-*riba* basis. State-ownership of banking institutions is another method of the elimination of interest from the economy in which case the state would ration the credit according to the requirements of the various sectors.[132]

If Islamic banking is neither a necessary nor sufficient condition for the existence of an Islamic economy, then what is the real significance of Islamic banks? According to Ahmed the answer to the question depends upon correctly understanding the nature of banking business and the prohibition of *riba* in Islam:

> "Banks are financial intermediaries which function as a bridge between the savers and investors if they are not the same people. They mobilise the saving of the people and provide it to those who have productive outlet for these funds. Traditional commercial banks perform this function on the basis of interest. The significance of Islamic banking institutions is that they aspire to perform the same functions as those of modern commercial banks without indulging in *riba*. To this extent, Islamic banks provide an alternative to interest-based banking for religious reasons . . . But it would be presumptuous to think that mere establishment of a few Islamic banks would automatically lead, through market forces or otherwise, to the establishment of an Islamic economy."[133]

The prohibiton of *riba,* therefore, implies an alternative approach to pricing the factors of production and time value of resources, and an alternative approach to the institution of 'lending.'[134]

'Islamic Banking' is in itself an oxymoron according to those who would repeatedly attack the Arab Islamic Banking movement as a camouflage for

---

[132]Ausaf Ahmed, *"Evolution of Islamic Banking,"* a paper from *Elimination of Riba from the Economy, op. cit.*, p.366.

[133]*Ibid.*, p.367.

[134]M. Fahim Kahn, *Essays in Islamic Economics,* (The Islamic Foundation, Leicester,) 1995, p.117.

capitalism. Merely using the word 'Islamic' does not produce, overnight, an Islamic economic system, but does it change the nature of the banks themselves? How different is 'Islamic' banking compared to non-Islamic banking, and how does the concept of *riba*/usury fit in to its structure? Can the Islamization of a nation's institution, operating in accordance with Islamic principles, exist in the Arab world, not to mention the secular West? What does it offer to individuals or communities that which is different or 'better' i.e. more ethical – again in terms of the *riba* prohibition? Even the word 'bank' is disliked in some Arab institutions because it comes from the Italian word 'banco' which means a 'table,' as in the past the money-changers from Lombardy would place their money on a table. This practice is considered inappropriate in Islamic financial transactions which are based on trust, therefore, some Arab Islamic institutions are called houses rather than banks, such as the Kuwait Finance House and the Dar al-Maal al-Islami - Islamic House of Funds (DMI).[135]

As established in quoting the Qur'anic sources, the practice of *riba* is contrasted with commercial selling in order to condemn *riba* and promote trade (Surah ii.275), and the Islamic scholars commended trade-oriented banking (such as it was) in place of traditional interest-bearing credit oriented banking. The major system of interest-free banking is the two-tier *mudarabah*. Of the four schools of Islamic jurisprudence outlined above, the Maliki and Hanbali accept *mudarabah* as a variant form of *shirkah* – partnership. *Shirkah* means participation of two or more persons in a certain business with defined amounts of capital according to a contract for jointly carrying out a business and for sharing profit and loss in specified proportions; *mudarabah* means that one party provides capital and the other utilises

---

[135]Rodney Wilson, *op. cit.*, p.183.

it for business purposes under the agreement that profit from the business will be shared according to a specified proportion.[136] It is two-tier in so far as there is one *mudarabah* between the financial institution and the depositors (the surplus economic users) in order to replace interest-bearing contracts between the savers and the bank; and another *mudarabah* between the financial institution and the defecit economic units in order to replace interest-bearing contracts between the banks and the ultimate users of funds. In this way the banks can negotiate deposits and loans on the basis of profit-sharing ratios. The *mudarabah*, therefore, is a business contract negotiated on the basis of profit-sharing ratios between two profit-seeking parties, so that Party A provides funds to Party B who independently manages the business according to agreed terms, the most important of which, from the banking point of view, is an advance agreement on a ratio in which realised business profits are shared, viz:

> "An Islamic bank lends money to a client – to finance a factory, for example – in return for which the bank will get a specified percentage of the factory's net profits every year for a designated period. This share of the profits provides for repayment of the principal and a profit for the bank to pass on to its depositors. Should the factory lose money, the bank, its depositors and the borrower all jointly absorb the losses, thereby putting into practice the pivotal Islamic principle that the providers and users of capital should share risks and rewards."[137]

---

[136]Muhammad Nejatullah Siddiqi, *Partnership and Profit-Sharing in Islamic Law,* (The Islamic Foundation, Leicester), 1985, p.15.

[137]Muhammad Anwar, "Reorganisation of Islamic Banking: A new Proposal," *The American Journal of Islamic Social Sciences*, Vol. 4, Number 2, Dec. 1987, p.303.

Thus, banking based on the principles of profit-and-loss-sharing (known as PLS) fulfills the Qur'anic requirements on *riba* by introducing trade-oriented activities in place of credit activities and eliminating interest from the banking system. In effect, interest-bearing loans are replaced by profit-seeking investments and *qard hasanah* (loans on zero interest).[138] For many Islamic banks, however, the main problem has not been to attract depositors, but to find credit-worthy customers by offering equity sharing *mudarabah*, or to service with trade credit through *murabaha*, or profit sharing *musharaka*, which will be discussed in more detail further on.[139] The replacement of interest rates by profit-sharing ratios has profound macroeconomic consequences for labour contracts, inflation, stability, growth, and income distribution. This is a fine arrangement for channelling surplus funds for investment, but problems persist when it comes to handling liquidity under a fractional reserve system, which virtually all Muslim economists would consider unjust for the following reason.

One of the ways in which banking evolved was because people used to deposit a medium of exchange, especially gold, with goldsmiths for safety. This would be surrendered in exchange for a certificate of financial credits (called financial claim) issued by the goldsmith. Rather than withdrawing their gold whenever the depositors wanted to buy commodities, which was a bulky operation, the financial claims issued by the goldsmiths came to be accepted in lieu of gold itself, and the goldsmiths (financial institutions) were used as trusts for the safety of the deposits. As it was a safe assumption that not all the gold would be withdrawn at once by all the depositors, the goldsmiths started loaning out a fraction of the

---

[138]Anwar, *ibid.*, p.298.

[139]See Rodney Wilson (ed.), *Islamic Financial Markets,* (Routledge, London, 1990), p.15.

deposited gold lying idle in their vaults, on interest, without permission from the owners of the deposits. In essence financial institutions would become wealthy by retaining only a fraction of the deposits, loaning out the rest of them, and charging interest on the loans.

Chapra maintains that the creation of credit in this way, which is in addition to the money supply, provides a subsidy – known as *seigniorage* – to the banks at the expense of society. Therefore he argues that:

> "the net income arising from derivative deposits should be passed on to the state after allowing for the *mudarabah* share of commercial banks, determined in accordance with an agreed formula. This entire income should be used by the state for social welfare projects, particularly those that benefit the poor." The challenge is, he further remarks, "how to design and run a money and banking system that is in harmony with the nature of Islamic ideology, eliminates *riba*, and helps realise the socio-economic goals of Islam."[140]

Islamic Banking: a Model

Most Muslim economists would agree, in principle, with Chapra, that the *seigniorage* should be used for the welfare of society rather than letting it be appropriated by the banking public, privileged borrowers, or bank stockholders, and Anwar suggests a dual banking system to meet this challenge in eliminating *riba* from the practice and transferring *seigniorage* from the private sector to society.[141]

---

[140]Chapra, *op. cit.*, pp.92-93 and 28.

[141]See also Michael Rowbotham, *The Grip of Death*, (Jon Carpenter Publishing, Charlbury, 1998) where it is maintained that as a result of our fractional reserve banking over 90% of our money supply is loaned into existence by commercial banks and thus must grow by enough to at least pay the interest on the loan by which it was created. Today's money system boils down to institutionalised theft.

Basically, Anwar suggests that financial institutions should be classified into two independent categories, private banks and social banks, according to the nature of deposits and intermediations (banks provide four distinct types of intermediations: denomination; maturity; risk diversification; and liquidity).[142] Some depositors possess funds beyond their consumption and therefore make savings and time deposits in order to make profits. Since they possess resources above their current needs they have the ability to bear risks, and positive returns are therefore not guaranteed on savings and time deposits in an Islamic society. Anwar proposes that these savings and time deposits should be solicited by private banks, and these banks may continue denomination, maturity and risk diversification, but not liquidity, functions in order to maximise profits for themselves and their clients. But the private banks may only function like all private business ventures, that is, on the basis of *mudarabah, musharaka,* and other profit sharing schemes. (Under *musharaka* the bank enters into a partnership with a client in which both share the equity capital – and perhaps even management – of a project or deal, and both share in the profits or losses according to their equity shareholding.)[143] Private banks should be barred from receiving demand deposits and the public should not expect charitable services such as *qard hasanah* from the private banks. The banks will have the same legal status as any other business enterprise. Therefore, savings are closely tied with investments and private banks will essentially become business banks fulfilling the Qur'anic injunctions against *riba* and in favour of trade.

Social banks, however, may be organised by local communities, but, should be authorised by the central bank of the country to manage all sorts of public

---

[142]See Anwar, *op. cit.*, p.296.

[143]*Ibid.*, p.303.

accounts especially *zakat, sadaqah* (charity or voluntary contribution for a good cause), and *awqaf* (charitable or family trust) funds. Social banks, according to Anwar, should accept all demand deposits and extend interest-free loans to finance welfare projects of their respective communities. The benefits being that people will be encouraged to use banking facilities in Muslim countries, whereas before it was viewed with suspicion; and, equally, social banks will participate in local welfare projects by financing local educational, housing, medical, and other necessities; developing a local infrastructure; and creating jobs for the unemployed in their neighbourhoods. Surplus social banks could cooperate with defecit social banks after meeting their reserve requirements. In this way:

> "Social banks are unlikely to extend undue credits because of the
> absence of the profit maximization incentive. Conservatism of social
> banks in extending loans, compared with the profit-seeking
> commercial banks, will also help to check inflation in addition to
> creating employment. Therefore the organisation of social banks for
> liquidity intermediation will not only transfer *seigniorage* to society
> but also contribute towards the achievement of several other socio-
> economic objectives of an Islamic economy."[144]

This proposition appears theoretically, and theologically, to have tremendous potential for helping the poorer elements in an Islamic society. Under this dual banking system private banks would continue their usual intermediation activities efficiently and would widen the scope of profit-sharing schemes, although their power to create money would be transferred to social banks. Reorganisation of the financial system in this way would transfer *seigniorage* from the private sector to society, and would assist in the realization of other socio-economic goals as well.

---

[144]*Ibid.*, p.301.

However, whether this altruism would actually work in practice depends on how much the private banks would be willing to relinquish the role they now play in respect of transferring those powers to the social banks. It is in theological terms an enlightening proposition. Hopefully, in the spirit of Islam, and *ummah*, it is a concept not too removed from practical implementation, whilst at the same time it would be upholding the Qur'anic injunction on *riba*, as long as the surplus of the *seigniorage* is a result of surplus credit requirements to meet demand deposits, rather than the accumulation of interest bearing loans from the fractional reserve, which was the main objection in the first place.

Islamic Banking: Micro-enterprise

How an effective credit system in line with Qur'anic teaching can operate successfully at the grass roots level in the Muslim world, can be seen if we examine, for instance, a project run by 'Save the Children' for the Bani Hamida farmers in Jordan; a credit system based on the principles of *murabaha, musharaka,* and *mudaraba.* Save the Children developed a strict lending system based on purely Islamic financial methods, basically because they found themselves stuck between headquarters who were refusing to foster an interest-free loan project, and the Bani Hamida farmers who felt they were being pressed by a western organisation to go against their religion. A lending project was established in Bani Hamida and run by Naim, the loan officer; an assistant from Bani Hamida who had recently graduated in agriculture; a bookkeeper/collector who was a village-council treasurer; with a part time input from an accountant and the SCF financial manager Samir Bseiso – a former Citibanker in Saudi Arabia for eleven years with the right credentials to help develop the scheme. For two years he went to Bani Hamida Mountain twice a month to train the village council heads on how to review and handle applications, while coaching the team and handling the system as well. Each loan granted was based on either *murabaha, musharaka,* or *mudaraba* principles which operate in the following manner.

Under *murabaha* (based on the Arabic word for profit) the borrower receives the *goods or animals* purchased by the loan, instead of money. Two or three people – the borrower, a committee member, a loan officer, or a vet – make the purchase. The borrower then repays the purchase price of the goods plus a six percent service, not interest, charge. As repayments are on a monthly or quarterly basis, the effective rate is around eleven percent; and the charge of a percentage is acceptable in *fiqh* for technical assistance, transport etc. *Murabaha* is the nearest to traditional banking methods, and is used when the committee does not want to take a high risk. Regardless of the outcome the borrower must pay back the loan, including the additional six percent. This method ensures that the loan is spent on what it was originally intended for. In addition the purchaser draws on expertise from the team to obtain the best quality at the lowest price. So far, in Bani Hamida *murabaha* loans have been given to farmers to build fences around orchards or construct water tanks to irrigate them.

In *musharaka* (joint venture) a partnership is made between the borrower and the lender. The borrower provides part of the capital needed (usually about thirty percent) and is responsible for managing the project. The loan officer provides the remaining capital, supervision and technical assistance. At the end of the project, normally two thirds of the profit goes to the borrower for his efforts. The remaining third is split between him and the fund, according to the amount of capital each contributes. Here the feasibility of the project, rather than the credit worthiness of the borrower, is the key for the approval of the project. The average return to the loan fund can be higher and any inflation that occurs is offset by increased profit from the project. Also in this type of joint enterprise, the project team is encouraged to provide the borrower with the technical assistance and managerial skills needed, for example, bookkeeping, handling purchases, marketing, etc., to increase the potential for profitability. This method is used for short-term income generating projects, such as lamb fattening, and ewe and Shami goat raising, in which the animals of offspring are sold at the end of the project.

Finally, under *mudaraba*, which I discussed as a two-tier system, and which is the third system used in Bani Hamida, the loan fund finances the whole cost of the project. The borrower contributes only the management and must keep careful records of all the expenses and income throughout the project. At the end the net profit is shared between the loan fund and the borrower, according to the percentage previously agreed upon, the downside is that any loss beyond the borrower's control must be absorbed by the loan fund. This method is used for exceptional cases involving very dependable borrowers with excellent ideas and capabilities who lack the capital needed to implement the project.

By 1992 (from 1986), 175 loans had been granted without a default. The loan fund which had grown to forty thousand dollars had granted eighty five thousand dollars in loans ranging from one hundred and twenty dollars to one thousand and thirty seven dollars. Repayment rates have often been as high as ninety eight percent in a country where other organisations' repayment rates have been very low. The original loan committee of a cumbersome ten has now only four members, each of whom is the head of a village council. Farmers are queuing up to obtain loans.

How and why has this project into an Islamic banking loan system, contra *riba*, with no defaults, managed to be so successful? There are several reasons: the system suits the beliefs of the participants: community representatives participate in decision making; a simple but sound managerial and credit system is in place, with experienced staff operating procedures who are respected by the community; repayments are collected house to house and are scheduled on a monthly or seasonal basis or a combination of both according to the projected cash flow; no collateral is required but each borrower must provide two guarantors; and as the projects are small, problems are addressed as they arise. As an experiment in Islamic lending, albeit on a small scale, this project is, therefore, proving a huge success in relative terms to these people, and there is much to be said for the non-governmental organisations working overseas in this field.[145] What is commendable about the work of the SCF in Jordan is that by operating financial assistance in specific Islamic terms it has won the support and approval of the Muslims there. By comparison, a Christian initiative for micro-enterprise financing in Pakistan has met with hostility and suspicion.

The Alfalah Development Institute was formed in 1986 by Church leaders, business people and professionals as a Christian development organisation to meet the challenge of poverty and unemployment in Pakistan. It specializes in micro-enterprise development providing people with access to credit and training and small scale enterprises (and, incidentally, to ameliorate the condition of the children working in the brick kilns). In an interview for the 'Christian Action Journal,' Bishop Nazir-Ali, one of its founders and at that period General Secretary of the

---

[145]From a report by Rebecca Salti, formally the Director of Save the Children in Amman, Jordan, in *"What's New: An Independent Voice for NGO News and Views."* (Published by CDI, Co-operation for Development International, 118 Broad Street, Chesham, Bucks.), 1995. After meeting with Amanda Rowlatt (First Secretary, Aid and Economics, in the British Embassy in Guyana from 1989-1991), now working with CDI, I have been very grateful for the information she has continued to send to me including an extremely interesting video tape entitled 'Small Business Matters in the Middle East' which focuses on the work of community-related credit programmes in the West Bank and Gaza Strip.

Church Missionary Society, admitted that they had touched on the difficulties of a Christian NGO working in a predominantly Muslim country:

> "Islamic fundamentalists oppose Alfalah for they see it as a threat even though Alfalah makes loans to both Muslims and Christians. . . The question of interest hangs like a sword, because charging interest in Pakistan is illegal. We offer loans attached to which is a service charge to help with the administration and training costs of Alfalh, but any Christian NGO involved in this work lays itself open to the accusation of usury. However, we retain good relations with large sections of Muslim society. Our banking and legal advisors are Muslims. Loans are made to Muslims as well as Christians."[146]

It is interesting to compare these two operations with regard to non-usurious funding in Islamic countries. In Jordan the outcome has been very successful because the Islamic nature of the undertaking has been given serious thought by the SCF, in so far as funding arrangements are being provided using Islamic terminology, and emphasis has been laid on the non-*riba* implications of the contracts. This not only suits the beliefs of the local people, but it would appear that their faith values have been taken into consideration as part of the methodology of extending loan facilities. In Pakistan, a Christian organisation is viewed with some distrust, because athough the loan system is based on a sort of *murabaha* contract, with a service charge percentage included – with money provided rather than goods or animals – it has not been translated as such into Islamic terms to allay the suspicions of the local community appropriating the service. And, although the bankers and legal advisors to Alfalah are Muslim, this does not seem to have

---

[146]From an interview with Bishop Michael Nazir-Ali in *"Opportunity: Christian Action Journal,"* St. Anselm's Church Hall, Kennington Cross, London. Autumn 1993. pp.12/13.

dispersed their anxiety about usury. The wisdom of this intervention, however well intentioned it might be, is equally queried by Kurshid Ahmad when he states that development economics is passing through a period of crisis and re-evaluation, and there are those who consider "the application of a theory based on Western experience to a different socio-economic situation, as it is being done in the less-developed countries, inappropriate and injurious to the prospects of development."[147]

It is a point very worthy of consideration. Contextualisation is a very important issue, especially when one considers that the countries with majority Muslim populations are all, without exception, in the Third World. This does not necessarily mean that all are poor, there are those economically bouyant on oil based revenue, but there are two serious issues to address: one is, not only the theological obligation, but also the practicalities, of providing interest-free, or at the very least, low-cost credit finance for the poor in terms of microeconomic activity – remembering at the same time the axiom that 'credit is also debt'; and, secondly, the issue of crippling Third World debt. These important issues will be addressed in my conclusion, especially with regard to agencies such as the Grameen Bank, Cashpor, and other NGO's working in this field, but it might appear a more sensitive solution for any specific religious organisation, other than Islamic, aimed at financing Muslims, whether in Britain or elsewhere, to provide an *Islamic economic* framework in which to operate in terms of providing funds for local communities. This would in no way compromise the beliefs of Christians, or other religious groups, but it would ensure a basis of trust in which local Muslims could operate, especially if, as in the case of Alfalah, Muslim bankers and/or legal advisors are used. Otherwise, as

---

[147]Kurshid Ahmad, *Economic Development in an Islamic Framework*, (The Islamic Foundation, Leicester), 1979, p.10.

Bishop Michael mentioned in his interview, the owners of the brick kilns, for instance, co-operated if the Church entered, 'did religion' and left, but resisted as soon as more than that was attempted. One other interesting point, in terms of community, which was highlighted in the Alfalah operation, was that initially co-operative models of enterprise development were experimented with, but these foundered on the communities' individualistic orientation, so microenterprise aimed at individuals and their families provided a more appropriate working model. This approach, according to Bishop Michael, could address poverty within a community by harnessing the individual talents of its members. (This model is particularly reflected in the work of LETS, local exchange trading scemes, which can cut across both religious and secular divides, and which I shall mention briefly further on.)

It is one thing, however, to propose these ideals in terms of Qur'anic values in relation to providing Muslims with access to financial credit (debt) at a micro-enterprise level in poor Islamic countries – as Rodney Wilson maintains: "It is clear that the application of Islamic ideas at the grassroots is much more advanced than at a higher level,"[148] it is quite another to address the issue in terms of the acceptance of non-usurious Islamic Banking in major cities, not least the City itself, but that does not mean to say that it is not a viable option.

Islamic Banking: Macro-enterprise

A very important point which Muazzam Ali, the vice chairman of Dar al Mal al Islami, London, makes, in a paper on existing Islamic Banking, is that one has to consider an Islamic economic order in the context of the existing international economic order. The former is still in the process of evolution, whilst the latter

---

[148]R.Wilson, *Islamic Banking and Finance, op. cit.*, p.186.

controls and dominates the world, and although in comparing the two systems it is most common to differentiate between them in terms of the one being *riba* free, and the other *riba* oriented, it is to completely over-simplify the concept of an Islamic financial system. Most importantly, *riba* is just an instrument, and its elimination does not automatically convert a non-Islamic financial system into an Islamic one because, as I have discussed above, the idea of an 'Islamic economic order' is based on a set of principles constituting the concept and philosophy as recited explicitly in the Qur'an. This, therefore, provides for an economic philosophy based on an Islamic system and concept of social justice:

> "The Islamic financial system, therefore, cannot be introduced merely by eliminating *riba* but adopting the Islamic principles of social justice and introducing laws, practices, procedures and instruments which help in the maintenance and dispensation of justice, equity, fairness, and human considerations."[149]

It is, I feel, a very important consideration as it makes the whole concept of Islamic Banking an even more complex operation to put into practice, especially with regard to instituting it in the Western world – it has been slow enough developing in the Muslim world. For example, in 1952 when the SAMA (Saudi Arabian Monetary Agency) was created by a royal decree in Saudi Arabia, it was probably the first time that prohibition against interest was figured in an official document of any Muslim country in modern times.[150] Until the early part of the twentieth century Islamic Banking was more or less an abstract theoretical concept, although, as has been

---

[149]Muazzam Ali, *"Existing Islamic Banking, Investment and Insurance Institutions and their Operations,"* Islamic Banking Conference, London, 1984.

[150]Ahmed, *op. cit.*, p.351. For reasons for slow evolution and practice of Islamic banking in the Islamic world see Section III, pp.347-355.

noted, an Islamic understanding of economic principles existed with regard to *riba* transactions concerning lending and borrowing since the time of Muhammad. Its early initiation was, not surprisingly, at the grass roots level. On a very modest scale some pioneering Islamic banks were established in Egypt in the 1960's, which operated as rural social banks in the Nile Delta, where banking did not exist as such until these small scale Islamic banks were put into operation. The Mit-Ghamr Savings Bank in Egypt founded in 1963 and later superseded by the Nasser Social Bank attracted deposits from an influential group of pious farmer landlords, and backed some significant agro-industrial ventures.[151] Their remit was as much to encourage savings as to promote interest-free banking, i.e. within the *murabaha, musharaka,* and *mudaraba* conceptual framework, confirming the view that this operation is particularly effective at the grass roots level, and an indication of the potential applicability of Anwar's social bank model; and although highly successful in the beginning it did suffer a setback in the period from 1967 to 1971. Owing to the political atmosphere (June 5th saw the outbreak of the six-day war in the Middle East) and to different political currents in the administration of the Egyptian government at that time, the Mit Ghamr Bank and its branches were put under the direct control of the state administration and consequently lost their operational autonomy. In the second half of 1967 the operations of the bank were undertaken by the National Bank of Egypt and the Central Bank, the operations of which were run on an interest basis. Operational policies were therefore changed and the basis of interest-free banking was abandoned. It was not until 1971, when President Sadat

---

[151]Rodney Wilson, *Islamic Banking and Finance, op. cit.*, p.182.

came to office, that the experiment of the Mit Ghamr Savings bank was revived with the creation of the Nasser Social Bank.[152]

It was the late King Faisal bin Abdul Aziz Al-Sa'ud of Saudi Arabia who initiated the Organisation of the Islamic Conference, formally proclaimed in May 1971.[153] It was at the second Islamic Conference in 1974, held in Lahore, that a proposal was sponsored calling for a study of an International Islamic Bank for Trade and Development together with a Federation of Islamic banks. It was recommended to replace interest-based financial systems with participation schemes linked with profit and loss sharing, the nature of which have already been discussed. In addition an Association of Islamic Banks was to be established in order to act as a consultative body in the field of Islamic economics and Islamic banks, and, to promote *riba*-free banking internationally. The International Association of Islamic Banks was established in 1977 under the chairmanship of Prince Muhammad Al-Faisal Al Sa'ud, acknowledged as the most singular and pioneering effort in this field. The association has been functioning mainly to provide Islamic countries with technical assistance and expertise necessary for the establishment of their own Islamic banks, but it has the potential to become a viable organisation on a world-wide basis. As well as being recognised by the Central Banks and Monetary Authorities of Islamic countries, its status is also accepted by all the major

---

[152]See Rodney Wilson, *Islamic Financial Markets, op.cit.*, p.61.

[153]The OIC expresses the determination of Islamic nations to "preserve Islamic social and economic values." Its primary goals are to "promote Islamic solidarity among member states; to consolidate cooperation among member states in economic, social, cultural, scientific and other vital fields of activity, and to carry out consultations among member states in international organisations; to endeavour to eliminate racial segregation, discrimination, and colonialism in all its forms; and to support international peace and security founded on justice." See Golam Choudhury, "Organisation of the Islamic Conference: Origins," in *The Oxford Encyclopedia of the Modern Islamic World, op.cit.*, vol.3, p.261.

international organisations such as the United Nations Conference on Trade and Development; and the Economic and the Social Council of the United Nations. Among the Islamic instruments which are being used at present to establish *riba*-free banking are *mudaraba* (financing participation); *musharaka* (mutual financing participation); *qard hasanah* (Islamic loan financing for commercial use); *ijara wa Iktina* (lease purchase financing); and *takaful* (the Islamic alternative to contemporary insurance). It is these features which provide the future non-*riba* economic order based on principles of equity and social justice.[154]

In effect, therefore, there has been a sea-change of public opinion with regard to banking in the Arab world, even during the last half century. Arab-owned commercial banks were only founded in the 1920's in the Middle East, those being the Banque Misr of Egypt and a Palestinian institution, the Arab Bank. Up until then most of the activity was dealt with by foreign banks which constituted trade finance, and not dealings with local Muslims.[155] In the case of Egypt a number of small-scale financial institutions had been created in Cairo, at the turn of the century, alongside the major foreign banks which were based on an imported model that had little concern for the religious sensitivities of the population. One of these small money-houses, the Administration of the Posts, established a 'Savings Fund' (*Sunduq at-*

---

[154]Muazzam Ali, *op.cit.* p.25.

[155]The early (mid-nineteenth century) commercial banks in the Islamic world were all European owned – the Imperial Ottoman Bank being an Anglo-French venture, and the Imperial Bank of Persia was British owned and managed. Much financial intermediation in the Ottoman territories was in the hands of Greek Christians or Jews rather than Muslims. The Imperial Banks served the government and the trade of the European empires rather than the local Muslim business community or the wealthy landlord class. The management of the Ottoman debt was a major undertaking and the Imperial Ottoman Bank acted on behalf of the Sultan in arranging bond issues in London and Paris. See Rodney Wilson: "Banks and Banking" in *The Oxford Encyclopedia of the Modern Islamic World*, *op.cit.*, vol.1, p.191.

Tawfir) which yielded a return to the depositor/saver in the form of a fixed interest.[156] Banks, therefore, were regarded as institutions serving infidels rather than an institution in which a devout Muslim should get involved and breaking through this barrier has been one of the problems which Islamic banking has had to contend with in the Muslim world, even before convincing non-Islamic institutions that it has something viable to offer.

Following the oil price rises of 1973/74, it has been the devout Muslim merchants of the Gulf who have been largely responsible for the rapid expansion of Islamic Banking. Reluctant to use the services of the conventional commercial banks they nevertheless required some type of financial intermediation. As a result institutions avoiding *riba* transactions were established (with the state taking minority share-holdings) such as the Dubai Islamic Bank (1975), the Kuwait Finance House (1977), and the Bahrain Islamic Bank (1979):

> "The banks' market penetration is considered a success, given that they represent a new type of institution adopting innovative financial techniques. Although there have been setbacks, notably as a result of dealings in precious metals, the track record of the Islamic banks has

---

[156]This polemic over *riba* in the Posts Savings Fund developed into the *'Sunduq at-Tawfir'* affair. Over three thousand of the depositors refused out of religious conviction (*tadayyunan*) to take their interest fixed by the decree of the Khedive. The Mufti, Muhammad Abduh, was asked by some men in the government and by the director of the Administration of the Posts if there was a legal way that would authorise Muslims to take their profit earned by their monies in the Savings Fund. Rashid Rida who related events as they took place in 1903 said that Abduh was dissastisfied with the system introduced by the Savings Fund and in no way could the *riba* be accepted. Indeed, since this money was exploited from the people rather than borrowed out of necessity, Abduh ruled that it could be put to use on the basis of the commenda partnership (*sharikat al-mudaraba*). The re-emergence of the debate on *riba* thus started again in Egypt and culminated in the discussion on their Civil Code. It involved the best lawyers in Egypt including the most famous jurist in the Arab world, Abd al-Razzaq as-Sanhuri. Avoiding *riba* was central to Sanhuri's concern, and he went to great lengths in explaining how the Egyptian Civil Code (as well as most other Arab Codes which were modelled after it in Syria, Libya, Kuwait, and Iraq) was consonant with the *Shari'a* in this respect. For an account of this see Mallat, *op.cit.*, p.158-162.

been favourable so far. . . many customers maintain accounts with both the new Islamic banks and conventional commercial banks. In this sense the Islamic banks complement rather than replace conventional banks. Nevertheless, the ultimate objective for the Islamic banks is to provide a comprehensive range of banking services as a complete alternative to *riba* finance."[157]

An interesting point was made in the case of Saudi Arabia which only later adopted the concept of specific Islamic banks (although maintaining considerable support for them) as all banks in Saudi Arabia are supposed to operate according to Islamic principles. The Saudi Arabian Monetary Agency saw no need to licence specially designated Islamic banks, as it was thought that granting such licences would, in fact, place the already existing commercial banks in an invidious position. Most Saudi citizens, however, do not have accounts with the commercial banks in the Kingdom, they use moneylenders and money-changers. Working on a *murabaha* principle, interest is not earned on loans which are very often in kind rather than cash. One such moneylending family has grown to become the third largest financial institution in Saudi Arabia – the al-Rajhis. All their business has been built up on the basis of *riba*-free transactions, and in 1985 the Saudi Arabian Monetary Agency officially licenced them as deposit-takers and exchange dealers. Under pressure to register as a commercial bank in 1983, as (unlike the commercial banks) they neither held reserves with the Saudi Arabian Monetary Agency nor were regulated in any way, the al-Rajhis preferred to seek Islamic banking status. In 1988 they became a public company and sold a half of their shares outside the family. With the registration of the moneylenders as Islamic banks, the Saudi Monetary Agency has conceded that Islamic financial principles can be interpreted in different ways; and,

---

[157]Rodney Wilson, *Islamic Banking and Finance, op.cit.* p.183.

therefore, plurality does exist, as both the conventional commercial banks, as well as the moneylenders, and the Islamic banking institutions, all claim to conform with Qur'anic principles, even though their operating methodologies may considerably differ.

It was also felt by Prince Muhammad that it was desirable to establish an Islamic presence in Western financial markets based on *riba*-free transactions, and to this end the Dar al-Mal al-Islami – the House of Islamic Funds (DMI) – was founded in Geneva in 1981. Despite severe losses during the 1983/84 financial year there appears to be little problem in attracting deposits. The problem that does arise is deciding on the appropriate choice of liquid financial instruments, as Islamic institutions cannot hold government bills or bonds which yield interest. In practice, therefore, DMI functions as a kind of investment company, with most of its funds in equity markets and in property, although it does hold some short-term assets in the form of cash and commodities.

Everything, however, has not been plain sailing for Islamic finance in the Muslim world. In 1988 the Egyptian Islamic investment house, Al-Rayan, collapsed. The Central Bank refused to intervene and thousands of small investors lost their savings.   Confidence in that sector has therefore been shaken, although it must be noted that the crash affected an investment company, not the Islamic banks themselves, though some investors have not always been clear about the differences.[158] In Pakistan many Muslims who were very active in the Islamic finance movement and many of whom worked for Islamic banks in the Middle East, have equally been seriously demoralized since the demise of the Zia regime.

---

[158]Rodney Wilson, *Islamic Financial Markets*, *op.cit.*, p.225, f.n.4.

There is little doubt, however, that despite set-backs or slow progress in the Muslim world, Islamic financial institutions will want to be increasingly represented in Western financial markets. The al-Rajhis have an office in London, not only for exchange dealings but also to provide investment services for their clients from Saudi Arabia. The al-Rajhi name, however, can cause some confusion. In 1982, the Saudi money-changer Abdullah Salah al-Rajhi was declared bankrupt forcing the SAMA to tighten up supervision of this sector. At the same time, the al-Rajhi Company for Currency Exchange and Commerce applied for an Islamic banking licence which was granted in 1983. This company shared a name but nothing else with the company that went bankrupt. The experience of the head of the group, Suleiman Abdul Aziz al-Rajhi, since 1954, and his employees, make it perhaps the most powerful force in Islamic finance, and it is a subsidiary of this – the al-Rajhi Company for Islamic Investments – which was formed in London in 1981. The al-Barakas, another Jeddah-based group are also in London, and they are also a significant force in Islamic finance as one of the fastest growing Islamic enterprises in the stages of expansion and organisation.[159] The al-Rajhi, al-Baraka, and Kuwait Finance House – which has earned the respect of the banking fraternity by its innovation, competitiveness with *riba* banks, and above all the integrity of its accounts (in 1983 when there was a 19% loss in earnings there was no attempt to disguise this by 'creative accounting') – are also all major shareholders in the Islamic Banking System International. One of its first subsidiaries, the Islamic Bank International of Denmark, was the first Islamic Bank permitted to operate alongside *riba*-banks in the

---

[159]See Chapter 3: 'Al-Baraka International Bank Limited: The Experience of an Islamic Bank in England' in *Islamic Banking: Theory, Practice and Challenges*, Fuad Al-Omar and Mohammed Abdel-Haq (Zed Books Ltd., London, 1996).

European market, although it is not easy at present to compare the Danish Islamic Bank's return with that of *riba*-banks in the same market.[160]

Beside DMI, The Kuwait Finance House, al-Rajhi, and al-Baraka, a further group of Islamic Banks can be designated as "Independents." These, according to Auton, operate outside the sphere of direct influence given by the other institutions named above. They include the long established Dubai Islamic Bank, the state dominated Bank Islam of Malaysia, and the Cairo based Nasser Social Bank. At the smaller end of the scale are the Shura Trust Limited in South Africa and the Dar Al Ulcom Banking House of Uttar Pradesh in India.[161] This is one of the smaller banks operating at a grass-roots level, serving economically unsophisticated urban and rural communities. The introduction of Islamic finance here has provided a valuable source of cheap liquidity where previously most of the communities were restricted to a choice between the rather large and daunting *riba*-based banks or the traditional moneylenders.[162] Their experience corrolates strongly with the findings in Bani Hamida where the methodology of Islamic finance also utilises the same ideological base that exists in these Muslim communities. As they are a development from the

---

[160]Bernard Auton, *"A Review of Islamic Financial Institutions,"* Islamic Banking Conference, London, 1984, p.26.

[161]*Ibid.*, p.27.

[162]In connection with moneylenders in India, Dr. Howard Jones has written a fascinating account of moneylending in a Hindu community after living with a moneylending family in a Rajasthan village during 1983 and 1989/90, observing the effects of the introduction of banking loan facilities to a Hindu/Jain community, where traditionally the Jains are the Indian equivalent to the moneylending Jew of Europe. Although not in Judaic, Christian, or Islamic terms, this does, however, provide a fascinating insight on the existance of moneylending classes in other major belief systems, and I am grateful to Dr. Jones for pointing this out to me in March, 1995. Howard Jones, *"Women's access to Informal and Formal Finance in a Rajasthan Village,"* paper from 'Finance Against Poverty,' a conference at Reading University, March, 1995.

society's religious and social structure, terminology and method require less explanation, and are, therefore, more readily accepted, and as Auton remarks: "The equity and welfare benefits of their long term operations indicate that the methodology of Islamic banking could have a major role to play in the development of the Third World."[163]

According to Al-Omar and Abdel-Haq there are currently five categories of operating Islamic Banks:

1.   The Islamic Development Bank - which is considered to have been the kick-start for the second phase after the demise of the Mit Ghamr banks.

2.   Those banks which operate in countries where the whole banking system has been converted to operating on Islamic principles and whose operations are overseen in some way by religious bodies e.g. in Pakistan.

3.   Those banks which operate in Muslim countries and which co-exist with interest-based banks. e.g. in Jordan, Egypt and Malaysia.

4.   Islamic banks in non-Muslim countries whose monetary authorities do not recognise their Islamic character e.g. the Al-Baraka International Bank in London and the Islamic Bank in Durban in South Africa.

5.   Islamic banks which exist in non-Muslim countries whose monetary authorities do recognise their Islamic character e.g. the Faisal International Bank (FIB) based in Copenhagen, Denmark and registered under the Danish Banking Supervisory Board.[164]

---

[163]Auton, *op. cit.*, p.27.

[164]Fuad Al-Omar and Mohammed Abdel-Haq, *Islamic Banking: Theory, Practice and Challenges*, (Zed Books Ltd., London, 1996), p.22.

I believe that in defining an ethical, social and Islamic economic financial system *riba*-free banking has a crucial part to play in the development of Muslim communities within not only third world countries but also first and second world. It provides a banking paradigm which an economist working in the Treasury in this country, and writing from a Christian perspective, advocates, in terms of providing better treatment for the poor. The banking which Paul Mills recommends is not defined as Islamic, but it has all the hallmarks of Islamic banking i.e. in terms of risk-sharing, and is cited as a model for a more just system of banking, although, of course denying its distinct religious roots based on Islamic principles.[165] With specific regard to Islamic banking, however, Mills maintains that if lenders were to lend on a profit-share basis they would have more of an incentive to lend to borrowers offering the best prospects of high returns, rather than to those who posed the least risk, and this, in fact, might lead to a more efficient allocation of finance than an interest-based alternative – assuming that profitability is an acceptable indication of efficiency. He quotes *The Economist* as saying that Islamic banking in some cases is not merely consistent with capitalism in terms of a market-driven allocation of capital, labour and other resources, but may even be *better* suited to it than Western banking.[166] If this is the case, then, the way has always been wide open for the development of a capitalist economy operating successfully in the Islamic world. The question is, therefore, what has prevented this from happening? Is it, as Ruthven suggests, the fact that Islamic law had no formalised conception of the legal personality of a corporate body which proved the stumbling block to the

---

[165]Paul Mills, *"The Ban on Interest: Dead Letter or Radical Solution?,"* Cambridge Papers, volume 2, number 1, March 1993.

[166]"Banking behind the Veil," *The Economist*, April 1992, p.76.

development of capitalism, rather than the ban on interest as such? Or is it that, in fact, as Muhammad Baqer as-Sadr implied, Islam provides a *via media* or middle axiom which lies somewhere between both capitalism and socialism?

Dr. Gaafar Abdel-Salam Ali, head of the public law department at Al-Azhar University in Cairo argues that because the 'golden mean,' or moderation, is a fundamental principle of Islamic economics it enables it to lie half-way between the capitalist and socialist systems. In the capitalist system, he maintains, free enterprise is guaranteed for anyone who can make an addition to the nation's wealth, whereas, in the socialist system, the opposite is true, an individual should work for the interest of the group, an ideology which has proved impracticable. However, the Islamic system is more realistic as it allows for individual ownership and exhorts man to work for a living. At the same time there are restrictions on man's actions, in particular, the theory that man is God's viceroy on earth and commissioned to run its affairs: *istikhlaf.* In doing so, man should follow the teachngs of the *Shari'ah*, which prohibit wastefulness and hoarding, as well as *riba*, and provides for the payment of *zakat.* Occasionally the Islamic system is placed closer to the socialist system by some on the grounds that *takaful*, social solidarity, is also a prerequisite in Islam; but, according to Ali, the important point is that Islam, and Islamic economics, provides for the 'golden mean' between the two other systems.[167]

Other Islamic writers echo this very important distinction. Muhammad Qutb maintains that although some of the outward manifestations of Islam appear on the surface to resemble those of capitalism or socialism, in fact, it is far from being one or the other:

---

[167]GafaarAbdel-Salam Ali, *Al-Ahram,* 23rd February-1st March, 1995, p.3.

"It retains all the good characteristics of these systems, yet it is free from their shortcomings and perversions. It does not extol individualism to that loathful extent which is the characteristic of the modern West. It was from this germ that modern capitalism sprang and institutionalized that concept of individual's freedom where man is allowed to exploit other individuals and the community only to serve his personal gain. Islam guarantees personal freeedom and provides opportunites for individual enterprise but not at the cost of society or ideals of justice. The reaction to capitalism has appeared in the form of socialism. It idolizes the social basis to the extent that the individual is reduced to an insignificant cog of the social machine, with no existence whatever of its own outside and independent of the herd. Therefore, the community alone enjoys freedom as well as power; the individual has no right to question its authority or demand his rights. The tragedy of socialism and its variants is that they assign to the state absolute powers to shape the lives of the individuals."[168]

Islam, on the other hand, according to Muhammad Qutb, strikes the balance between the extremes of capitalism and socialism. It harmonises the individual and the state in such a way that individuals have the freedom necessary to develop their potentialities and not to encroach on the rights of their fellow human beings, and this harmony is maintained by giving the community and the state adequate powers to regulate and control the socio-economic relationships. Most importantly, this unique system of life as envisaged by Islam was not the result of any economic pressure, but revealed as an ordained system of life at a time when man attached no particular importance to economic factors – both the modern concept of socialism and capitalism are much later developments.

Equally, Chapra maintains, that any attempt to show the similarity of Islam with either capitalism or socialism can only demonstrate a lack of understanding of

---

[168]Muhammad Qutb, *Islam and the Crisis of the Modern World,* (The Islamic Foundation, Leicester, 1979), p.18.

the basic characteristics of the three systems. The commitment of Islam to individual freedom distinguishes it sharply from socialism, or any system, which abolishes individual freedom. Recognition by Islam, however, of the freedom of enterprise, along with the institution of private property and profit motive, does not make the Islamic system akin to capitalism. The difference is due to two important reasons. Firstly, as Qutb points out, even though property is allowed to be privately owned in the Islamic system, it is to be considered as a trust from God. Secondly, and consequentially, because the wealth a man owns is a trust from God, he is therefore bound by the conditions of this trust with regard to the moral values of Islam, particularly the values of *halal* and *haram*, brotherhood, social and economic justice, equitable distribution of income and wealth, and fostering the common good..[169] It would appear, therefore, that Islam can possibly exist as a middle axiom between capitalism and socialism, it needs neither to conform to one nor the other. The task before the Islamic leadership, intellectual as well as politico-economic, is to clearly formulate the objectives and strategy of change, and the ways of achieving it, and also to establish institutions and inaugurate processes through which these policies could be actually implemented. (It interestingly appears to correlate to the 'Third Way' that is being so strongly advocated by world leaders such as Tony Blair and Bill Clinton in the West today.) In terms of Islamic Banking this might be easier to formulate in Islamic environments, but how difficult would it be to operate in non-Islamic environments?

---

[169]Chapra, *Objectives of the Islamic Economic Order*, (The Islamic Foundation, Leicester, 1979), pp.23, 24.

Islamic Banking: Non-Islamic Environments

There are problems which inevitably arise when Islamic financial institutions attempt to operate in non-Islamic environments. In a paper on Islamic financing, *"The View from the City,"* Frank Steele maintains that Islamic Banking was met, in the early 1970's when the first rise in oil prices made more funds available, with a welcome intermingled with caution, and a certain degree of scepticism. It was welcomed because, although traditionalist in some respects, the City also has to respond to new concepts and developments with a certain amount of innovation to keep its place as one of the leading financial centres in the world. The caution covered the concern over new and unfamiliar terminology in which the City had to be educated, coupled with the fact that even within the Muslim community there did not seem to be any clearly defined views and positions on Islamic banking; and the scepticism (amongst the most sceptical being Muslims operating within the traditional system) revolved around *hiyal* - transactions which were in effect *riba* but dressed up not to look like it, and the risk element, where instead of working in the traditional banking system to minimise risk, the City was being asked to work with a method of banking in which risk was an essential part of the system.

In the 1990's, however, the City has become more educated and is working with the Islamic banking system. Problems persist, however, with regard to the role of the Bank of England as a supervisory body, and the difference in concept between the two systems. Supervisory bodies are intended to protect the security of depositors and to minimise risk in the system, whereas the Islamic banking system, based on Qur'anic teaching, is based on profit-sharing and risk. The Bank of England is also governed by the Banking Act of 1979 which obliges the Bank to repay the precise amount deposited, from an Islamic point of view, if a venture fails then the deposit is not returnable. It is also difficult in banking terms to value the assets of an Islamic institution, such as, for example, a share in a joint venture. The traditional banking system has much of its assets in fixed interest instruments and it is comparatively easier to value, also, the valuing of such assets in Islamic terms then gives rise to the problems of ensuring that there are adequate capital ratios, liquidity, reserves, etc.

There is no easy solution. As Islamic banking practice continues to evolve, in what way should British banking legislation and regulations change, when the Islamic world's own monetary authorities have not yet agreed upon how to supervise and control Islamic banks? If the 1979 Act was altered to make provision for the entrepreneurial and risk-taking nature of Islamic banking, it might, in fact, make loopholes which the less scrupulous traditional banks could be tempted to exploit.[170] It would appear, however, that for the present, Islamic banking is here to stay. It must be remembered though, as Steele points out, that, in the City, it is not a question of two separate groups of people with Muslims on one side and non-Muslims on the other, there are non-Muslims, e.g. Westerners, working in Islamic houses, and there are Western banks operating the Islamic system of finance as well as traditional banking practices, even though there are still many problems to solve working

---

[170]The Bank of England has two major duties: to supervise the institutions authorised by it; and to keep under review the operation of the Banking Act. It must be satisfied with the capital, liquidity, management and corporate structure of every bank in London. Eddie George, governor of the Bank of England addressed the Arab Bankers Association in March, 1994 stating that: 'Some forms of Islamic Banking not only can be accommodated within our system of banking supervision but actually have been. Nevertheles there are problems we have to solve together in facing requests that institutions be permitted to offer more general Islamic banking facilities here. One is how to classify Islamic funds in terms of our own legal framework . . . A second issue is risk . . . I do not believe that these are inseparable problems, either for the banks concerned or for their supervisors . . . Our role as supervisor is to judge what is prudent banking and also what is acceptable in terms of the UK Banking Act, under which we have statutory responsibilities." See Al-Omar and Abdel-Haq *op.cit.* p.35.

together;[171] whether there are any Westerners actually preferring to bank with an Islamic institution is not known. It would still appear at the moment, however, as Wilson points out, that although the Islamic financial movement has matured it seems more likely to remain an *alternative* for Muslims rather than the sole means of conducting financial transactions.[172]

In moving toward an Islamic understanding of usury, therefore, and in the light of the above historic outline and practical applicability of the Qur'anic teaching with regard to *riba*, is it possible, in twenty-first century terms, to define an Islamic economic system?

Even within the Islamic community there are differing opinions as to what the definition of an 'Islamic economy' as a viable concept might be, and how, if it exists, it might interact with the world economic system. In Egypt, for example, Dr. Said El-Naggar, professor of economics at Cairo University, and the Mufti at that time, Sheikh Mohamed Sayed Tantawi (later Grand Imam after the death of Sheikh Gadd-al-Haqq), insist that 'interest' in general is not necessarily *riba*. Interest, they would maintain, is very important for the functioning of any economic system; and although an Islamic economy may be defined by various factors, such as: Islamic banking free of interest; *zakat*; and the elimination of poverty; and it may be limited to certain kinds of activities to distribute the risk between the investor and the bank, to say that an Islamic economy means banning interest altogether is a big mistake; likewise, to claim that there is an Islamic economic science as distinct from a

---

[171]Frank Steele, (Kleinwort Benson Ltd., London), *"View from the City,"* Islamic Banking Conference London, 1984.

[172]Wilson, *Islamic Banking and Finance, op. cit.*, p.186.

Western economic science, is an exaggeration. Dr. Said El-Naggar is reiterating an Abduh/Rida argument when he maintains that:

> "The science of economics which has been developed in the West has nothing to do with religion, in the sense that it is based on generalisations which are true and applied to all human beings, whether Muslims, Christians or Jews. The foundations of Western economics are based on general assumptions. As such, Western economic science is relevant to our own society; we have the right to develop it according to the recommendations of social sciences, including economic science . . . Some people interpret Islam in a way which means going back to what was applied in the seventh and eighth centuries, while others think that our religion is capable of development in order to go hand in hand with progress in general."[173]

This proposition, however, would negate the very arguments discussed throughout this chapter with regard to a specific Islamic economic system, particularly with regard to the prohibition of *riba, based on the very firm foundations of its religious teaching and interpretation.* Likewise, in the context of arguments I have made here and elsewhere,[174] I have argued that the science of economics which has developed in the West, has at least *something* to do with religion, especially with regard to the Judaic and Christian teaching with regard to 'usury.' What is ironic, in a sense, is that although the assumption that there is a strong interdependence between religion and morality is but the remains of the now lost hegemony of Christianity over Western culture, many of Western societies' moral attitudes and

---

[173]Said El-Naggar, *"Al-Ahram,"* Cairo, 23 February-1 March, 1995, p.3.

[174]See *"A Theological Examination of the Religious Teaching on 'Usury' within Judaism, Christianity and Islam and its Relevance for the World Today"* (Ph.D Thesis, S.L.Buckley, University of Aberdeen, 1996) and *Usury Friendly? – The Ethics of Moneylending – A Biblical Interpretation,'* (Grove Books Ltd., Cambridge, July, 1998).

practices are still based on Jewish and Christian beliefs, which in themselves have been discarded as irrelevant or false in themselves. The situation does not necessarily provide an argument for the continued viability of religious practices, but it may indicate that as a culture the implications of generating a genuine secular morality has not been fully faced.[175] Perhaps the most enlightened work being done at the moment is by Professor Hans Kung and his 'Global Ethic Foundation' in Tubingen. His book 'Global Responsibility' with its plea for a consensus on basic ethical values among those of all religions and no religion led to a 'Declaration Toward a Global Ethic' which was endorsed by the Parliament of the World's Religions held in Chicago in 1993. In a book edited by Kung in 1995 a remarkable group of international figures including heads of states and world organisations, religious leaders (including from the world of Islam: Muhammad El-Ghazali; Hassan Hanafi; Mahmoud Zakzouk; Muhammad Talbi and former Crown Prince Hassan Bin Talil), scholars and writers made their own contributions toward the vision of a global ethic. His latest book deals with the concept from both an economic and a political perspective: 'A Global Ethic for Global Politics and Economics. '[176]

Dr. Gaafar Abdel-Salam Ali, equally argues that *Islamic* sciences, including Islamic economic science, differ from man-made economics on this point – that revelation *is* a basic foundation of the Islamic economy. If the Qur'an and the *sunna* provide certain rulings related to selling and buying all these form an integral part of

---

[175]Stanley Hauerwas/Alasdair Macintyre (eds.), *Revisions*, (University of Notre Dame Press, London), 1983.

[176]See Hans Kung: *Global Responsibility*, (SCM Press Ltd., London 1991); *Yes to a Global Ethic*, *(ed.* SCM Press Ltd., London 1996); and *A Global Ethic for Global Politics and Economics*, (SCM Press Ltd., London, 1997). I am very grateful to Professor Kung for providing me with a copy of this prior to publication and for his insightful comments when he kindly invited me to meet with him in Tubingen on July 18th, 1997.

the science. Islamic economics are based on the Qur'anic teaching and the *Shari'ah,* naturally, therefore, Islamic economics has been greatly influenced by Islamic jurisprudence, but, although there are those at Al-Azhar University who deny that Islamic economics is an independent science on the grounds that it is included in jurisprudence, jurisprudence alone cannot explain all economic phenomena and problems of the present time, although obviously, for Islamic economic scholars, it has proved highly influential.[177]

In terms of the Islamic teaching in the Qur'an, with regard to *riba*, this book has tried to define the existence of a distinct Islamic economic system. This has been shown to exist within the context of the Qur'anic and *Sunnah* teaching with regard to the prohibition of *riba*, and within the provision of an interest-free Islamic banking model in terms of a profit-and-loss-sharing partnership. This has enabled us to move toward an Islamic understanding of the concept of usury – *riba*, and its attempts to conform to this teaching in the economic and religious clime of the twentieth century. There are those, however, who envisage the whole exercise as effectively unenforceable in a large, heterogeneous society, and question whether Islamic economics/banking can offer any viable alternative; or, even more improbably, an economic and social solution to the economic ills of today, in terms of brotherhood, equality and justice. In Islam itself, according to Ahmed, the *ummah* is inchoate, and the West is suspicious. Can 'Islamic Banking' or an 'Islamic economic system,' offer an authentic working model to the West, not just as a supplement but, perhaps astonishingly, as a substitute? Data suggests that the Islamic banking movement is a dynamic movement and even the characteristics described above are already changing, for example, reliance on *mudaraba* has started to decline in certain banks,

---

[177]Gafaar Abdel-Salam Ali, *op.cit.*, p.3.

and more reliance is being put on *musharakah* as a financing technique. Newspaper reports often explore the phenomenon of Islamic banking in Britain, with headlines such as: "A growing interest in Islamic banking;"[178] and, "Interest grows in banks that lend money with no interest."[179] It would appear that for the present Islamic banking is here to stay; it certainly produces a distinctive economic model with regard to its religious teaching on usury, as does a Judaic and Christian model which I have discussed in detail above. What sort of model, therefore, is appropriate in terms of combatting exploitative usurious lending, for the twenty-first century? Are religious models of any use, and in particular in this case, an Islamic model? Or do we have to abandon these in favour of a secular model – do we, indeed, have to go, for want of a better neologism, in search of an ethical 'seconomic man' i.e. secular economic man?

The question I now address in my conclusion, is, this: what relevance, if any, does the concept of 'Islamic Banking' as a potential 'Third Way' paradigm for the future have as we move into the twenty-first century? Do we try to produce a working, secular economic model devoid of specific religious teaching, but none the less imbued with moral considerations, in order to bring about debt relief; the alleviation of poverty; the fair distribution of wealth and, equally, opportunities for its creation; justice; and access for the poor to finance and financial institutions? Or is it still possible to address – in theological and Islamic terms – an ethical banking system which could have an enormous economic, social, and political impact in our 'global village' for all concerned?

---

[178]*Financial Times,* Friday, October 7, 1994.

[179]*The Independent,* November 9, 1994.

Islamic Banking – A Paradigm for the Future?

The thrust of this discussion has been to see whether the model of 'Islamic Banking' defined within its religious tradition can possible act as a paradigm – a blue-print – for the future in terms of advancing an economic system which might attempt in the future to, not only, alleviate, but possibly eradicate poverty throughout the world, in moving toward a more compassionate and tolerant society where the dignity and worth of every human being is to be acknowledged, not least in the sphere of finance, and provided with accessibility to ways and means with which to earn a decent living and care for one's family and community, on a local, national, and global scale. Is it possible to address this issue in terms of promoting a theological interpretation onto an economic model in a secular, yet, at the same time, pluralist and multi-faith society? Can the concept of 'Islamic Economic Man' in terms of 'Islamic Banking' have any effect whatsoever on the poor, and on the global economy, at the beginning of the twenty-first century?

This may seem either a presumptious or a naieve, or indeed, both, proposition. And as a theologian, albeit one who has addressed the issue very seriously in its economic consideration, I have been chiefly concerned in this study to set the arguments within the context of theological and theoretical implications. I have defined and determined the concept of 'Islamic banking' with regard to Islam's religious teaching specifically on the concept of *riba*/usury, as taught in the Qur'an and the *Sunnah*, and interpreted in *hadith* and the various schools of law, and as discussed above also within the context of *ummah*, and the communal responsibility of mutual aid collected and distributed as *zakat*. Both are expressed in the idea of *tawhid*, the unicity of God,[180] with its corollary that persons should not

---

[180]See Malise Ruthven, "Islam: A Very Short Introduction," (OUP, 1997), Chapter 3: 'Divine Unicity.'

be compartmentalised in their actions. Although, from an economic point of view, *hiyal* (legal fictions) were invented down through the ages to get around the implementation of interest-free loans, the teaching with regard to the proscription on usurious lending remains at the heart of a 'new' Islamic economic system today, in terms of inaugurating a specific Islamic banking system with this as its underlying ethic. There are, however, bound to be reservations expressed by some as to the viability of an economic system based on this premise. One such voice of scepticism belongs to Timur Kuran.

Kuran does concede that profit-sharing constitutes a useful scheme, indeed, in many markets it is a preferred option for allocating returns even when interest is a legally viable option.[181] However, his criticism is that it hardly follows that profit-sharing should be the basis for all productive ventures. Kuran's reservations concern the redistribution not just of returns but also of risks as some segments of society are better able to bear this than others. He cites the case of a handicapped octogenarian who relies on his/her savings for a living, or at least the interest payable on the capital sum saved. But there are alternative schemes which could be built into the system for the elderly and more risk averse: for instance, the compulsory savings scheme toward a pension which is being implemented in Australia (and partially advocated in Britain); or the improvement of state pensions for the elderly and greater benefits distributed to the handicapped. In this case the element of risk could be overcome, although in an inflationary economy some form of indexation would be necessary. These methods do not have to rely on an interest-based economy.

---

[181]See Timur Kuran, "The Economic System in Contemporary Islamic Thought: Interpretation and Assessment," (*The International Journal of Middle East Studies*, Vol. XVIII, 1986).

His second objection lies in the opportunism that informational asymmetry might afford to the more unscrupulous – the borrowing enterprise knows its revenue and cost structure whereas the lender can only estimate, in which case the borrower could understate profit and overstate costs, or, deliberately, let costs soar in order to grant high benefits to employees, and effective monitoring by a bank can obviously be costly. Kuran also points out that employees should share in the risk by banning fixed wages otherwise all the risks are borne by the shareholders. But this in fact may be an excellent idea. If this is what a 'stake-holder' economy is all about, it would encourage the work-force to work to the best of its ability, foster a sense of community (and loyalty) within the work-force, enhance shop-floor and management relations, and even provide some form of security. In more productive times the 'feel good factor' can be distributed among the work-force as a bonus, and, in any event, is not some wage better than redundancy and no wage at all? Even though Kuran quotes Syed Aftab Ali of the Bureau of Statistics in Ottawa who detects the inconsistency in allowing fixed wages, but not interest and, therefore, advocates wages for employees tied to the profitability of their firms, Kuran summarily dismisses it because he maintains that some people prefer fixed wages anyway, and a ban on fixed wages would be unenforceable. To address this anomaly, however, a guaranteed minimal wage could be implemented which also had the possibility of producing profit bonuses. It is an interesting proposition. One might refer to it as a 'kitty-economy' – redistributing fairly what is available in the 'kitty' to all concerned.

As to the bank's monitoring costs, Paul Mills outlines proposals with regard to a more 'relational' method of co-operation between the two parties which might alleviate the costs involved – long-term relationships between the bank and the borrower would help to build up trust[182] and knowledge of the operations in progress; and the bank could gain inside information by being represented on the boards of companies in which it has a profit-share stake, as happens with German banks.[183]

In his paper, Kuran, in trying to define and critique the concept of an Islamic economic system ties together the prohibition of *riba, zakat,* and behavioural norms. Although I have considered *zakat* because of its important dimension as one of the five pillars of Islam, I am only concerned with trying to define an Islamic economic system in terms of the whole concept of the prohibition on *riba,* and the possible implementation of the concept of 'Islamic banking' based upon it. There have obviously been ways in which this prohibition has been, and still is, legitimised by *hiyal,* and there will be those opposed to the idea and concept whatever the validity or not of their arguments – and other writers more qualified than I have addressed these issues.[184] It is impossible to derive an entire blue-print for an Islamic economy from the Qur'an or *Sunnah.* But the moral principles expounded in the Qur'an, and the normative ideals worked out in the *Sunnah* are still ones which can undergird a specific Islamic economic framework, without compromising the teachings of the Prophet, Muhammed, or trying to return to an economic situation based on seventh

---

[182]See also Francis Fukuyama, *Trust,* (Hamish Hamilton 1995). Fukuyama argues that free markets, competition and hard work are not the sole precursors for prosperity, there is another key ingredient – *trust.* He explains how trust and culture have affected economic and political life.

[183]Paul Mills, "Interest in Interest: The Old Testament Ban on Interest and its Applications for Today," (Jubilee Centre Publications Ltd.), 1993, p.47.

[184]See, in particular: *Islamic Banking: Theory, Practice and Challenges,* F.Al-Omar and M.Abdel-Haq, (Zed Books Ltd., London, 1996); and *RIBA: The Moral Economy of Usury, Interest and Profit,* *Ziaul Haque* (Ikraq, Selangor, 2nd. edition 1993).

century Arabian ideals, 'a golden age' which did not even exist at the time of Muhammed as institutions were abandoned or modified as circumstances warranted.

With regard to 'Islamic Banking' there is one huge distinction and caveat which should be made. If most people were asked to broadly define the concept of 'Islamic Banking' they would probably define it as the expansion of financial institutions which can be characterised as Islamic in that they do not deal in interest-based transactions. However, in a sense, it must be maintained that authentic 'Islamic banking' must be in consonance with the teachings, ethos and value system of Islam. Interest-free banking, by contrast, is a narrower concept, denoting a number of banking instruments or operations which avoid interest. Islamic Banking in its true essence is expected not only to avoid transactions on the basis of interest but also to participate actively in achieving the goals and objectives of an *Islamic* economy and society.[185] This I think is a very important point and one often missed in the discussion of 'Islamic Banking.'

In suggesting 'Islamic Banking' as an economic paradigm I fully maintain that it is the principles of Islamic teaching and thought which fully undergird this model for an ethically functioning new economic system for the future, which is why I have taken great care to define it within these parameters. However, in terms of an interest-free banking system, Islamic Banking as a financial model could serve to provide society with the means of alleviating the poverty engendered as a result of interest bearing loans. These could be implemented with especial regard for the poor, both at home and in low income countries, by giving them a stake in society, and providing financial institutions which may more justly distribute wealth, and give the poor the opportunity to create it for themselves, in terms of providing access

---

[185]Al-Omar and Abdel-Haq, *op.cit.*, p.21

to low cost finance; training, skills and equipment. In all this there has to be the constant reminder of the worth and dignity of every human being in society constantly in mind. As we are reminded:

> "Some ways of distributing are demeaning and destructive; sharing
> that is grudging, or patronising, or demands that the recipient shows
> himself to be 'deserving,' humble and grateful, is fatally flawed . . .
> Some modes of allocation create dependency, limit freedom and
> destroy dignity and self-respect; others encourage a proper balance
> between independence and interdependence so that within the
> community care and respect for one another flourish."[186]

I suggest this model of Islamic banking therefore, as a paradigm not only within Islam itself and its concomittant Islamic ethos, but one from which non-Muslims, too, may learn and appreciate. If accepted and initiated as a role model it could establish a more just, profit-sharing economic system, where, in principle, a sense of community and responsibility is engendered and facilities are established to help the poorer members within society. I want to conclude finally by addressing two financial operations which on the face of it may appear to be at opposing ends of a spectrum but are not as far removed as one might imagine: the work of the Islamic Development Bank in the Third World and the concept of Venture Capital in the First.

Although the presence of Islamic commercial banks in the Third World is relatively recent, and their impact minimal as yet, the Jeddah based Islamic Development Bank has a much longer and more significant development. Despite its name the IDB is primarily an aid agency rather than a bank, as its aim is to

---

[186]*Just Sharing*," eds. Duncan Forrester and Danus Skene, (Epworth Press, Church and Nation Committee of the General Assembly of the Church of Scotland, 1988), p.62.

provide concessionary finance to low income and middle income Islamic countries. It charges no interest, whereas with other aid agencies the concessionary element in their lending represents the difference between their low fixed interest rates and fluctuating, but generally higher, commercial bank rates for borrowing:

> "It makes loans subject only to a small charge to cover administrative overheads, or invests directly in the equity of the project it backs, or purchases the item required and leases it to the user. In none of these cases is the bank's objective to make a profit, rather it only aims to break even and recoup its advances eventually, so that other projects can in turn be aided."[187]

It is by far the largest Islamic financial institution, the most sophisticated and well-run, co-financing development projects and collaborating with multilateral aid agencies such as the World Bank. Although not charging interest itself it will assist projects in which other agencies provide loans on an interest basis, a very co-operative attitude. It can also give technical assistance with the design and implementation of projects.

The substitution of equity for debt finance is advocated by many development agencies and participatory finance is especially suited to small business. For example: as Mr. Poonawalla pointed out in relation to the development agency AKFED (the Aga Khan Federation) the difference between AKFED and other institutions (e.g. the International Finance Corporation, the Commonwealth Development Corporation, and the German Development Corporation) is that AKFED is more equity oriented. The portfolio of other agencies would show 10-20% by way of equity and the remaining portion would be by way of loans. "Equity

---

[187]Rodney Wilson, *Islamic Business: Theory and Practice,* (The Economic Intelligence Unit, Special Report No. 178, London, 1985), p.46.

is there for long term . . . because the money is part of your own equity you want to ensure the success of the project you are investing in, and that means more commitment on our part."[188] This level of service indicates just how far Islamic finance has evolved. As Rodney Wilson remarks, those who regard it as some quaint inheritance from the past should think again, as it has certainly entered the modern banking world despite the problems that remain to be tackled.[189]

A very interesting comparison can be made at the more affluent end of the spectrum with respect to 'VC: Venture Capital' in terms of technology funding. Apparently VC is the key to America's technological lead in the world marketplace. Second to the USA in world importance the UK industry is the largest and most developed in Europe accounting for nearly fifty per cent of total annual European VC investment. Very simply, VC is money invested in start-up companies to help fund the development of new products or services. In return venture capitalists receive a stake in each company they help finance. If the start-up company succeeds and prospers, the venture capitalists who backed it realise a profit. Of course many VC backed companies will fail, and that can mean significant loss of capital. However, unlike other investors who hope to profit from fluctuations in the public markets, venture capitalists profit by building value. Investment managers play an active, dynamic role in all of the fund's portfolio companies, providing value-added management skills, long-term investment discipline and professional risk management to its emerging growth investments. There does appear to be a strong correlation between both equity funded PLS contracts and Venture Capital

---

[188]Quoted from the transcript of an interview between Poonawalla and Malise Ruthven. I am very grateful to Dr. Ruthven for providing me with this information.

[189]Wilson, *op.cit.*, p.47.

investment. As far as VC goes, one has only to consider the history of Silicon Valley to realise its potential.

In 1957 eight young men left Shockley Semiconductor Labs to start their own company because they thought they could build a better product. Fairchild Semiconductor Corp. became the first company to make computor chips exclusively out of silicon. Ten years later, two of these men left Fairchild to start a company they called Intel, and another Eugene Kleiner launched one of the region's first venture capital firms. Forty years later there are some 7,000 electronics and software companies in Silicon Valley with an estimated eleven new companies forming every week. In 1996 alone Silicon Valley firms created fifty thousand new jobs at wages five times the national average.[190]

In a perfect world, equally in a perfect Islamic world, economic considerations should be subordinated to moral consideration, in terms of social, political and economic justice. The relevance of Islamic Banking to ethical banking generally is that it offers a number of alternative approaches to the banker-customer relationship. It helps to stimulate new ideas for alternative banking in the context of seeking ethical solutions to emerging problems, such as coping with the problem of how to help the society by financing small businesses based on networks or communes.[191] Equally, as I have already emphasised, the general objective of Islamic Banking would be to develop the economy within and according to Islamic principles, and, therefore, no bank would engage in the payment or receipt of interest (nor, incidentally, in investment in the alcoholic beverage trade, in the gambling

---

[190]Information taken from the Internet: http://www.techfunding.com/text/what.shtml http://www.brainstorm.co.uk/BVCA/UKStats.html

[191]Al-Omar and Abdel-Haq, *op.cit.*, p.26.

industry or in the pork meat trade, or in any other specifically Qur'anic prohibited activities even if such activities were conducted under PLS contracts).

In suggesting Islamic Banking as an economic paradigm for the future, therefore, one could do no better than to quote the public statement of the International Association of Islamic Banks as a clear expression of the duty of Islamic banks toward the society in which they operate:

> "The Islamic banking system involves a social implication which is necessarily connected with the Islamic order itself, and represents a special characteristic that distinguishes Islamic banks from other banks based on other philosophies. In exercising all its banking or developmental activities, the Islamic bank takes into prime consideration the social implications that may be brought about by any decision or action taken by the bank. Profitability – despite its importance and priority – is not therefore the sole criterion or the prime element in evaluating the performance of Islamic banks, since they have to match both between the material and the social objectives that would serve the interests of the community as a whole and help achieve their role in the sphere of social mutual guarantee. Social goals are understood to form an inseparable element of the Islamic banking system that cannot be dispensed with or neglected."[192] (IAIB, 1990)

---

[192]Quoted *Ibid.*, p.27.

Conclusion

This book has examined the way in which the religious teaching on 'usury' affected the historical development of an economic system within the three great monotheistic traditions of Judaism, Christianity, and Islam, and concludes that three distinct models of Judaic, Christian, and Islamic 'economic man' are distinguishable as a result. The questions which now need to be addressed in conclusion, are: will any of these models serve as a blue-print for society in the future in an attempt, not only, to alleviate, but also to eradicate poverty throughout the world; or do we need a new model upon which to work, and, if so, how will that model differ? Can we put a theological interpretation onto a model in a secular, yet at the same time, multi-faith, society? In moving toward a more compassionate and tolerant society, where the dignity and worth of every single human-being is to be acknowledged, how can a theological interpretation on the religious teachings on usurious lending, within the three monotheistic traditions of Judaism, Christianity, and Islam, have any effect whatsoever on the poor, and on the global economy, at the dawn of the twenty-first century?

I have examined the way in which the model of what I term, 'Judaic economic man,' evolves as a result of the pentateuchal teaching with regard to usurious lending. Usury was considered, not in twentieth century terms as exorbitant interest, but as any, even minimal, payment taken as profit on a loan. In Exodus 22:25 and Leviticus 25:35-37, in addressing concern for the poor, the Jewish 'brother' is enjoined to extend interest-free loans to one another. Deuteronomy 23:19-20 extends this principle to all moneylending within the Jewish community,

309

whilst at the same time it excludes interest-free loans to the 'foreigner.' In theological terms this would appear to represent the very important aspect of the covenantal relationship between God and his 'chosen people' and his concern as they were about to enter the 'promised land' which he had brought them to, however literally or symbolically that might be translated. This, unfortunately, as Paul Johnson points out, resulted in a calamitous position for Jews in their relations with the rest of the world. They were burdened with a religious law which forbade them to lend at interest among themselves, but permitted it towards strangers. Thus, although the proviso seems to have been to protect and keep together a poor community whose chief aim was collective survival in an alien land, as Jews later became small, diasporan communities in a gentile (not gentle) universe, it not only permitted Jews to serve as moneylenders to non-Jews, but in a sense positively encouraged them to do so. When Jews were themselves financially oppressed and reacted by concentrating on moneylending to gentiles, their unpopularity and persecution increased; and so Jews were trapped in a vicious cycle.[1]

Whether one defines usury in terms of the Hebraic *neshekh* as 'advance interest,' or *marbit* or *tarbit* as 'accrued interest,' or the Talmudic *ribbit*, the Talmudic rabbis laid a great deal of emphasis on all sins of 'moral' usury. A loan from one Jew to another should not only be an act of loving kindness without the least expectation of profit, but is also a legal obligation associated with righteousness within Judaism – *chesed.* From the earliest days of Jewish society, therefore, these interest-free loans were an integral part of the Jewish economic world, and according to Tamari, are still operative in Israel today.[2] The provision for the release from debt

---

[1] P. Johnson, *A History of the Jews*, (Phoenix, London), 1995, p.172ff.

[2] M. Tamari, *With All Your Possessions: Jewish Ethics and Economic Life*, (Free Press, New York).

expressed in sabbatical and jubilee years is also evidence of the theological significance that was placed upon the care for the poor in early Israelite society.

I have maintained that Jews were engaged, from the very early days in the Temple, not only in money-changing activity, but also moneylending, and in this respect I have detected an embryonic 'spirit of capitalism.' Jewish economic life developed throughout most of medieval Europe dominated by Christianity in the West, and Islam in Spain, North Africa, and the Middle East, and the ensuing Ashkenazi and Sephardi Jewish economic life tended to develop parallel to the economic fortunes of the countries in which they lived. I have suggested that although the argument is normally formulated that Jews were forced into moneylending because of persecution from a hostile society, barred from owning land, serving in the army, and other occupations, and even expulsion from these countries, there did exist from early times an endogenous quality which developed from the money-changing and moneylending activity in the Temple, although I am not, as Cantor comes close to, investing Jews with some innate genetic superiority.[3]

I conclude that the model of 'Judaic economic man,' therefore, is a synthesis of various factors: the essential moneylending Jewish characteristic which originated in the Temple and fostered from an early time an embryonic 'spirit of capitalism'; the logical reaction to economic opportunities with regard to trade, commerce and banking, plus initiative and entrepreneurial ability; and more especially the precise religious teaching on the concept of usury that led Jews into business, and more specifically into the role of moneylending; and that it was not just as a result of the external pressures and persecution which were brought to bear on Jews in exile. In

---

[3]Norman Cantor, *The Sacred Chain: A History of the Jews,* (Harper Collins, London) 1995, p.423: "The Jews are a superior people intellectually and as long as Jewish genes exist, the extraordinary impact Jews have had in twentieth century thought will continue indefinitely."

this respect the model of 'Judaic economic man' stands as a direct result of pentateuchal teaching, especially that expressed in Deuteronomy 23:19. If justified in theological terms as emphasizing God's covenantal relationship with his 'chosen people,' and in political terms as protecting a vulnerable community in an alien land, in social and economic terms it alienated a people by promoting the 'brother' at the expense of, in Levinas' term, the 'other.'[4] This seems a harsh conclusion to reach in light of the suffering of the Jewish people throughout history, but it appears to be one that has developed historically through two thousand years of Diasporan exile. It was a model which developed from the Deuteronomic teaching in the Torah, and although it was essentially political it had a serious affect on the social and economic situation of the Jewish people. It was a model which served its purpose for a given time, but it does not have to represent the Judaic model of the future, if indeed, a future is plausible.

In his book, 'Vanishing Diaspora,' Bernard Wasserstein argues that what is now destroying Jews in Europe is their own apathy:

> "We witness now the last scene of the last act of more than a millennium of Jewish life in Eastern Europe . . . We witness now the withering away of Judaism as a spiritual presence in the daily lives of most Jews in Europe . . . We witness now the end of an authentic Jewish culture in Europe . . . We are, then, witnessing the

---

[4]Emmanuel Levinas who died in Dec. 1995, was a philosopher who tried to connect philosophy and religion within the ethical dimension. He studied the way in which the 'other' can become depersonalised. Existence, he argued, should be understood in its ethical as well as its existential dimension, at the heart of his thought lay the basic concept of the encounter between human beings. More than Buber's 'I-Thou' encounter in which a true meeting of minds is said to take place, Levinas stresses the concept of the 'face' of the other – a 'face' which helped to define each individual in the 'epiphany' of being addressed by the other in person; this provides the distinction between the existence and the existent. In religious terms it became man's awareness of his ethical responsibilities to other people. "Emmanuel Levinas," Obituaries, *The Times*, January 19th, 1996, p.21 and E. Levinas, *Collected Philosophical Papers*, (Martinus Nijhoff Publishers, Dordrecht.) 1987, p.44.

disappearance of the European Diaspora as a population group, as a cultural entity and as a significant force in European society and in the Jewish world."[5]

Similarly, Cantor prophesies the demise of the Jewish community as it now exists in the United States:

"Population trends signal the approaching end of Jewish history as we have known it. Fifty years from now there will be about the same number of Orthodox Jews in America – not more than fifteen percent of the current five million – as there are today. There is no way their Halakic behaviour can appeal beyond a population level that this difficult lifestyle appeals to today. As for the other eighty-five percent of Jews in America, they are on a one-way ticket to disappearance as a distinct ethnic group."[6]

Apart from apathy, the falling birthrate and increasing intermarriage are also undermining the Jews of Europe and America – Israel, at this time, is an unknown factor in predictability. Wasserstein suggests a way out of the apathy by the replacement of Jewish religious observance with Jewish culture – a 'cultural politics of the diaspora.'[7] Rabbi Julia Neuberger, equally, thinks this may be a way to solve

[5]Bernard Wasserstein, *Vanishing Diaspora: The Jews in Europe since 1945*, (Hamish Hamilton Ltd., London), 1996, p.283f.

[6]Cantor, *op.cit.*, p.426.

[7]In 1972, Arnold Toynbee was suggesting that we need the Jewish diaspora as a model of civilisation for the future. He maintains that the 'annihilation of distance' by the progress of technology applied to communication embraces the whole surface of the planet and unites the human race in a single comprehensive society. In such an ecumenical society, diasporas, not territorially compact local units, seem likely to be the most important of the global society's component communities, and, he states: "we may guess that the majority of these future diasporas will not be the products of the dispersal of communities that were originally local, and that they will not be held together by ethnic or even religious bonds. Their spiritual bond will be some common concern or common profession. The world's physicists already constitute one global diasporan community; the world's musicians are another; the world's physicians and surgeons are in process of becoming a third . . . the network of global diasporan communities is growing rapidly . . . now that the world is becoming one city, we

the problem, if Jews can get away from an obsession merely with surviving, and begin to see a purpose in their survival:

> "If we find messages in Judaism about the nature of the family, community, and society to be shared with others irrespective of our personal belief in God or lack of it, then we might be able to create a 'cultural politics of the diaspora' . . . The survival, should it happen, has to come out of our own conviction that there is within Judaism – its history, its cultures, its moral values, its religion, any aspect of its being – that which is worth preserving . . . if we cannot find anything worthwhile in our heritage, or do not even look, then we will disappear."[8]

The economic model of the future for Jews, therefore, will exist in the light of this 'vanishing' phenomenon – if it continues to take place. Perhaps Neuberger is prophetic in foreseeing the continued existence of Jewish community defined in a different way, one in which the community is not assimilated into its surrounding culture, as has happened in some cases, but one which is clearly defined, yet tolerated. This is the new economic model I would like to predict for Jews, as also for Christians and Muslims, within a pluralist twenty-first century culture. One of the most important aspects is not only to maintain identity, but also a sense of this identity. If the hallmarks of postmodern life are to be observed in terms of tolerance and synthesis, the synthesis must not encourage syncretism. People can be combined socially, politically, and economically into a community without having to combine

---

may expect to see associations based on neighbourhood come to be overshadowed by others based on spiritual affinity; that is to say, by diasporas in the broadest sense of the term in which this includes ubiquitous scattered minorities that are held together by religious and other ties of all kinds that are independent of locality." See A.Toynbee, *A Study of History*, (Oxford University Press and Thames Hudson, 1972), pp.65-67.

[8]Julia Neuberger, "The Purpose of Survival," *The Times*, January 18, 1996, p.40.

their beliefs. Tolerance of other people's belief systems, or none, as the case may be, must be the trademark of the next millennium's society, and the freedom to express those beliefs. As Wasserstein points out: 'would disappearance by murder and emigration in Eastern Europe be matched in the West by dissolution into a society that killed by kindness?'[9] 'Judaic economic man' must retain his identity, but the model will change. With regard to moving toward a Judaic understanding of the concept of usury, the introduction of *'hetter iska'* in allowing partnerships in joint ventures where risks are shared, is something that can be extrapolated out of the whole history of the development of the Judaic teaching on usury, especially in relationship to the Deuteronomic principle in terms of the 'brother' and the 'other,' to provide a positive economic framework, within which Jews can function in harmony with the rest of humankind, as also humankind will interact with Jews.

I have already mentioned the very important Judaic religious concept of *chesed,* which fostered an attitude toward needy members of the community, be they Jew or non-Jew, associated with the idea of righteousness. It was more than an act of charity. This was to be expressed in non-usurious loans to one another; it was a system which developed in diasporan communities and as I have mentioned still operates within Judaim today.

Another integral aspect of Jewish life is also the concept of *tzedaka* or charitable giving. One tenth of profits should be set aside for charitable giving, although as Norman Solomon points out: "the 'tenth' is a matter of conscience, not a tax levied by the community . . . the idea of the tithe comes from Scripture: the Bible lays down that farmers in the land of Israel should set aside tithes of cattle, sheep, and produce, for priests and levites who were a public charge and for the

---

[9]Wasserstein, *op.cit.*, p.279.

poor."[10] In his book *'The Kabbalah of Money,'* Rabbi Nilton Bonder states that the word charity is used to translate the Jewish concept of *tzedekah:*

> "The nature of *tzedekah,* however, is not related to the literal meaning of charity, which comes from the Latin *caritas* 'love.' The Jewish meaning is associated with the Market and should be translated literally as 'justice' *(tzedek)* . . . *Tzedekah* is a key issue in Jewish tradition . . . all interactions are taxed proportionally to our various levels of interdependence . . . the co-responsibility that we all share demands that our day to day life be filled with 'justice adjustments,' *tzedekah*. . . Judaism says that all kinds of wealth are interconnected. And if wealth doesn't seek to ameliorate poverty, then by definition it impoverishes itself. There can be no neutrality in poverty."[11]

To understand charity, therefore, in terms of justice, in the Judaic sense *(tzedekah)* is an important contribution to the debate on making available finance to the poor, indeed gifts rather than loans. *Tzedekah,* however, is much more than that as Rabbi Bonder explains further. It is not only a concept but a practice, a technique. As an art it cannot be practiced literally, that is to say that it does not mean mechanically setting aside a percentage of one's profit for donations at the end of a fiscal year – for how in fact might that be worked out – net/gross/expenses? It demands above all else involvement, creativity and wisdom because the dynamics of *tzedekah* are linked to gratitude. "Gratitude," says Rabbi Bonder "is the measure you should use to tax your gains."[12] It is something that the Christian church might also again bear in mind as inclusive of its own inheritance, where tithing now, too, seems an unexplored means of giving in a consumerist society.

---

[10]Norman Solomon, *Judaism, A Very Short Introduction,* (Oxford University Press, 1996), p.82.

[11]Nilton Bonder, *The Kabbalah of Money,* (Boston and London: Shambhala, 1996) pp.63-64

[12]*Ibid.*, p.67.

In a sense, therefore, the model of Judaic economic man proves to be something of a paradox. On the one hand, theologically, the Deuteronomic exemption succeeded in stressing the covenantal and protective element in the relationship between God and his 'chosen people,' but at the same time it alienated the Jew within its own economic clan ethic and resulted in the stereotypical history of the Jew as money-lender, a fascinating but brutal journey of anti-semitism and persecution, not least by the Christian church. It is a sad irony that in persecuting Jews, surely Jesus as Jew, is also again persecuted? On the other hand, within its religious teachings and traditions, Judaic economic man incorporates the admirable, and universalistic qualities of *chesed* and *tzedekah,* ideals which could translate into a secular and humanistic framework, even though in Judaic terms, they are not so much a concept as a technique, demanding involvement, creativity and wisdom, and above all else gratitude. There is much to be gleaned from this model.

The model of 'Christian economic man,' derived from the teaching with regard to usurious lending in the Bible, is different again to the Judaic model. This model reflects the more universalistic teaching of Luke 6:34,35 in the New Testament, which is used by Christians to modify the usury prohibition in the Hebrew Bible. The struggle of the Christian Church with the Judaic model, and in particular the 'horns of the dilemma' it found itself impaled upon with regard to the Deuteronomic 'exemption,' is surely proof enough – for those who try to discount the importance of the particular Deuteronomic text – of the tremendous effect, and problem that the Judaic teaching produced.

The historical development of the Christian Church's stance regarding the biblical interpretation on the concept of usury has been outlined above in terms of: the patristic position and the early Church Councils; the medieval period and the development of scholastic thought with particular reference to the work of St. Thomas

Aquinas and his divergence from the Aristotelian theory; the right to interest and the contracts of the *societas, foenas nauticum,* and *census*; the establishment of the pawn shops of the *montes pietatis* supported by the Franciscans; the controversy of the triple contract – the *Contractus Trinus*, the casuistry of the nominalist, John Major, and the position of the Jesuits forty years after Eck's defence of the triple contract. The Reformation and Calvin brought a counter-theory, and after the Reformation the Church was no longer able to stand in the way of the growth of commercial capitalism. Canonist thought ceased to represent an analysis of existing society as well as a code of conduct, although the Victorian 'Christian Socialists' responded to the forces of urbanisation and industrialisation in Great Britain with a new economic vision of 'co-operation.' The question of proscription and prescription concerning usury evolved into a question of regulation, and financing the poor through low-cost facilities. The problems and solutions with regard to the church's position on the prohibition of usury have, therefore, been reiterated and expounded above with regard to both scholastic and canonist interpretation, as well as that of the secular state. The Early Church condemned it for its greed and uncharitableness; the Medieval Church believed interest to be inherently unjust, largely because it was equivalent to the charging of rent for the use of money which ceased as soon as the borrowed money was spent. From around the early sixteenth century, as trade increased, the strong attack on interest became less intense. The Church allowed greater exceptions to the rule so as to fully compensate a lender for any loss incurred through the process of lending – risk and time were factors to be taken into consideration. Calvin rejected the view that interest was inherently wrong and this opinion became widespread, whilst at the same time, as I emphasised, the qualifications that Calvin made were ignored and then forgotten. Commercial developments were combined with the weakening of the influence of the Church over

Western society, and the dilution of anti-interest beliefs, to produce financial systems that were predominantly interest-based. The subject of economic enquiry then became not whether interest was licit, but rather, what determined the rate of interest and to what level it should be restricted. The model of 'Christian economic man,' therefore, changed from one that would have looked very similar to an Islamic model in terms of the forbidding of usurious lending, i.e. that which was added to the principal, to one which eventually, not without much struggle, abandoned the principle altogether, fostering a capitalistic spirit, based more on usurious lending and the development of trade and profit, than on Weber's thesis with regard to the 'Protestant ethic.' The Christian Church, therefore, acquiesced in this drift away from any biblical teaching, although the inauguration of a 'co-operative movement' by 'Christian Socialists' tried to engender a more universalistic spirit akin to the teaching in Luke 6:35; but today little contemporary Christian economic thought even bothers to raise the issue, although in a now famous speech to the General Assembly of the Church of Scotland in 1988, Margaret Thatcher stated that : "It is not the creation of wealth that is wrong but love of money for its own sake. The spiritual dimension comes in deciding what to do with the wealth. How could we respond to the many calls for help, or invest in the future, or support the wonderful artists and craftsmen whose work also glorifies God, unless we had first worked hard and used our talents to create the necessary wealth?"[13] Where however, does that leave the Church's position, and that of the politician and the economist, with regard to usury today?

---

[13]Margaret Thatcher's speech to the General Assembly of the Church of Scotland on May 21st, 1988, quoted in full in *Christianity and Conservatism*, ed.Michael Alison and David Edwards, (Hodder and Stoughton, London, 1990), pp.333-338.

In a paper entitled: "*Interest in Interest: The Old Testament Ban on Interest and its Implications for Today*,"[14] Paul Mills, an economist working at the Treasury, and writing from a Christian perspective, states that Christians have accepted the dualistic world view that separates ethics from economics, rather than challenging economic structures from a biblical viewpoint. He believes that the institution of interest is morally wrong and destructive of the economic paradigm that the Bible sets out. He proposes a reform of the Western capitalist economic system particularly with regard to the features of an interest-free banking system, in the hope that this line of argument will be convincing enough to ensure that the prohibition of interest is not dismissed as naive wishful thinking but comes to be regarded as an essential ingredient of a God-centred economy. He cites the experience of Medieval society and of contemporary Islamic profit-share banks as giving tentative support to this conclusion. Therefore, as this interest-free system is indeed comparable with the concept of Islamic banking, which I addressed in my third chapter, its economic proposals will be discussed here.

The key features of a practical replacement of the Western financial system upon non-interest lines are the elimination of all returns on monetary loans; the legitimacy of hire and rental charges; and the financing of commercial investment through profit-share arrangements. These three aspects have been common to rabbinical, medieval Christian and Islamic schools of thought at varying times in their history, and at present the only serious work in this area, as I have suggested, is being conducted by Muslims convinced of the need to strictly obey Qur'anic teaching and the Shari'ah.

---

[14]Paul Mills, "Interest in Interest: The Old Testament Ban on Interest and its Applications for Today," (Jubilee Centre Publications Ltd.), 1993.

In passing, it is interesting to note that some writers have come to the speculative conclusion that the interest prohibition was positively *beneficial* for medieval commerce, since it had the effect of diverting loans away from consumption and into productive enterprise. The most compelling evidence comes from F.C.Lane, who estimated that by the early thirteenth century, ninety-one percent of Genoese commercial investment contracts were of the partnership form. The interest ban was particularly effective in this respect in Venice since there was no land to invest in or to act as security for consumption loans. He concludes that:

> "The doctrine created pressure on men possessed of liquid wealth to find some way in which to make their wealth yield income. It thus encouraged the flow of capital into commerce. It is logical to conclude, then, that the usury doctrine, insofar as it was effective, stimulated economic growth."[15]

The Church can be praised, therefore, in its attempt to promote a credit system that recognised the need for flexibility of return. This principle is taken to its logical conclusion in the Islamic model of an interest-free system. What then are the properties of a modern interest-free system, which the Christian Church could promote and sanction in the twenty-first century? According to Mills, these are: an interest-free bank; parallel forms of finance; efficiency in the allocation of funds; the reaction of savers; the reaction of borrowers; the stability of a non-interest banking system; and cycles and inflation. Because of the importance of promoting an interest-free financial economic system in the light of the theological teaching which I have considered above with regard to the prohibition of usury; and because Timur Koran paints a rather pessimistic view of the potential success of Islamic banking in

---

[15]F.C.Lane, *Venice and History: The Collected Papers of F.C.Lane,* (John Hopkins Press, Baltimore), 1966, p.68.

this respect, these will each be addressed in a little more detail. I hereby acknowledge a specific debt to Dr.Paul Mills and his work, and to Dr.Michael Schluter who drew my attention to it. As so little, to the best of my knowledge, has been written from a positive Christian perspective on the possible inauguration, and the potential benefits of adopting an interest-free banking system, I closely follow his economic expertise. As far as an interest-free bank is concerned, Mills maintains that:

> "if a moral stance is taken against interest, a bank can neither lend or
> borrow with returns unrelated to the profitability of the use to which
> such funds are put or which do not constitute a hire charge for the use
> of property."[16]

The working principle of such a bank, therefore, is that of partnership; and as I discussed above with reference to *mudaraba* and *musharaka* in Islamic terms, that means that when money capital is provided for commercial investment, any profit or loss is shared on a pre-specified proportionate basis. The bank may also, in addition, engage in commodity and share-trading, finance real estate purchases or engage in leasing property or equipment. When a depositor designates his deposit for investment purposes it is added to the bank's overall portfolio and allocated a share of any profit or loss that the bank makes on its investments. In essence the investment side of the bank's business becomes equivalent to that of a unit trust with returns on deposits being related to profitability. Also like a unit trust the depositor could lose part of the money if the portfolio proves to be loss-making. However, like conventional banks and unit trusts, the non-interest bank can diversify its investments so as to reduce the potential for loss; equally, as I mentioned in connection with

----

[16]Mills, *op.cit.*, p.44.

Islamic banking, the bank would be very careful as far as it could be with its investments. There are then two ways in which the bank could conduct its business:

> "It could use a proportion of its demand deposits for investment purposes and so be able to provide current accounts to its customers with few charges. If this practice was widespread, the central bank would have to specify reserve requirements and provide a 'lender of last resort' facility to maintain public confidence in the transactions mechanism and to prevent any losses on the bank's portfolio from affecting its ability to honour its current account liabilities. Alternatively, the bank could simply hold transactions deposits in cash and highly liquid assets or use a proportion to provide interest-free short-term overdrafts to its profit-share borrowers. This option most closely resembles proposals for a 100% reserve banking system which would dispense with the need for state deposit insurance and remove the bank's ability to create money.[17]

The bank can also be responsible for supplying parallel forms of finance. Interest prohibition is designed to eliminate certain types of loan, the most obvious being that of consumer credit at interest. The permissability of hire purchase contracts means that consumption could be achieved without the prior need for saving, and although the purchase of a consumer durable may cost just as much with a hire purchase scheme as with a loan at interest, the hire purchase form has the advantage that the purchaser is never 'in debt' with the option of returning the goods if the payment cannot be maintained, and the hire charges are determined by the price of the goods involved rather than the overall level of interest rates in the economy. Mills further expounds on the benefits of retailers' interest-free credit offers being financed by banks in order to share in the extra profit generated by the extra custom, whilst at the same time complementing these forms of consumption finance by

---

[17]Mills, *ibid.*, p.45.

interest-free loans provided for poverty relief and financed by a proportion of bank current accounts, or even local taxation, in the hope that these more convoluted forms of financing consumption before saving would lessen the current preoccupation with borrowing as much as one's income can serve.

Similarly, the prohibition of interest eliminates the possibility of mortgage finance for house purchase. The devising of alternatives, however, is quite simple in terms of the existence of rent. Mills outlines the policy, thus:

> "Either the bank can buy the property in question and let it out to tenants who pay in excess of the market rent whenever they wish or on a contractual basis and gradually accumulate an ownership share in the property or finance intermediaries to do this on a profit-share basis. The advantages of such a scheme over those of mortgage-finance are that the buyer is not necessarily committed to buy the whole property but could just purchase a portion, the buyer is not forced to accumulate ownership if his or her circumstances worsen and the price paid for houses would be primarily determined by the conditions in the housing market rather than the influential money markets influencing rates."[18]

I would agree that given the problems that mortgage finance has caused in the British housing market, especially in terms of negative equity, such an alternative has attractions.

In discussing the efficiency in the allocation of funds it is interesting that Mills quotes from Siddiqi's work on issues in Islamic banking,[19] where Siddiqi discussses profit-sharing between the entrepreneurs and the suppliers of capital. The function of equating the supply and demand of loanable funds that the interest-based

---

[18]Mills, *ibid.*, p.45.

[19]See Mills; and N.M.Siddiqi, *Issues in Islamic Banking,* (The Islamic Foundation, Leicester), 1983, pp.101-110.

system claims it performs is emulated in the interest-free system by the banks altering the profit-shares that they charge from borrowers and offer to depositors. Hence, the allocative properties of a profit-share system need not be derided and could possibly prove more beneficial than those of its interest-based counterpart.

Perhaps the most important element in all this is both the reaction of not only the borrowers but also the savers. If people only save in order to receive interest this would lead to a large reduction in saving. But, people also save for the psychological desires for security and wealth, or to finance consumption in the future. The problem with a profit-share arrangement is that returns on savings are not eliminated but they might be more uncertain depending on the profitability of the underlying investment. The more crucial point is the risk averse factor. The realised real return on profit-share deposits, however, need not necessarily be more uncertain. The pooling of bank investments, a diversified bank portfolio, and the use of reserves should ensure that investment deposits only suffer in a severe cyclical downturn. Equally, if a profit-share system relates the return on savings to the inflation rate then as profits rise in inflationary conditions, this will pass on to the savers through the profit-share mechanism.

The major benefit of the non-interest system for the borrower is that it shares the risk of profit-failure between the bank and the commercial borrower, and a risk averse borrower will tend to prefer the bank to undertake some of these risks. When profits are unexpectedly low, the borrower is not saddled with fixed interest payments, and when profits are unexpectedly high, they are shared with the bank. This seems a far more sensible way of allocating risk than the interest system whereby the borrower carries the risk of profits not matching up to interest payments and the risk of variable interest rates rising unexpectedly. Here the potential for bankruptcy is high, particularly for small businesses and farmers dependent on a single market or product. There are two disincentives, however, in lending to small businesses or farmers. There is the potential that the borrower might not maximise profits or put in as much effort as the bank will be taking a share; and a profit-share bank would have to incur large information-gathering costs in assessing the viability of ventures and verifying declared profits. Long-term relationships between the bank and the borrower would help to build up trust and knowledge of the operations in progress, as is done in the Japanese financial system; or, the bank could gain inside information by being represented on the boards of companies in which it has a profit-share stake, as happens with German banks.[20]

These problems are not insuperable, and they could even work to the borrower's advantage since profit-share banks would have an incentive to use their business experts to vet projects and to provide advice and financial assistance if the borrower runs into trouble or needs help to develop a business. Therefore, the risk-sharing benefits of a non-interest system may be weighed against the possible disincentives effects and the extra costs of conducting bank business on a 'relationship' basis, which I also discussed with regard to Islamic banking. In his thesis, Mills also maintains that there would be more stability with an interest-free banking system because the flexibility of the value of savings deposits ensures that the bank's solvency is not threatened by a loss-making portfolio since the shortfall is passed on to the depositors; and, also, with regard to cycles and inflation, although difficult to assess, the potential for an interest-free system to prove inflationary would appear less than its interest based counterpart. The higher reserve requirements for transactions deposits should ensure less scope for banks to create money, or even eliminate this prerogative altogether.

---

[20]Mills, *op.cit.*, p.47.

This analysis of an interest-free system is not, however, wholly hypothetical. Both Iran and Pakistan have theoretically abolished interest since the early 1980's. Whilst some interest-bearing contracts have been replaced by those carrying arrangement fees and transaction charges, and conventional government debt persists, progress has been made in moving toward a profit-share banking system – particularly on the deposit side of the business. Where interest-free banks have been established they have been warmly welcomed by Muslim depositors and have performed as well, if not better, than their interest-based competitors. There certainly are disadvantages with regard to greater information-gathering costs and weakening entrepeneurial incentives, and some forms of finance would disappear altogether. However, the rewards for such an upheaval would be found in a more allocatively efficient and robust financial structure which diversifies risk to a greater extent and does not amplify movements in the levels of production activity or prices. Therefore, although the prohibition of interest may strike everyone as a revolutionary notion it need not be impractical.

Having evolved from a model which represented at first the Church's ban on usurious lending to one where interest as a form of compensation for loss was permitted, and the concept of justice, as implied in Luke 6, became an integral part of working out arrangements to help finance the poor, the model of 'Christian economic man' with regard to its religious teaching on usury might, in the future, revert to a model more akin to the Islamic paradigm where *'riba'* transactions were specifically forbidden in the Qur'an, and this proscription was upheld in *hadith* teaching. It might also be time for the Christian church to reconsider the universalistic and ethical attitude toward lending expressed in Luke 6, as well as remembering its Judaic heritage and roots in reconsidering the 'Jubilee' teaching that I discussed in Chapter One. Organisations such as 'Jubilee 2000' have highlighted the interest/usury issue once more, specifically with regard to Third World debt. It is good to see that the Christian church is not burying its head in the sand. Recently a group of thirty of the world's leading religious figures representative of the Baha'i, Buddhist, Christian, Hindu, Jain, Jewish, Muslim, Sikh and Taoist faiths met with the free-market economists of the World Bank. This meeting was hosted jointly by George Carey, the Archbishop of Canterbury, and James Wolfensohn, the President of the World Bank, to discuss the relationship between religion and development.

Cynics might argue that religion is just being used to add a certain amount of respectability to unpopular agenda but it is interesting to note, as Paul Vallely commented, that Wolfensohn 'confessed' that in the past the Bank's Structural Adjustment Programmes had not always been sufficiently conscious of the need to protect the Third World's poorest people; and grandiose schemes for dams and power stations further enriched the wealthy caste in poor countries, or increased trade or GDP, but did nothing to help the really poor. The plan is now to set up a number of joint Bank-Faith action groups alongside practical projects which will necessarily have monetary considerations at their core and which will protect the interests of the poor. It is a visionary yet practical assignment, long overdue, and one which should reinstate the role of the mainstream Christian church with regard to its stance on the whole issue of 'usury' in terms of its commitment to the poor. In this sense a concept that was so hotly debated by the church in the sixteenth and seventeenth centuries once again rears its head.

The model of 'Islamic economic man,' therefore, can equally be defined and determined with regard to its religious teaching on the concept of '*riba*'/usury, as taught in the Qur'an and the *Sunnah* and as discussed above within the context of the *ummah*, and the communal responsibility of mutual aid collected and distributed as *zakat*. Both are expressed in the idea of *tawhid*, the unicity of God, with its corollary that persons should not be compartmentalised in their actions. Interest-free loans were enjoined here also, and although, as with the Judaic and Christian traditions, *hiyal* (legal fictions) were invented to get around the prohibition, the teaching with regard to the proscription of usurious lending is at the heart of the 'new' Islamic economic man today, in terms of inaugurating a specific Islamic banking sytem with this as its underlying ethic. There are, however, reservations expressed by some as to the viability of an economic system based on this. As I suggested at the end of Chapter Three one such voice of scepticism belongs to Timur Kuran. In view of summing up this particular section in terms of defining a specific Islamic economic man, I will repeat the argument from Chapter Three especially as Paul Mills has provided counter claims.

Kuran does concede that profit-sharing constitutes a useful scheme, indeed, in many markets it is a preferred option for allocating returns even when interest is a legally viable option. However, his criticism is that it hardly follows that profit-sharing should be the basis for all productive ventures. Kuran's reservations concern the redistribution not just of returns but also of risks as some segments of society are better able to bear this than others. He cites the case of a handicapped octogenarian who relies on her savings for a living, or at least on the interest payable on the capital sum saved. But there are alternate schemes which could be built into the system for the elderly and more risk averse, for instance, the compulsory savings scheme toward a pension which is being implemented in Australia; or the improvement of state pensions for the elderly and greater benefits distributed to the handicapped. In this case the element of risk may be overcome, although in an inflationary economy some form of indexation would be necessary. These methods do not have to rely on an interest-based economy.

His second objection lies in the opportunism that informational asymmetry might afford to the more unscrupulous – the borrowing enterprise knows its revenue and cost structure whereas the lender can only estimate, in which case the borrower could understate profit and overstate costs, or, deliberately let costs soar in order to grant high benefits to employees, and as I have suggested, effective monitoring by a bank can be costly. Kuran also points out that employees should share in the risk by banning fixed wages otherwise all the risks are borne by the shareholders. But this, in fact, may be an excellent idea. If this is what a stake-holder economy is all about, it would encourage the work force to work to the best of its ability, foster a sense of community within the work-force, enhance shop-floor and management relations, and even provide some form of security. In more productive times the 'feel good factor' can be distributed among the work-force as a bonus, and, in any event, is not some wage better than redundancy and no wage at all? Even though Kuran quotes Syed Aftab Ali of the Bureau of Statistics in Ottawa who detects the inconsistency in allowing fixed wages, but not interest and, therefore, advocates wages for employees tied to the profitability of their firms, Kuran summarily dismisses it because he maintains that some people prefer fixed wages anyway, and a ban on fixed wages would be unenforceable. To address this anomaly, however, a guaranteed minimal wage could be implemented which also had the possibility of producing profit bonuses. As to the bank's monitoring costs, Mills outlined proposals above with regard to a more 'relational' method of co-operation between the two parties which might alleviate the costs involved. Kuran also points out that with regard to interest-free consumption loans in all societies it is reasonable to expect them to be made within a small community of family and friends, as with the Judaic model, or within the confines of *ummah*, but interest-free loans to strangers constitute another matter. But if it is built into a new economic system the relationship changes from that which exists between family or friend, to that between consumer and institution, which does not mean to say that the relational aspect has to change too. In any event, in terms of a non-interest loan formulated as rental, as outlined above by Mills, this also becomes viable within an interest-free economy. Mills also has responses to Kuran's final objection, the possibility of excess demand for interest-free loans (see above).

With regard to Islamic banking Kuran does maintain that impartial investigators have verified that the Islamic banks have been successful from the standpoint of both owners and clients. However, his scepticism returns when he cautions that both the dividends of the Islamic banks and the interest rates offered by traditional banks are controlled by monetary authorities who may well be under special orders to enhance the attractiveness of the Islamic banks, and he maintains, that since *mudarabah* accounts are riskier few people would be attracted to them unless they provided higher yields, and one cannot conclude that everyone would be better off using this method, in particular the risk averse. Kuran maintains that the people holding *mudarabah* accounts would in fact in a more developed economy be holding stocks. In countries where Islamic banks are in operation the stock market performs inadequately, and therefore for the saver/investor the *mudarabah* accounts serve the same function as stocks, although one could conclude that the establishment of Islamic banks in these countries has stimulated savings by introducing a new financial service. Also, according to Kuran, none of the Islamic banks had ever provided an interest-free consumption loan, and one bank had invested almost exclusively in short-term commercial deals, which suggested that Islamic banks were operating as personal-profit maximisers, not as social-welfare maximisers intent on upholding Islamic principles of justice.[21]

In his paper, Kuran, in trying to define and critique the concept of an Islamic economic system ties together the prohibition of *riba, zakat* and behavioural norms. Although I have considered *zakat* because of its important dimension as one of the five pillars of Islam, I am only concerned in trying to define 'Islamic economic man' in terms of the whole concept of usury – *riba*, and the possible implementation of an Islamic economy in terms of Islamic banking based on it. There have obviously been ways in which this prohibition has been, and still is, legitimised by *hiyal*, and it is impossible to derive an entire blue-print for an Islamic economy from the Qur'an or *Sunnah*. But the moral principles expounded in the Qur'an, and the normative ideals worked out in the *Sunnah* are still ones which can undergird a specific Islamic economic framework, without compromising the teachings of the Prophet Muhammad, or trying to return to an economic situation based on seventh century Arabian ideals, "a golden age" which did not even exist at the time of Muhammad as institutions were abandoned or modified as circumstances warranted.

In the light of the above discussion, therefore, in terms of an interest-free banking system, there are in existence Judaic, Christian and Islamic models which could serve to provide society with the means of alleviating the poverty engendered as a result of interest bearing loans. These could be implemented with especial regard for the poor, both at home and in low income countries, by giving them a stake in society, and providing financial institutions which may more easily redistribute wealth, or give the poor an opportunity to create it for themselves, with

---

[21]T.Kuran, "The Economic System in Contemporary Islamic Thought: Interpretation and Assessment," (*The International Journal of Middle East Studies*, Vol. XVIII, 1986), p.157.

the constant reminder of the worth and dignity of every human being in society constantly in mind. As we are reminded in *"Just Sharing"*:

> "Some ways of distributing are demeaning and destructive; sharing that is grudging, or patronizing, or demands that the recipient shows himself to be 'deserving,' humble and grateful, is fatally flawed . . . Some modes of allocation create dependency, limit freedom and destroy dignity and self-respect; others encourage a proper balance between independence and interdependence so that within the community care and respect for one another flourish."[22]

There is also, often the mistaken assumption that the poor have no savings at all when, in fact, what they often lack is access to an opportunity to be able to do something with them. At the same time this does not destroy the entrepreneurial opportunities for those with wealth, indeed, it may even foster a more compassionate sense of responsibility within a community which 'Islamic economic man' should symbolize.

In search of a new economic paradigm, therefore, in terms of interest-free or low-cost loans, I propose a synthesis of these ideas in order to establish the model of an ethical, humanist and universalistic 'seconomic man' – 'Secular economic man,' with its potential to alleviate poverty as we progress into the next millennium.

The neologism 'seconomic man' epitomizes the prototype for a new, post-modernist model of 'economic man' in the multi-faith, culturally pluralist, secular society of the late twentieth/early twenty-first century. The concept of secularization itself is not devoid of religious meaning although the term 'secular*ism*' signifies that

---

[22]*"Just Sharing,"* eds. Duncan Forrester and Danus Skene, (Epworth Press,Church and Nation Committee of the General Assembly of the Church of Scotland, 1988), p.62.

which is not religious.[23]   The English word 'secular' derives from the Latin word *saeculum*, which initially meant 'this age' or 'generation.' As Harvey Cox maintains, the history of the interpretation of this word *'saeculum'* in the West is a parable of the degree to which the biblical message has been misunderstood and misappropriated.[24] Because it is such an important concept within the context of this book, and also because it is the most insightful definition I have encountered, I have reproduced Cox's interpretation of it (See *Appendix1*). Secularization, therefore, finds its roots in biblical faith and has a wide and inclusive usage; it implies an historical process and liberating development – "an authentic outcome of the impact of biblical faith on Western history." I use the terminology 'secular,' therefore, within the context of the above definition as determined by Cox, acknowledging the word's biblical heritage, its interpretation as the passing of certain responsibilities from the ecclesiastical to political authority, and more recently, as the irreversible historical process on a cultural level which is parallel to the political one.   In determining 'secular economic man,' therefore, I bring the use of the word 'secular' into the domain of economic secularization with regard to the concept of 'usury.' By definition this denotes the disappearance of the significance of the Judaeo/Christain religious teaching on this issue in the West, but equally acknowledges its roots in the biblical faith. (Although, interestingly, an organisaton calling itself 'Jubilee 2000' is actually reviving the usurious concept and raising its profile considerably by calling on the First World to remit the debts, the interest repayments of which are crippling Third World countries. Many supporters, however, may not be aware that the foundation of this sentiment is rooted in the Judaic/Hebraic scriptures of the 'Old

---

[23]See D.Smith, "Secularism," in *The Encyclopedia of Modern Islamic Thought, op.cit.*, p.20.

[24]Harvey Cox, *The Secular City,* (The Macmillan Company, New York, 1965), p.18.

Testament.') What is significant is that, as Cox maintains, secularization arises in large measure from the formative influence of biblical faith on the world, an influence mediated first by the Christian church and later by movements deriving from it. It is in this sense of historical progression within a religious tradition, therefore, that I use the word 'secular.' In acknowledging its biblical roots, it is equally open to the influence that the religious teaching of Islam might have now, and in the future, on the reinterpretation of the usury issue in terms of interest-free banking. Rather than signifying that which is non religious, therefore, 'secular economic man' does in fact, refer very much to its roots in a religious tradition in the West, and at the same time, remains equally open to the influence of a religious tradition in the (Middle) East (although one could equally argue that all three monotheistic traditions emanated from the (Middle) East and were 'highjacked' or rather, appropriated, by the West!). It is an interesting point made by Ernest Gellner that when the world of Islam had industrialisation thrust upon it, it turned not to secularization but to a vehement affirmation of its own tradition:

> "In the world of Islam . . . though long endowed with a commercial bourgeoisie and significant urbanisation, this civilisation failed to engender industrialism; but once industrialism and its various accompaniments had been thrust upon it, and it had experienced not only the resulting disturbance but also some of its benefits, it turned, not at all to secularization, but rather to a vehement affirmation of the puritan version of its own tradition . . . On the evidence available so far, the world of Islam demonstrates that it is possible to run a modern, or at any rate modernizing, economy, reasonably permeated by the appropriate technological, educational, organisation principles, *and* combine it with a strong, pervasive, powerfully internalised Muslim conviction and identification. A puritan and scripturalist

world religion does not seem necessarily doomed to erosion by modern conditions. It may on the contrary be favoured by them."[25]

Secular society has never existed in a vacuum, and certainly not one devoid of theological influence. It may even surprise itself in the West where rather than imagining it has shaken off the hegemony of its Judaeo/Christian heritage, it is still reiforced by it, whilst at the same time informed in a new and different way by the teachings of Islam. 'Secular' economic man proves, paradoxically, to be more 'religious' than its implied terminology suggests.

The term 'Economic Man' found its first literary expression in the *homo economicus* of Adam Smith and his school, embodied in the assumption that self-interest is what really motivates human beings,[26] although as Andrew Skinner argues while Smith did devote a good deal of attention to motives which relate to self-interest narrowly defined, he also argued in his *"Theory of Moral Sentiments"* that the pursuit of gain has a social reference.[27] In his book *"The End of Economic Man"* Peter Drucker, writing in 1939, discusses the fact that the only basis for 'Economic Man,' or for any society based upon it, is the promise of the realisation of freedom and equality. This realisation was first sought in the eleventh to the thirteenth centuries in the spiritual sphere. It saw and understood man as 'Spiritual Man,' and

---

[25]Ernest Gellner, *Postmodernism, Reason and Religion,* (Routledge, London and New York, 1992), p.22.

[26]A comparison could be made with Richard Dawkins' *"The Selfish Gene"* where the world of the selfish gene is one of savage competition, ruthless exploitation, and deceit and yet there are acts of apparent altruism in nature – the bees who commit suicide when they sting to protect the hive. The selfish gene is also a subtle gene, however, and Dawkins holds out the hope that our species, alone on earth, has the power to rebel against the designs of the selfish gene. (Oxford University Press, Oxford, 1976).

[27]Andrew Skinner, "Adam Smith and Self Love," in *Finance and Ethics Quarterly,* (No. 2, Christmas, 1993). I am very grateful to Professor Alan Main for passing this article to me.

his place in the world and in society as a place in the spiritual sphere. When this order collapsed, freedom and equality became projected into the intellectual sphere. Drucker traces an evolutionary process whereby the Lutheran creed, "which made man decide his fate by the use of his free and equal intellect in interpreting the Scriptures" was the supreme metamorphosis of the order of 'Intellectual Man.' After its breakdown freedom and equality became projected into the social sphere. Man became first 'Political' and then 'Economic Man.' Freedom and equality became social and economic freedom and social and economic equality, and man's nature became a function of his place within this order. Writing prophetically in the darkness of totalitarian fascism in Europe into which the collapse of 'Economic Man' had manoeuvred her, Drucker finally asks whether it will ever be possible to find a positive 'Free and Equal Man'?[28] Freedom cannot be exercised except by people who are equal. The freedom of the strong at the expense of the weak is not truly freedom. Freedom in terms of equality is the freeedom from want and oppression, and the opportunity to participate fully in society. But one has to tread with care. As Gorringe points out, "the socialist dream of the early Marxists became the nightmare of Stalinism. The attempt to create a more 'equal' society led to Lubyanka and the camps and Tiananmen Square ... Can we recognise that the only genuine 'economic man' is a *social* creature?"[29] Instead of self-interest, it will be rights, obligations and needs, as we specifically saw in the Judaic model, that are at the heart of a new economics, and the major concern will be to enable people to meet their needs and develop themselves. However, there is nothing intrinsically wrong with enterprise,

---

[28]Peter Drucker, *The End of Economic Man: A Study of the New Totalitarianism*, (William Heinemann Ltd., London, 1939), pp.23-55; 251.

[29]Timothy J.Gorringe, *Capital and the Kingdom: Theological Ethics and the Economic Order*, (Orbis, New York/SPCK, London, 1994), p.165.

initiative and ownership. "What is wrong is when these are harnessed to profit, power, self-aggrandisement, and inequality. There is scope for both initiative and co-operation in many areas – in production and consumption, housing, land, savings and finance."[30]   Far from being a socialist daydream, co-operation is now seen as essential for survival:

> "Fundamental to the new economics will be that *decentralisation* which makes democracy in production possible. The local economy . . . will be the central focus of interest, rather than the national or multinational economy. Local economies may even be able to use local currencies, related to national ones. Central planning for things like transport, energy and heavy industry will remain a necessity. Given that fact, the task in an alternatively structured society is to see that bureaucracy does not get in the way of responsibility and accountability, and that, if private ownership of the means of production is abolished, industries owned by the community are answerable to both workers and consumers. Planning is inescapable, and is essential to the survival of the planet."[31]

In terms of planning different economic structures for the future, therefore, what can we extrapolate from the Judaeo, Christian, and Islamic teachings on usury that could be of relevance in an attempt to create a more just economic system? To allow any structure to function, however, the economy must be surrounded with the appropriate framework of institutions, and I see no reason why both competitive and co-operative markets should not operate side by side in some form of mutually advantageous, symbiotic exchange.[32] In any event they are not mutually exclusive

---

[30]*Ibid.*, p.166.

[31]*Ibid.*, p.166.

[32]See also 'Co-opetiton' – a revolutionary mind-set that combines competition and co-operation. The Game Theory strategy that's changing the game of business (Adam M. Brandenburger and Barry J. Nalebuff – Currency Doubleday, N. Y., 1996).

concepts, as H.B.Acton realistically points out: "Welfare planners wish to force everyone to integrate, but in such a community of forced friends there would still be competition, both to obtain a maximum of the services provided and to obtain special benefits."[33] The main criterion is that the basic structure for a social and economic system as a whole must be just. I have argued throughout this book that religious teachings have made comment on the financial obligations pertaining to both individuals and institutions in the past, and they should continue to do so within whatever social, religious, political or economic system they function. The problem that Islam faces is that there are no concepts of 'mosque' and 'state' as specifically religious and political institutions. Religion and state are believed to be fused together, the state is conceived of as the embodiment of religion, and religion as the essence of the state.[34] In an Islamic state, therefore, 'Islamic economic man' operates as a function of both religious and state institution within the community or *ummah*, and embodied in every aspect of an individual's private and public life within the concept of *tawhid*.

In terms of 'Secular economic man' and concerning the usury issue, there are ways in which interest-free, or low-cost, finance could be implemented for the poor and needy. These could result in a more economically just re-ordering of society. I shall consider five options which all high-light the concept of banking. These are the Islamic *riba*-free banking institutions; the co-operative movement; credit unions; local exchange trading schemes; and the question of Third World debt.

---

[33]H.B.Acton, *The Morals of Markets,* (Longman Group Ltd., London, 1971), p.100.

[34]Rodney Wilson, *Islamic Financial Markets,* (Routledge, London, 1990), p.34.

In this century one of the official ecclesiastical pronouncements relating to the usury theory occurred in the remarks of Pope Pius XII to the employees and directors of the Bank of Rome in 1950. The Pope took the opportunity to define his view on the unhealthy and oppressive opinion which held that the banking system was by nature stained with guilt, that the banking profession inevitably exposed one to the danger of losing eternal salvation, and that bankers ran a great risk of becoming too attached to material riches.[35] The Pope vigorously repudiated this opinion. He acknowledged that banking can be, and has been, abused, but he found no inherent iniquity in the *system*. A banking system has power, utility, and responsibility and is essentially honest, and bankers earn their livelihood honestly. The suggestion the Pope was refuting being that there exists an impersonal system going on like clockwork with no kind of moral conduct in it, such as le Mercier de la Riviers's world that 'goes on its own,'[36] and a world quite distinct from the economic world, in which moral conduct does occur. However, moral conduct does take place in the market place and does not need to be imported into it, for people can be just or unjust, honest or dishonest, and these are moral characteristics.[37] How one tries to explain moral obligation is another matter and not necessary for the nature of this book,[38] other than assuming that in theological terms the teachings with regard

---

[35]J.Noonan, *op.cit.*, p.392.

[36]le Mercier de la Rivier, *"L'Ordre Naturel et Essentiel des Societes Politiques,"* (London, 1767), Vol. 2, p.444, cited in Acton, *op.cit.*, p.17.

[37]Acton, *Ibid.*, p.19.

[38]See C.Stephen Evans, *Philosophy of Religion,* (InterVarsity Press, Leicester,1982), p.72. Naturalistic humanism tries to show that moral obligations can exist even if there is no God. This can be done in two ways: 1) one can claim that the existence of moral obligations is simply an ultimate fact which needs no explanation; or, 2) one can try to give an alternative explanation for the existence of moral obligations. Three common views are held – moral obligations are grounded in self interest; or grounded in natural instinct; or explained as a result of evolution.

to the concept of usury in the three monotheistic traditions of Judaism, Christianity, and Islam, have provided a moral framework within which to orientate oneself ethically.

This I have shown with regard to the moral framework in which Islamic Banking can operate in accordance with its Qur'anic and *hadith* instruction, not only in countries with a predominent Muslim population, but also where they are a minority. It is also a model which could be adopted in secular society as Rodney Wilson points out:

> "Although the Islamic banking movement has been tremendously successful, it is important not to be complacent and merely review the encouraging progress of the 1970's and 1980's. There has already been much imaginative thinking in the field of Islamic finance, and some of the ideas have given non-Muslim observers considerable food for thought. Indeed, many of the economic problems of the Western world may stem from an excessive reliance on *riba* finance, and the narrow and unhealthy obsessions which that seem to bring."[39]

Firstly, therefore, I suggest this model as a paradigm for establishing a more just, profit-sharing economic system, where in principle, a sense of community and responsibility is engendered and facilities are established to help the poorer members within society. Although the presence of Islamic commercial banks in the Third World is relatively recent, and their impact minimal as yet, the Jeddah based Islamic Development Bank (IDB) has a much longer and more significant development. Here again, to refresh the memory, I reiterate its potential as I discussed at the end of Chapter Three in comparison with venture capitalism. Despite its name the IDB is primarily an aid agency rather than a bank, as its aim is to provide concessionary

---

[39]Rodney Wilson, *Islamic Financial Markets*, (Routledge, London, 1990), p.17.

finance to low income and middle income Islamic countries. It charges no interest, whereas with other aid agencies the concessionary element in their lending represents the difference between their low fixed interest rates and fluctuating, but generally higher, commercial bank rates for borrowing. "It makes loans subject only to a small charge to cover administrative overheads, or invests directly in the equity of the project it backs, or purchases the item required and leases it to the user. In none of these cases is the bank's objective to make a profit, rather it only aims to break even and recoup its advances eventually, so that other projects can in turn be aided."[40] It is by far the largest Islamic financial institution, the most sophisticated and well run. It co-finances development projects and collaborates with multilateral aid agencies such as the World Bank. Although it never charges interest itself, it is prepared to assist projects in which other agencies are providing loans on an interest basis. It is also in a position to give technical assistance with the design and implementation of projects. The substitution of equity for debt finance is advocated by many development agencies and participatory finance is especially suited to small business.[41] This level of service indicates just how far Islamic finance has evolved. As Wilson remarks, those who regard it as some quaint inheritance from the past

---

[40]Rodney Wilson, *Islamic Business: Theory and Practice,* (The Economic Intelligence Unit, Special Report No. 178, London, 1985), p.46.

[41]As Poonawalla points out in relation to the development agency AKFED (the Aga Khan Fund for Economic Development) the difference between AKFED and other institutions (e.g. the International Finance Corporation, the Commonwealth Development Corporation, and the German Development Corporation) is that AKFED is more equity oriented. The portfolio of other agencies would show 10-20% by way of equity and the remaining portion would be by way of loans. Whereas AKFED will be just the reverse, with more than 90% by way of equity and the rest by way of loans. "Equity is there for long term . . . because the money is part of your own equity you want to ensure the success of the project you are investing in, and that means more commitment on our part." Quoted from the transcript of an interview between Poonawalla and Malise Ruthven. I am very grateful to Dr. Ruthven for providing me with this information.

should think again, as it has certainly entered the modern banking world despite the problems that remain to be tackled.[42]

Secondly, I consider again the work of the co-operative movement and co-operative banking as it has developed since its inception by the 'Christian Socialists.' The Christian Socialists – Maurice, Ludlow, Neale, Kingsley and Hughes had devoted themselves to the formation of workmen's societies of producers, and their main interest was in providing an intermediate agency between these and the retail stores. In 1864 agitation for a Wholesale Society culminated in the creation of the North of England Co-operative Wholesale Agency and Depot Society Ltd. In 1872 its name was changed to the Co-operative Wholesale Society. The Christian Socialists saw the need for a co-operative link between production and distribution but they were opposed to the Wholesale becoming a manufacturer; that they believed to be the function of special societies of producers. Their view was not accepted by the retail societies which financed and controlled the Wholesale, and in 1871 the rules of the Wholesale were amended to permit manufacturing:

> "Whatever its ultimate ideal it was now to strengthen its position within the existing economic system. The alternative it offered its members was not a community physically set apart from and dedicated to the communal way of life, but the spread of the co-operative system horizontally and vertically throughout Britain. Beginning with the making of biscuits and preserves the CWS passed on to boots and shoes, furniture and textiles, flour-milling and farming, banking and insurance, and a multitude of activities including the establishment of depots in Ireland and elsewhere overseas."[43]

---

[42]*Ibid.*, p.47.

[43]J.Bailey, *The British Co-operative Movement,* (Hutchinson and Co. Ltd., London, 1955), p.48.

While the consumer arm of the Co-operative Movement has proved the most popular and efficient, it is run a close second by credit institutions. Two particular types of co-operative credit institutions should be distinguished: those owned and run by working class institutions such as trade unions or consumer co-operatives; and those whose members are individual workers linked by some common interest for example, employees of a large company, students, farmers, or members of a local community or religious group. The Bank für Gemeinwirtschaft in Germany is an example of the former type – founded after World War II by the trade union movement in partnership with consumer co-operatives; in the United Kingdom the Co-operative Bank Ltd. is a wholly owned subsidiary of the Co-operative Wholesale Society. The Paris Caisse Nationale de Credit Agricole, on the other hand, Europe's largest bank, is an administrative umbrella for three thousand or so agricultural credit institutions whose members are individual farmers. The advantages of such an institution to a common interest group should be underlined as the deposits of some members generate credit available to others. "Since it is a common interest grouping, the bank will have a special undersatnding of its members' needs and problems; a member is assured that his request for financing will receive particularly sympathetic attention, and in some circumstances the bank may be able to extend credit at favourable interest rates."[44]

I have already examined the foundation of the modern co-operatives in the early nineteenth century when society was being radically transformed by new methods of production and where in the new industrial world large factories and

---

[44]See *Worker-Owners: The Mondragon Achievement: The Caja Laboral Popular and the Mondragon Co-operatives in the Basque province of Spain*, (A Report financed by the Anglo-German Foundation, and prepared by Alastair Campbell, Charles Keen, Geraldine Norman, and Robert Oakeshott, 1977), p.17.

shopkeepers were more often impersonal, and the employers regarded labour as a commodity. The answer by the pioneers of this movement was to organise co-operatives to tackle the problems of the day and they were particularly concerned with the provision of services to members based upon fair prices, honest dealings and safe and unadulterated goods. They were also based on the 'co-operative principles' of voluntary and open membership, democratically based control, the equitable use of any profit, and payment of limited interest on capital. Co-operation is often discussed as if the benefits of ownership must be largely financial and there has been much debate over the incentive effects of different kinds of reward for capital, but the history of the worker-co-operative suggests that the first priority has always been jobs – jobs worth doing, in decent conditions, for decent wages.

Throughout the century new forms of co-operation were developed to meet new needs in society. In the beginning consumer co-operative societies sprang up all over the world, but membership of a worker co-operative was much more demanding. It asked their members to take the not inconsiderable risk of investing their labour and their savings in the same enterprise and to subordinate their personal ambitions to the collective greater good. One of the best known examples within the co-operative movement was that set up in Spain, and much admired by Jo Grimond in his book 'The Common Welfare,' who thought every Liberal should study the experiment. It was established at Mondragon in 1941 by Don Jose Maria Arizmendiarrieta, a Catholic priest inspired by his brand of Basque social Christianity. Today the Mondragon co-operatives operate not only a wide range of manufacturing industries, but also consumer, housing and agricultural co-operatives, as well as having their own bank, schools, a technical college, health care services, pensions and unemployment benefit schemes. Factors contributing to the group's success have been itemised as: "quality of leadership and management; emphasis on technical competence and training; the commitment which comes from the members' capital stakes; the mutual support which the group provides through Lagun Aro (the social security organisation) and in other ways; and the Caja Laboral Popular – the Group's bank."[45] Indeed the base of the operation was the group's own saving bank.

The Caja Laboral was set up in 1959 to provide financial services for its associated co-operatives and their members. It collected savings from co-operative workers and re-invested them in the associated co-operatives. In the earliest days it had built-in advantages of roots in a close-knit community. As a savings bank, even though it paid the best rate of interest, it was able to borrow cheaply. Under Spanish law the depositors in a credit co-operative cannot at the same time be shareholders, but the Caja Laboral effectively treats them as such by holding depositors' general meetings. Since there are no private or institutional shareholders who might invest in the bank for income, a high proportion of the profits can be ploughed back into investment, and Caja Laboral has an admirable record of prudent investment. The Caja Laboral's first objective is to keep the co-operatives in being, and although lending to co-operatives is normally on profitable commercial terms, interest can be reduced or even waived in cases of hardship.[46]

However, in response to recession, technological change, and Spain's entry into the European Union, Caja Laboral has had to restructure, but the new structure represents the best available compromise between hard realities and the aspirations of the co-operatives' members to own and control their enterprises. It is not derived

---

[45]Hans Wiener with Robert Oakeshott, *Worker-Owners: Mondragon Revisited*, (a project of the Anglo-German Foundation for the Study of Industrial Society, 1987), p.67.

[46]*Ibid.*, p.28.

from dogma and thus imparts a salutary lesson that like everything else at Mondragon it will be regarded as an experiment and when necessary will be changed.

The variety of applications of the co-operative model on a global scale shows an amazing range of activities. For example, in Switzerland there are many agricultural co-operatives and co-operative stores trading under the name of 'Migros.' In South Africa now that majority rule has been established there is a great deal of interest in getting the black population involved in the economic life of the country. In the former Soviet bloc prior to the communist takeover many Soviet states had blossoming co-operatives which are slowly re-emerging with the break-up of the old Soviet empire and the abandonment of centrally planned economies, e.g. in Uzbekistan. And in Japan one of the most novel dynamic co-operative enterprises is the 'Han group' where a group of about ten members combine to make group purchases from co-operative shops.[47] Community co-operatives have also been established as neighbourhood development trusts engaged in providing services for which there is local demand but no public or private provision. They are also being used to regenerate entire areas of major cities with direct communal involvement. The number of community co-operatives are growing rapidly and they are heavily concentrated in rural and urban Scotland. Their success suggests that other inner city and rural areas in Great Britain could benefit from the Scottish experience.

It would be foolish to pretend, however, that co-operation offers the best solution to every economic problem, and unrealistic to believe that it will solve such problems as unemployment or urban decay, but it does represent a different pattern for the forging of new relationships between the state and society. Co-operation is neither sentimental nor Utopian, it is a practical approach to practical needs, needs

---

[47]See *The Co-operative Opportunity,* (The UK Co-operative Council, 1994).

which are frequently ignored or badly served by the alternatives of public or solely commercial provision. There is a need for a variety of forms of enterprise which work within the framework of a market economy, especially when long-term investment decisions may not always be taken in the best interest of the community, the nation, and future generations. The desirability of having alternate forms of business provides a compelling reason for co-operatives to be encouraged as a matter of public policy. They can provide protection for weaker parties; give members control and choice over the services which they require – working with others not for others; they may compensate for failures of supply which are not sufficiently profitable for commercial interests; and most importantly they offer the possibility of self-development – in knowledge, skills, confidence and responsibility. They are established to benefit and to be accountable to a defined community, and their aim is to satisfy an unmet need and to trade for profit but not to accumulate capital.[48]

The co-operatives of the twenty-first century will have to meet the needs and aspirations of a society that is espousing a different set of values to those promoted by the post-war generation of 'trickle-down' economists and entrepreneurs. The dominant factor affecting future economic activity will be environmental sustainability and the relationship that exists between our material standard of living and the planet's resources. If the First World is to share its wealth with the rest of the globe and we are all to live within the planet's renewable resources, there will have to be some adjustment to the way our business is conducted. The co-operative system, with its roots in 'Christian Socialism' offers a viable alternative to interest based financial operations with its ethos of equitable profit-sharing and payment of limited interest on capital.

---

[48]*Ibid.*

A third option is to consider the development of savings and loans co-operatives known as community credit unions. They began in Germany in the 1850's and 1860's when Herman Schultze-Delitzche – to whom I referred in Chapter Two – set up his 'peoples' banks,' whilst at the same time, and quite independently, Friedrich Raiffeisen, a local mayor, launched the idea of financial co-operatives. The idea spread quickly to Italy, then in 1900 to Canada, and in 1909 to the USA. They were also established in Africa, Australia, the Caribbean, and parts of Asia. By 1959 Ireland had two hundred. The first credit union was set up in England in Wimbledon in 1964, and in Scotland in Drumchapel in 1970.[49] By 1992 there were sixty thousand credit unions in eighty-nine countries. Credit unions are self-help organisations which were originally set up to provide loans at low rates of interest to the poor and still follow the same basic co-operative principles that only members can borrow; loans should only be made for productive or provident purposes; members own, control and administer the society; and the character of the member is the most important security for the loan. They also encourage members to *save* regularly. But their philosophy goes beyond cheap loans and regular savings. "Credit unions are principally about people; people helping each other and working together for themselves and their community." Members help, support, and are answerable to each other. Any 'profit' is returned to the members and used for their

---

[49]Quoted from the *The Community Credit Union Handbook*, p.4. I am extremely grateful to Mr. D. Simmers, President of the Grampian Regional Council Employees Credit Union Ltd. for putting me in touch with Ms. Jackie Burns and Mr. B.Mearns working for the social strategy unit; and for the time they took to explain to me their vision for the development of credit unions in the North-East of Scotland, and for providing me with very useful information including their handbook in April 1995. On March 18th, 1995 a conference was held in Aberdeen to develop North-East credit unions. There were two operating locally: the St. Machar Credit Union and the above mentioned, with others in an embryonic state of formation. One year later there are credit unions, or credit union steering groups, established in Forres, Fraserburgh, Kemnay, Mastrick, Rosemount, Peterhead, and the Royal Mail Employees Credit Union Steering Group in Aberdeen.

benefit. They do not discriminate, and they continually provide training for members. The philosophy is summed up by their motto: "Not for profit . . . not for charity . . . but for service."[50]

Credit unions require twenty-one people who share a 'common bond' based either on domicile, association (e.g. church, or trade union), or employment to set up one of these non-profit making organisations. The common bond exists to promote loyalty and a sense of belonging as well as a shared responsibility amongst members. The members rely heavily on voluntary labour to organise the credit unions which are vital organs in some places where building societies and banks have reduced their community service role. Also in some areas people have little or no other access to credit and financial services because of their small or irregular incomes. In for example, Canada, Ireland, and Australia, credit unions are mainstream financial institutions competing with other commercial organisations but in Britain they are heavily regulated. The business of credit unions is restricted by the Credit Union Act of 1979, but Angela Knight, economic secretary to the Treasury, said: "Credit unions have told the government that they have too many restrictions. They have asked for changes . . . I want to see credit unions grow and bureaucracy shrink while keeping the necessary protection for members."[51] The government proposes that the limit on a member's shareholding – or saving – will be relaxed so that in addition to the £5,000 (the limit for both saving and borrowing) there will be the alternative of 1.5% of the credit union's total shareholdings at the last balance sheet date if this produces a higher figure. There is also a proposal to increase the maximum repayment period

---

[50]*Ibid.*, p.3.

[51]Angela Knight quoted in *The Daily Telegraph – Credit Unions Set to Take Off,* (July 15th, 1995), p.B15.

for unsecured loans from two to four years and for secured loans from five to ten years. If the new rules become law the limit on membership will double to £10,000.

Much of the support for credit unions have come from development workers, mostly employed by local authorities to provide advice services or debt counselling. Building a credit union is often a slow process of creating confidence and fostering new skills but the potential is great and the results can be very rewarding. It is unfortunate if support is withdrawn and the development workers drop out – the loan sharks or, 'tally men,' move in. Indeed, Mike Cullen's recent play 'The Collection,' performed at The Traverse in Edinburgh, was set in the offices of a debt collecting firm, the business end of a loan sharking operation. Its theme follows the lives of its three employees for a few weeks and as a savage satire it shows the power of money to enslave and brutalise those in its thrall in a bleak social landscape.[52] The potential therefore, to help the more disadvantaged members of society with this banking model of low-interest loans and savings schemes is tremendous; and it remains to be seen how they might develop under greater governmental deregulation. It is certainly an indication that far from being a 'dead letter' the whole concept of usurious lending is one that is still firmly under investigation today.

Perhaps a little more controversial is a fourth option known as the 'LETS' scheme. It was created originally in the early 1980's by a Canadian, Michael Linton, and known as the 'Local Exchange Trading Schemes.' Since then LETS systems have proliferated around the world mainly in English speaking countries, such as Canada, Ireland, Britain, New Zealand, Australia and the USA. In Great Britain in 1990, hardly anyone had heard of Local Exchange Trading Schemes, now an

---

[52]Mike Cullen's 'The Collection' was performed at 'The Traverse' in Edinburgh on May 13th-21st, 1995.

estimated twenty thousand people are exchanging skills, services and goods in up to four hundred local LETS shemes.[53]

LETS are local, nonprofit 'exchange' networks in which all kinds of goods and services can be traded without the need for money. A LETS network uses an interest-free local credit or 'currency' so that direct exchanges do not have to be made. A LETS member may earn local credit by doing e.g., child care or computer work for one person, and spend it later on food, hiring equipment, plumbing or carpentry with another member of the network. LETS currencies have their own local names (and cheque books) – *Ideals* in Bristol which operates one of the largest schemes in the country; *Readies* in Reading; *Groats* in Stirling; *Trugs* in Lewis; *Bobbins* in Manchester; *Naaris* in Leicester; *Acorns* in Totnes, Devon; and *Cockles* in Exmouth – to name but a few of the three hundred and fifty local currencies operating in Great Britain alone. These trading schemes can offer new hope in areas of high unemployment and rebuild communities. LETS can help a wide cross-section of the community – individuals, small businesses, local services and voluntary groups – to save money and resources, and extend their purchasing power. Other benefits include social contact, health care, tuition and training, flexible ways of working, support for local enterprise and new businesses, and a revitalised community.

Any group or community can start a local netwotk; each LETS is independent, self-managed and non-profit making. The cost of running a local

---

[53]Statistics provided by Letslink Development Agency for 1995: 61 Woodcock Road, Warminster, BA12 9DH. I am very grateful to Nicholas Colloff, director of 'Opportunity Trust,' Oxford, for drawing my attention to this area and for providing me with very useful material. Opportunity's mission is to provide opportunities for people suffering chronic poverty to transform their lives; their strategy is to create jobs, stimulate small businesses and strengthen communities among the poor; and their method is to work through indigenous Partner Agencies that provide small business loans, training and counsel. Opportunity programmes respond to Jesus Christ's call to serve the poor.

network can be covered by local membership fees of between £5-10 per year, and the only equipment required is access to a photocopier and home computer. Account balances are updated periodically and each member is sent a statement of account showing his or her transactions for the period. However, as an article in The Sunday Times pointed out: "The Inland Revenue, worried that idealism may be leading to tax evasion, is busy monitoring the new exchange systems. It expects people to declare their acorns or face prosecution."[54] It will be interesting to monitor the future development of these local exchange trading schemes. It is a simple, but quite revolutionary 'seconomic' model for developing appropriate low-cost methods for any group to establish and maintain its own interest-free system of exchange as a popular grassroot initiative in a cashless community. At at the same time it mobilises all kinds of skills and resources to meet local needs. In terms of the usury issue, it is a place where 'seconomic man' could officiate most efficiently.

Finally, I turn once again to the issue of Third World debt which I critiqued briefly in Chapter One. As far back as 1981 the Brandt Report highlighted the need for international negotiation to deal with rising unemployment, persistent monetary instability, exorbitant interest rates, insupportable payments deficits and unprecedented debts within the Third World, and the Report called for 'additional finance flows to ensure the stability of national economies strained by precarious balance of payments and mounting debts."[55]

Ten years later when Third World countries are still struggling to meet debt repayments, Belinda Coote writes:

---

[54]Quoted from *The Sunday Times*, March 26th, 1995, Section D, p.1.

[55]*Handbook of World Development: The Guide to the Brandt Report*, Compiled by GJW Government Relations and Peter Stephenson, (Longman Group Ltd., Essex, 1981), p.vii.

"Debtor countries should not be expected to pay more to service their debts than they can afford without damaging their economic development. As a development of the Government's Trinidad Terms initiative, all creditor governments could agree to early implementation of significant debt reduction for the poorest, most indebted developing countries. Creditor governments, when requiring debtor nations to conform with structural adjustment programmes, should not insist on rigid adherence to IMF-approved schemes if the debtor nations can devise alternative programmes that prioritise social and environmental needs alongside economic growth. Similar terms for official debt reduction could be extended to other indebted Third World countries, together with more significant reduction of commercial debt, and action to ease the burden of debt service on loans from multilateral institutions."[56]

Likewise, Timothy Gorringe maintains that there are possible alternatives in order to deal with Third World debt if the political will is there, and although he does not outline any substantive measures (apart from advocating 'creative rescheduling') he does draw on Biblical exegesis to underline two fundamental considerations which demand church pressure for a different economic order. Instead of one market controlled by the rich and powerful for their own benefit he cites Paul's message that if one member of the body suffers, all suffer together (1Cor.12:24-26). Secondly, he brings us around full circle to the principle of the remission of debts. The Jubilee year, he states, is a fundamental part of our scriptures. Jesus himself specifically addressed the question of debt and advocated its remission (Mt.18:24ff.). The idea that this teaching might have import for our personal behaviour but no bearing on what society does, rests on the entirely artificial individualism that has been created

---

[56]Belinda Coote, *The Trade Trap,* (Oxfam UK and Ireland, Oxford, 1992), p.189.

in the West. The building of a new social order must begin with addressing the issues of the global economy within the household of God.[57]

Similarly the voice of Islam in a religio-ethical response to the problem of the external debt in Nigeria speaks about a 'return to God':

> "We are of the view that the current economic crisis and debt problems confronting Nigeria are not only indications of the failure of capitalism and related economic theories but they are also clear manifestations of the emerging dominance of materialism over spirituality. Because of the fact that in Islam it is difficult to separate the individual from his actions, we can conclude that the idea, process and practice of external borrowing among nations can not be condemned per se. However, where those on whom authority is rested to lead, negotiate and decide on our behalf choose to deviate from the course of God, policies associated with debts are bound to lead to disaster. There is no better solution than a 'return to God' by allowing all moral and spiritual precepts and other injunctions in the Qur'an and Hadith to guide our conduct in private and public life."[58]

There are responsibilities on both sides. Belinda Coote calls on governments in the South to reduce poverty and respond to popular demands for more democratic and accountable government by respecting human rights, tackling the massive inequalities in the distribution of wealth *within their own systems*, as well as pursuing economic reforms and meeting the basic needs of the poor for food, shelter, education, employment and health.[59] Of course this can create a Catch-22 problem because until the Third World is relieved of its crippling debt it is difficult to make

---

[57]Gorringe, *op.cit.*, p.141.

[58]Dr. M.T.Talib, "Islam and the Debt Question in Nigeria," in *The Church and the External Debt: Report on a Conference held in Jos, Nigeria,* (Institute of Church and Society, 1990), p.68. I am very grateful to Rev. Dr. Henry Awoniyi for drawing my attention to this report and loaning me a copy.

[59]Coote, *op.cit.*, p.187.

provision for its own people. Brian Griffiths writing to defend the Christian morality of capitalism goes so far as to maintain that the causes of Third World poverty are cultural differences, political factors such as corruption and incompetence in Third World governments, and the adoption of non-monetarist economic policies.[60] Whatever truth there may be in that, it does not however negate the responsibility of the developed world, nor condone the right to foster its indifference, to the problems of the Third World. As the year 2000 marks a Jubilee Year, the cancellation of Third World debt might inaugurate a new spirit of equality and freedom for 'seconomic man.'

Harold Lever and Christopher Huhne suggest three criteria for a solution to the debt problem. The first must be that "it is adequate in its scope to end the negative flows from the Third World to the industrial countries. Without some means of ensuring that the debtor countries become net recipient of funds, the deflationary impact of their outstanding debt cannot easily be remedied." For a reversal of flows the banks must have time, perhaps over a decade, to write off the present debts out of profits, without impairment of their capital and their ability to lend. Secondly any 'new money' over and above that required to neutralize present interest payments should be used to build up the productive capacity of the borrowing countries and their capacity to earn foreign exchange. In this respect the commercial banks in the developing countries should remain the main point of distribution and allocation. Thirdly, related to the second criterion is that regulation must govern commercial banking flows with targets conditional on the pursuit of sensible domestic economic policies. They conclude that:

---

[60]Brian Griffiths, *Morality and the Market Place,* (Hodder and Stoughton, London, 1982), p.135/6.

"there are many different ways of resolving this problem. The details of a new reform are less important than the mustering of political will in the advanced countries to change a perilous and unsustainable situation. The political pressures which the debtors currently face, having lost what may amount to a decade of development as a result of the mismanagement of the reaction to the shocks of the 1970's, should not be underestimated. The volcano of the debt crisis is dormant but far from extinct. The authorities of the advanced countries have little time in which to ensure that it does not once again heave and erupt. At stake are not merely the well being of the populations of the debtor countries but the living standards of each and every nation that is reliant for its prosperity on the health of the world's trading and financial system."[61]

The model for the future, therefore, of 'Seconomic Man' – secular economic man, will not be as devoid of religious motivation as one might imagine. Although 'secularization' has been used as a descriptive, value-neutral category to describe cultural developments, nothing could be further from the truth. However one may reject the faith of the culture into which one has been born, the undergirding principles and ethics of that faith still impinge on the culture of the people, so that, as I have remarked, even though Christianity may have lost its hegemony over Western civilisation, its underlying belief system is still the moral structure which undergirds society, and even though that may have been rejected by the majority of the people they never the less still pay implicit lip service to it. Therefore, in suggesting a model of 'seconomic man' in terms of an interest-free economic system, it is a model which could serve as a middle-axiom. In Islam it will exhibit both intrinsically and extrinsically the teaching of the Qur'an; in Judaism it will represent the teaching in the Hebrew Bible of the love of brother for brother, specifically

---

[61]Harold Lever and Christopher Huhne, *Debt and Danger: The World Financial Crisis*, (Penguin Books, Middlesex, 1985), pp.133-144.

within the context of *chesed* and *tzedekah*, having let go of the Deuteronomic principle which no longer need apply; in Christianity it will, above all, represent attitude: Christ's teaching in the New Testament with regard to a universalistic love for all; and in secular society it will be representative of all three religions, incorporating teaching from all three scriptures, although unbeknown to those who no longer follow the God-given teachings of a specific 'book.' In this respect, therefore, 'seconomic man' is the sum of all the parts, and can appeal to all humankind, whatever his or her non-belief or belief system might be, in advocating an interest-free economy, or at the very least, providing low-interest financial incentives for the disadvantaged, based on the reasonings derived from the above examination of the monotheistic religious injunctions against the voluntary taking of profit on a loan – usury.

According to Akbar Ahmed what the postmodernist age offers us by its very definition is the potential, the possibility, the vision of harmony through understanding.[62] Peter Drucker writing in prophetic vein again over fifty years after *"The End of Economic Man"* states: "I consider it highly probable that within the next decade or two there will be new and startling 'economic miracles,' in which poor, backward, Third World countries transform themselves, virtually overnight, into fast-growth economic powers."[63] If the rich of the world are to see, in Levinas' term, the face of the 'other' in the poor of the world, and in them see also the face of the 'Other' – in either the sense that Christ is in all, or in the Islamic sense of Oneness and *tawhid* – and respond to that with Judaic loving kindness 'righteousness,' *chesed*, embodied in the new 'seconomic man,' then there is hope for all mankind. I have

---

[62]Akbar Ahmed, *op.cit.*, p.261.

[63]Peter Drucker, *Post-Capitalist Society,* (Butterworth-Heineman Ltd, Oxford, 1993)

followed the religious teaching on the concept of usury through three of the world's greatest religious traditions, with all its vicissitudes, applications and rejections. I have proposed ways in which the ethic involved in non-usurious lending, or at the very least low-cost finance, could help to alleviate the suffering of the poor. If we believe that the issue of usury today is still a dead letter, we all must think again.

The 1980s have been called the lost decade in the fight against poverty.[64] The year 1990 saw the publication of the first World Bank report on poverty for ten years and although consumption per capita rose by seventy per cent in some countries and life expectancy, child mortality, and educational attainment have improved in many countries, still more than one billion people in the world were living in abject poverty on incomes of less that $310 per *year*. Under present conditions more than fifteen to twenty million people die yearly from malnutrition and hunger related diseases, including twelve million children – the equivalent of a Hiroshima every two days.[65] The year 1996 was designated by the United Nations as the year of the eradication of poverty, as we move into the twenty-first century we are no nearer eradication. What does the future hold for the poorest people in the world in the twenty-first century? It is not too strong a point to make that there is genocide by debt being carried on in the Third World today:

> "Without being radical or overly bold, I will tell you that the Third World War has already started – a silent war, not for that reason any the less sinister. This war is tearing down Brazil, Latin America and practically all the Third World. Instead of soldiers dying there are children, instead of millions of wounded there are millions of unemployed; instead of destruction of bridges there is the tearing

---

[64]Gorringe, *op.cit.*, p.129.

[65]*Ibid.*, p.129.

down of factories, schools, hospitals and entire communities . . . It is
a war by the United States against the Latin American continent and
the Third World. It is a war over the foreign debt, one which has as
its main weapon INTEREST, a weapon more deadly than the atom
bomb."[66]

Actions speak louder than words. What are we going to do about it?

---

[66]A Brazilian Labour leader speaking in1985, quoted *ibid.*, p.139. (Italics mine).

Appendix 1: Secularization vs. Secularism

Because this is a very important concept for this book I am quoting Harvey
Cox's differentiation between secularization and secularism in order to root my
concept of 'seconomic man' – secular economic man in its biblical foundations.

"The English word *secular* derives from the Latin word *saeculum*,
meaning "this age". The history of this word's career in Western
thought is itself a parable of the degree to which the biblical message
has been misunderstood and misappropriated over the years.
Basically *saeculum* is one of two Latin words denoting "world" (the
other one is *mundus*). The very existence of two different Latin
words for "world" foreshadowed serious theological problems since
it betrayed a certain dualism very foreign to the Bible. The
relationship between the two words is a complex one. *Saeculum* is a
time-word, used frequently to translate the Greek word *aeon*, which
also means age or epoch. *Mundus*, on the other hand, is a space-
word, used most frequently to translate the Greek word *cosmos*,
meaning the universe or the created order. The ambiguity in the Latin
reveals a deeper theological problem. It traces back to the crucial
difference between the Greek spatial view of reality and the Hebrew
time view. For the Greeks, the world was a place, a location.
Happenings of interest could occur *within* the world, but nothing
significant ever happened *to* the world. There was no such thing as
world history. For the Hebrews, on the other hand, the world was
essentially history, a series of events beginning with Creation and
heading towards a Consummation. Thus the Greeks perceived
existence spatially; the Hebrews perceived it temporally. The tension
between the two has plagued Christian theology since its outset.

The impact of Hebrew faith on the Hellenistic world, mediated through the
early Christians, was to "temporalize" the dominant perception of reality. The word

became history. *Cosmos* became *aeon*; *mundus* became *saeculum*. But the victory was not complete. The whole history of Christian theology from the apologists of the second century onward can be understood in part as a continuing attempt to resist and dilute the radical Hebrew impulse, to absorb historical into spatial categories. There have always been counter-pressures and counter-tendencies. But only in our own time, thanks largely to the massive rediscovery of the Hebrew contribution through renewed Old Testament studies, have theologians begun to notice the basic mistake they had been making. Only recently has the task of restoring the historical and temporal tenor to theology begun in earnest. The word *secular* was an early victim of the Greek unwillingness to accept the full brunt of Hebrew historicity.

From the very beginning of its usage, secular denoted something vaguely inferior. It meant "this world" of change as opposed to the eternal "religious world." This usage already signifies an ominous departure from biblical categories. It implies that the true religious world is timeless, changeless, and thus superior to the "secular" world which was passing and transient. Thus the vocation of a "secular priest", one who served in the "world", though technically on the same level, was actually thought of as somehow less blessed than that of the "religious" priest who lived his life in the cloister, contemplating the changeless order of holy truth.

The medieval synthesis resolved the tension between Greek and Hebrew by making the spatial world the higher or religious one and the changing world of history the lower or "secular" one. The biblical assertion that under God all of life is drawn into history, that the cosmos is secularized, was temporarily lost sight of. In its first widespread usage, our word *secularization* had a very narrow and specialised meaning. It designated the process by which a "religious" priest was transferred to a parish responsibility. He was secularized. Gradually the meaning of the term was widened. When the separation of pope and emperor became a fact of life in Christendom, the division between the spiritual and the secular assumed institutional embodiment. Soon, the passing of certain responsibilities from ecclesiastical to political authorities was designated "secularization". This usage continued through the period of the Enlightenment and the French Revolution and obtains even today in countries with a Catholic cultural heritage. Consequently, for example, when a school or hospital passes from ecclesiastical to public administration, the procedure is called secularization.

More recently, secularization has been used to describe a process on the cultural level which is parallel to the political one. It denotes the disappearance of religious determination of the symbols of cultural integration. Cultural secularization is an inevitable concomitant of a political and social secularization. Sometimes the one precedes the other, depending on the historical circumstances, but a wide imbalance between social and cultural secularization will not persist very long . . . In any case, secularization as a descriptive term has a wide and inclusive significance. It appears in many different guises, depending on the religious and political history of the area concerned. But wherever it appears, it should be carefully distinguished from secular*ism*. Secularization implies a historical process, almost certainly irreversible, in which society and culture are delivered from tutelage to religious control and closed metaphysical world-views. We have argued that it is basically a liberating development. Secularism, on the other hand, is the name for an ideology, a new closed world-view, which functions very much like a new religion. While secularization finds its roots in the biblical faith itself and is to some extent an authentic outcome of the impact on biblical faith on Western history, this is not the case with secularism. Like any other 'ism', it menaces the openess and freedom secularization has produced; it must therefore be watched carefully to prevent its becoming the ideology of a new establishment. It must be especially checked where it pretends not to be a world-view but nonetheless seeks to impose its ideology through the organs of the state.

Secularization arises in large measure from the formative influence of biblical faith on the world, an influence mediated first by the Christian church and later by movements deriving partly from it."

Harvey Cox, *The Secular City: A Celebration of its Liberties and an Invitation to its Discipline*, (The Macmillan Company, New York, 1965) pp.18-21.

Bibliography

Books:

ACTON H.B. *The Morals of Markets* (Longman group Ltd., London) 1971

AHMAD Khurshid *Economic Development in an Islamic Framework* (The Islamic Foundation) 1979

AHMAD Ziauddin *Islam, Poverty and Income Distribution* (The Islamic Foundation, Leicester) 1991

AKBAR S. Ahmed *Postmodernism and Islam: Predicament and Promise* (Routledge Press, London) 1992

AL-AHSAN Abdullah *Ummah or Nation? - Identity Crisis in Contemporary Muslim Society* (The Islamic Foundation) 1992

AL-AZMEH Aziz *Islams and Modernities* (Verso, London) 1993; *Ibn Khaldun* [The American University in Cairo Press, 1993; (Routledge, London, 1982)]

ALISON Michael and EDWARDS David (eds.) *Christianity and Conservatism* (Hodder and Stoughton, London) 1990

ALT Albrecht *Essays on Old Testament History and Religion* (tr. R.A.Wilson, Blackwell, Oxford) 1966

ANWAR Muhammad *Modelling Interest-Free Economy* (The International Institute of Islamic Thought, Vancouver) 1987

APPLEYARD Bryan *The Pleasures of Peace* (Faber and Faber Ltd., London) 1989

AQUINAS Thomas *Opera omnia - Quaestiones disputate de malo. Vol. xiii* (ed. P.Mare and S.E.Frette, Paris) 1871-1880

365

ARISTOTLE *Works* (tr. B.Jowett, William Benton, Chicago) 1952

ASAD Muhammad (tr.) *The Message of the Qur'an* (DarAl-Andulus Ltd., Gibraltar) 1980

ATHERTON John *Christianity and the Market* (SPCK, London) 1992; (ed.) *Social Christianity: A Reader* (SPCK, London) 1994

BACKSTROM Philip *Christian Socialism and Co-Operation in Victorian England* (Croom Helm Ltd., London) 1974

BAILEY Jack *The British Co-operative Movement* (Hutchinson and Co. Ltd., London) 1955

BARCLAY William *The Gospel of Matthew* (The St. Andrew Press, Edinburgh) 1975

BENTHAM Jeremy "Defence of Usury" in *Economic Writings* (ed. W. Stark, G.Allen and Unwin, London) 1952

BLENKINSOPP J. *The Pentateuch* (SCM Press Ltd., London) 1992

CALVIN John *Opera, vol. x* (ed. W. Baum, E. Cunitz and E. Reuss, Brunswick, Braunschweig) 1863-1900

CANTOR Norman *The Sacred Chain: A History of the Jews* (Harper Collins, London) 1995

CHAPRA M.Umer *Towards a Just Monetary System* (The Islamic Foundation, Leicester) 1985; *Objectives of the Islamic Order* (The Islamic Foundation) 1979

CHARPENTIER E. *How to Read the Old Testament*, (tr. J.Bowden, SCM Press Ltd., London) 1988

CLEMENTS R.E. *Deuteronomy* (JSOT Press, Sheffield) 1989

COOTE Belinda *The Trade Trap* (Oxford UK and Ireland, Oxford) 1992

COULSON N.J. *A History of Islamic Law* (Edinburgh University Press) 1964

COX Harvey *The Secular City* (The Macmillan Company, New York) 1965

CRONE Patricia *Meccan Trade and the Rise of Islam* (Blackwell Oxford) 1987; *Roman, provincial and Islamic law* (Cambridge University Press) 1987

CRONE Patricia and HINDS Martin *God's Caliph* (Cambridge University Press, Cambridge) 1986

DAWKINS Richard *The Selfish Gene* (Oxford University Press, Oxford) 1989

DAWOOD N.J. *The Koran*, (Penguin Books, London) 1990

DRANE J. *Introducing the Old Testament* (Lion Publishing, Herts.) 1987

DRUCKER Peter F. *Post-Capitalist Society* (Butterworth-Heineman Ltd., Oxford) 1993; *The End of Economic Man* (William Heinemann Ltd., London) 1939

EDWARDS Norman *The Victorian Christian Socialists* (Cambridge University Press) 1967

ETZIONI Amitai *The Spirit of Community* (Harper Collins, London) 1993

EVANS Stephen *Philosophy of Religion* (Inter Varsity Press, Leicester) 1982

FIELDS F., HALLIGAN L., OWEN M. *Europe Isn't Working* (The Institute of Community Studies) 1994

FORRESTER Duncan and SKENE Danus (eds.) *Just Sharing* (Epworth Press, London) 1988

GELNER Ernest *Postmodernism, Reason and Religion* (Routledge, London and New York) 1992

GOLDBERG David J. and RAYNER J.D. *The Jewish People: Their History and Their Religion* (Penguin Books, London) 1987

GORRINGE Timothy J. *Capital and the Kingdom* (SPCK, London) 1994

GRECO Thomas H. *New Money for Healthy Communities* (Thomas H. Greco, Jr. Publisher, Arizona) 1994

GRIFFITHS Brian *Morality and the Market Place* (Hodder & Stoughton, London) 1982

GUILLAUME Alfred *The Life of Muhammad: A Translation of Ishaq's "Sirat Rasul Allah,"* (Oxford University Press, London) 1955; *Islam* (Penguin Books, London) 1954

GUNDRY R.H. *A Survey of the New Testament*, (Zondervan, Michigan) 1981

HANNA Nelly (ed.) *The State and its Servants* (The American University in Cairo Press) 1995

HARVEY David *The Condition of Postmodernity* (Blackwell, Massachusetts and Oxford) 1990

HAUERWAS Stanley and MACINTYRE Alasdair *Revisions* (University of Notre Dame Press, London) 1983

HIGGINSON Richard *Called to Account* (Eagle (IPS) Ltd., Surrey) 1993

HIRO Dilip *Islamic Fundamentalism* (Paladin, London) 1988

HOLLAND Muhtar *The Duties of Brotherhood in Islam* – Trans. from the *Ihya of Imam Al-Ghazali* (The Islamic Foundation, Leicester) 1975

HOURANI A. *Arabic Thought in the Liberal Age 1798-1939* (Oxford University Press, London) 1962

IQBAL Munawar and KAHN M. Fahim *A Survey of Issues and A Programme for Research in Monetary and Fiscal Economics of Islam* (Jeddah and Islamabad) 1981

JOHNSON Paul *A History of the Jews* (Phoenix, London) 1995

JOHNSTONE William *Exodus* (JSOT Press, Sheffield Academic Press) 1990

JOMIER Jacques *How to Understand Islam* (SCM Press, London) 1989

JONES Donald (ed) *Business, Religion, and Ethics* (Oelgeschlager, Gunn and Hain, Publishers Inc., Massachusetts) 1982

KAUFMAN Y. *History of the Religion of Israel*, (Vol.IV, Union of American Hebrew Congregations, New York) 1970

KELLER Werner *Diaspora: The Post-Biblical History of the Jews* (Pitman Publishing, London) Eng. tr. 1969

KHAN M. Fahim *Essays in Islamic Economics* (The Islamic Foundation, Leicester) 1995

KHAN Muhammad Akram *Rural Development Through Islamic Banks* (The Islamic Foundation, Leicester) 1994

KHAN Waqar Masood *Towards an Interest-Free Islamic Economic System* (The Islamic Foundation, Leicester) 1985

KIDNER Derek *Ezra and Nehemiah* (Tyndale Pld Testament Commentaries, Intervarsity Press, Leicester) 1979

LAWRENCE Bruce *Defenders of God* (I.B.Tauris & Co.Ltd., London) 1990

LEVER Harold and HUHNE Christopher *Debt and Danger: The World Financial Crisis* (Penguin Books, Middlesex) 1985

LEVINAS Emmanuel *Collected Philosophical Papers* (Martinus Nijhoff Publishers, Dordrecht) 1987

LIPSEY R.S. *Positive Economics* (Oxford University Press, Oxford) 1989

MAUDOODI Maulana Abul A'la *Capitalism, Socialism and Islam* (Islamic Book Publishers, Kuwait) 1987

MAURICE Frederick *The Life of Frederick Denison Maurice* (Macmillan, London, second edition, volume 1) 1884

MAWDUDI Abu'l A la *Islam: An Historical Perspective* (The Islamic Foundation) 1974

MENDENHALL G.E. *The Tenth Generation: The Origins of the Biblical Tradition* (The John Hopkins University Press, Baltimore and London) 1973

MILLER P.D. *Deuteronomy: Interpretation* (John Knox Press, Louisville) 1990

NASR Seyyed Hossein *Ideals and Realities of Islam* (The American University in Cairo Press) 1989 *Traditional Islam in the Modern World* (Kegan Paul International, London) 1987

NELSON B. *The Idea of Usury* (The University of Chicago Press, Ltd., London) 1949

NOONAN John *The Scholastic Analysis of Usury* (Harvard University Press, Massachusetts) 1957

NORMAN Edward *The Victorian Christian Socialists* (Cambridge University Press) 1987

O'BRIEN George *An Essay on Medieval Economic Teaching* (First edition: Longmans, Green and Co., London 1920. Reprinted: Augustus M.Kelley, New York) 1967

PANNENBERG W. *Christianity in a Secularized World* (SCM Press Ltd., London) 1988

POBEE John S. *Who are the Poor? The Beatitudes as a Call to Community* (WCC Publications, Geneva) 1988

PRESTON Ronald H. *Religion and the Rise of Capitalism* (Penguin Books, Middlesex) 1992; *Church and Society in the Late Twentieth Century: The Economic and Political Task* (SCM Press Ltd., London) 1983; *Religion and the Ambiguities of Capitalism,* (SCM Press Ltd., London), 1991

QUTB Muhammad *Islam and the Crisis of the Modern World* (The Islamic Foundation, Leicester) 1990

RAUSCHENBUSCH Walter *A Theology for the Social Gospel* (Macmillan, New York) 1917

RIPPON Andrew *Muslims - Their Religious Beliefs and Practices,* Vol. I (Routledge, London) 1990

RODINSON Maxime *Islam and Capitalism* (Allen Lane, London) 1974

ROLL Eric *A History of Economic Thought* (Faber and Faber Ltd., London) 1938

ROSE Gillian *Judaism and Modernity: Philosophical Essays* (Blackwell, Oxford) 1993

RUSHDOONY Rousas John *Politics of Guilt and Pity* (The Craig Press, New Jersey) 1970

RUTHVEN Malise *Islam in the World* (Penguin Books, London) 1984

SCHAACHT Joseph *An Introduction to Islamic Law* (Oxford University Press) 1964

SCHLUTER Michael and CLEMENTS Roy *Reactivating the Extended Family: from Biblical Norms to Public Policy in England* (Jubilee Centre Publications, Cambridge) 1986

SCHLUTER Michael and LEE David *The R Factor* (Hodder and Stoughton, London) 1993

SCHUMACHER Christian *To Live and Work: A Theological Interpretation* (MARC Europe) 1987

SIDDIQI Muhammad Nejatullah *Partnership and Profit-Sharing in Islamic Law* (The Islamic Foundation, Leicester) 1985; *Issues in Islamic Banking* (The Islamic Foundation) 1983; *Banking Without Interest* (The Islamic Foundation) 1988

SMITH Adam *An Enquiry into the Nature and Causes of the Wealth of Nations* (1776) eds. R.H.Capbell and A.S.Skinner (Clarendon Press, Oxford) 1976 Vol.1

SOMBART W. *The Jews and Modern Capitalism* (tr. M.Epstein, Burt Franklin, New York and London) 1913

STEVENSON J. (ed.) *A New Eusebius* (SPCK, London) 1987

STOTT John *Issues Facing Christians Today* (Marshall Morgan and Scott, 1984, Marshall Pickering, London) 1990

TAMARI Meir *"With All Your Possessions" - Jewish Ethics and Economic Life* (The Free Press, A Division of Macmillan Inc., New York) 1987

TAWNEY R.H. *Religion and the Rise of Capitalism* (Penguin Books, Middlesex) 1922

TOYNBEE Arnold *A Study of History* (Oxford University Press and Thames Hudson) 1972

TREVELYAN G.M. *History of England* [Longman Group Ltd., London, (first edition 1926) 1973 edition]

TROELTSCH E. *The Social Teaching of the Christian Churches*, (Vol.2, tr. O.Wyon, Allen and Unwin, London), 1931

VAISEY John *Revolutions of our Time: Social Democracy* Weidenfeld and Nicholson, London) 1971

WASSERSTEIN Bernard *Vanishing Diaspora: The Jews in Europe since 1945* (Hamish Hamilton Ltd., London) 1996

WATT W.Montgomery *Muhammad at Medina* (Clarendon Press, Oxford) 1956; *Muhammad at Mecca* (Oxford University Press, Oxford) 1953; *The Influence of Islam on Medieval Europe* (Edinburgh University Press) 1972

WEBER Max *The Protestant Ethic and the Spirit of Capitalism* (Unwin University Books, London) 1930

WEINFELD Moshe *Deuteronomy and the Deuteronomic School*, (Clarendon Press, Oxford), 1972

WIENER Hans with OAKESHOTT Robert *Worker-Owners: Mondragon Revisited* (Anglo-German Foundation, London) 1987

ZUBAIDA Sami *Islam, The People and the State: Political Ideas and Movements in the Middle East* (I.B.Tauris, London) 1989/93

Bibles and Commentaries:

Authorised Version of the Bible (Cambridge University Press)

New Revised Standard Version Bible (Collins, London), 1989

Peake's Commentary on the Bible (ed. M.Black and H.H.Rowley, Van Rostrand Reinhold (UK) Co. Ltd.), 1962

The Babylonian Talmud, "Seder Nezikin II, Baba Mezia" (Translated into English under the Ed. Rabbi Dr.I.Epstein, (The Soncino Press, London), 1935

Encyclopeadias:

Encyclopaedia Judaica, Vol.16 (Keter Publishing House, Jerusalem Ltd.) 1972

Encyclopaedia of Islam, Vol.III (E.J.Brill, Leiden; Luzac & Co., London) 1936

Encyclopaedia of Islam – New Edition, Vol.III (E.J.Brill, Leiden; Luzac & Co., London) 1971

Encyclopaedia of Religion and Ethics, Vol.xii (ed.) J.Hastings, (T.&T.Clark, Edinburgh) 1921

The Shorter Encyclopaedia of Islam (eds.) H.A.R.Gibb and J.H.Kramers (E.J.Brill, Leiden) 1974

Encyclopaedia of the Bible (ed.) D.&P.Alexander, (Lion Publishing, Tring) 1973

The Jewish Encyclopedia, Vol. xii, (Funk and Wagnells Co., New York and London) 1905

Evangelical Dictionary of Theology (ed.) W.E.Elwell, (Marshall Morgan and Scott Publications Ltd., Hants.) 1984

The Oxford Encyclopedia of the Modern Islamic World, Vols. 1-4   (ed.) John Esposito (Oxford University Press) 1995

The Concise Encyclopedia of Islam   (eds.) N.Drake and E.Davis (Stacey International London) 1989

PhD. Thesis:

TAHIR Hailani Muji *Islamic Budgetary Policy in Theory and Practice,* (Aberdeen University, 1988)

EL-KARAKI Mohammad   *The Agricultural Credit Systems in Jordan*   (Wye College, University of London, 1994)

Papers:

From *Elimination of Riba from the Economy* (published by the Institute of Policy Studies, Islamabad), 1994:

   AHMAD Khurshid *"Elimination of Riba: Concept and Problems"*

   AHMAD Ausaf   *"Evolution of Islamic Banking"* and *"Contemporary Experiences of Islamic banks: A Survey"*

From *Studies in Islamic Economics* ed. Prof. Khurshid AHMAD (International Centre for Research in Islamic Economics, King Abdul Aziz University, Jeddah), Conference held Feb. 1976:

   UZAIR Muhammad *"Some Conceptual and Practical Aspects of Interest-Free Banking"*

   AHMAD Khurshid *"Economic Development in an Islamic Framework"*

From *Money and Banking in Islam* ed. AHMED Ziauddin; IQBAL Munawar:

KAHN M. Fahim (Jeddah and Islamabad), 1983:

From an International Conference Report on Islamic banking, London, 1984:

RUTHVEN Malise *"The Evolution of Islamic Principles in Relation to Financial Dealings: An Historical Perspective"*

KAMEL Ibrahim *"Money Management and General Trading Under Islamic Banking Procedures"*

MUAZZAM ALI *"Existing Islamic Banking, Investment and Insurance Institutions and their Operations"*

AUTON Bernard *"A Review of Islamic Financial Institutions"*

STEELE Frank *"View from the City"*

From a conference held at Reading University, March, 1995, *Finance against Poverty:*

JONES Howard *"Women's Access to Informal and Formal Finance in a Rajasthan Village"*

WILSON Rodney *"Islamic Banking and Finance"*

MILLS Paul *"The Ban on Interest: Dead Letter or Radical Solution"* Cambridge Papers, Vol. 2, No.1, March 1993; *"Interest in Interest: The Old Testament ban on Interest and its Implications for Today"* Jubilee Centre Publications Ltd., 1993

"Families in Debt," Jubilee Centre Research Paper No.7, Jubilee Centre Publications Ltd., Cambridge, 1988:

TALIB M.T. *"Islam and the Debt Question in Nigeria"* in *The Church and the External Debt*, Jos, Nigeria, 1990

Journals:

The Muslim World, Vol. LXXXIV, No. 3-4, July-October, 1994:

AL-AZAMI Tarik Hamdi *"Religion, Identity, and State in Modern Islam"*

The Muslim World, Vol. LXXXV, No. 3-4, July to October, 1995:

MADIGAN Daniel A. *"Reflections on Current Qur'anic Studies"*

JANDORA John W. *"The Rise of Mecca: Geopolitical Factors"*

The American Journal of Islamic Social Studies, Vol. 4, No. 2, Dec. 1987:

ANWAR Muhammad *"Reorganisation of Islamic Banking: A New Proposal"*

MIRAKHOR Abbas *"The Muslim Scholars and the History of Economics"*

MIECZKOWSKI Bogdan *"Ibn Khaldun's Fourteenth Century Views on Bureaucracy"*

Journal of the West Asian Studies Society, 1986:

SHAGHIL M. *"Islamic Economics: A View"*

The International Journal of Middle East Studies, Vol. XVIII, 1986:

KURAN Timur *"The Economic System in Contemporary Islamic Thought: Interpretation and Assessment"*

The Nat. West Quarterly, November, 1987:

EVANS J.W. and TAYLOR T.W. *"Islamic Banking and the Prohibition of Usury in Western Economic Thought"*

Finance and Ethics Quarterly, No. 2, 1993

SKINNER Andrew *"Adam Smith and Self Love"*

Opportunity: Christian Action Journal – interview with Bishop Nazir-Ali in connection with Alfalah Project in Pakistan:

What's New: An Independent Voice for NGO News and Views –Report by Rebecca Salti with regard to Bani Hamida project in Jordan.

The Annual of the Society of Christian Ethics:

KEENAN J.F. "The Casuistry of John Major: Nominalist Professor of Paris (1506-1531)"

DURKAN J. "John Major After 400 Years, (*The Innes Review* 1), 1950

REID W.S. "Jean Calvin: The Father of Capitalism," (*Themelios*, January, 1983)

Newspaper Articles/Magazines:

Press and Journal, March 20th, 1995
Al-Ahram, Cairo, 23 Feb. - 1 March, 1995
Financial Times, October 7th, 1994
The Independent, November 9th, 1994
The Economist, April, 1992
The Economist, April 13th, 1996
The Times, January 18th, 1996
The Sunday Times, March 26th, 1995
The Daily Telegraph, July 15th, 1995

Index

✳

TEXTS AND STUDIES IN RELIGION